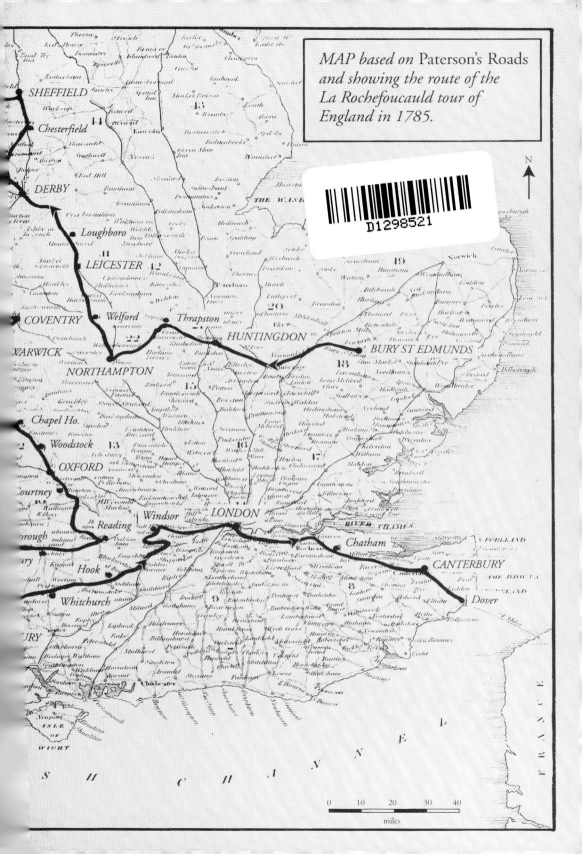

MAP based on Paterson's Roads
and showing the route of the
La Rochefoucauld tour of
England in 1785.

Innocent Espionage

THE LA ROCHEFOUCAULD BROTHERS' TOUR OF ENGLAND IN 1785

Dover quayside c. 1785, by Thomas Hearne. Town and castle stand beyond the basin and the bridge: an elegant family alight and await embarkation.

Innocent Espionage

THE LA ROCHEFOUCAULD BROTHERS' TOUR OF ENGLAND IN 1785

NORMAN SCARFE

THE BOYDELL PRESS

First published 1995
The Boydell Press, Woodbridge

ISBN 0 85115 596 0

The Boydell Press is an imprint of Boydell & Brewer Ltd
PO Box 9, Woodbridge, Suffolk IP12 3DF, UK
and of Boydell & Brewer Inc.
PO Box 41026, Rochester, NY 14604–4126, USA

British Library Cataloguing-in-Publication Data
Innocent Espionage:La Rochefoucauld
Brothers' Tour of England in 1785
I. Scarfe, Norman
914.20473
ISBN 0–85115–596–0

Library of Congress Cataloging-in-Publication Data
La Rochefoucauld, François, duc de, 1765–1848.
    Innocent espionage : the La Rochefoucauld brothers' tour of
England in 1785 / edited and translated by Norman Scarfe.
        p.   cm.
    Includes bibliographical references and index.
    ISBN 0–85115–596–0 (alk. paper : hardback)
    1. England – Description and travel – Early works to 1800.   2. La
Rochefoucauld, François, duc de, 1765–1848 – Journeys – England.
3. La Rochefoucauld, Alexandre de – Journeys – England.   4. England –
Social life and customs – 18th century.   5. French – Travel – England –
History – 18th century.   6. England – Foreign public opinion, French.
I. La Rochfoucauld, Alexandre de.   II. Scarfe, Norman.   III. Title.
DA620.L33   1995
914.204'73–dc20   94–42907

This publication is printed on acid-free paper

Printed in Great Britain by
St Edmundsbury Press Ltd, Bury St Edmunds, Suffolk

Contents

To the memory of
Edmée de La Rochefoucauld
1895–1991
inextinguishable spirit
most lapidary of reflective writers
kindest of staunch friends

L'homme imagine, réinvente sans relâche son passé . . . Nous ne nous lassons pas d'essayer de voir *ceux qui nous ont précédés.*

'I find it very courteous of them to show their processes to strangers who can do no harm to their business; or at least very little harm, at a long time in the future, by establishing these processes at home . . . Their compatriots, in appropriating a novel idea, might do them real, immediate and serious damage.'

François de La Rochefoucauld, in Mr Swift's cotton-mill at Derby. Ten years later, his brother did set up such a mill in France: by then, England and France were again at war.

Illustrations

Credits

Author and Publishers are very grateful to the following owners and trustees of copyright for their permission to publish:

Frontispiece: Mrs Hilary Teare (photograph Courtauld Institute)

1, 23, 26, 35, 45:   G.F. Cordy

2, 3, 5:   The La Rochefoucauld family

4, 56, 57:   Mme G. Etienne, Directeur des Archives départementales de l'Oise, Beauvais

6:   Sir John Ruggles-Brise, Bt., and the Paul Mellon Foundation for British Art

7, 55:   Christopher Reeve and the St Edmundsbury Museums Service

8:   A private collector

9:   The Marquess of Northampton

10, 11:   Leicestershire County Council

12:   University of Reading, Rural History Centre

14:   The Trustees of the Science Museum

In text, p. 43:   Françoise Monet, Directeur, Service de la Bibliothèque de l'Assemblée Nationale, Paris

15:   Richard L. Hills

16:   Richard Childs, Principal Archivist, Sheffield Central Library

17, 34, 47, 50, 51:   The Trustees of the British Museum

18, 19:   David Taylor, and Manchester Central Library, Local Studies Unit

20, 21:   Alan Davies, and Lancashire Mining Museum, Salford

22:   Joseph Sharples, and National Museums & Galleries on Merseyside

24:   City of Aberdeen Art Gallery & Museums Collections

25, 38, 39:   Le duc d'Estissac

27:   The Trustees of the Wedgwood Museum, Barlaston, Stoke-on-Trent, Staffordshire

28, 60:   Birmingham Museums & Art Gallery

29:   Yale Center for British Art: Paul Mellon Collection

30:   Warwickshire County Record Office

31:   Edwin Smith

32: Jeremy Whitaker

33: Courtauld Institute of Art

37: John Somerville, Sotheby's

40: Devon County Council, Westcountry Studies Library

42: Roger Peers, and Dorset County Museum, Dorchester, Dorset

43: Nick Griffiths, and Salisbury & S. Wiltshire Museum

44: Stuart Piggott

46: The Royal Collection © HM The Queen

48: The Theatre Museum, by Courtesy of the Board of Trustees of the Victoria & Albert Museum

49: The Royal Academy of Arts, London

52: National Portrait Gallery

53: Whitbread plc

58: The Metropolitan Museum of Art: Mr & Mrs Charles Wrightsman. Gift in honour of Everett Fahy, 1977

62: Musée du Louvre, Département des Arts Graphiques

We are especially grateful to the library of the National Assembly in Paris, and to Mme Françoise Monet its librarian, for permission to use the manuscript volumes numbered 1249 bis, ter and quater; the principal source of this book. We are also grateful to the British Library Board for allowing us to publish in translation a large part of Add. MSS. 42095, the chief source of chapters 11 and 12.

Note on the Translation

As with my earlier book, *A Frenchman's Year in Suffolk, 1784*, I have not thought it desirable to create some notional 1780s English: where 'it is' seems too formal, I have invariably preferred 'it's' to 'tis'. Within the limits of 18th-century manners, these journals are very informal, like letters home. In Chapters 11 and 12, Lazowski's letter-book is more consciously formal, as from a highly-trusted servant-friend of the family. I'm relieved to hear these slight tonal differences between the three writers as I read my translation. Like François de La Rochefoucauld who became one, I have been imperfectly consistent over presenting particular dukes with a capital D.

NS

Notes on Measurements and Currency Values

Arthur Young travelled extensively in France in 1787–90, and his observations are invaluable in interpreting the prices and measurements noted by his three French friends during their English tour in 1785. Constantia Maxwell grouped Young's reckonings in her edition of his *Travels in France* (CUP, 1929), on pp. 405–07.

Currency

In Young's day the *livre*, which equalled 20 *sous*, or *sols*, was worth 10$\frac{1}{2}$d (10$\frac{1}{2}$ 'old' English pennies, before the decimalization of our coinage). A *livre* was thus worth seven-eighths of one English shilling. The three Frenchmen used the English word 'shilling' instead of trying to convert it into the precise French equivalent. And a *sou* was equal approximately to a halfpenny (half of one 'old' penny).

24 livres	=	the French *louis d'or* (or the English guinea).
23 livres	=	the English pound sterling.
6 livres	=	the French *louis d'argent*, or *écu*, which was equal to the English crown, or 5 shillings (25 'new' pence).

How many debased modern English pounds a 1785 pound sterling was worth is hard to calculate.

Measures

Young wrote: 'In France, the infinite perplexity of the measures exceeds all comprehension. They differ not only in every province but in every district, and almost in every town, and these tormenting variations are found equally in the denominations and contents of the measures of land and corn.'

In these journals of their English tour, it is clear that the Frenchmen, well aware of the variations (which were not confined to France), tended to equate the *arpent* with the acre, and use the French and English words interchangeably, though at one point (*A Frenchman's Year in Suffolk, 1784*, p. 27) François reckoned an *arpent* varied between $\frac{1}{2}$ and $\frac{5}{6}$ of an acre.

In linear measurement, these are the basic measures (variable, of course):

1 *pied de roi*	=	.3267 of a metre = (roughly) 1 foot
6 *pieds*	=	1 *toise* (a fairly common measure)
20 *pieds*	=	1 *perche*
2,200 *toises*	=	1 *lieu* (or league)
1 *lieu*	=	4,400 yards = 2$\frac{1}{2}$ miles

And in 1790, Dorothy Wordsworth and her brother, walking through France, reckoned one lieu (or league) = 3 miles (E. de Selincourt, *Dorothy Wordsworth*, Oxford, 1933, p. 27).

Foreword

François et Alexandre de La Rochefoucauld sont encore de très jeunes gens lorsque, en 1784, accompagnés par leur précepteur M. de Lazowski, ils partent faire le tour de l'Angleterre. Pourtant, ils ne sont pas dépourvus d'expérience. Grâce à leur père, le duc de La Rochefoucauld-Liancourt, humaniste et grand maître de la garderobe de Louis XVI, ils ont fait d'excellentes études et ont déjà beaucoup voyagé. En effet, deux ans auparavant, ils ont visité tout le sud de la France; et l'année précédente, ils ont passé plusieurs mois à Bury St Edmunds auprès du fameux agronome Arthur Young, et rayonné dans les comtés de Suffolk et de Norfolk.

Familiarisés avec la langue anglaise, ils profitent pleinement de leur voyage et font preuve d'une curiosité insatiable tant en ce qui concerne l'agriculture, étudiant le rendement et le prix des terres, l'élevage des moutons de Lincolnshire, que l'industrie naissante: filatures, où la condition des enfants et des femmes les attristent – François remercie le Ciel de n'avoir pas à travailler dans ces conditions – manufactures de porcelaine (Wedgwood gardera jalousement ses secrets), ou aciéries de Sheffield.

Mais les deux frères aiment aussi visiter les curiosités touristiques; la maison de Cromwell, le château de lord Scarsdale dont les soixante chambres d'invités l'éblouissent, les hôpitaux où il remarque que chaque patient dispose d'un lit pour lui seul, le port de Liverpool, ou à Stratford, la maison natale de Shakespeare, les bains à Bath ou, non loin de la cathédrale de Salisbury, les magnifiques et étranges ruines de Stonehenge.

Il faut rendre grâce à M. Norman Scarfe, excellent historien, d'avoir traduit, publié et annoté avec tant de soin et d'intelligence ces journaux de voyage qui présentent un passionnant tableau pris sur le vif de l'état de l'Angleterre à la veille de la révolution française.

Solange Fasquelle,
ancienne Présidente du
PEN Club Français

Preface and Acknowledgements

We never tire of trying to *see* people of earlier generations: nous ne nous lassons pas d'essayer de *voir* ceux qui nous ont précédés.

It is hard to see our 18th-century predecessors with even a fraction of the familiarity we take for granted as we view our contemporaries; it is still harder to know what they were thinking, especially about themselves. Topographical draughtsmen and engravers proliferated, from Samuel and Nathaniel Buck through to Rooker and Rowlandson, Paul Sandby, Thomas Hearne, Edward Dayes: a widening fraternity, with the ingenious Wright of Derby, and Philip de Loutherbourg, at their heart. They help us to focus on externals, and these in themselves tell a gripping and still often surprising story; starting with great houses and formal gardens and avenues laid out in the working countryside – Blenheim, Chatsworth and Hampton Court perhaps pre-eminent – and the old walled towns all girt still by market-gardens and fields; and ports bustling with loaders and off-loaders and bristling with sea-defences; and then all this perceptibly, and sometimes swiftly, changing into a new world of irresistibly self-confident industries of all kinds, powered by unprecedented ingenuity in technology, and cross-fertilising with commerce and capital and ideas of profit and benefit.

How do we see under the surface of these images? We can only read our way under. And before we start constructing our own descriptions of England in the 18th century, we look for contemporary writers who have travelled the roads and observed the varying elements in the landscape with sympathy and curiosity, and described them intelligently.

The most famous of these is Daniel Defoe, whose *Tour through the Whole Island of Great Britain* appeared in the 1720s. G.D.H. Cole, who edited the serviceable Everyman edition, reckoned it 'by far the most graphic contemporary account of the state of economic and social affairs near the beginning of the 18th century'. He added that it succeeded in 'conveying an impression which no derivative history, however brilliant or scholarly, is ever likely to convey'. After Defoe, there is a gap of an entire century before we come to anything comparable: the *Rural Rides* of William Cobbett, full of tiresome idiosyncrasy and prejudice, but, like Defoe's *Tour*, highly readable, and appropriately published for Everyman. Of course, his were essentially *rural* rides. He hated the new machinery that destroyed the labourers' wages; he deplored the miseries of the French wars that subsidized the garrison towns and threatened liberty; and he groaned at the great multiplication of gaols, like Leicester's, newly-crowned by turrets like Warwick castle, as if it were a building to be proud of.

A large number of English *Tours* has been published – two of the best of them coming just before Defoe: Celia Fiennes in the late 17th century and Sir John Percival

(University of Missouri Press, 1989 – a handsome publication), who toured England in 1701 in preparation for the obligatory Grand Tour of Europe. But what is there, like this, of vivid, valuable description of town and country, between the 1720s – when the revolutionary changes in farming and industry had hardly begun – and the 1820s, when the changes were ordaining the flight of the villagers from the arable lands and the inexorable growth of the towns? In many ways the best of them – and among the most congenial travel-books – are the Hon. John Byng's diaries of his fifteen leisurely, unaccompanied tours in parts of England and Wales during the period 1781–1794 (John Byng, *The Torrington Diaries*, ed. C.B. Andrews, 1934–8 and reprinted 1970; 4 vols). Byng's excursions, mostly on horseback, were made entirely for 'the pleasure of Touring'. His itineraries coincide at surprisingly few points with those followed in 1785 by the La Rouchefoucauld brothers. But there is a more fundamental difference: he detested the world of business and manufactures, which for them supplied some of the most pleasurable excitements of their English tour. (Compare Byng's dismissive remarks: 'How eager was I to get from the insolence of Birmingham: a town wherein I should be crippled in a week from want of flagstones' – III, p. 150 – with those on p. 114 below tempered in footnote 20.)

There are two books – one for the 1770s and the other for the 1780s – that do very substantially enable us to view through the eyes of highly observant foreigners our landscape and its people in the two middle decades of that long and dynamic century.

The first, which appeared as lately as 1992 under the aegis of the British Academy, was *An American Quaker in the British Isles: The Travel Journals of Jabez Maud Fisher, 1775–9*, ed. Kenneth Morgan. Fisher's father, a Philadelphia businessman, sent his 25-year-old son over here to avoid the embarrassment of having him at home: his sympathies in the War of Independence were with Britain, and if his book is a shade joyless it is because he was not only a Quaker, but he lamented the 'unnatural war' that prevented his getting back home to Philadelphia: after failing to get through the lines, he returned to the Friends at Leeds, and died at 29 of scarlet fever. In the interests of the family firm, which the war closed down, he made lists of the manufacturers in the various towns over here, the prices of their products, adding shrewd notes on the business qualities of the makers themselves and the distributors. He naturally got to know the Quaker network, usually travelling with one or more Friends, and staying mostly in their houses. They included William Cookworthy, the discoverer of china-clay, and Abraham Darby III, who showed him the model of the famous iron bridge they were about to build at Coalbrookdale. He noted the conditions of road and canal transport, the docks at Liverpool, and the tremendous industrial activity in Sheffield, Manchester and Birmingham. More surprising, he responded with some feeling to 'the sublime and the beautiful' in the scenery of Wales and around Perth; and he responded to the gardens at Hagley and the Leasowes, Painshill and Clifton. Finally, he formed an opinion of the English and of humanity generally, also a memorable way of expressing it. (How much his opinion was conditioned by an acquaintance limited to Quakers one can only guess.) Of the English he wrote:

In adversity, they aggravate the picture of their misery, and fancy destruction impends. In prosperity, they rack their brain for some source of unhappiness . . . This is too much the case with human nature in general, but particularly with the November-spirited English.

The book that helps fill the gap between Defoe and Cobbett for the 1780s is the one that follows: I have pieced it together from the travel-journals of two young Frenchmen and their tutor, as I describe in the Introduction. Just as Jabez Fisher's commentary has the valuable objectivity of a friendly American with particular business interests, so these Frenchmen were admirably equipped to spot and describe what was of vital interest for the English, and therefore presumably the French, industrial economy and society. The two Frenchmen were young, but knew very well what to watch out for. They had travelled widely in France during two years, and then spent thirteen months making friends in Suffolk, in Bury St Edmunds, before looking at the industrial Midlands and the West Country. Both they and their tutor had in mind their father, the influential and philanthropic duc de Liancourt, when they wrote their journals: this gives them something of the vividness of letters, indeed of speech. Their father, the duke, had already founded the first of the French *Ecoles des Arts et Métiers*. When the Napoleonic War was at last over, he became co-founder of the *Caisses d'Epargne et de Prévoyance*, from ideas that may well have germinated in his mind on reading his sons' reports of the Benefit Clubs and Box Clubs they saw in the inns of Suffolk in 1784 (see my book, *A Frenchman's Year in Suffolk, 1784*, 1988).

I have called this present book *Innocent Espionage* because, as I read the detailed description of the processes in the famous cotton-mill, and in the very secret wool-spinning mill, in Derby, and then the mills of Sheffield and Manchester, and the foundries of Abraham Darby and John Wilkinson in the Ironbridge Gorge, the thought inevitably crossed my mind that – in view of their father's closeness to Louis XVI – there might have been a serious element of industrial spying. It seemed curious, though, that the English manufacturers were so willing to allow these three Frenchmen to inspect very closely – presumably sometimes making notes on the spot – their highly secret processes. Jabez Fisher was firmly denied access to Richard Arkwright's mill at Cromford. It may have been thought that young French aristocrats would be incapable of comprehending technical details: mostly, they understood, as may be seen in their delighted journals. (Indeed François discusses this very question in chapter 2, p. 40. As we see in my Epilogue, the younger brother actually succeeded in setting up a cotton-mill in France, after coming to terms with the Revolution.) In this question of 18th-century industrial spying, Professor J.R. Harris of Birmingham University, the leading English authority on the subject, shares my conclusion. He has been immensely kind and helpful, too, over the part played by Lazowski, the boys' tutor, in supplying statistics on British agriculture to the failing French administration in 1786.

A brief list of my Acknowledgments follows.

First, I acknowledge the debt I expressed in the dedication of *A Frenchman's Year in Suffolk, 1784*. Without the work of the late Jean Marchand, 1894–1988, Archivist and Librarian to the French Chamber of Deputies and National Assembly, who edited the early travels of François de La Rochefoucauld and his brother in France during the years 1781–83, and who projected some such volume as this one, I would have been much less confident of my reading of François' manuscript journals, the major text on which my book is based. I had not long been grappling with François' imperfect hand (see p. 43) in the Library of the National Assembly, when word came that Mlle Françoise Marchand would like to discuss my researches with me. Her father was then gravely ill, and with immense generosity she entrusted me with his transcripts, in his immaculate scholarly hand. She then arranged with the duc d'Estissac for me to transcribe Alexandre's notebooks at the Jockey Club, of which he is President: not easy work (see p. 158), but a necessary complement to François' much fuller account. My debts to Mlle Marchand and her late father, and to the duc d'Estissac, are immeasurable. My chief hope is that M. Marchand would have approved and enjoyed this book; my chief regret, that he and Edmée de La Rochefoucauld, to whom I have dedicated it, died before it could appear.

My detailed obligations to scholars are recorded in the text, and I can only register my general thanks to all of them here. But some historians and librarians and museum curators have been exceptionally kind. I must mention John Harris again, for his careful comments not only on matters touching industrial espionage but also on the iron-working processes, his other great expertise. Both he and Barrie Trinder helped greatly over the Ironbridge chapter. I am equally much in Richard Hills' debt: without his comments on the various textile processes, this book would have been seriously defective. He even made time to travel down from Manchester to the Science Museum's overflow storerooms at Olympia to meet me and show me precisely what it was the brothers were watching in Derby in 1785. Several other friends have been most generous. In Birmingham and the West Midlands, Stanley Sellers and Richard Butt joined in the pursuit of the brothers, not only in Birmingham and its marvellous museums, but at Edgbaston and Soho, and over at Coalbrookdale and Viroconium, Chapel House and Heythrop. Similarly, in Liverpool and Worsley, Alan Swerdlow and Jeremy Greenwood introduced me to museums and record offices. Alan Davies, curator of the Lancashire Mining Museum at Buile Hill Park, Salford, supplied a remarkable commentary to François' description of Worsley's underground canals. Writing this book after long association with museums, public libraries and record offices, has made me feel even prouder of their public services all across England. Dr Tony Bennett showed me his native Bristol and the Goldney grotto at Clifton, and kindly came on a tour of Plymouth and Mount Edgcumbe. In France, I must thank Georges Ausset and Patrick Sarrois for constant kindness; also M. Georges Martin of Lyon, and Mme. Geneviève Etienne, at Beauvais. Richard Wilson and Hugh Belsey guided me in their realms of economic and art history. I've enjoyed working with Richard and Helen Barber and their Boydell team: notably Joan Jordan, Pam Cope, and Pru Harrison. While Gillian Delaforce was creating the index in Brighton, in Woodbridge Jeremy Greenwood was being vigilant with proofs, and Paul Fincham kind as ever.

Introduction

This tour of England by three intelligent and observant Frenchmen, in 1785, is notable for their candidly envious attention to new industrial processes in textiles and in iron, for their delight in the busy traffic on the roads, and in the hospitality of country inns; for their care to record precise differences in regional farming, and to describe the beauties and curiosities of English gardens; for the surprise they expressed in London at the great ponds occupying the middles of the squares – St James', Bloomsbury, etc. – and at the ingenious urban invention of 'the area', unknown in Paris; and at the comparative excellence of our art, and the classic Commons debate, Pitt versus Fox, on the state of the country's finances. They declared: 'We have no-one with whom Mrs Siddons can be compared'; and in describing how she moved them, they help us to understand, and almost experience, the theatre of their day. As Paris slipped down into Revolution in 1789, an English friend of theirs described its theatre as 'the first in the world'.

We see that the tour was carefully planned. Two of the Frenchmen, François and Alexandre de La Rochefoucauld were sons of a remarkably public-spirited duke, the duc de Liancourt, a member of the senior branch of the La Rochefoucauld family. (They have been traced back to about 1060; and developed 26 main branches, down through 28 or 29 generations. In her recent delightful history of her family, *Les La Rochefoucauld*, Librairie Perrin, Paris, 1992, Mme Solange Fasquelle imagines an even earlier start, c.980.) When he sent his sons over to England in December of 1783, he had already founded above the village on his great estate at Liancourt – among woods near the Paris-Amiens road – the first of France's *Ecoles des Arts et Métiers*, schools in which the children were encouraged to discover and develop their true ability, their *métier* for life: it was not a bad principle. The two sons, almost exactly two years apart, were first sent out, at barely 14 and 16, with their 33-year-old tutor-companion, Lazowski, to look at and record what we should call the economic landscape of France. That was between late-1781 and mid-1783, a few months before they left for England. The observations of the elder brother, François, were edited by the late Jean Marchand and published in two octavo volumes in 1933 and 1939 by the *Société de l'Histoire de France: Voyages en France de François de La Rochefoucauld, 1781–1783*. Their orthography was not good, but nor was their father's: language, as usual, was changing: the Physick Garden (Pl. 54) was already looking old-fashioned with its 'k'. What they saw, they learnt to describe precisely and with an infectious commitment: and what they saw on those early French travels gave them a standard against which to set England.

Later in the 1780s, which ended so cataclysmically in France, an engaging Englishman, Arthur Young, already devoted to what he called 'Political Arithmetic', came to France three times, travelled all over it in the years 1787–90, and wrote such a vivid account of what he saw that, when it was translated into French in 1793, the

Convention ordered 20,000 copies to be distributed free throughout the Republic, and new editions followed. Young was no revolutionary, was indeed horrified by what he already saw in 1789. Two years earlier, when he began his *Travels through France*, he was already firm friends with members of the La Rochefoucauld family. The Duke and Duchess made him welcome at Liancourt and at their town house in Paris, the Hôtel Liancourt, now no. 58 rue de Varenne, and at the Duke's apartments in the palaces of Versailles and the Tuileries (for he was Grand Master of the King's Wardrobe): quite a good home-base for his French travels. The boys and their tutor not only welcomed him warmly, they accompanied him on parts of his journeys. (One wonders if they ever showed him the manuscript of their own travels written in 1781–83.) That they and Arthur Young met and got to know each other so well is a very remarkable example of serendipity.

When they reached London in December 1783, on their first visit to England (see *A Frenchman's Year in Suffolk, 1784*, 1988, Introduction and p. 15), the boys and their tutor intended to go on to Bristol 'to get hold of the language'. By mere chance, one of their London acquaintances was the Hon. Thomas Walpole, a banker with interests in Paris; he advised them most strongly against Bristol, as a place where they would find many people who spoke French, and where English was badly spoken; and where it rained twice as much as it did anywhere else in England. He recommended Bury St Edmunds: 'Suffolk was a province where English was spoken best, and where it rained least'. The last claim is often true, but they found the weather in Suffolk deplorable that year. On the other hand they quickly met Arthur Young, who lived only four miles down the road from Bury. If they had not been deflected from Bristol by Thomas Walpole, they might never have met Young, and thereafter shaped one another's lives as they did. We can hardly doubt that Young helped with the planning of the 1785 tour through England. Nor can he have failed to influence the direction of their observation: on the *wheat*-straw thatch, for instance, covering the mud-walled houses of part of Northamptonshire; or on the quality of the clothing and the horses of the hundreds of country folk hurrying along the wintry road to Chesterfield cattle-fair.

The story of the fourteen months spent by the three Frenchmen in Bury St Edmunds (with only three brief excursions) is told in *A Frenchman's Year in Suffolk, 1784*. Their five-day excursion in Young's company that July was something of a turning-point in all their lives, familiar as they all were with observant travelling. François wrote:

> Such is the summary of my tour in Suffolk made with the man who, perhaps in all England, was the most agreeable and useful of travelling companions . . . It gave me the most enormous pleasure: it was not merely that all I saw was new and interesting to me, every single thing was agreeable, and I was quite discontented on the sixth day to get back home to Bury.

Young himself found the tour 'pleasing from the conversation and politeness of my companions who, I have no doubt, are convinced of the real importance of attending to the agriculture of the countries through which they may have occasion to travel'.

2. *François de La Rochefouchauld, drawn by his wife.*

3. *François' father, the duc de Liancourt, attributed to the baron Gros.*

The journals of the remainder of their travels – two weeks in Norfolk in 1784, then three months in the Midlands and West Country in early 1785, the main matter of this book – demonstrate beautifully that Young's teaching and his example had entirely succeeded.

I must mention Lazowski here. Introducing the 1784 book, I quoted at length Young's very endearing picture of him (from *The Autobiography of Arthur Young*, ed. M. Betham-Edwards, 1898). The boys' father, the Duke de Liancourt, was colonel of a regiment quartered at Pont-à-Mousson, in Lorraine, and there fortuitously met Maximilien de Lazowski, son of a Pole who had come to Lorraine with King Stanislas, apparently as a cook. The Duke was so struck with the young man's manner and conversation that he resolved to cultivate his acquaintance and engaged him as tutor for his sons – 'not for the common purposes of education but to travel with them'. They were deflected to Bury by Mr Walpole (*not*, as Young came to imagine, because they had heard he lived nearby!) Mr Symonds, Professor of Modern History at Cambridge, who volunteered as their kindly host for most of their stay in Suffolk (see Pls 7 and 55), brought them from Bury over to Young's home at Bradfield: 'from that time, a friendship between me and Lazowski commenced, and lasted till the death of the latter'. Young unaccountably says nothing of the date of Lazowski's death, which as I show in the Epilogue to this book, seems to have occurred sometime during 1794–95. Young thought him 'about 40 years of age' when he came to Bury, but he was a month short of 36.

This is perhaps the moment to describe Lazowski's contribution to this book. It will be seen that there are three main contributors. François' journals supply the basis of the first ten chapters, fairly frequently supplemented by his younger brother who quite often mentioned something overlooked by François – sometimes it was something fundamental, like the name of the great Birmingham 'japanner' who personally showed them his factory, Henry Clay: often it is just a different personal view-point that Alexandre expresses. He chimes in as something of a foil to François. Not that François' monologue ever seems monotonous; of the three, he is the most natural writer.

François' principal shortcoming is that, near the end of the tour, he completely and finally dried up on Salisbury Plain, having given a fairly full account of Stonehenge, but unable to write a word about Wilton, seen on the same day. His journal stops there, without a word of explanation. One can only guess at the sort of fatigue we all experience, those of us who try to keep notes of our travels. Wilton presents a formidable challenge to any writer. François must have been deeply impressed but wrote nothing about it. To read more of his writing, we have to jump to *Souvenirs du 10 Août, 1792*, and this I attempt a little, in the Epilogue. Meanwhile Alexandre kept going, no doubt rather smugly – presumably knowing that his brother had given up. But then Alexandre fizzled out at Windsor. It was only when I was half-way through this translation and edition of their journals that I made an amazingly lucky discovery. Catalogued rather misleadingly, a volume of Lazowski's incomplete journals of this same tour (in the form of a letter-book) was placed on my desk in the British Library's Department of Manuscripts. It begins mid-sentence at Glastonbury, and ends mid-sentence: but not till they are all at Dover, waiting to go aboard and sail for France on 10 May.

4. *The ducal château at Liancourt before the Revolution. The building on the left, the handsome* laiterie *built by François' mother, is all that survives today.*

5. *Hôtel de Liancourt, Paris, late 17th century. Now no. 58, rue de Varenne, opposite the Hotel Matignon.*

It is an asset to any book, to have both a beginning and an end! Ending with Alexandre at Windsor was going to be difficult, manfully though he composed his last sentence. In his case it was't his last, either, for he resumed his notebooks the following March on his journey with Lazowski through Scotland and Ireland.

Arthur Young introduced his *Travels through France* with the dictum: 'There are two methods of writing travels; to register the journey itself, or the result of it'. He means the day-by-day journals, such as François and Alexandre illustrate in the first ten chapters of this book – and this includes descriptions in the form of letters – which also covers this book: for the journals are 'imagined' by both the Duke's sons as daily reports, letters home to their father. Young's second method, 'which usually falls into essays on distinct subjects', is the form Lazowski used here to describe, manageably, at one sitting, the very full week they spent in London before riding out through Kent to Dover (where daily descriptions resume – hop-growing, Chatham, etc.).

François had used this second method, short essays on distinct subjects, to report to his father on their year in Suffolk in 1784: he called it *Mélanges sur l'Angleterre* because it included a few pages on London and Cambridge and Norfolk: I ventured to translate his title as *A Frenchman's Year in Suffolk, 1784* because that was where his year of observation was almost entirely spent. The essays were lively, but his two brief tours, on the Suffolk-Essex border and up in Norfolk, seemed to me fresher and livelier, a natural result of travelling and changing scenes. I must mention here that when *A Frenchman's Year in Suffolk, 1784* went to press in 1988, the vital pages devoted by Lazowski to the Norwich textile industry were missing. They were found in Norwich and published in a joint essay by me and Richard Wilson, Director of the Centre of East Anglian Studies, in the professional journal, *Textile History*, 23, pp. 113–20, 1992. Dr Wilson is impressed – we both are – by the 'exceptional acuteness' of Lazowski in his observation of the wool textile industry in Norwich. We can only deplore that Lazowski's (presumed) letter-book for the earlier part of the 1785 tour – covering the major industrial towns, from Leicester round to Birmingham and Coventry – are missing: yet how invaluably serious and involved François is in, for instance, Mr Swift's cotton mill at Derby, and at Manchester and Coalbrookdale and Birmingham. If the earlier part of Lazowski's letter-book had survived, this account of the La Rochefoucauld tour would have become unmanageable in one volume.

The survival of François' travel-journals is fairly miraculous. When he got home after the '85 tour in England, the nine notebooks, probably bought in England, were bound into three hard-back volumes and handed over to his father, the Duke, to whom they were really addressed. We presume they stood on the shelves of the great library in his town house in the rue de Varenne. After his departure to England in 1792, he was declared an émigré and his collections were sequestrated. A list survives of those of his books chosen by Citoyen Ameilhon, a member of the monuments commission, for transfer to the dépôt in the Hôtel de Nesle: the list is dated 21 September 1793. It includes these journals under the title *Voyage en Angleterre*, also François' journals of their early travels through France.

6. *Arthur Young. Pastel by John Russell.*

These manuscripts were then transferred to a great depôt at the Cordeliers, which contained as many as 262,189 volumes, of which nearly 150,000 came from 217 libraries of émigrés. The Duke de Liancourt's library contributed a thousand volumes of history and literature, occupying Bay II of the second gallery.

On his return, the Duke was authorised in 1800 to search in the depôt of the Cordeliers for the books that had belonged to him, but he found nothing. The Administrator of the combined literary depôts recorded that literary works from the libraries of the émigrés had been subjected to the most active and continuous plundering over six years: all had been removed from the depôts and were to be sought 'in the libraries of Paris'. I have based these two paragraphs on the researches of the late M. Jean Marchand, librarian and archivist to the National Assembly. He concluded that, sometime between 1796 and 1800, the celebrated archivist Camus picked out François' *journals* to enhance his newly organized collection for the library of the Corps Législatif, which became the Chamber of Deputies and then the National Assembly. One is at least grateful that the journals were preserved through these years of plunder, and that they were brought to light, and devotedly transcribed, by my friend Mlle Françoise Marchand's late father. This is their first public appearance.

Alexandre's eighteen *cahiers* – small notebooks numbered I to XVIII, with XV unfortunately missing – measure approximately 7 inches in width by 4 inches tall, and are conveniently interleaved with blotting-paper. See Pls 38 and 39 on pp. 158–159. His handwriting is much less careful than that of François, perhaps to conceal uncertainties of orthography and syntax: for instance, words one might expect to end in -é, or -er, or -ez, are very often written -ez – it is a convenient squiggle, possibly just a shorthand trick for speed? These seventeen notebooks faced fewer vicissitudes than those of François. At least, they have presumably never been separated from the family, and I am delighted to be beholden to Alexandre's direct descendant, the present Duc d'Estissac, for permission to transcribe and use his young forebear's resolute and independent travel-records. I have outlined in an Epilogue the lives of the three travellers in the months and years leading up to and through the Revolution – very briefly indeed thereafter.

The identification of Lazowski's letter-book was a remarkable stroke of luck. When I first saw it, it was described as *An Account of a Tour in Ireland*, and I see that the first pages are unhelpful; the top page soiled, creased and obviously not originally the first page. The first words are 'except for the château of Blois, this is the tallest and most considerable'. After some lines, I began to see that this was part of a description of Glastonbury Tor: I suddenly realized that here was a third account of the last leg of the brothers' tour. A more puzzling clue was, and remains, the library record that the volume was presented to the Museum by 'M. Charles Dollfus'. Can this M. Dollfus have some connection of the late M. Jacques Ferdinand-Dreyfus, who published a serous life of the Duc de Liancourt in 1903, entitled *Un Philanthrope d'Autrefois*? For it was he who lent M. Marchand typescript copies of the various letters by Lazowski I was able to use in *A Frenchman's Year in Suffolk, 1784*. The originals of those letters have so far not been traced. That book, *A Frenchman's Year in Suffolk* now in its third printing, with a new Appendix of Lazowski's account of

Norwich's textile business, provides the fullest introduction to the present one. I have supplied short introductions to each of the following twelve chapters. The three Frenchmen who set out early in 1785 to see the England that interested them were not the most intimate of friends, as we soon learn. This temperamental difference may well have contributed to their remarkable concentration on what they were seeing; and to the strength of their descriptions. Seven years later, on 10 August 1792, as the kingdom of these young patriots foundered, their great personal peril brought them close together. Thereafter, as my epilogue shows, the brothers went very separate ways. The reader can now safely turn to the first chapter – 'Leaving Suffolk'.

1

Leaving Suffolk

First they headed west, for Huntingdon, Northampton, and Leicester. There they arrived in snow one afternoon and left on the following afternoon in time to travel 11 miles to Loughborough through dense snow and fog. What they managed to see of Leicester and its chief industry in those few hours perfectly illustrates their astonishing energy, endless curiosity and candour. Loughborough, or rather Robert Bakewell's world-famous stock-breeding establishment at nearby Dishley, was one of the great objects of their tour: to it and to their meeting with Bakewell, François devoted as much space as he did, in turn, to the revelations of Worsley and Ironbridge, Birmingham, Bristol and Plymouth.

After living for over a year in Bury St Edmunds, both François and Alexandre found they had grown strongly attached to the little capital town of West Suffolk: it was hard to leave. Alexandre gives a hint of heated arguments they had had before setting out, as to whether they should carry through their original intention of seeing as much as possible of England in the time available; or whether, as so much time had been taken up with illness in Bury since October, it would be better to head home to France direct. Which of them was ill, and what ailment it was, isn't said; but later, as they drove in very bad weather through the north Midlands, François referred to anxieties about the health of both Alexandre and their French servant Chaveron. Alexandre seems to have suffered from feverish chills. François, possibly asthmatic, himself admitted to becoming quite seriously ill before they had managed to complete the half-mile of garden-walk they laid out and made for their host, Professor Symonds, during 1784's cheerless summer. In 1785, the combination of severe early-Spring weather with their relentless itinerary would have tested the most robust constitution. François' opening sentence reveals the melancholy truth that he did not find his younger brother and their mentor the most congenial of travelling companions. Alexandre's diary provides a better starting-point.

Alexandre: After being ill at Bury, and being held back two months by the last illness, we were finally ready to take off on the longest tour we could manage in the two months left. Our time was growing short, and the squabble [*la guerre*] had been fought over our desire to get back to France: already it is February, and we need to be home in April.[1] We finally decided on the tour, and left Bury on [Wednesday] 16 February, 1785.

---

[1]   They sailed to France from Dover on 10 May.

11

I can't help remarking how painful it was to leave this town in which I'd spent a year: I had stayed too long to be able to leave. I had friends I miss, and who were sorry to see us go. For us, the name of this town will never be forgotten. Anyway, after much difference of opinion, we left on the 16th at 10 in the morning. We slept at Newmarket: nothing to say about it.

François: It's very hard to leave acquaintances and friends, and devote oneself to travelling from town to town, with no hope of enjoying the company, or the laughter, of anybody one could freely open one's mind to. After living for about fourteen months in Bury, which we hardly left in all that time, we were so used to being there that we began to think we were in France. And so today we are leaving a second home [*patrie*]. All these ideas occupied me from Bury to Newmarket; sadness prevented me from talking as we went along; I spent a very gloomy first day.

Alexandre: We had two cabriolets[2] – one for ourselves, the other for the servants, one of whom was French, the other English. Our third horse was a saddle horse, which I rode and thus I left Bury. We mustn't forget to mention our dog, a general companion for our journey.

François: The weather was fine enough; we had a little sun, only the wind was tiresome. It made M. de Lazowski's ears very red, and he often complained. We went only as far as Newmarket, wanting to spare the horses on the first day (14 miles). The road is good, though rather dirty; the hills[3] we kept having to climb slowed us down; we scarcely managed to trot. As for the land, it is dry and uncultivated. The last ten miles especially are uncleared waste. The soil is a fine sand which, however, will support trees as several good partridge-coverts show.

We are travelling in the same cabriolets that took us to Norfolk, with the same two horses, and my brother is on horseback. We are all in good fettle; we hope to keep up a brisk pace and so see something more of the country in the time left to us in England.

---

2   The previous September, they had bought 'two cabriolets, known as *gigs*, for our great journey, our projected tour of England', and tried them out very successfully almost at once on their fortnight's tour of Norfolk (*A Frenchman's Year in Suffolk, 1784*, p. 156). So we think of them setting out in two 2-seater gigs, with three horses, one for each gig and one to be ridden. The cabriolet that later developed as Hansom's 'cab' and as a hackney vehicle seems to have derived from the English gig. For François and Alexandre, the *cabriolet* was clearly synonymous with *gig*. However, W. Bridges Adams, *English Pleasure-Carriages* (1837), p. 240, declared that the cabriolet 'much used in the present day, is in reality a regeneration of the old one-horse chaise'. The Curators of the Museums and Galleries of both Hull and Maidstone have been very helpful in sorting out the nature of this carriage.
3   Gradual, but in a motoring age we forget the effect of a steady incline, and indeed decline, on horse-drawn traffic.

7.   *Angel Hill, Bury St Edmunds, 1777: second state of J.S. Lamborn's print. The newly remodelled Angel Hotel stands just above the coach-horses on the right; at the left edge, St Edmund's Hill, the house in which Professor Symonds was host to the three Frenchmen.*

8.   *A one-horse gig draws up at a country inn. 'After' Henry Bunbury.*

Newmarket[4]   It was 16 February. Newmarket is a very small town, with no trade. The horse-racing and the large numbers of horses training there all the year round, and of people employed in that business, is what the inhabitants live on. The King and several grandees have houses in this town, where they live during the race-meetings. Its situation is on a north-east slope.

Huntingdon 17 February 1785   Our second day, the 17th, Newmarket to Huntingdon – 29 miles. The weather was so bad, it froze; and it snowed so hard that it was impossible to see the landscape, but I was missing very little. I had travelled the same road in summer, and seen nothing but heath and grassy waste over a great expanse. A little further on from Newmarket, all the land is cultivated, but its sandy nature[5] impedes fertility. This district is cultivated entirely in the French way: no enclosures; the fields simply worked in length, ignoring the natural slope for water-drainage. The sole difference is that [with us] the land never lies fallow; it's productive every year. It seems awful to abandon these immense acreages of heath to a few sheep that could be feeding themselves as part of crop-production.[6] What can be the explanation? They would prove as good as the neighbouring lands which *are* cultivated, and would justify the cost as *they* do. It seems unforgivable that, in England where the public interest is so powerful an incentive, so great an area should be left out of cultivation.

I have already spoken of Cambridge, and even in some detail when I described the brief visit I made last summer; so I will say nothing of it now except to complain of the high cost of the turnpikes, on which one has to pay 12 French sols for a one-horse cabriolet and 6 sols for a saddle-horse.[7]

The awful weather did not abate during our lunch at Cambridge. We found it just as bad when we left the inn, and it came with us all the way to Huntingdon, a distance of 17 miles. The road itself is one of the finest I have seen anywhere;[8] the sandy soil is very favourable to it but nothing has been spared to make it as fine as a road in a park: such roads are worth so much more than our cobble-stones. The horses and carts can go longer on them, and the travellers are less worn-out. These roads are made for travellers, for horses and carriages. The country is flat and – seen through the wretched weather – it looked rather poor and the farming indifferent.[9]

---

4   The towns they named (like this) in the left margin may usually be taken to be the towns in which they were staying when their journal-entries were being made. They sometimes added the day of the month. I have added Sundays and Wednesdays as useful markers of the week, without wrapping them in scholarly square brackets.

5   It is chalk, rather than sand.

6   He was remembering, for instance, the way the very light lands of the Sandlings, the coastal heath district of Suffolk, were, by a 4- or 5-year rotation of crops, able to provide fodder for a great many animals that, in turn, manured the soil: see e.g., *A Frenchman's Year in Suffolk, 1784*, p. 137.

7   *Ibid.*, pp. 91–6, where he had also thought the turnpike tolls excessive. For French and English 'sols' see p. xiv.

8   Its basis was Roman.

9   T. Stone's *General View of the Agriculture of Huntingdonshire*, 1793, pp. 8, 15, 17, showed two-thirds of the county in open fields. 'The sheep of the common fields are of a very inferior

Two miles before reaching Huntingdon, you go through a place called Godmanchester which was once a very considerable town. Today it is reduced to one parish and a few inhabitants.[10]

The last half-mile is a causeway raised to a height of almost thirty feet, forty or fifty feet wide. At places where water passes under the road there are two bridges, each of eight arches: a third, a little less massive and very ancient, crosses the river. The road and the first two bridges [causeways] have been built about six or seven years.[11] As we passed alongside the river, I saw the course where races are held twice a year. There are several such race-courses: some Newmarket horses come here.

HUNTINGDON

Huntingdon is a very small town, not more than five hundred souls.[12] It is well built; I have seen more than fifty very pretty houses.[13] The trade is in wool, which is spun and combed there.

In the middle of the market place is a Town Hall newly built [1745] by the county at the cost of the duke of Manchester[14] and Lord Sandwich,[15] the two principal

sort; from the neglected state of the land on which they are depastured, and the scanty provision for their support in winter . . . their wool is also of a very inferior quality'. It is hard to square this with François' account of the fine Lincolnshire sheep 'spread generally across Huntingdonshire'. See below, p. 16 note 18.

10 It was a Roman town (24 acres) at a major road and river crossing, but in the Middle Ages never more than one flourishing royal manor and agricultural parish. Today it is charming.

11 The main bridge over the Ouse *is* very ancient, pre-1322, and very narrow, and has lately been bypassed by two deplorable concrete bridges. The approach-causeways, apparently lately rebuilt in 1785, were constructed to take the traffic across the meadows when the Ouse was in flood. A plaque on a surviving brick bridge of eight arches records: 'Robertus Cooke, Ex Aquis Emersus, Hoc Viatoribus Sacrum, DD 1637'. The height of the causeways above the meadows is nearer 3 ft than 30: an English foot and a French *pied* are similar, yet François wrote *trente pieds*. He may well have meant 30 inches (*pouces*).

12 Huntingdon was an Anglo-Saxon *burh* (fortified town). The Normans built a small castle here, and it became the county town of Huntingdonshire, with several parish churches, reduced to two since the 17th century.

13 Many of those pretty houses are now destroyed or disfigured: the bypass came too late, and there are now mediocre shopping and housing developments.

14 Robert Montagu, 3rd duke, 1710–62, lived nearby at Kimbolton Castle, designed for his father, the 1st duke, c.1707 by Vanbrugh, who had designed Blenheim Palace for Marlborough: see below p. 132.

15 John Montagu, 4th earl, 1718–92, lived just outside Huntingdon at Hinchingbrooke, a big rambling house, medieval, Tudor and later. He was a businesslike First Lord of the Admiralty. The sandwich is said to be named after him: he once sat 24 hours at the gaming table eating only slices of cold beef between slices of toast: the word was in use in the 1760s. The Town Hall they saw survives, with its four Hanoverian portraits and three fine chandeliers in the ballroom; the small card-room is now the Mayor's Parlour. Allan Ramsay's full-length portraits of George III and Queen Charlotte in their coronation robes are splendid. George II's portrait in coronation robes is by the court painter John Shackleton: Queen Caroline's is almost certainly a copy of the Goodwood Vanderbank, 1736, made in 1784 by Gainsborough's nephew and assistant, Dupont. There is also an engaging portrait of Sandwich himself by Thomas Beach,

landowners. It contains the court of Quarter-sessions and that for the Assizes, both quite large, painted and suited to their functions. Above is the Assembly Room where there are balls five or six times a year, and daily while the races are on: it is very beautiful, 60 feet by 30; adorned by four portraits, all life-size: the King, the Queen, the Prince of Wales and another lady of the blood royal.[16] There are two chimney-pieces and several chandeliers. The card-room is small. There is a market at Huntingdon once a week, on Tuesdays I think.

We certainly didn't forget to visit the house where Cromwell was born [25 April 1599]. The front on to the road has been entirely rebuilt: the back of the house is the only part remaining of the old building. We were taken to the room where he was born – a small room, low and uncomfortable. The house belongs to a private family, very willing to let us see the room and part of an old stone wall.[17] I suppose they are equally polite to all strangers. The duke of Manchester has complete sway in this town. He nominates whom he pleases as Members of Parliament representing the freeholders of the borough – 'free', as their name suggests.

The bad weather and the continuation of the snow could not hold us fast in Huntingdon: as travellers we are too intrepid to be discouraged by the rotten climate. We left next morning in weather as bad as we had the previous day, but soon afterwards we grew more cheerful: the snow stopped and the weather cleared: there remained only the icy wind that I found very painful.

The cold was such that we could not stay in the cabriolet: we would have perished. All we could do was to get down and walk. That day we did more than half the journey on foot.

I saw for the first time the fine sheep of these parts: they are of the Lincolnshire breed, spread generally across Huntingdonshire. They are extremely fat, their fleece very long: they are white all over and polled [their horns removed]. Their heads are so small and their fleece so long that their eyes and their noses seem to spring directly from their necks.[18]

after Gainsborough. (See J.F. Kerslake in *The Connoisseur*, May 1955.) Hitherto, the earliest reference to the existence of the Corporation's pictures has been Brayley and Britton's (*Beauties of England and Wales*) in 1808.

[16] Gainsborough Dupont's copy of the portrait of Queen Caroline was commissioned by Sandwich in November 1784, and the portrait of Sandwich himself was Thomas Beach's copy, 1793, of Gainsborough's portrait in the National Maritime Museum.

[17] The birthplace is now entirely built over, but the 12th-century stone building which served as Cromwell's school is now a most remarkable small museum, vividly recalling him to mind, with portraits and such memorabilia as the hat, with enormous brim, he is thought to have worn when dissolving the Long Parliament, and the apothecary's cabinet, made by Nicholas Kolb, that went with him on active service.

[18] This is interesting. It flatly contradicts the description of the sheep in Huntingdonshire given in the *General View* by T. Stone (1793): footnote 9 p. 14 above. François and Lazowski were friends and pupils of Arthur Young: their observations are not easily dismissed. Their knowledge of the value of the long fleece of Lincolnshire sheep was gained first in Norwich. See 'Norwich's textile industry in 1784, observed by Maximilien de Lazowski', *Textile History*, 23, 1992, and 3rd impression, 1995, of *A Frenchman's Year in Suffolk*.

I notice that the breed of all the animals is stronger than those in Suffolk; the cows are perceptibly larger and more handsome.

This countryside must be very pleasant in summer, crossed by hills, valleys and streams. We went through several well-built villages but with names so uncouth [*baroque*] that I've already forgotten them.[19]

The George at Spaldwick   The horses were getting weary with the frequent jolting caused by the road, so we stopped in a village called Spaldwick, which stands a short distance from Kimbolton, the principal seat of the duke of Manchester, where Queen Catherine, of Spain, took refuge after her divorce from Henry VIII.[20]

The innkeeper, inclined to be talkative, was unusually intelligent. He told us that the part of the county we had just come through was enclosed only a short time ago, and, in fact, we had noticed that the hedges were very newly planted.[21] He told us the land was leased at thirty shillings an acre. The greater part is in pasturage. They have many cows and send the butter and cheese to Huntingdon, and from there to London via Lynn: Lynn is the chief centre of communication for this whole region. The river Ouse is navigable as far as Northamptonshire, and on all sides are canals leading to all parts of the county and its neighbours.[22]

Commonly, a farmer has between 12 and 20 cows in his yard: he needs ¾ of an acre of pasturage to feed each one. The cows sell on the hoof at from 3 to 6 guineas. All land that makes good pasture is left as pastures, and every six years they plough them, and sow clover and sainfoin and ray-grass [*ivraie vivace*]; and so on for six more years.

A day's work earns a shilling, evening out the wage over summer, winter and harvest. I've seen on the farms a large number of hens, larger than in those parts of England I've seen so far.

After a light lunch we resumed our journey. I was obliged to take along with me

---

[19] Not particularly uncouth by Anglo-Saxon standards: Ellington and Spaldwick, now by-passed by the A14, lie in the meadows beside a winding east-flowing stream. Bythorn, with its former toll-bar house, is on the slopes of the watershed that marks the Hunts/Northants boundary, before the road descends to Thrapston at the crossing of the Nene river.

[20] Kimbolton Castle had been rebuilt (see p. 15 above) since Catherine of Aragon was strictly confined there by the King in 1534 for not helping him to repudiate her and her daughter Mary in favour of Anne Boleyn. She sickened and died there early in 1536.

[21] The walls of an upper room of the George at Spaldwick retain painted secular figures, including an archer of Henry VIII's time. Enclosure maps of 1775 and 1776 show the progress of subdivision of the fields of Spaldwick: parts of them are still under permanent pasture as they have been since 1776. See Peter Bigmore, *The Bedfordshire and Huntingdonshire Landscape*, 1979, p. 177. Perhaps this explains the fine beasts noticed by François and Alexandre, and the discrepancy with Stone's *General Description* of 1793 (see p. 16 opposite).

[22] In fact Northamptonshire was fed by the network of the *Nene* Navigation, through Wisbech and then Lynn and London. The *Ouse* Navigation network fed the counties south of this – Bedfordshire, Huntingdonshire and Cambridgeshire – through Lynn. The confusion is under-standable. They were approaching the watershed between the two systems and at Thrapston reached the Nene itself.

a poor dog that was so tired it could hardly stand. It was so longing to come into the carriage and so appealing that I took pity on him and let him come in.[23]

The very bad weather resumed: it was extremely cold as we arrived at Thrapston, the first town within the boundaries of Northamptonshire.

Thrapston   Thrapston lies in a funnel-shaped dip formed by hills of some height. It's a very small place: although it has a weekly market, it has no more than 250 inhabitants. It is all in one parish, of which the houses, though stone-built, look poorer than we have seen elsewhere. The 250 are employed in spinning wool and in some lace-making.

The innkeeper was a character.[24] He amused me the more because he irritated M. de Lazowski so much. He is a prattler of the most incorrigible kind. He is in the habit of visiting all his guests to chat with them; so, after entering the adjoining room to talk to the visitors, and honouring them with a little song which his rough voice made very pleasing, he came into our room. He held forth at length against the American War and against those who brought it on, Lord North, etc.; he wished them in hell, as the English do; and, after talking for more than an hour, he told us how vexatious it was that he couldn't speak French and that he couldn't understand our English – because we might have had a little conversation. Notice that we had been talking for a whole hour, and that he had understood us very well! I learnt afterwards that he was drunk. He said he was going to drink some rum and water and go to bed; but he came back to tell us, with laughter, the story of his wife, who fell as she went down to the cellar, and broke her leg badly!

19 February 1785   On the 19th, when we got up, we saw that a lot of snow had fallen, but that it had stopped. Only the wind continued, and it was very cold. We took the Northampton road.

The road is perhaps one of the worst in England.[25] It is punishing for the horses. Once again we were glad that it had frozen as much as it had, because the frozen mud bore the weight of our horses, and without that I don't know if our carriages could have gone forward. Not only is the land very hilly, but the ground is so slippery and the gravel so scarce that there is no highway at all. The road is traceable, but that is all. If these metalled roads are better, when they are good, than our paved roads, they are worse when they are bad, or in places where sand and gravel are scarce.

I can say nothing of the agriculture: I saw none: snow covered everything. All I can say is that I very much regret not seeing this countryside at another time of year. The line of the hills, the various field-enclosures, which is all I have to judge by, gave me an idea of what this land might be like in summer.

23 François doesn't refer to the dog Alexandre says they brought from Bury for company: perhaps he travelled with the servants: page 12 above.
24 Paterson's *Roads*, 1826, gives two inns at Thrapston, the *George* and the *White Hart*.
25 In fact it had been turnpiked in the 1750s as far as Wellingborough, but, incomprehensibly, not from Wellingborough to Northampton until 1796.

Wellingborough   We stopped at Wellingborough, a small town, a single parish of about 1500 people. It stands on the side of a little hill in a fertile district of superb fields. The trade is lace, which they send to London via Lynn, and thence abroad. It is said that their profits amount to about 50 pounds sterling a week. There is a weekly market. The building stone is uniform: all the houses are built of it: a sort of imperfect sandstone, yet durable enough. Reddish brown,[26] rather small pieces. In buildings, I haven't seen them bigger than about one foot and a half square: they are found in shallow ground not more than two feet deep. They are used in drystone walls in place of field hedges, a distinct advantage for the ground is improved by the removal of the stones. What I see deriving the greatest beauty from the abundance of this stone are the bell-towers of the churches, which here are just like the majority of those in France, a very sharply pointed cone, sometimes with open-work embodied in the upper parts. They are very tall and one sees them from very far off. In the rest of England, the square towers containing the bells are brick-built, looking like a large dove-cote.[27]

On our way to Northampton we passed by a very considerable house[28] belonging to Lord John Cavendish,[29] with what seemed to me a superb situation. It is on top of a hill and overlooks a lovely large valley, neither too close nor too distant to please the eye. His farm, with several fine improvements I noticed, had the look of having been taken in hand by the owner himself: it stands on a hillside and in an amphitheatre looking out over the rest of the countryside, and must be a delicious situation in summer.

---

[26] It is a Liassic rock, or marlstone, coloured by iron oxide, and so more of a rusty brown, and is usually known as ironstone. It gives a warmth and interest to Wellingborough and to a district running mainly from North Oxfordshire through western Northants and Rutland, into Kesteven.

[27] It is not surprising that François noticed the spires for which the Midlands (and especially Northamptonshire with no fewer than eighty of them) are famous. Modest, sturdy and beautiful examples begin as soon as you go west of the river Cam, and it is much to Alexandre's credit that he took note of one – it would have been Fenstanton's – 'when we were about 7 miles from Cambridge: since that village, all the churches are different from those of Suffolk, where the bells hang in towers: here they are all *en pointe*' – spires. *Alexandre* did not suppose Suffolk's towers were all 'brick-built'. What *can* François have been thinking of? Not Bury or Sudbury, Woodbridge or Framlingham, which have stone towers the equal of almost any in Christendom. Like François, Alexandre enjoyed the road through Spaldwick, 'un joli pays'. So, till lately, it was, and the spires of the little villages such as Ellington and Spaldwick you never forget once you've seen them: but the traffic on the adjacent A 14 wrecks the quiet sense of being in the country: at least it no longer pounds through the villages themselves.

[28] Billing Hall, Great Billing, stood above the church, east of it. 'A handsome old house with pleasant gardens' in 1720. In c.1776, Lord John Cavendish 'completely transformed it'. It was apparently a large plain house designed by Carr of York in the local Kingsthorpe stone (Barker, *History of Northamptonshire*, I, 24). It was the home of the singer Gervase Elwes (d.1921), and was pulled down in the 1960s in the interests of suburban development.

[29] 1732–96, he had shown himself a competent Chancellor of the Exchequer, but only during the younger Pitt's brief absence from that post: five months in 1782, and then for nine months in 1783. Burke described him as 'one of the oldest and best friends I ever had, or that our common country possessed'. He was called 'the learned canary bird' from his good memory and small stature.

The park is notable for a grove of very large and very old trees, rare in England and very pleasant for walking on a hot day.

A little further along the same road is the house of Squire d'Arby, also pleasantly situated.[30]

NORTHAMPTON

Northampton   When I arrived I was astonished to find a broad and handsome street, straight, with good buildings, and with pavements and street-lighting as in London. I'd heard it was a pretty town, but hadn't thought it was so elegant. It is not very large: only two parishes.[31] The market-place is one of the finest I have seen: a great square.[32] In the middle stands an obelisk, or pyramid, which disfigures more than it embellishes: erected by voluntary subscription, it is small and not at all adequate to its position.[33] From the four corners of the market-place, four roads lead out towards the four points of the compass, corresponding to different routes, and beginning to create suburbs. The town is completely built of stone. It is the capital of Northamptonshire.

The market is very considerable: the outlet for all the produce of the countryside – butter, cheese and grain on its way from here to Lynn by river, and then on to London or to foreign parts. [Alexandre adds coal to the list of exports to Lynn.] The Prince of Wales and the Duc de Chartres are expected to pass through the town tomorrow on their way for a few days' hunting with a gentleman of this county,[34] but the frost will spoil their sport.

We stayed in Northampton only long enough to see the town. Nothing else stirred our curiosity. The evening and two or three hours next morning were enough. We left after lunch.

Here Alexandre adds a little to the picture of their brief stay in Northampton, which he thought 'tres grand et tres joli'.

30 Abington Hall, conceivably by Francis Smith of Warwick, is now one of Northampton's museums. In 1785 it was owned by Squire Thursby, who had the kind of name a Frenchman finds difficult. A pleasant building: downpipes dated 1743.
31 In fact, there are still four early medieval parishes: by 1200, there were nine. The widening and straightening of the streets followed a great fire of 1675 which destroyed four-fifths of the town.
32 It was moved to this site by Henry III. In 1712, John Morton had claimed it was 'lookt upon as the finest in Europe' (*Natural History of Northamptonshire*). In 1958 the once splendid Charles II Peacock Hotel was finally destroyed to make way for an enormous supermarket. Since 1971, the familiar medieval and 17th-century street-pattern has made way before the gods of motor-traffic.
33 It was replaced by a cast-iron fountain in 1863, scarcely an improvement. Now the market-place is wholly disfigured.
34 The Prince of Wales, later Prince Regent, and King George IV. Duc de Chartres, later 'Philippe-Egalité', guillotined 1793, father of King Louis-Philippe. They were clearly delayed by the weather. The *Northampton Mercury* of 28 February announced: 'His Royal Highness the Prince of Wales is expected to pass through this town, accompanied by the Duke de Chartres, as soon as the weather alters, on their way to Mr Meynell's Hunt at Quarndon in Leicestershire. Sixteen Horses and nine Grooms belonging to His Royal Highness are now in waiting at Market Harborough'. At Quarndon, on the edge of Charnwood Forest, Hugo Meynell reigned, 1753–1800, over the most celebrated Leicestershire hunt, 'the Quorn'. His house now belongs to Loughborough University. Arthur Young deplored the Duc de Chartres' 'readiness to titter' – see Epilogue, p. 245.

9.   *Northampton Market-Place: south view. James Blackamore, surveyor, after 1761.*

10.   *Cyparissus pavement, Leicester.*

Alexandre: The town is mostly built of stone with very little brick. The four main streets leading from the market place are superb. The banks of the Nene are composed of beautiful meadows intersected by trees, and must be very delightful in the summer. Covered by the snow, the beauty is lost to view of a very pleasant landscape, especially in the surroundings of the town. There are two squares, one presided over by the church[35] which is built of a beautiful stone: its main entrance has a frontispiece adorned with a fine colonnade. Above the frontispiece, which is simple, without ornament, is an inscription saying that King Charles II had given money for the building. There is a statue of the King, and a very beautiful dome over the church. There is an inn that is more like a palace than an inn.[36] The central square is regularly laid out, with a promenade in the middle. The town is magnificent.

François: The snow that fell overnight made it increasingly difficult to see the countryside: what little we were able to see made us constantly regret that we weren't travelling in a different season. The views must be delightful. We drove for about four miles along a ridge above two valleys which, on either side of us, ran almost parallel with our ridge, like two ditches beside our road. The road is perhaps half-a-mile wide, and reasonably high. The valleys looked prosperous and are well populated. However, the houses are small, and look poor: most of them are built only of mud,[37] upon a few lower courses of rough stone. However, the mud-building is better than that in many of our regions. I've examined it carefully, and not only is the mud-walling very compact, but instead of grass-thatch they use wheat-straw.

AN ENGLISH INN

Welford, Sunday 20 February   Unable to reach Leicester, we stopped at an excellent inn in a little village called Welford.[38] Our host told us that the fields had been enclosed about

35 All Saints was very largely rebuilt after the great fire of 1675: its west end was removed to make way for the town's busy traffic. This explains the Frenchmen's pleasure in the town plan. What the inscription actually says is that Charles II gave 'a thousand tun of timber' for the rebuilding of All Saints. The statue shows the king oddly arrayed in his long wig over Roman armour, and is disproportionately small, perhaps in the vain hope of creating a sense of height and distance.
36 Probably the George, which Defoe described in the same words: 'more like a palace . . . and cost above £2000 building'. But both the Red Lion and the Peacock also had about 40 rooms. The George was demolished in 1921 to make way for a new Lloyds Bank.
37 Naseby, in this part of Northamptonshire, was said to have consisted almost entirely of mud buildings until about 1850 (C.F. Innocent, *The Development of English Building Construction*, 1916, p. 145).
38 In Northamptonshire, but near the Leicestershire boundary. *Paterson's Roads*, 1826, in the index at p. 76, shows that post-horses were available at the Talbot, clearly their 'excellent inn'. A sturdy Elizabethan-Jacobean stone-built house, with 18th-century remodelled and stucco'd front, survived a demolition of more than half the inn in 1957. It has been converted into a private house. Staircases and fireplaces of the 17th century survive, and parts of the stables are now farm-buildings. John Spencer, their host in 1785, advertised in the Northampton Mercury 17 July 1772 that he had 'greatly enlarged and completely fitted up the said House'. I owe this reference to Mr Geoff Pitcher, of Braybrooke.

21 years, which tallied with my noticing that the hedgerows weren't very thick. The main income of the farmers comes from feeding cattle, but they don't rear them: they are driven down from Derbyshire, further north. The rent evens out at a guinea an acre.

It is extraordinary what inns there are even in the smallest English villages. The contrast between the inns of their *big towns* and our large hostelries is too much to our disadvantage, but nothing like so much as when you compare the smaller inns of our two countries. We had in that little village a good, spacious house, all its doors and windows freshly painted, shutters and blinds with green cords and copper[39] pulleys; bells everywhere. Our dining room (for one never has meals in the bedroom) was very neatly wainscotted and with a prettily papered ceiling, mahogany tables and chairs, a good supper and then an excellent bed. We were as comfortable as if we were in a very grand hotel, and everything as clean. And yet this was in a village on a not-very-busy road. The stables amazed me even more than the houses as to cleanliness and good arrangement: each horse has its stall, partitioned off by wood, very roomy, perhaps seven or eight feet wide, the racks, mangers etc. in good order, and with halter, well fitted, and no lack of litter for each stall. How often have I found in France stables in which our five horses,[40] packed together, hardly had room to lie down beside each other, and where a ladder served as rack, and the manger was so badly holed that the oats fell out at the back; and we had scarcely straw enough to cover the floor. The difference between us and the English, which I am constantly made aware of, sometimes grieves me: we are inferior to them in a great many ways. I make this reflection not only in regard to inns; I am speaking much more generally.

21 February 1785   On the 21st, we left early to go to Leicester, only seventeen miles away, with the idea of stopping at a little inn on the road, the only way to make some useful enquiries: the snow and frost did not let up, but there were compensations: we stopped at Wigston, the first village we went through in the county of Leicestershire.[41] It is a very large country-town with two parishes.[42] It has a considerable trade in yarn-spinning and in stocking-manufacture: there are perhaps 500 frames making stockings that are sent to Leicester (4 miles) by cart, to be washed (*blanchis*) and then sent on. Our innkeeper is a farmer, a butcher, and a good fellow. We asked him to our room, gave him some punch, and talked about the land.

---

39 *cuivre*: it may be that *cuivre jaune* – brass – was meant.
40 They evidently used 2-horse carriages on their travels through France.
41 He missed Husbands Bosworth; perhaps it was snowing!
42 He wrote 'Whetstone' which is indeed a village just south of Leicester, but it lies just west of the Lutterworth road, and some miles west of the Welford road by which they were approaching Leicester. Furthermore, Whetstone, like most Leicestershire villages, has only one ancient parish; but Wigston is distinguished by having two, and was indeed known as Wigston-two-steeples. W.G. Hoskins wrote a classic social and economic history of Wigston, *The Midland Peasant*, 1957. Enclosure had put paid to its medieval open field farming in 1766. By 1801, when the first census was made, 1,020 of the 1,658 people of Wigston were working in trade or industry, only 113 in agriculture. François called it 'un très gros bourg', which suggests a town rather than the over-populated 'industrial village' it was. One would like to identify the good farmer-butcher-innkeeper. The French travellers can't have spent more than an hour or so in Wigston: they called on Mr Peares in Leicester that same evening.

The farms are large, generally of five or six hundred acres which, on average, are let for a rent of one guinea. Meadowlands are worth up to 42 shillings, a prodigious sum.[43] They usually cut the hay, then turn the cattle on to the meadows till winter. The meadows are always left as meadows, but there are also artificial meadows (for there couldn't be enough natural meadowland), and these are sown with clover and ray-grass for three years and the cattle are allowed to graze them, partly on the hoof, partly in the field during winter: a haystack is made and the hay distributed to the cattle when the pasture has been completely cropped. They have few turnips. When the three years are up, they plough the artificial meadows and scatter lime and dung over them, then for three years put them down successively to oats, barley and oats. If the soil is suited to wheat, then they sow a crop of wheat. It's only about thirteen years since these lands were enclosed, which has caused a rent rise of ten shillings an *arpent*, on average.[44] They raise all their cattle themselves: they buy none from outside. The cows are fine and quite large: they give milk from the age of 18 months, 4 gallons a day. The sheep are superb: their wool is extraordinarily long and very white: their heads are completely covered in it, and polled (hornless). They yield ten pounds of wool a year.

A good cow fetches about 8 guineas: the return it makes is seven [guineas] a year. Their milk is made into butter and cheese (excellent), which are sold at Leicester, and which, from there, are sold abroad. They fatten the beef, cows and sheep on oats, which is not at all economical, and won't allow much profit. Three *arpents* of pasture feed two cows all the year.

It was already easy to see that I was in another county: the breed of the animals is noticeably bigger, the horses especially are strong and handsome. We have seen several teams of farm-horses and waggons, the finest in the world, drawing with surprising strength and vigour, and most of them black.[45]

LEICESTER

Leicester is the capital of Leicestershire, a fairly large, rich and pleasant county. The town is made up of six parishes, of which two are without churches:[46] they fell, over two centuries ago, and haven't been rebuilt. Leicester lies in a plain,[47] and is well built. The majority of its inhabitants are merchants.[48]

---

43 These are interesting figures, and add to W.G. Hoskins's picture of 'Farming after the Enclosure', *op. cit.*, pp. 261–7.

44 It was nearly nineteen years since the actual Parliamentary Enclosure Award of 1766. The French *arpent* could vary between 1 and 1½ acres. See Notes, at p. xiv above. Here, François is probably translating our acre straight into the French word *arpent* without considering the precise measurements. He may have thought of it generally, as a very similar measurement.

45 Sixty years earlier, Defoe wrote of the 'great black coach horses and dray horses . . . continually brought up to London' from Leicestershire.

46 Puzzling: there are five good medieval parish churches: his sixth may have been the abbey of St Mary-in-the-Meadows, which certainly fell soon after Wolsey came to lay his bones there? Or perhaps the Newarke church, also destroyed in the 16th century.

47 Almost a flood-plain: the Soar winds slowly through it, and only in the time of this French visit was the city beginning to clamber up the slope to the south-east.

48 Well, that was his impression.

The market-place is rather fine, though very irregular in shape. In the middle is a building that serves as corn-hall[49] and the upper floor serves for the assizes. The assembly room is on another side; it is said to be very fine; it sometimes serves as a theatre.

The Romans had fortified this town. One sees remains of their buildings, which are always recognizable. One of the castle gates is in a long stretch of wall entirely built by them:[50] their big stones are bonded with their cement, which is impermeable to the weather. We also saw, in a private house, a piece of mosaic of perhaps four square feet. It shows a stag between two children in different postures; but it isn't, by a long way, perfect in either design or colour, compared with those we saw at Lyons and in other French towns.[51]

We noticed, in passing, the biggest gate of the castle, which is of gothic architecture, a very flat vault with several curves boldly arranged.[52] We didn't forget to visit the hospital for the sick, founded by voluntary subscription with the money of the inhabitants of the town and neighbourhood and many legacies. It holds about forty patients but is far from full.[53] There are two physicians, four surgeons and a resident apothecary employed by the house. Even sick children are admitted. Everyone who has contributed £5 is entitled to nominate a patient for a bed: those who've given more may nominate more.

There are four servants living in. There's no shortage of baths or anything needed for the various treatments: the building, of brick, is large and elegant.[54] During the past year an entire wing has been added to confine the insane, who will pay a little for their board. My one reservation concerns the luxuriousness of this building: not only that, on all sides there are consulting-rooms (a kind of parlour) for considering, they say, each type of illness, as though one room would not do for all: for, as well as their being magnificently furnished, they do occupy space and they cost money that could be used to help a greater number of sick: instead of five guineas, four would be enough.

---

49 'halle pour mettre les grains à couvert.'
50 He may be referring to 'the Jewry Wall', a noble and unmistakeably Roman length of stone, laced with red brick courses, and some 24 feet high; but it is by no means associated with any gate – of the castle or of the town.
51 (Pl. 10) It was discovered c.1675 in High Cross Street, near All Saints church, and is now in the Jewry Wall Museum. It shows a youth fondling a stag, while Cupid aims an arrow at them. John Nichols, a decade later (*History and Antiquities of Leicester*, I, 1795, p. 9), rehearsed some fairly improbable classical interpretations, which had clearly not been tried out on the French visitors. The present museum label, much more satisfactory, suggests that the youth is probably intended to represent Cyparissus, who accidentally killed his pet stag when he was out hunting. Out of compassion, the gods turned him into a cypress tree, a symbol of mourning. Sure enough, the youth does seem, towards the right of the mosaic, to be beginning to be identified with a sort of tree.
52 Difficult. He may have been thinking of the early 15th-century Magazine Gateway, which has a low vault, but no very bold curves! A castle gateway of 1422 was partly destroyed in a riot in 1832.
53 Alexandre says '35 beds, not counting those for the insane, of whom there are few'. He describes a disagreeable odour.
54 It was erected in 1771 to the design of Benjamin Wyatt: V.C.H. *Leicestershire,* IV, 1958, p. 372, which contains a bare outline of the infirmary's beginnings. It is now rather hidden among extensions (Pl. 11).

11.   *South view of Leicester infirmary and asylum. Longmate, 1796.*

12.   *Robert Bakewell on his cattle-pastures at Dishley.*

The English are not as economical as we are in their public establishments: the wards are large but not very clean; each patient has a bed.[55]

Near this infirmary is the public promenade,[56] which is delightful, under the trees. The land belongs to the corporation; so does a very large common[57] where all the *freemen* of the town are allowed to pasture a horse or a cow from September right through the winter without paying a farthing. This corporation is immensely rich: it lodges the Recorder, whose house is near the common. They say that in summertime it's charming to see the fashionable people of the town walking beneath this fine avenue of trees.

Mr Symonds gave us a letter for a Mr Peares, a lawyer, whose son is a successful merchant.[58] We found the father, after dinner, drinking beside his fire; he was in that state of English drowsiness that immediately follows a meal, and his belly was so roundly extended that he could scarcely move. If it were not so unpleasant, I would add that standing up cost him the most painful efforts and much breaking of wind, which the English generally take no trouble to control. He received us very politely, had glasses brought for us, and we drank with him. He told us many things about the town, and sent for his son, who soon arrived. We continued to drink, and our conversation extended to the business of the town.

It is very considerable. It is the entrepôt of all the yarn spun in the county and of the stocking manufacture, woollen, cotton and silk; woollen stockings easily surpass in quantity the trade in the others.[59] The majority are sent to Spain and Africa. They are all different: for this last market, their quality is coarser: they are blue, with large white or yellow clocks representing two flowers. Mr Peares assured us that if they weren't made precisely to this pattern they wouldn't sell.

The rest of their output is for England, though a little goes to France. All sorts of jumpers and woollen vests are made here, and are very cheap. Lately they have started up a branch of Manchester trade, a kind of knitted cotton and silk which makes very pretty waistcoats and has become very fashionable. A single waistcoat sells at 6

---

55 John Howard criticised the inadequate ventilation in 1789: the architect John Johnson supervised improvements (Nancy Briggs, *John Johnson, 1732–1814*, Chelmsford, 1991, p. 133).
56 A boundary path between the medieval south and east fields. Known as 'the Queen's Walk' when it was walked by the Corporation in 1785. Now known as the New Walk, about a mile long and unique in England, according to Pevsner, *Leicestershire*, p. 137. And see W.G. Hoskins, *Leicestershire*, 1957, p. 103.
57 Still known as the Freemen's Common.
58 See Introduction, p. 4, for Mr Symonds. 'Mr Peares' may perhaps be the father, also, of Thomas Pares, junior, a Leicester solicitor for whom correspondence and bills survive for the late 18th and early 19th centuries (Cradock-Hartopp Papers, Leicestershire Record Office, 10 D 72): Thomas Pares, junior, was living in Cank Street in 1775 and Friar Lane in 1800. I am grateful to Mr K.L. Ovenden, Assistant Keeper of Archives, for these references. See p. 64, fn. 14, for another reference to the Pares family.
59 John Throsby, *History and Antiquities of Leicester*, wrote in 1791: 'In Leicester there are upwards of seventy manufacturers called hosiers, who, it is computed, employ 3,000 frames. Out of 14,000 souls in Leicester, 6,000, it is conjectured, are employed or depend on one branch or other of this great business'.

shillings. The stuff is made on a stocking-frame, to which has been added a new invention which has the advantage of never stopping the thread. The manufacturer was kindly willing to explain it to me.[60] He stopped the workman and got him to go on very slowly, but the mechanism of the whole machine is so complicated that, as I've never examined in detail a stocking-frame, I'm in no position to describe what I saw, and could only begin to explain it if I had a simple stocking-frame in front of me: yet I examined it for half-an-hour with the greatest attention.

Leicester manufactures are worth about £200,000 sterling a year: most of it is for export. The spinning is spread throughout the countryside. There are [middle] men who buy the wool and supply work to several parishes, then sell the yarn to the manufacturers: it's a kind of trade. I should add that everything made at Leicester is made with combed wool, none of it is carded. As for the yarn, spinning it is peculiar; I've never seen spinning like this; the women spin with each hand yet as fast as if they were only operating with one hand. They reckon to spin a pound of wool in six hours, and earn 8 *sols* (16 French *sols*).[61] Their wheels are simple and low down, a foot-wheel placed on a small board and wound round by a leather thong which passes over the spindle of two little bobbins set in front of the woman, above the wheel, and level with her stomach. Above the bobbins is a distaff which is no more than a little double fork on which one lays the wool, which divides in two, each half going to a bobbin. This neat arrangement is easy for the woman to work: she doesn't get tired by having to lift her hands too high. The movement of the pedal is generally slight: they spin with the greatest speed I ever saw.

Leicester is well populated: it contains a great many gentlemen of considerable fortune, but there is a preponderant number of merchants.

We saw Leicester to its great disadvantage: all the streets were covered with snow, which fell unceasingly. I forget to say that there are many poor in this town, as in almost all towns where there are manufactures. The contribution that has to be paid to the poor, which is called 'the poor rate', is five shillings in the pound, exactly a quarter.

22 February 1785   On the 22nd we left Leicester for Loughborough in very bad weather: it was foggy and the snow fell so densely that I could scarcely see anything at fifty feet.[62] So I can give no account of the countryside, which is said to be very

---

[60] Mr Peares' openness with three foreigners about this 'new invention' is remarkable. He may have felt confident that the complexity of the knitting machinery would baffle them. François' candour over his failure to grasp these intricacies is engaging. Professor Harris tells me M. Bruno Jacomy has pointed out that the only Arts et Métiers item in the Encyclopédie that Diderot insisted on writing himself was that on the knitting frame: he didn't trust anyone else to do it.

[61] Here he means '8 pence' (i.e. 8 'old' English pence), which is roughly what 16 French *sols* were worth: see Measurements and Currency Values on p. xiv above.

[62] Loughborough is 11 miles from Leicester. In view of all that they managed to see in Leicester (which they can have reached only the previous afternoon), they must have left for Loughborough in the afternoon – in fog, but evidently before dark.

fine. I was only extremely bothered by the number of cartloads of coal which they carry in blocks, like ashlar, from Loughborough to Leicester and neighbouring places: it is very good coal and comes from Derbyshire,[63] costing very little and burning very well. These carts are a great nuisance to the cabriolets, which have to get off the road to let them pass. We went through a large village[64] called Mountsorrel[65] where there are several good inns and many charming houses. The road is entirely paved in this village, which is something one doesn't often find in England.

Loughborough   Loughborough is a very small place with a weekly market. It has nothing to commend it, nothing in the least interesting to see[66] apart from the coal dock, connected with Derbyshire and high Leicestershire by the river. This canal, built by subscription, is 7 or 8 miles long as far as the place where it enters the river. Those who subscribed share in the revenues and the rights over the canal and are at present well paid in interest on their money. A great many flat-bottomed boats arrive.

VISITING MR BAKEWELL AT DISHLEY

Our sole purpose in coming to Loughborough was to see Mr Bakewell, this industrious farmer living two miles from the place on a farm belonging to Sir Henry Gosson.[67] We didn't present ourselves to him on the night of our arrival as it was a shade too far out. We were content to walk in the town and look at the buildings, well worthy of a village.

Wednesday 23 February   Next day we went over there early, but not early enough, as he had just ridden off to lunch in the town. We found his sister, who was very kind and

---

63   The river Soar, which ran north into the Trent at Leicestershire's boundary with Derbyshire, had been made navigable as far south as Loughborough in 1778 as François goes on to say. It immediately brought the price of Derbyshire coal down, though the canal didn't reach Leicester itself till 1794; which explains these dangerous carts. The west Leicestershire coalfield was a 19th-century development (W.G. Hoskins, *op. cit.*, p. 111).

64   Again, as at Wigston, he uses '*gros bourg*' for what was a large village: the snow made it hard to judge its size. He calls it a *village* in the next sentence.

65   He makes an intelligent guess at the place-name's meaning, spelling it 'Mount Soar-Hill'.

66   Alexandre's verdict was: 'the town is ugly and badly built'. Nevertheless, the 1826 edition of *Paterson's Roads* lists four inns supplying post-horses in Loughborough, as against only three in Leicester itself. And *The Leicester and Nottingham Journal* of the time suggests a surprisingly full social programme in Loughborough: apart from lectures on experimental physics (see below), there were the usual concerts, assemblies and balls, card-parties and florist's feasts, cock-fighting, and so on: all organized by the inn-keepers.

67   This famous farm at Dishley, lying 2 miles out along the Derby road, is now an equestrian centre run by Mr A.G. Gilbey. It belongs to the estate of the Squire de Lisle, of Quenby Hall over in east Leicestershire, who kindly informs me that 'Sir Henry Gosson' must be a misrecollection of Sir William Gordon, KB. Mr Gilbey showed me, in the adjoining meadows, the ridges representing Bakewell's elaborate water-courses, described by François. The Squire de Lisle, a leading authority on Robert Bakewell, has commented helpfully on François' text. Only Worsley and Coalbrookdale gain more of François' space and attention than Dishley.

offered us lunch, dinner, etc., and when we declined, sent for an intelligent servant to show us Mr Bakewell's farm.[68]

This man of genius had often noticed that the part of the bullock that the butcher sold for the best price was the back, the sirloin and fillet (or the saddle of mutton) for roasting; 'gentlemen's meat.' Supposing my drawing, instead of showing this pathetic animal, showed a proper bullock,[69] we might draw two horizontal lines across it: the top section is the most costly, the middle less so, and the rest only fit for the army. He had noticed that generally the bullocks are fattened in all their parts equally, and that it would follow that if someone could develop the greatest amount of meat where the most expensive joints are found, that would be bound to be beneficial. From then on, for over 30 years, he has raised a species of horned beast with the largest possible back – where the best meat is – and the leanest possible lower parts: and in this he has perfectly succeeded. I've seen his bulls and his cows, with backs perhaps a foot and a half across, and practically flat: they are prodigious, and their bellies form a sort of triangle, with very little meat fit for the army! He has done even more: by dint of research, and since he has come to have an entire breed which is always semi-fat [i.e. has a thin covering of fat], the calves are semi-fat and the two-year-olds also – they work on the farm[70] without growing thin. The cows give milk in their state of fatness, and they are semi-fat when they go to the butcher.

After a calf is born, it stays with its mother for a month and a half; sometimes it is put to feed from a cow whose milk isn't as good as its mother's, being fed on turnips or on rotten hay. After this period they are fed by hand with milk and water. When the young cows are a year and a half old they are tethered to a manger where they are fed turnips, straw and hay, and where they stay for about six months. At two, they take a male until they have a calf. Then they are put in the manger, give milk, are sold, then fattened and eaten. The cows give 4 gallons of milk a day (16 bottles), like all the cows of this area. Their great advantage is that they eat no more than other cattle, are always semi-fat and become so in very little time and on very ordinary feed when one wants to fatten them for the table. What I saw of cows applies also to the bulls.

I found it hard to understand how such a race of cattle has been brought into being.[71] He has told me he selected the finest animals he could find in England and

---

68   They had already met Mr Bakewell at Mr Symond's house at Bury St Edmunds the previous year: see *A Frenchman's Year in Suffolk, 1784*, pp. 149–51, q.v. Five years later, in 1790, Professor Symonds followed his French friends to Bakewell's establishment. What pleased him most were the advantages derived from flooding the lands. He, too, mentioned Bakewell's trouble with his uncooperative neighbour. Gordon Mingay has printed some brief selections from letters addressed by Symonds to Arthur Young on this tour of the North Country and Scotland, July – October 1790, in a *Festschrift, On the Move: Essays in Labour and Transport History presented to Philip Bagwell*, ed. C. Wrigley and J. Shepherd, 1991, pp. 9–21. See also fn. 9 on p. 81 below.

69   His little sketches of a bullock and – perhaps – a sheep are very vague and truly dismal.

70   See below, p. 32.

71   Cf. *A Frenchman's Year in Suffolk, 1784*, p. 150: 'I don't really understand it, but I believe

Flanders, those with the biggest backs, then he bred from them: he sought out, sorted out and coupled, several different types until he found what was needed. These he half fattened and in that state he produced the breed. The young took after their parents, coming into the world fatter than the others and, little by little, by dint of trials and the coupling of what he discovered to be the best animals, he came in the end to create the most superb breed of animals I have ever seen.

His object is to sell them. That is the basis of his principal business, and he sells at a very big price, so generally are his breeds admired. He told us that last year he sold a cow for a full sixty guineas, and he wouldn't have sold her for less. He sold for a hundred or a hundred and fifty a fine bull, but not for anything in the world would he sell its calves: he would profit more from leasing them out. There are a great many people who hire them during a campaign to couple them with their cows and so produce a breed much better than their own – but never as good as that of Mr Bakewell who has both the male and the female. The price of a bull for one season is from 20 to 40 guineas, so convinced are people of the advantage to be derived from them, for he lets out regularly all those he has.

The breed of sheep is equally fine in its way. It isn't for their wool – they yield 20 pounds of wool a year and their wool sells at 6½ English, 13 French, sols,[72] more or less like all the other Leicestershire sheep – but that they're fatter, generally producing two lambs a year and fattening in very little time when one wants to fatten them. He showed us a joint from a sheep he had raised; it was a piece of ribs, where the joint is generally very little fat. The fillet [? cutlet: fillet comes from the saddle] of his mutton was five and a half inches thick. M. de Lazowski measured it. I was there: it's such an extraordinary fact that I wouldn't state it if I hadn't seen it. Another advantage of these sheep is their very small bones, which enables them to sell a pound of their mutton dearer than other people's. A pound of theirs contains more meat.

It seems to me that his breed of sheep is even more refined than that of his cows. He won't sell rams and lets them out at a mad price. I have seen him with a farmer who gives him a 100 guineas to have one of his rams for a season. One of these rams can serve 140 ewes.

All his sheep are regularly so plump that we have measured several of them and found them broader than they are tall.[73] They are so well-covered that, although this is lambing time, our fingers could not feel their spines beneath their wool; they have on each side a great lump of fat which the farmer called *clovant flan* [? cloven flank], which isn't to be found in any other breed.

---

it, as I believe in Religion, because I've been told that you have to believe it, and that everyone believes in it.'

72 See *Notes*, p. xiv above. He rates a French *sol* at about half an 'old' English penny.

73 Arthur Young (*Le Cultivateur Anglois*, tome IV, p. 73) recorded H. Stanford's statements at Dishley, 17 March 1790: 'Today I measured one of Mr Bakewell's rams, a 3-year-old: I found it 5ft 10ins in girth and 2ft 5ins tall; the neck, at the base of the ears, 1ft 4ins broad; the breadth at the shoulders, 1ft 11½ins; at the ribs, 1ft 10½; at the haunches, 1ft 9½.'

'Measured today a ram, 2 years old, who has not yet coupled; height, 1ft 11; girth 5ft 9; height of dewlap above ground, 4 inches. I was prevented by a fall of snow from measuring his breadth.'

He won't sell any of his sheep since he finds he can let them out at such profit. However, his man told us he will sell to foreigners, being less afraid that their offspring will destroy the price of his own. Formerly he sold them at 100, sometimes 150, and even 200 guineas each. But now, his breed of sheep is so esteemed that he is unwilling to distribute it. He takes the greatest precautions that no one acquires his sheep, and even when he sells them fattened up for killing. For fear that the butcher breeds from them, he kills them at home and sells the butcher only dead meat for which he pays much more than the current price of mutton. At London, his bullocks and sheep fetch a price very much higher than any other breed.

He has also raised a fine breed of cart-horses. I've seen eight of his stallions which are truly magnificent. All are black, their coats are short and glistening although they are never groomed. They are almost six French feet high; a long and powerful neck, with a small head and lively eyes gives them a majestic appearance; they are extremely short, broad-breasted, their legs low-jointed and strong; they are strong enough to pull a house along. These stallions never work, so one can't tell how good they are; but Mr Bakewell has many others of the same breed, which are as good as they are handsome. He lets them out at about 60 or 80 guineas for a season. It's after a great many trials that this degree of superiority is reached, and he has the glory of being the only man in England, perhaps in the world, who has reached such great perfection in cattle, sheep and horses. I think he has reached the point he was aiming at and no longer seeks to improve them, only to lease them out.

He has about 300 cows, bullocks and bulls, great numbers of sheep and mares with as many horses as are needed to work the farm. I said that the bullocks and cows worked, so that a large number of horses isn't needed. The 300 cows, bullocks or bulls are divided among two farms. All are tethered to a small manger made so that one can go in front of them and behind to see them. Mr Bakewell thinks it much better to keep them tethered than to let them roam in the farmyard where they trample on their fodder which they then won't want to eat, which is very wasteful. There is an abundance of muck, better than if the cattle roamed about in the yard, and they eat all they're given. There's less risk of clashes and injury from horns. He is sure it is better to cart the dung on to the land than to let the cattle loose to manure it unevenly. The expense of servants to look after them, and of the manure that one always has to add to what the cattle provide, is greater than getting in the harvest from the field, bringing it to the stable and spreading the muck on the land; in this way, nothing is lost, all is eaten, and the manure is better rotted.

The layout of this farm, which is immense, gave me the greatest pleasure. All is in tremendous order, everything arranged to avoid wasting time in carting from one place to another. The cows are in a great barn, disposed all round parallel with the walls, head towards the middle. You can walk between their rumps and the wall. The carts arrive in the middle to deposit the straw, hay and turnips. The piles of hay are on the floor, behind the cattle stalls. Another place is intended for the working animals. Here are the milking cows; further off, those that calve, with several little stalls for the calves, according to their different ages. The cattle go into the meadows only for exercise. I've said nothing of neatness and spruceness: it's impossible to have any in so big an establishment; it can be had only as a luxury and expense, but everything you see here is in order. One sees only a few farm-workers, all occupied; and as their jobs are all different they are on their own, with little chance of talking and time-wasting. Anyway, he said his servants were good, that he chose them carefully when he took them on, and on principle looks after them well in order to keep them. Also there are six who have been with him twenty years, who are faithful, and in whom he has complete confidence. He told us he pays them well, and they all seem to like him.

This picture of rustic life pleased me. It was touching to see an old man[74] who, as much from pleasure as self-interest, liked to be liked by his men and to make them happy. I well believe what he told me, that, without good farm-workers it is impossible to run a farm well. He himself was convinced of this truth.

His sister's realm was indoors, the running of the house was hers. It was done with scrupulous cleanliness and simplicity.

Back to Loughborough   After we had been shown over the whole of the farm by his servant, we returned to Loughborough. Mr Bakewell had to be there himself at four in the evening to hear a lecture on experimental physics. We went to see him there and asked him back to supper. His conversation was instructive in his own way all through supper. He showed us how well, beneath a heavy and rough exterior, he had been making observations, and studying how to bring into being his fine breed of animals with as much care as one would put into the study of mathematics or any of the sciences. We arranged to visit the farm with him the following morning.

24 February   Next morning, the 24th, we left Loughborough early to go to breakfast with Mr Bakewell, who lives on the road to Derby, our next destination. He had already walked round his farm. We breakfasted with him. His sister was an even earlier riser, having had her own breakfast some hours before, although it was still no more than 9 o'clock. We saw staying here a young man the Empress of Russia had sent to spend some years studying English agriculture. There are two of them: the other was out in the fields and we saw only one.[75]

After breakfast, we walked over the farmlands. His principal interest, that is to say Bakewell's, is in cattle, and he has as much land as possible down to pasture. So his principal harvest is hay, but for the good of the land itself and of the hay he has to plough his pastures every four years and then for three years running. He sows oats, wheat and barley, and sometimes cabbages and turnips. Only about a quarter of the farm is strictly arable. A great many of his meadows are in the valley-bottom with a

74 He was sixty, and had ten years to go.
75 The Empress had sent over seven or eight young men, who were examined by Arthur Young at the end of their stay in England. Apparently her imperial farm was never established, and on their return the men were 'turned loose, some to starve, some driven into the army, and others retained by Russian noblemen' (Young, *Autobiography*, pp. 124–5). Young's only son went, in 1805, to make an agricultural survey of the province of Moscow for the Tsar: in 1810, he was able to buy a 10,000 acre estate in the Crimea, where he died in 1827 (*op. cit.*, chapters 15 and 16).

damp soil that he can never plough. This means a reduction in the quarter that he ploughs yearly. He has 500 acres,[76] on which he feeds over 400 beasts, which is prodigious. His system operates with many enclosures: all his fields he has divided by hedges and ditches, into small patches of six or ten acres.[77] But here I noticed something I never saw in Suffolk or Norfolk: in both those counties the hedges are planted on the bank where the earth from the ditch was thrown, but here the hedge is planted on the other side. By this method, it is more difficult for the horses and cattle generally to break out, so this is better. As for the small enclosures, I think they are also best. It is easier to vary the cropping, and the cattle put to graze in small fields feed more evenly. In several fields we saw how he is able to make comparisons between his breed of sheep and those of a large part of the kingdom. From each county he has bought a model sheep and these he turns out into the same field and with the same feed and treated in the same way as many sheep of his own breed. He demonstrates the comparison to everyone who visits his farm, and it is undeniable that the others are thin and lean compared with his, which are large and well-covered. It is a clear demonstration in his favour.

His land is fairly moist. However, in the knowledge that water is the best possible nourisher and, above all, that, mixed with manure, it would double the yield of his farm, he has made at his own expense, on land that he only rents, a canal perhaps fifteen feet wide by eight or nine in depth which skirts a hill and brings water to all his fields, which he can irrigate whenever he needs to. This canal is perhaps two or three miles long.[78] From it, the water is spread by smaller channels to all parts of the farm and in the valley-bottom, where the soil is black and where one might have thought it more necessary to dry out rather than to water. One's bound to feel that this is an immense undertaking that must have cost an enormous fortune. There are, I'm certain, more than ten or twelve miles (4 or 5 *lieus*) of canals[79] of one size or another, dug for his irrigation scheme. In several places he has had to lead his channels on little wooden aqueducts above streams running at a lower level. In the meadows where the slope is gentle, the works were not very great: he has led the water in one or two channels. But in those meadows where there is no slope he has had to make a large number of little conduits with a slope calculated to distribute the water evenly. And as he realizes that stagnant water is worse than having no water at all, in parallel with all his conduits he has made deeper ones which bring the water and discharge it into canals of a lower level, either purpose-made or that happened to have been nearby. In some meadows he has left rather large areas unwatered: others are not watered but are manured to see which works best for those meadows. We noticed that in a black unrewarding soil growing nothing but turf or those small rushes that make very poor hay, those parts that were watered and manured were better than any of the others. There, even the grass has somehow changed its nature and become

---

76 Here he uses the word *acres*.
77 Here he uses the word *arpents*. It is clear that he thinks of these two words as interchangeable, and rather imprecise: I shall therefore stick to acres.
78 It wanders through Hathern from the river Soar at Zouche Mills, due north of Dishley.
79 About 10 miles seems right to the present occupier of Dishley.

more established. The meadows are improved, and in the parts that are either left to themselves or merely manured, there the grass is neither so rich nor so green: that is obvious to the eyes of everyone.

It is about ten years since he began these works of irrigation. His meadows are greatly improved, but his neighbour, who is a very bad one, and who sees this very clearly, will not accept that this is the result of irrigation. In consequence, he will not allow any water to invade his land; and Mr Bakewell has been forced to undertake much needless work in order to prevent his water from spreading over the land of his fatuous neighbour, who would certainly benefit from it. The hay from the water-meadows is richer and heavier than that from other meadows. Mr Bakewell weighed the hay from an acre of water-meadow, which weighed 89 pounds; that from a nearby meadow left unwatered weighed 13 pounds. This year he means to try irrigating his ploughlands.

He has had an extraordinary idea for his canal, which rather surprised me: he wants to make it navigable. He is having a boat built that will carry a cartload of grain or of turnips from one side of his farm to the other, and as the canal has to skirt right round a hill, this would establish good communications between all parts of the farm. It is amusing and satisfying to be such a farmer. Admittedly, it is the branch of agriculture I myself most enjoy – perfecting the breed of the essential animals. But to take on the whole subject and carry it to such perfection is a fulfilment granted to very few people.

The financial affairs of Mr Bakewell have long been in a very bad way: he let many of his beasts to the Irish who have never paid up, so that he was ruined without its being his fault. He is so widely respected and his breed of animals so generally esteemed that a public subscription was opened and now he is abreast of his affairs. I'm afraid he isn't yet making much profit, but there is reason to hope that he will in future, and, in truth, I hope so with all my heart.

He has given us a letter of introduction to take to Derby. After seeing over his farm, we got into our carriages and went swiftly to Derby. The time one spends on the road in weather so awful is time entirely lost, for although it was thawing, the landscape was still snow-covered.

Two days later, Bakewell reported to Arthur Young that they had 'set forward for Derby at about noon' on the second day of their visit, and that they were very attentive – not an overstatement. Bakewell continued: 'I have many experiments now making on different kinds of horned cattle and sheep . . . I wish you to come soon that you may see some of the horses before they go out – and compare them with the Suffolk kind.' H.C. Pawson printed the letter in full (Robert Bakewell, 1957), but misdated it 26 Feb. 1783.

2

Getting into their Stride

North of the Trent and into Derby, with famous riverside silk mill and adjoining cotton mill: here, faced by Mr Swift's new cotton-carding machines, François provides, with his own rough drawings, perhaps the only detailed contemporary description in existence of the early machinery Arkwright developed for processing cotton before the first spinning. Hoping to miss no part of the process, they dashed over in a postchaise to see the Curzons' house at Kedleston during the factory's dinner-break. North again next day they stopped for breakfast and to ask details of farming practice before pressing on over a bumpy, narrow road to Matlock Bath. In a blizzard, after dark, they passed (perhaps intentionally, after seeing so much at Derby) Richard Arkwright's own great mills, Cromford and Masson, and reached the Matlock Bath Hotel for the night. François wished they had time to climb these picturesque cliffs, but they advanced to Chesterfield. It was Sunday. They spent an idle afternoon, probably trying to catch up with their journals; and ventured out to evensong and to have a sight of the ladies: they somehow failed to note the disconcerting spire.

Next morning, on the road to Sheffield, they met 2,000 (they said) well-clad, well-mounted people heading for Chesterfield's cattle fair: quite a scene, anyway. At Sheffield, as at Derby, they were in their element: new market-place, new inn 'looking like a playhouse'; tombs 'not magnificent' in old church; guided by friendly cloth-merchant to see, first, a plated-button factory belonging to their guide's sister and nephew, then a cementation-steel works; and ending with an evening at home with their guide.

Back to the Trent:

Cavendish Bridge. François: We crossed the river [Trent] on rather a fine bridge of freestone masonry. Close by is the junction of two canals.[1] It is called Cavendish

---

[1] It is a pity the weather and visibility were so poor. Going north across the Trent is, traditionally, entering 'the North Parts'. With its canals, the Trent is visibly an artery of the England of the Industrial Revolution. One sees it today in the first Derbyshire parish, Shardlow, and soon crosses the Trent and Mersey canal, or 'Grand Trunk', which goes west through Burton to Gt Haywood in Staffs. There it branches to go north to the Mersey, where we meet it again, and south to the Severn at Bewdley. The Trent and Mersey was built 1766–77: Cavendish Bridge replaced a ferry in 1771. It survived till the floods of 1947, and was rebuilt. The list of tolls François complained of, carved in a stone pediment with rococo decoration, was brought to its present site on the Shardlow side in 1960. The crossing would have cost them a shilling for each of the two gigs, and a penny for their third horse.

Bridge.[2] Near it stands a great warehouse for the loaded and unloaded canal goods. May I renew my complaints about the dearness of the tolls.

DERBY AND MR SWIFT'S MILL

25 February 1785   Derby stands happily on a south-facing slope and on the flattish top of the hill: six parishes, well peopled.

The market-place is very well built and square: the assembly-rooms are at the bottom, large and attractively designed with columns.[3] The other houses fronting on the market-place are also good, but the rest of the town is very mediocre except for a street on the outskirts called *High Row Green*, with a great many pretty houses.[4]

The whole town is well lit, and everywhere provided with pavements for pedestrians. The many houses of the manufacturers are not really part of the town, but spread out some distance along the river, which flows through the outskirts.[5]

The letter Mr Bakewell had given us was to a manufacturer, but we had no need of it, for when we arrived the people at our inn[6] told us we could go and visit all the factories without any letters of recommendation. However, we went in the evening to see his factory, and I will tell you about it later. As we made no useful acquaintance at dinner, we found out nothing about the general business of the town. I will put down only the details of things I saw.

The manufacture of porcelain is important to the town. It employs about 300 people. The paste is light and the glaze not especially good – the fault I found with it is that it is rather too glassy;[7] its good qualities that it is very light and cheaply priced. It is painted and gilded but without great perfection. Their workmen are not terribly good. Generally, they send their whole output to their agent in London, who sells great quantities. I saw an entire dinner-service, gilded and painted attractively, for eighteen guineas. The cup I bought, which is very pretty, cost me only 8 shillings.

The methods of manufacture are precisely the same as those of other such factories.[8] I will note only that there are three bakings: once for twelve hours with a

---

2   Named after one of the Cavendishes, dukes of Devonshire but a leading Derbyshire family.
3   1763, burnt down 1963.
4   Derby has, still, one street of very fine 18th-century houses in its outskirts (the way to Ashbourne). It is called Friargate, but was once in the area known as Nuns Green. Its breadth suggests that it was built along an enclosed Green. No Derby street was ever called High Row Green: François may have misheard and amalgamated 'High Road' with 'Green'.
5   The fast-flowing Derwent powered the early textile mills here.
6   The two great Derby coaching inns were the King's Head and the George, both gone. But the genial, kindly countenance of Old John, the head waiter at the King's Head, with roses in his button-hole, suggests first-class hospitality in his surviving delightful portrait, c.1780, by Wright of Derby (No. 140, Tate Gallery 1990 Exhibition Catalogue).
7   *vitrifié*: a criticism made by John Fleming and Hugh Honour, *The Penguin Dictionary of Decorative Arts*, 1977, p. 234. It had been going since c.1750. Since 1784 it had been 'Crown Derby', marked by a crowned D. William Duesbury II took over from I in 1786.
8   Cf. Lazowski's description of the Lowestoft factory, *A Frenchman's Year in Suffolk, 1784*, pp. 216–17. As with Lowestoft ware, the late Mrs M. Bell of Norwich, a correspondent of M. Jean Marchand, communicated these short paragraphs to John Twitchett, the historian of the Derby

coal fire; then the colours are applied, and the porcelain rebaked with a wood-charcoal fire in a large reverberatory-oven;[9] finally, after the glazing, the porcelain is again rebaked on a slow coal fire in a very small oven.

The porcelain factory is delightfully situated near the river, at the end of the bridge, so as to enjoy the view of the water and of the whole town.

We left the porcelain factory and went to a cotton and silk factory belonging to a Mr Swift, a very rich merchant.[10]

We entered without asking anyone's permission. We were brought by the servant from our inn. We found the [manager?] of works and, without the least difficulty, he took us into the workshops.

The first one we saw is the silk mill. One knows that the silk arrives from China, Italy or France so extremely fine, so perfect,[11] that it had to be boiled and spun, thrown and doubled, sometimes trebled, to render it workable. This mill is built on the lines of those I have seen in France, except that it is on a rather bigger scale. However, as I didn't observe any particular machinery there, I shall not offer any authentic detail.

The whole mill is worked from one water-wheel, perhaps 30 feet in diameter. It turns with great speed. The movement is transmitted from the wheel to each storey of the building, and to the machines of an immense establishment, by gear-wheels and lantern-wheels.[12] Everything is made in oak-wood of a precision and lightness that amazed me; but it is this precision in the proportions that avoids friction and secures the durability of a machine longer than one which is under strain.

This water-wheel turns about three hundred different wheels, whether reels for skeins,[13] or bobbins. The movement is regular and rather slow, which loses a little time, certainly, but *does* spare the threads which would break if the mill went faster.

The workshops are large and the bobbins are distributed so as to lose no power. For example, I saw in one room six of these large reels for skeins [or hanks] which doubled and threw the silk as well – so far as I could see[14] – as twelve would do. They are perhaps twenty feet high and eight in diameter. There are forty-eight rows or storeys of bobbins, and twenty-four in each row. A single workman watches two of them.

manufacture, who printed them without observation in his standard work, *Derby Porcelain*, 1980, p. 49.
9   'So constructed that the flame is forced back upon the substance exposed to it, 1672' OED.
10   This famous waterside mill worked by the Derwent river in Derby is usually thought of as the factory where the celebrated Lombe family introduced their silk-throwing machinery in 1719. Thomas Lombe, cousin of the founder, was knighted, and died in 1739. The lease was transferred to Richard Wilson. 'These premises were occupied for many years by Mr Swift who made many important additions to the machinery': Stephen Glover, *History of the Borough of Derby*, 1843, p. 77. So far, I have found no other reference to Mr Swift.
11   *sommée.*
12   A form of cog-wheel, OED.
13   *dévidoirs.* The cocoons of silk had already been immersed in hot water to soften the gum, and wind the threads from six or eight cocoons on to a reel, to form a skein. The next stage was performed by this machine.
14   Handwriting baffling here: *d'autant* is mere guesswork.

13.   *Derby: Mr Swift's silk and cotton mills, 1798 from earlier drawing.*

14.   *Arkwright's cotton-carding machine, 1775.*

There are about two hundred people occupied in this factory. The majority are small children and women. They earn from one shilling to six shillings a week, and work ten hours [a day].

After the silk mill, I asked to go into the cotton mill that I'd seen on the other side of the building. But we were refused on the grounds that only Mr Swift could allow us to go in. Luckily for us, he arrived as we were on the point of leaving. Mr de Lazowski asked his permission. He replied that, seeing that we were foreigners, he asked nothing better than that we should satisfy our curiosity, though he certainly would not admit an Englishman; and we entered by an iron door double-bolted.

I report at length the courteous and hospitable behaviour of this manufacturer only to offset what I should probably have to write of the jealousy of the majority of manufacturers, who refuse all entry to strangers. At least, I've been assured that I shall come across plenty of examples in the course of my journey. I find that it is very courteous of them to show their processes to strangers who can do no harm to their business; or at least very little harm, and a long time in the future, by establishing these processes at home. It is very natural that they should want to exclude their compatriots who, in appropriating an idea not already established, might do them real, immediate and serious damage.[15]

The door that they opened for us, and the wall that separates the two mills, are both of iron so that, if fire were to take hold in one of the mills, the ruin of the whole building might be averted.

I heard it said some time ago in France that the English invented the method of carding cotton by machine. I have seen one near Rouen which Mr Oulkerque established, at Oissel,[16] but that machine had little in common with the one we saw here, which is more complicated and doesn't involve more work. I have been assured that it is impossible to spin cotton by machine, and yet that is precisely the purpose of this mill.

The cotton is first washed, then beaten with switches, then picked by the women to get rid of everything too coarse – then it is taken to a card, i.e. a carding-machine.[17] This machine is simple. Imagine a cylinder one and a half feet thick and two in length, bristling with several bands of cards. The cylinder is placed horizontally, its

---

15   The idea behind François' reasoning is that, in England, the skilled workpeople were on hand to operate new machinery: he was probably unaware of the degree to which French industrial espionage extended to attracting skilled British operatives to France: see following note.

16   See *Voyages en France de François de La Rochefoucauld*, Jean Marchand ed., Société de l'histoire de France; Professor John Harris showed me that 'Mr Oulkerque' is John Holker, the Jacobite Manchester textile manufacturer recruited by the French minister Trudaine. In 1755 he was made Inspector-General of Foreign Manufactures, with responsibility for introducing English methods and English workers: H.T. Parker, *The Bureau of Commerce in 1781 and its Policies with Respect to French Industry*, Durham, N. Carolina, 1979, and A. Remond, *John Holker, manufacturier et grand fonctionnaire en France au XVIII siècle, 1719–1786*, Paris, 1946.

17   Its job is to part, comb out and set in order the fibres. Erasmus Darwin, physician, polygrapher, a friend of Arkwright, Priestley, member of the Lunar Society, grandfather of Charles, was wonderfully inventive but not a great poet. He published *The Botanic Garden*, some

axis resting on two supports. The kinds of bent wire-pin called, I think, the teeth [or points] of the card, are on a band about four inches wide along the cylinder, from one end to the other. Another little cylinder, with finer cards, also placed horizontally and beside the larger one, so that the teeth [or points] engage with those of the other cylinder, turns, consequently, the opposite way, by means of a leather belt laid across the two pivots of the cylinders.

On the little cylinder a small iron rod is fixed, on one side to a spring and on the other to a little crank, so that it leans, with a regular motion, on the card and causes the cotton to fall in little tongues [*languettes*] into a basket placed to receive them.[18] Notice that it is a little child, of seven or eight years, who puts the cotton on the cylinder: the one thing to watch is that it is placed fairly equally along the length of the cylinder.

After being carded this first time, the cotton is weighed in order to calculate what needs to be carded all together and what should be spun by weight into thread. Two children weigh it, then roll it between two cloths of the same breadth as the second cylinder, where it will soon go.[19]

4,500 lines, in 1791. It does describe in layman's terms the cotton-carding machine, and the revolving-can frame for turning the tender skeins, or slivers, into twists or spirals:

> – First, with nice eye, emerging Naiads cull
> From leathery pods the vegetable wool;
> With wiry teeth *revolving cards* release [his italics]
> The tangled knots, and smooth the ravell'd fleece;
> Next moves the iron-hand with fingers fine,
> Combs the wide card, and forms the eternal line;
> Slow, with soft lips, the *whirling can* acquires
> The tender skeins, and wraps in rising spires;
> With quicken'd pace *successive rollers* move
> And these retain, and those extend the *rove*;
> Then fly the spoles [i.e. spools], the rapid axles glow; –
> And slowly circumvolves the labouring wheel below.

The rove, or roving, was the strand softly twisted in the 'whirling can': as a 'sliver' it had been drawn out by rollers, then into the can which twisted it. The roving was then wound round a bobbin and spun into yarn.

18 Here, and two paragraphs further on, François is describing precisely the way Arkwright solved the problem of carding, which was how to get the cotton off the final drum, or cylinder; he did it with this 'little crank' (and an attached comb). Arkwright patented his famous machine (see Pl. 14) in 1775, so in 1785 the patent still had four years to run before expiring. Dr Richard Hills, on reading this, reckons that Swift's machines were early copies of Arkwright's (the one preserved in the Science Museum, apparently dating from 1775, has three cylinders compared to Swift's two). Dr Hills supposes that Swift was using these machines without paying the large patent dues that made Arkwright's fortune. This would explain Swift's reluctance to admit English visitors to his cotton mills.

19 Pl. 3 in *Power in the Industrial Revolution*, 1975, by Richard L. Hills, shows a machine for doing this, where only one cloth was used, as the cotton was spread evenly along it; and it was then rolled up. The amount of cotton was weighed at this stage to give the correct 'comb' of spun yarn at the end of the spinning processes. It was a form of quality control. Similar methods were quite recently in use, as Richard Hills tells me.

One of the children brings the rolled cotton between the two cloths and attaches it behind the large cylinder of the second card[-ing machine] so that the cloth unrolls by itself and the cotton charges itself by the movement of the cylinder without the help of any human hand. Above all, one should note that the bands of cards of this second machine are no longer based on the length of the cylinder: they are always about three inches wide, but crosswise like the rings of a cask. The little cylinder is constructed the same way and turns the opposite way. The rod that causes the cotton to fall is no longer held by a spring: it is fixed here, so that the card charged with the cotton, coming into contact with the rod, discharges itself and produces as many bands as there are bands of teeth on the card and the bands of cotton are continuous like kinds of ribbon.

These two card[-ing machine]s are the same size. The large cylinder of each is about three feet in diameter and is as long: the small cylinders are half a foot in diameter and three feet long. The toothed wheels that make all these small pieces go by means of the water-wheel are all made of iron – a few of brass in order to ease the friction.

I don't know if I am making myself clear. The movement of the two card[ing machine]s is the same. The two cylinders of each are horizontally placed and their movement is contrary. The first machine's sole object is to divide and clean the cotton: the teeth of the cards are placed in 3-inch bands the length of the cylinder; in this manner, more or less,[20] and each band has an inch-and-a-half interval from the next. The little cylinder is the same: the machine is mounted so that the rod leaning on the spring falls on the cylinder the moment one of the places empty of card-teeth passes in front, so that, leaning on the last teeth, and just when there aren't any, it drops the little tongues of cotton.

The teeth of the second card are finer and ranged the other way. The cylinder is the same thickness.[21] The little cylinder is like the little cylinder on the other one, but arranged like the last one I described, so that by means of the rod, a band of continuous cotton emerges, that I called ribbon [sliver].

This sliver of cotton without consistency is passed into an entirely different machine.[22] It is between two little cylinders of tempered steel. They are fluted and exactly joined, by means of which the ribbon takes on a little more consistency. The cylinders are not more than a half-inch in diameter and three in length. When the cotton emerges from between the two cylinders, it passes between two more of the same dimensions but made of wood covered with leather; a third, covered with bristles like a brush, was there so that the cotton, before entering between the two wooden cylinders, should be brushed and so cleaned of the coarsest dirt that always gets into it.

This last machine, made up of three cylinders, is beneath two steel cylinders in such a way that the ribbon passes continuously without human help: then it is twisted on large wooden bobbins. All the movements of so many little pieces are made of iron with astonishing precision. Two of the machines need only the supervision of a little girl, who has very little to do: all she does is remove the charged bobbins and replace them.

---

20 See facsimile opposite, above.
21 See facsimile opposite, below.
22 This is the drawing-frame.

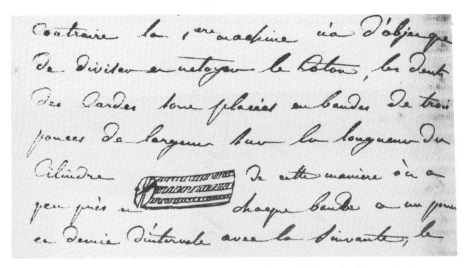

Xerox of Francois' manuscript, Library of National Assembly, 1249, bis, p. 45. See opposite, footnote 20.

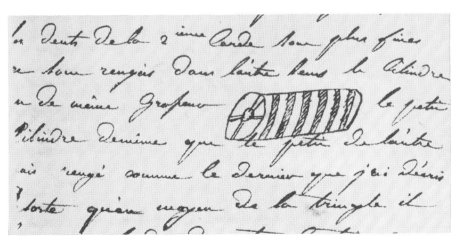

Xerox of Francois' manuscript, Library of National Assembly, 1249, bis, p. 46. See opposite, footnote 21.

The last operation is to place the bobbins on a frame. The sliver of cotton still passes between two iron cylinders, with fluting the same size as the first, then enters a round tin can of about four inches in diameter and a foot tall.[23] It is fixed on a little wooden tray carried on a pivot. The sliver goes in, passes between two very small joined iron cylinders; as big as a key-hole. They are fixed to the can and turn the reverse way, and thus get the sliver to enter and be stretched.

These little cylinders rotate on their axis and in reverse, but as they are fixed to the can they share its movement. This latter also turns on its axis by means of a leather thong which passes over its pivot. It is the complexity of these two movements of the last little cylinders which twists the sliver of cotton, compressing and extending it, and forms the thread. This motion substitutes exactly for that of the fingers of the woman who drew the cotton to present it as untwisted thread, or that of the little wheel that twists it and winds it round the bobbin.

As it leaves the machine, the cotton thread is thick and stays in the tin can: to be finished, it passes twice more into other cans where the cylinders are finer and which turn faster.[24]

One must have an idea of the complexity of such machines, of the number of little wheels, of the variety of movements and of the precision with which they must be made. I've watched it several times, with great admiration. Most of the movements requiring the greatest accuracy are made of brass.

The largest working parts are of wood. This whole cotton-mill is worked from a single water-wheel, and it is all so well made that one can stop any particular part whenever one wants. This establishment contains a great number of machines of the kind that turn all together, at once: each piece is separate.

They must spin a great quantity of cotton every day. I asked how much it might be. The workmen didn't know. There are not more than 100 people employed, and of the hundred, ninety are children and little girls twelve years old – so useful is such a mill!

The letter Mr Bakewell gave us for Derby was for a very talented man whom we went to see after dinner. He has invented a new machine of which I can form no precise ideas except at his house. It's a machine for spinning wool, like the mill I've just been describing for the spinning of cotton. He assured us that no-one has done it before him, and his mill isn't yet finished.

He is extremely jealous of his invention. That's why, although the walls are not of iron, they are impenetrable to the eyes of the curious, and it is the greatest favour, as he told us, that, on Mr Bakewell's recommendation, we were allowed in.[25]

We saw very few workshops. The wool isn't carded there, as the cotton was at the other mill; it arrives already carded. It is passed between several little cylinders and

23 This is the 'revolving can frame' Pl. 15.
24 This very accurately describes the work of the revolving can frame.
25 Robert and Thomas Barber were the proprietors (see R.S. Fitton, *The Arkwrights, Spinners of Fortune*, 1989, pp. 141–43). Professor John Harris, who put me on to this fine posthumous book, notes that the woollen machine seems very early, and expresses his amazement that both Swift and Barber allowed the French so close a look at their machines.

through tin canisters like the cotton I've described. All the cylinders and the little wheels are of tempered steel. They follow closely the construction of those in the cotton mills: oil runs everywhere to moisten the wool and prevent it from overheating.

We went down below to see the water-wheel that works the whole mill: it is a prodigious size, and a size related to the supply of water, of which there is no great quantity. The cog-wheels, lantern-wheels – in a word all the pieces made to communicate to the different parts of the mill – are of cast iron, the strength has to be so much superior to that of a cotton mill.

They spin the wool very fine: the majority is employed on camlets, brocades (*baracants*) and even cloths for clothes. Some of their thread is good enough for the making of crape.

The river in Derby [the Derwent] is beautiful and fast-flowing: it is this river that powers a great many silk and cotton mills which are built all round the town, which the river doesn't enter.

The population of the town must be very considerable, like the trade, but as we don't know who would know, exactly, I won't report the hearsay of people in the inns.

They sell here a great many vases in a thousand different antique shapes, made from the marble dug out in all parts of this county. It is very pleasant to look at from the variety and liveliness of its colours: its core, in places, has the appearance of crystal. [Here, Alexandre accurately describes it as 'a sort of alabaster' and speaks of 'vases and pyramids sold very cheaply'.]

KEDLESTON

Near Derby, within about four miles, Lord Scarsdale has a superb country house named Kedleston, that we were determined to see. We chose the moment when the workpeople of the [Derby] factory were at dinner, in order to do as much as possible in a short time and to spare ourselves a second unprofitable stay. We went by post-chaise, the weather was the nicest it had been so far since we left Bury. I felt warm, and the sun shone, though without glory. The English climate is extraordinarily varied and unreliable. The previous day we were cold, and had a little snow, whitening the landscape, and today it is warm and the snow entirely melted.

The entrance to Lord Scarsdale's[26] house is magnificent. As we crossed the park a moment before arriving, we had the front of the house before us, a fine grass slope stretching from the foot of the wall to one of the most beautiful artificial rivers I've yet seen, and a mass of woods on top of a rise close to and behind the house, giving shade to the picture. As we looked to our left, we noticed a little valley, in the bottom of which we saw something of the town of Derby: the slopes are covered with houses, some of them erected by Lord Scarsdale to enrich his view. Turning to our right, the view is no longer so rich, but there are several hills rising one above another with varying slopes. There are few houses, but the fields are enclosed and everywhere one sees good farming.

---

[26] Sir Nathaniel Curzon, 5th baronet, started building the house in 1758, and became 1st lord Scarsdale in 1761.

15. *Revolving-can frame, Higher Mill, Helmshore.*

16. *Lord Surrey's new shopping-mall at Sheffield, 1785 see p. 52.*

Whichever way one looks there is a beautiful valley, sometimes full of houses, sometimes devoted to farming, giving such pleasure to the view. The façade of the house is in the shape of a horse-shoe, the aisles running east and west.[27] There are about thirty bays across the front, and two storeys. It is of freestone, embellished with columns. We first entered the hall, which is large, but low and furnished with enormous pillars supporting the whole house.[28]

Above this lower hall is what is called the hall, which divides the house exactly in two.[29] The proper entrance is by a double staircase leading up to the front, and at the foot of which one steps into one's coach. This hall is of the greatest magnificence. Eight columns of fluted marble of the composite order[30] along each side support the most richly decorated cornice. The frieze is carved with the greatest taste, and so is the ceiling which is pierced in the middle to let the daylight in. Its form is oblong: eight marble columns long and four wide, which makes about 80 feet by 40: the elevation is perhaps 40 feet.

In the middle of the long sides, two chimneypieces of the whitest marble Italy can produce are sculpted with all the delicacy of the finest artists.

The marble is local, quarried from the owner's lands: it is white, veined with red and a flesh colour, which makes an effect as beautiful as it is striking. From the hall one can walk into the two pavilions which form the wings on either side of the front. The front of one [west: right as you approach] contains the kitchens, offices of great beauty: the other, 21 rooms, among which are the apartments of the master and mistress. The corridor by which one reaches the detached pavilions leads in its two directions from the front entrance. It is furnished with the taste and elegance belonging more to a gallery than a corridor. One's sight of the room where the mistress received company, a part of her apartment, is delightful. We saw out over the way by which we approached the house, a long gentle slope of grass embellished with innumerable deer and sheep; a pretty river running at the foot, with two well-planted islands; a freestone bridge built magnificently and over which one arrives; above it is a fine stretch of water to keep the level up to the height of the banks: even though the canal may be supplied only by a very small spring and by driblets from the earth and from the flow of rain-water, and although there is no steady replenishment, the water is clear and its flow looks perfectly natural. The whole place owes what is beautiful to art: formerly a road passed close to the spot where the house now stands; and a village stood exactly where the bridge is today. Lord Scarsdale demolished the village and rebuilt it elsewhere: the road was re-routed around the park-pales and he has almost entirely removed a hill, the steep slope of which seemed to spoil the view. He himself enclosed the entire park, which is perhaps

27 The approach is from the north. The original plan was Matthew Brettingham's, with four subsidiary wings based on Holkham Hall. This north front was completed by James Paine, from whom the whole interior design, and that of the south front, was taken over by Robert Adam. Brettingham's two southern wings were never completed.

28 This is the lower entrance hall, at ground floor level, for use in bad weather, and informally.

29 He may mean that it leaves equal portions on either side, but, from north to south, the hall occupies exactly two-thirds of the depth of the house, the saloon one-third.

30 Ionic on Corinthian.

nine miles round. It was all finished about five or six years ago under the direction of Mr Adams, a famous architect.[31]

I won't give a more detailed description of the arrangement of the house. It is something that interests few people,[32] and description gives none of the pleasure one feels in seeing for oneself so much magnificence united with the most elegant taste. The house is extremely large: it contains sixty guest-rooms.[33]

Similarly, I don't see that it would be any more possible to describe the beauties of the garden.[34] The distribution of the clumps of trees, the slope of the hills, the course of the river are moulded into beauties that it would be as tedious to record as they are delicious to see.

26 February 1785, Matlock   Our curiosity being satisfied after one day's stay in Derby, we went on our way towards Matlock on the 26th, but wanting to get some knowledge of Derbyshire and of its farming, after six miles we found a little inn in a village and went in for breakfast.[35]

The part of Derbyshire that isn't mountainous is extremely agreeable, as much for the number and great variety of its valleys as for its good farming: the fields are enclosed by good hedges and the enclosures are small.[36] The soil is strong and rich: most of the land is artificial water-meadows, with clover and ray-grass; the longest the pastures stay in good condition is generally three or four years – then they plough them and sow them with wheat, sometimes twice, and with barley or with oats and turnips, then grass again. Their land has to be as good as it is if it is to be continuously fertile with that kind of farming; but they are so good that their harvests are one-third better than those of other counties. This large area of meadows raises a multitude of cows and young bullocks which go down south into neighbouring counties, some

31 The date of completion he gives for the whole work is interesting, not, I think, found elsewhere (as with his account of the work in progress at Heveningham the previous year): *A Frenchman's Year in Suffolk, 1784*, pp. 138–42.
32 This phrase is the first suggestion that he *might* have had an eye on publication, but probably he was just thinking of his father's tastes. Alexandre unluckily agreed that 'it would be boring to give an exact account of every room, so I shall just describe *la hall* '.
33 It is disappointing that he never anticipated our interest in his response to the details of this great house. It is particularly disappointing that he takes us out into Brettingham's two north wings – valuable though his account is – before he has gone from the hall into Adam's marvellous saloon, a most noble rotunda; from the basilica, or the atrium, of the hall into the vestibulum, or the pantheon, of the saloon. It would have been interesting to hear his reaction to the south front, of which the saloon forms the centre, approached externally, by one of the most beautiful carved double staircases ever designed. John Fleming, who showed exactly how Robert Adam came to take over from Brettingham and Paine, says Kedleston's south front 'of all Adam exteriors best exemplifies the quality of movement . . .' (*Robert Adam and his circle*, 1962, p. 312).
34 He uses the word here to mean 'park': see his explanation in *A Frenchman's Year in Suffolk, 1784*, p. 36.
35 This was Weston under Wood Inn, 6½ miles from Derby, according to *Paterson's Roads*: now, I fear, called Puss in Boots.
36 One so readily associates Derbyshire with dry-stone walling that it is hard to remember the more 'midland' landscape of southern Derbyshire where the Frenchmen still were.

for milking, others to be fattened and killed. Their sheep are fat and long-fleeced, good for spinning.

They also raise horses, good tall animals: I've seen several young ones on the road being broken in. They are fine and cut a very pretty figure. They are often in demand in Yorkshire.

The farms are small, the rents two guineas an acre and the poor rate one shilling and sixpence.

The weather, as I had accurately foreseen, had changed: it had been warm the previous evening, but the night brought a great change: freezing and icy. The snow fell and gave way only to a little draught of icy wind, extremely uncomfortable, and rendering extremely useless the occasional rays of sunshine.

The road was narrow and tiring for the horses, littered with loose stones, and we were constantly having to dismount. On the top of these hills, the soil lost its richness; it became much sandier, yet was still very fertile.

Before reaching Matlock, we went through a large village called Wirksworth, where there are several cotton-mills and a warm-water spring that runs through a man-made channel the length of the hill to the mills.[37]

The place is separated from Matlock by much-divided steep hills. At the foot runs a powerful torrent of crystal-clear water: it has passed Matlock and turned two cotton-mills on the way.

MATLOCK BATH

Matlock belongs to the Duke of Devonshire. It has quite a reputation for its warm waters that spring out of the rock. They are said to be sovereign against all nervous disorders, and crowds of people come here in the summer. We saw the baths. They are vaulted in the rock. One has as much water as one desires: it is almost warm, quite without taste, and very clear. [Alexandre referred to it as '*un endroit appellée* the old bath'.]

Matlock's situation is very picturesque, in an extremely narrow valley, at the bottom of which runs the torrent I mentioned. The hills are very high; the one opposite is covered almost to the summit in fairly thick coppice in the middle of which one sees several pinnacles of marble, pretty hard, I should think.

The hill on which the houses are built is more sterile – wooded only round the lower slopes: the rest is mostly quarries of a rather beautiful stone that is easily extracted for building.

---

37 He is actually describing Cromford, in the Derwent valley, between Wirksworth and Matlock, and could easily have thought he was in either. Cromford is now one of the Meccas of industrial archaeologists, for here Richard Arkwright established the first water-powered cotton-mill in 1772, only thirteen years before this visit by François. 120 feet long and seven storeys high, it was joined nearby, in 1783, at the entrance to Matlock Dale, by the greatest of Arkwright's mills, the Masson Mill. As they approached Matlock on that freezing cold, snowy night, they weren't in much of a condition to admire the reflection from a hundred windows in the river, and the din of the factory was probably obliterated by that of the weather and the wheels on rough roads.

The people at the inn where the baths are[38] have cut several walks through the woods on these slopes: they must be lovely in the summer. I like the wild atmosphere of this place, and I'd be thrilled to climb one of these peaks even though the cold would disagree with me.

If these waters were nearer London, they would be much frequented: they are said to be much better than those of Bath.[39]

Sunday 27 February 1785   The next day was one of the coldest one could ever experience: we found nothing but ice on the road, and the wind was terrible. I was frozen, and nothing could thaw me. We had several hills to surmount. I cannot imagine how the horses managed to draw us along. They slipped so much that they seemed to lose ground without gaining any, and I constantly expected to see them fall. We crossed some very high peaks and were never on flat ground.

The turnpikes never deserted us in these wild places; the roads cost little to make up, for they are little more than carved hillsides, and even so the carving has been necessary only at the summits where they haven't had to cut to depths of more than four or five feet. Anyway, we very often found ourselves on turnpikes, and they never failed to be dear. It certainly seems that if the revenue from the turnpikes exceeds the cost of road-maintenance, then that's legalized robbery of all the travellers, a serious robbery, which is the case here.[40]

Before arriving at Chesterfield we saw several coal-mines: there are very many in this part of the world. Coal is very cheap: eight shillings a ton at the pit-head. There are frequent accidents from landslips and fire and we are told that often men get killed.

Chesterfield   Chesterfield is quite a large town. The market-place is built regularly round a square. As the wind was very cold, and we had stayed chatting in the morning and were late, we abandoned our plan to get on to Sheffield for the night, and stayed where we were. Having nothing to do, we went to the evening service (for it was Sunday) to have a sight of the ladies of Chesterfield. There is only one parish, so there they all were, and we saw some rather pretty ones.

After church we strolled along the four or five main streets of the town, which are pleasantly built.[41] The countryside produces an abundance of coal and tin, which in turn produces an immense number of poor unfortunates who die young.

[38] Matlock Bath, separate from the small town of Matlock, is a picturesque residential settlement on the very steep rocky cliff to the left (west) as you enter from Cromford. The road now runs beside the river, but in 1785 seems to have climbed, past where the New Bath Hotel stands, to the Old Bath and Old Bath Hotel, both sites now hard to find. The 'several walks through the woods' are now inevitably dotted with houses dispelling 'the wild atmosphere'.
[39] See pp. 156–7 below.
[40] It is surprising to find such 'anti-market' feelings in François: he may simply have wanted to find fault with something.
[41] Arthur Young, *Le Cultivateur Anglois*, IV, p. 141, noted Chesterfield's celebrated twisted spire. It had been built c.1300, but no one knows when it grew crooked: it is as much as 7 feet 10 inches out of true to the south-west. The French may have had eyes only for the girls: it might have been too dark that evening to see the spire, but they would have seen it in prolongation of the very large market-place as they stood chatting.

28 February 1785   Next day, before leaving, we found a great number of cattle in the market-place, and people gathered for the fair, which lasts three days. I was told there were over 300 horses and a thousand cows and bullocks. Many London merchants came and bought horses for export to France and Germany: an immense number of horses is exported from here.

On the road from Chesterfield to Sheffield we met over 2,000 people on their way to the fair, most of them well mounted and all of them travelling fast. This chance review of a part of the county brought once more before my eyes the ease and freedom of the English peasants. One has no idea how so many are well dressed and well shod; their horses well bridled and saddled, much as those of gentlemen are in France – indeed I've seen many French gentry who couldn't normally be so well turned out.

The county of Derby reaches almost to Sheffield, which is in Yorkshire. Derbyshire is surely the English province that would be most interesting to study in detail: it produces copper, tin, iron, coal, marble, slate in great abundance;[42] it has great variety of landscape; one part is very hilly and it is that part which has the mines and the medicinal waters; the rest is plains and valleys with soil of the greatest fertility producing an extreme abundance of cattle for the southern counties.

As for their mines and factories, their superiority over us in the great numbers of their machines must be acknowledged. I saw several coal-pits; and even the poorest, those that mined proportionately the least coal, were always equipped with mining gear and one of those pulleys with five wheels which, in slowing down the speed, gain remarkably in power.

I saw in several villages small machines in the cottages of poor people who looked as if they should be receiving charity as paupers. Yet I saw there these same fairly complicated pieces of equipment for either spinning or carding the cotton. The machines are of iron, all well made and needing no more than a child to operate them. This is why, although manual labour is so dear in this country that the cost of living is high, they turn out a great quantity of manufactured goods which they sell in competition with the other nations, and which makes a living for everyone in the countryside as well as in the towns.

SHEFFIELD

'8 February 1785   On 28 February we arrived at Sheffield early, had lunch and, without losing any time, went to see a merchant of the town who had received a letter recommending us, and who walked round the town with us. He is 'Mr Stangforth', a draper.[43]

---

42 The nearest slate comes from Charnwood Forest, just over the border in Leicestershire: François should certainly have included lead.

43 '*Marchand de drap*'. Richard Childs, Principal Archivist, Sheffield Central Library, has kindly sent me photo-copies of Gales and Martin's *Directory of Sheffield*, 1787. Among several Staniforths, Samuel Staniforth & Son, linen-drapers, of Truelove's Gutter, were the only drapers of that name. Alexandre noted that it was their friend Mr Symonds, of Bury St Edmunds, who had sent the letter: he seems to have had an influential friend almost everywhere. Alexandre's

The town occupies a curious site, on the top and sides of a little hill which stands in the middle of a wide valley, so that although the town is large, it is impossible to see it properly. There is no view-point that could give you an overall view. There is an unevenness about the buildings which is disagreeable. The houses are mostly low and built with no great elegance, generally covered with large stones about an inch thick. Some houses are brick, some stone, and there is a fair number of pretty ones; but they are lost in such a multitude of shapeless huts and outlandish factory-buildings that Sheffield could never pass for a fine town. For some years now the town has been growing enormously. A whole district has been built in a very little time, and this is the finest part. Lord Surrey owns a great part of the land in this quarter, and he is the principal agent in its embellishment. At his own cost, he is at present building a market-place surrounded by shops and a kind of portico for strolling under cover:[44] it will be a great ornament to this place. He has obtained an Act of Parliament to secure rent for the market stalls. I saw the plan of the elevation of this building: it will be simple, convenient and large, and pleased me enormously.

Lord Surrey and forty-nine subscribers have each given 100 guineas to build a fine inn that is just finished. There are about 60 guest-beds and stabling for 80 horses. It all fits in well. They have let it to someone for seven years, 70 guineas for the first year, 80 the second, 90 the third and so on so that it will bring in 130 guineas by the seventh year, which rent they hope to fix for some years longer. They won't recover the value of their money, but they didn't subscribe to make a profit, only out of public spirit, through national enthusiasm. One finds examples of that in this country at every step.

Alexandre liked the new inn: he said it was 'more like a play-house than an inn'.

François continues: We saw an old church, which has the tomb of the dukes of Norfolk, not of great magnificence.[45] The last duke of Norfolk founded a hospital for thirty poor people (fifteen men, fifteen women): their houses are small, but

---

spelling is correct: *Staniforth*. The name suggests a close link with the Pattesons of Little Haugh Hall, Norton, near Bury, friends of the Oakes family in Bury, whom Symonds, Lazowski and the boys often visited. William Staniforth of Sheffield married Mary Macro, who in 1767 inherited Little Haugh from her father: her father's younger sister, Alethea, had married Samuel Staniforth of Darnall near Sheffield. (See *The Oakes Diaries*, I, pp. 232–35 and N. Scarfe, 'Little Haugh Hall, Suffolk', *Country Life*, 5 June 1958; also Andrew W. Moore, *Dutch and Flemish Painting in Norfolk*, HMSO, 1988, pp. 43–46.)

[44] A print shows it looking like an elegant, one-storey shopping 'mall', so inelegant in our recent times. Pevsner notes that south of Church Street and High Street a quarter was laid out c.1770 by the duke of Norfolk and gradually built over: it covered the area Pinstone Street – Fargate – High Street and Flat Street and Pond Street. Charles Howard (1746–1815) was styled Earl of Surrey 1777–86, when he succeeded his father as 11th duke of Norfolk. (Pl. 16)

[45] No, the Norfolks were buried in E. Anglia, the Shrewsburys in Sheffield: François had been looking at the effigies of the 4th and 6th earls of Shrewsbury (1538 and 1590).

pleasant, and they receive a half-crown a week.[46] It is only for old people. He built them rather a large chapel, hexagonal, the light let in from the top, and all built in rather beautiful stone.

Our walk took us near a silk and cotton mill, but as we had seen one at Derby and had very little time to see everything we particularly wanted to see in Sheffield, we didn't go in. All these factories stand beside the river formed by the junction of two small rivers,[47] above the town. They flow very rapidly, and it is to their waters and to the abundance of coal mined close to the town that the town owes the great abundance of factories of every kind gathered here.

The town consists of a single parish. There are only two churches, and the population is about forty thousand, all employed in manufactures and trade, for children who are still small already begin to earn something.

The first factory we saw made buttons and plate, and belongs to the sister and nephew of our guide.[48] I had already seen a button factory at Amboise, but the buttons were coarse and plain.[49] So this manufacturing process was new to me. You take a piece [an ingot] of fine copper which is exactly the shape of an octavo book; you apply a silver leaf, or film, of perhaps four *lignes* [50] and flatten it and stretch it by passing it between steel cylinders turning opposite ways, which pulls it through: this is operated by means of a water-wheel. When the process doesn't call for great power, then the machine works by man-power. Each cylinder is rotated by a man simply using a handle; the piece of copper is reduced to between half a *ligne* and a *ligne* in thickness, according to what is wanted in the substantial quality of the buttons, and the silver leaf thus incorporated with the copper and perfectly part of it.

A workman with a well-tempered steel punch, or cutting-out machine, cuts out roundels of the plate (of silvered copper) of the size required for the buttons, then beats them on a steel stamp of the desired pattern. The stamp is made up of two pieces; one is a little anvil on which the design of the button is hollowed out; the

46 It was actually founded in 1673 by Henry Howard, who became 6th duke of Norfolk in 1677. He was carrying out the wishes of his great-grandfather, Gilbert, 7th earl of Shrewsbury. (Henry was also a great benefactor of Oxford University and of the College of Arms.) Charles, earl of Surrey, the enterprising developer of Sheffield when François was here, became 11th duke of Norfolk the following year, 1786. In the NW corner of the Cathedral churchyard stands the Charity School for Poor Girls, built by subscription in 1786. Just to the north of this is Paradise Square, where in July 1779 Wesley had preached to the biggest weekday crowd he remembered.
47 The Loxley and Rivelin rivers.
48 From the reference to Mr Young a little further on, it looks as if this factory was Younge, Greaves and Hoyland, of Union Street, manufacturers of buttons, 'gilt and plated only' (Gale & Martin's *Directory*); also as if Mr Young's mother was a Miss Staniforth. Still generally called Sheffield plate, though superseded by cheaper 'Electroplate' c.1840. The process was discovered in Sheffield by Thos Bolsover c.1742, caught on in the 1760s, and developed in Birmingham by Matthew Boulton: see below, p. 111, and E. Wenham, *Old Sheffield Plate*, 1955 (also F. Bradbury, *History of Old Sheffield Plate*, 1912).
49 He described his visit to Amboise on 22 May 1783 but didn't mention the button-factory: *Voyages en France* ed. Marchand, II, p. 200.
50 Formerly a twelfth of an inch (*pouce*).

other is the same design embossed, made so that they fit together exactly. The embossed piece is fixed on the underside of a fairly heavy iron weight: this kind of 'drop-press'[51] is raised between two perpendicular wooden posts by means of a cord passing over a pulley and attached to a stirrup which a man works with his right foot. The man places the roundel of plate on the mould, lifts the drop-press and lets it fall so that the button is imprinted with the design.

The next process is to fix the little ring [the shank][52] that attaches the button. This is done with a small spring rather like a pair of tweezers in the middle of the copper face, on to which you pour some drops of a composition of copper with fairly strong dissolvent. Then a woman holds the button in the flame of a lamp which she directs upwards with bellows worked by her foot, dissolving the composition and fusing the ring and the button perfectly.

Over this side of the button you pass silver reduced in lime and water, which resembles whiting; then the button goes through the lamp-flame again and the silver reappears: this gives a silvery appearance much more economically than plate itself, and which is equally effective on the back of the button.

From there, the button goes into a turning-box on a wooden mould, and is polished with a very hard stone brought from America: then it is washed and, if it requires no more embellishment, it is finished. If it is to receive a pattern, it passes into the hands of another woman who works with a steel chisel and a little hammer. If they are open-worked, it is done with a pointed tool fixed to the underside of a press which the workman tightens with a very slight movement of the hand; they work them on a small anvil on which a hole corresponds exactly to a projection, so that the piece of button pricked will fall.

Yellow buttons are made the same way: they are gilded, not laminated with gold, but gilded with calcined gold.

The same manufacturer also made plate in great quantities. The processes are not very different. The plate, that is to say the silvered copper, is made as it was for the buttons: sometimes it is silvered on both sides, sometimes tinned on the inside, for tea-pots for instance. The pattern is pressed in by the drop-press, and the fusing is done by the lamp-flame: the open-work is done with the pointed tool, the patterned work with the chisel. The only difference is the greater intricacy of the plate, requiring greater care and workmen more skilled. The finish is given with the same small stone as with the buttons, and the final job is to put it into soapy water and rub it down with tools of polished steel. One must never fuse it over a fire, only on the flame of an oil-lamp, directed either by bellows or by a blow-pipe.

There are 120 workers employed in this factory; the greater part of their output goes abroad to France, Spain, Portugal and Germany – a little goes to Italy, but most to France. It is extraordinary that we don't succeed in an art so simple.

---

[51] *mouton.*
[52] Heaton had invented a machine for making the shanks of buttons in 1744 (C. Gill, *History of Birmingham*, I, 1952, p. 93).

The manufacturer, Mr Young,[53] was extremely kind: he not only showed us all his workshops, one after another, but he was careful to begin each with the workman explaining each process in the greatest detail; and as we were there with him five hours he invited us to take tea with his mother, which we did, and we all had a very enjoyable conversation.

Sheffield abounds in all sorts of factories. However, it is only those making plate and steel that are outstanding, and that we considered with attention. I shall now speak of the steel works.

This branch of industry employs not only a large number of workpeople in the town, but also a great many in the country, which to my way of thinking is more important. There are many iron-mines all around,[54] both in this part of Yorkshire and in Derbyshire close by. They always smelt the ore with wood charcoal, but soon they are going to try to do it with coke, which would be much cheaper, the mines gaping open at every step.

The iron is brought to town and bars of it are put into a furnace shaped like an oven: there it stays about ten days, six being fired and four being cooled; and so it becomes steel. It is a mystery, this change of substance, that I don't yet really understand. I know that the means of changing iron into steel is to harden those parts that were soft, to give it phlogistic,[55] or elementary, fire, but what phlogistic is and how it is instilled into iron I have no idea.

The furnace is constructed with doubly thick walls, the first of brick, the outer one by stone clamped by bands of iron, and the flames are so violent that the outer stone wall is calcinated. A lot of the brick is constantly reduced to cinders. The steel at this stage is either prepared for export or turned into knives, scissors, etc. To do this, the steel is again put into a furnace and the strips, red-hot, are fed between two steel cylinders turned opposite ways by a wheel and thereby flattened, stretched and broadened. As it emerges and falls to the ground, a workman picks up the end with tongs and steers it between two other cylinders turned by a water-wheel, but with the ridges and channels coinciding so that the strip is cut into as many little strips as there are ridges. One sees the degree to which the cylinders must be accurate and what effort must go into making them so.

These new little strips are no sooner cool than they are again put into the fire and passed on to a tilt-hammer, worked by a water-wheel, and of enormous strength and speed, which toughens the steel by beating it for some time.

[53] See footnote 48, p. 53 above.
[54] François' account here, and later at Ironbridge, is remarkable in giving the clear impression that local iron was used in steel-making. Yet the orthodox view is that *Swedish* ore only was used. David Crossley, FSA, of Sheffield University, kindly affirms that the late Ken Barraclough, author of *Steel-Making before Bessemer* (1984) found no evidence of local iron being used. François may have misunderstood: but then he repeated the misunderstanding, quite unambiguously, at Ironbridge.
[55] Phlogiston was a hypothetical substance or principle once believed to be part of the process of combustion.

Going through the different workshops where the fire, the heat, the smoke and the noise created a frightful impression, one saw the men thin, dirt-blackened and sweating,[56] and I couldn't stop thinking how much the comfort and convenience and even the mere fancies of some people cost in terms of the blood of millions of people; and how miserable they must be to have to use up their lives in earning what we throw away on pleasure; and I believe that in the moment of seeing, and being confronted by, men enduring so much, one might be tempted to renounce all the steel-goods in the world; but as soon as one came outside, one saw, quite simply, that the poor work to live, and that those who have money *by luck* [*par hasard*, underlined in François' manuscript] give it to have what they like.

To return to the steel. After being beaten again, and in small strips, it is divided among the workmen who make different goods: knives, scissors and razors are the main products of this town. The processes are well-known everywhere and are the same in England as in France, so I needn't describe them. The one thing I will say is that one can admire here the same desire for perfection that the English show in all their work. The steel is finer and better than ours only because they take the greatest trouble. Notice in passing that there are no regulations at all, no restraints to hold them up; that a merchant does well or badly as he pleases; these are his affairs and the buyer's, who is not taken in. There is nothing in England resembling all the commercial laws of France.

Our merchant was extremely accommodating and polite: he not only gained us admission to the better workshops of all kinds, he came round with us, and we passed the evening with him.

There are two weekly markets at Sheffield. The better is Tuesday, but it didn't seem very crowded.

The town is responsible for the maintenance of a large number of poor: this is partly because when the workers are young they know they will be fed in their old age, and so they eat all they earn; and partly because the men often leave the town, and leave their wives and children to the charge of the parish. The poor rate in Sheffield is a fifth – 4 shillings in the pound.

The workhouse for the poor is large, containing 130 poor or incurable. It pays for 76 infants being nursed out in the country, and pays different sums out for 350 poor people distributed through the town. To qualify for these charities one has to have one's settlement in the town or be a native of it.

---

56 Wm Lowry's beautiful engraving, c.1788, of the Broseley smelting-house (pl. 26) perversely conveys an air of leisure and calm.

3

Adventuring Underground;
The Making of Manchester's Black Velvet

With confused thoughts about the 'frightful' working conditions in the steel-mill, the effect of poor-relief on workmen's thrift, and then finding there 'the same desire for perfection the English show in all their work', they left Sheffield in freezing fog and boldly headed for Manchester across high Derbyshire. At Castleton, below Peveril's Norman keep, they plunged – like the summer day-trippers of that time over from Buxton – down into the spectacular sequence of caverns known, indelicately from the shape of its entrance, as the Devil's Arse: the aptness of the name was obvious whether you approached in the 1790s with the unerring pencil of Edward Dayes, or with a camera in the 1990s. Here François' candour enabled him to record his delight at the uneasy look on their bear-leader's face as, wrapped in straw in a narrow boat, he was propelled out of sight under a very low vault.

Edward Dayes' distant view of Manchester, engraved in 1795, showed the winding Irwell with its meadows and a mill-group in the foreground. In the middle-distance, the expanding town the Frenchmen so admired and the Derbyshire peaks they had left are almost obscured by the industrial smoke they didn't mention. On reaching the town, they had lunch with the eminent Dr Thomas Percival, an early promoter of Public Health, who warned them they would find the manufacturers wary of foreign visitors after having several inventions stolen, and notable attempts by the French Marquis de Crillon. Yet the doctor's son managed to show them over a factory making black cotton velvet and employing 2,000 people – 'the equal of over 10,000 when you take into account the number of machines at work'. Again, their description of the processes is found accurate by a leading modern authority.

That evening they walked out to see the entrance to the duke of Bridgwater's canal; and next morning, eager to reach his mines and underground canals at Worsley, they had their one serious accident, an encounter with a coal-cart set in a deeply-rutted road. Their axle repaired, they were soon being entrusted by the duke's General Manager to a guide to this remarkable network of canals and mines: twelve miles at that time, developing later into 52 miles at four levels. Worsley, a thriving inland port at the hub of all this, still preserves a glimpse of the character François described. Alexandre was furious: he had a slight chill, and Lazowski refused to let him enter the miles of tunnels. Before they had advanced 500 metres, François was quite sure they'd come a mile. They were soaked by the dripping vault: he developed a headache and 'felt very uneasy'. They went almost two

miles along these black waterways, and he gave an unforgettable description of the
subterranean work of the miners, many of them children.
    By bad road to Barton, then splendid paving from Prescot to Liverpool.

Wednesday 2 March 1785   When we got up on the 2nd we could see only snow, falling abundantly, and an extraordinary freezing fog.[1] We left nevertheless. We could see nothing in those first three hours, the fog prevented our being able to distinguish anything beyond our horses, until we arrived about 6 miles from Sheffield: the road descended a hill over 2 miles long, and very narrow. However, at this much lower level, we could see clearly and we enjoyed the view of a very wild valley opening out in front of us. The countryside we travelled was lonely and barren, with long grasses suitable only for sheep and which the owners generally let for rough grazing at 5 shillings an acre. They are working at clearing in several places, and instead of hedges establish dry-stone walls. Places on too steep a slope and inaccessible to the plough are left as grazing: the breed of sheep is very small. In this state the land lets at between one and two guineas an acre. We were assured that in a very short time this immense wilderness would be cleared, but what slowed down the progress was the enormous capital outlay needed. We were told that, on average, an acre costs ten pounds sterling to bring into cultivation. The valley[2] goes along as far as Castleton; very pleasant and well peopled.

CASTLETON

We stopped at Castleton only to see a famous cave commonly called the Devil's Arse. It is something that gave me the greatest pleasure.[3] The first outcrop of rock we came to before entering the cavern is 261 feet high – as high as an ancient castle of which no one knows the age. The first cave is 42 feet high, 120 feet broad, and 270 in length. Inside, there's a rope-factory making very fine ropes, and two little houses

---

[1] W.E.A. Axon, *Annals of Manchester*, 1856, recorded under the year 1785 that between 18 October 1784 and 15 March 1785 there were only 26 days in Manchester in which the thermometer did not stand somewhere between 1 and 18½ degrees below freezing point.
[2] Appropriately named Hope Valley, after one of its villages.
[3] I have given it the English name in use in that refined age. François uses *Cul du Diable*. Anyone approaching the cavern, then or now, would see the striking aptness of that name. But already the conventionally polite were calling it The Peak Cavern, which is its dull official name today. It is one of a number of caverns in this famous beauty-spot in the area known as the High Peak. Few would attempt its pleasures in the snows of an extremely cold winter. The castle, celebrated by Scott, was built by William Peveril soon after the Norman Conquest. François has nodded in his usually careful notice of county boundaries: Castleton is back in (the north tip of) Derbyshire. James Plumptre and his friend John Dudley visited the cave in August 1793 (*James Plumptre's Britain*, ed. Ian Ousby, 1992, pp. 67–9). They unfortunately coincided with a party from Buxton, 'hooping and hollowing about: the lights and noise of so large a party took off much from the horror and solemnity of the scene'. They were also subjected to a woman and a number of children in surplices, with tapers, singing psalms.

have been built.[4] From this cave you go perhaps 450 feet before reaching the water where the rock ceiling is very low, and the water has to be crossed by boat. The guide launches into the water which, like the boat, is no more than a foot deep, but one lies flat in the boat – each carrying a little candle with great care: you would not be very happy in pitch darkness. What with the boat and the horror of the place, the candle showed a scene that to me suggested the bark of Charon. I was delighted to see Mr de Lazowski, packed in straw, being rowed beneath this vault – the more because he showed a little the uneasy look of someone not quite sure where he was being taken. Once out of the water we entered an enormous cave – 120 feet high, by 210, by 270 – and came again to the same water, now 30 feet across. Here, there was no boat, and the guide had to carry each of us on his shoulders.

A little further on, we came to a small chamber called the rain-house,[5] because there is a gutter that spouts rain incessantly and noisily. Further still, you enter a cave and, turning round, you see another cavern high up and beneath which we came: it is possible to climb to it, but we didn't. They lit it up for us and the effect was charming. The next grotto we came to is called the Devil's Cave[6] because a great many people have written their names there. From there you descend over thirty yards of sand to a place where water that comes from further on disappears underground. This is exactly half-way.

A little further and one comes to the Arches where the rock forms three absolutely regular arches. From this place one hears perfectly the cascades made by the water within the rock where one cannot go. The next cave, small, is called the Bell of Lincoln,[7] for it is perfectly round and bell-shaped: soon rock and water meet and one can go no further. The entire cave formation is 2,742 feet, and 621 feet below ground: all the calculations have been made exactly. What is more astonishing is that in the first cave there is a round hole, about 2 feet in diameter, that goes right through the rock and comes out close to the castle; but it contains so many bends that if you throw a stone down it doesn't fall to the bottom. A child couldn't get through, but

4   They are shown in a drawing by Dayes engraved for *The Beauties of England and Wales*. The admirable Pastor Moritz, at the extent of his hike north from London (170 miles, he reckoned), was perhaps excited into exaggeration when he was greeted by a sort of Charon and led inside (*Travels of Carl Philip Moritz in England in 1782*, a reprint of the 1795 translation, 1924, pp. 185–93): he wrote that he had 'perceived in the hollow of the Cavern a whole subterranean village where the inhabitants, on account of its being Sunday, were resting from their work, and with happy and cheerful looks were sitting at the doors of their huts along with their children'. He saw a number of large wheels on which these 'human moles' made rope. Saint-Fond, the celebrated authority on the extinct volcanoes of the Vivarais and Velay, came here in 1784. He noted that each of the two houses in the cave-entrance was inhabited by 'several families': B. Faujas de Saint-Fond, *A Journey through England and Scotland to the Hebrides in 1784*, ed. Sir A. Geikie, Glasgow, 2 vols, 1907. See p. 247 below and Pl. 59.
5   Alexandre called it 'Roger's rain-house (*la maison de pluie de roge*)'. *The Beauties of England and Wales*, III, p. 464, calls it Roger Rain's House.
6   'Or Devil's Caldron' (Alexandre).
7   *Beauties of England and Wales*, III, 1802, p. 465, calls it Great Tom of Lincoln. Plumptre too called it Tom of Lincoln.

on lighting a good fire in the cave the smoke comes out through the top of the hole. All this mass of rock is of very hard black marble. You see several fossils and many stalactites.

It has been shown that the water flowing through these caves enters several miles away from where a little stream emerges from the hill-top. We often experimented by throwing oats or bran into the water and seeing it carried off through the cave: one had the distinct feeling that their course *was* being controlled by the Devil.

Disley   We slept at Disley[8] after our hardest day so far: thirty miles, including a great many hills and in bitter cold.

Our innkeeper is a great agriculturalist. Last year he was awarded a fine silver cup by the Agricultural Society of Manchester for having introduced the best turnips into the district. He is hoping to win another this year for his cabbages, which he grows successfully as a field crop.[9]

Stockport 3 March 1785   Before reaching Manchester we went through Stockport, a town with a great many cotton mills. Although it is a small place it has a very commercial appearance.

From here to Manchester, which is about seven miles, we saw nothing but houses. It is all one town, one continuous factory. Some of the houses belonging to the merchants are very fine.

In the suburbs of Manchester we passed the hospital, which is vast and contains several hundred patients. It is maintained by subscriptions from several parishes. In front of it, there is a wide canal and a terrace with tree-lined walks, which is the regular promenade of the ladies of the town.[10]

---

8   François and Alexandre both spelt it Dishley (thinking perhaps of Mr Bakewell's farm back in Leicestershire). They had crossed briefly into Cheshire, without noticing, here and at Stockport. In the 1820s, the well-known inn was the Ram (*Paterson's Roads*, 1826, 252, 511). Their Bury acquaintance James Oakes, at Disley in 1805, said the only house at Disley 'is the Lamb's Head, and a very neat, clean, pleasant house it is' (*Oakes Diaries*, II, 29 June 1805).

9   At Disley, the Ram's Head is still very welcoming, with pleasant garden and bowling-green in rear, where it is overlooked by the church. John Hancock was the landlord when Byng stayed here in June, 1790: 'a neater and more chearfully situated inn I never saw: the room I chose, looking upon a small garden and up to a pretty church, is like one of a good rectory. The stables are excellent; the brown bread, and cheese, so good; the water so cold; the decanters so clean; and the bedrooms so nice . . . I sat down to a good dinner of mutton chops, cold veal and gooseberry pye – In such a house there is a wonderful larder, viz. salmon, pigeons, mutton, veal, cold ham, etc'. (*Torrington Diaries*, II, 1935, pp. 182–85).

10   This is known as 'the Infirmary Pond' on C. Lauret's fine plan of Manchester, 9 December 1793, and as The Canal on Green's map of 1794: hardly 'in the suburbs'. The Canal fronted the Infirmary and the Lunatic Hospital: in the gardens, along Bath Street, the New Public Baths were added for subscribers. The Infirmary held about 70 in-patients: there were also 'out-patients' and 'home-patients'. The number of patients admitted in all three classes in the year 1794 was 6,704, and the sum subscribed that year was £2,449. The Lunatic Hospital held about 70 patients in 1795: J. Aikin, *A Description of the Country from Thirty to Forty Miles round Manchester*, 1795, p. 199.

17.   *Castleton, Le cul du Diable, Edward Dayes, 1794.*

18.   *Manchester Lunatic Hospital, Infirmary and Public Baths, 1787–1788.*

MANCHESTER

4 March 1785   After the capital, Manchester is the handsomest town we've seen in
England. It is well laid out; at least most of the streets are straight and the houses
admirably built, of brick; the pavements are comfortably broad, the street-lighting
good.[11] What makes the streets and squares finer than those of other towns is their
greater regularity. Most of the houses, being intended as workshops, are very large,
the windows numerous and broad. The population is about 37,000.[12] The trade is
very considerable, for the town is at the centre of all the cotton-manufacture spread
throughout the countryside for 30 miles around. The manufactures are mostly of
cotton or cotton and yarn; those of wool and yarn are few.

The cotton is spun by machines similar to those of Derby. I would have been glad
to see over one to check the observations I'd made in Derby. I asked if I could,
but was told it wasn't possible.[13] the merchants are afraid to let strangers in
because they have had several of their inventions stolen: among others, M. de Crillon
went through all these factories some years ago, and made off with several good
designs.

*It is characteristic of François to want to get at once into the detailed technology of
Manchester's famous cotton-mills, but very strange indeed that he makes no reference to
the source of his information about the industrial espionage of M. de Crillon; for his
source was Dr Thomas Percival (1740–1804), one of that group of nonconformist
intellectuals who were at the heart of the scientific and 'philosophical' discovery that seems
to have been closely linked, almost fused, with the technological invention of Britain in
perhaps its most creative age. They were the counterpart of those French philosophers
whose lives, like Liancourt's, the father of François and Alexandre, related so tragically
to the revolutionary destruction of Bourbon France. Thomas Percival, a Warrington boy
and one of the earliest students at its dissenting Academy, was taught by the great
Joseph Priestley (the subjects he taught there were languages, history and anatomy) and
went from there to Edinburgh; to one of the youngest Fellowships of the Royal Society,
and lasting friendships with William Robertson, the historian and cousin of the
architect brothers Adam, and with Hume, etc. He completed his medical studies at Leyden
before settling, as physician and author, in Manchester from 1767 till his death in 1804.*

---

11 James Oakes, an acquaintance of theirs from Bury St Edmunds, visited Manchester in
September 1785 and wrote: 'Building goes forward at an amazing rate at Manchester. There is
a street or two new building wherein some houses will lay the occupiers in from 3 to 400 rent
annually' (ed. Jane Fiske, *The Oakes Diaries*, I, 1990, pp. 238–39).
12 The population of Manchester with Salford at the end of 1788 was reckoned at 50,000,
having risen from about 20,000 in 1757 (Aikin, *op. cit.*, pp. 156–57).
13 Some years later, in 1799, Thomas Philip Robinson, 3rd baron Grantham, described the
operation of a cotton-spinning machine (illustrated by a rough sketch) in a large Manchester
factory (Bedfordshire R.O., L31/114/3, quoted in *The Observant Traveller*, ed. Robin Gard,
1989, p. 74). But in 1784, the distinguished French geologist Saint-Fond failed to gain entry
to any cotton mill: see p. 247 below.

19.   *Dr Thomas Percival, MD, FRS, 1740–1804.*

There, in his house, the celebrated Manchester Literary and Philosophical Society was founded in 1781.[14] *In Manchester he saw the dangers as well as the benefits of the new and rapidly expanding factory production. He was an early promoter of public baths,*[15] *public health and factory legislation. Was it through disapproval of this that François made no reference to him? Alexandre had no such compunction. Now, for the first time in his visit to England, Alexandre comes into his own. At Manchester he completely 'scoops' François.*

Alexandre: The entrance to Manchester is fine, noble and very agreeable . . . Our inn was situated over the market-place.[16] That same day we delivered a letter we had brought for Dr Percival from the Bishop of Llandaff.[17] The doctor was not at home but would be able to see us later . . . The doctor is a medical man, very well informed, and highly intelligent. He is in touch with all the great men living in England. He gave us much detailed information about Manchester which was very useful to us. As we were not staying with him, we went home to write our journal and didn't go out that evening. The doctor asked us to lunch with him, and we had a conversation between Mr de Lazowski and him. He spoke of a new society [the Manchester Literary and Philosophical Society: see above] established only in the last few years, and which is designed on better lines than any other.

14 An example of the extent of such intellectual and commercial networks is Samuel Greg, one of the giants of the cotton industry with his famous Quarry Bank mill, near Wilmslow. He became a member of the Manchester Literary and Philosophical Society in 1790. His wife's sister, a Liverpool Unitarian, married Thomas Pares of the Leicestershire banking family, with textile interests in Derbyshire see p. 27 above.

15 Pl. 18 shows the Public Baths alongside the Infirmary and Lunatic Hospital in an engraving of 1787/88 (through the kindness of David Taylor, Local Studies Unit, Manchester City Council Department of Libraries and Theatres). The 'wide canal' mentioned by François is seen in the foreground, though not the 'tree-lined walks'.

16 Probably the Bull's Head. Seven weeks later, on 21 April, Manchester's two successful delegates returned from the House of Commons with the news that Mr Pitt, seconded by Mr Fox, had moved the repeal of the tax on fustians and all bleached cotton manufactures. They alighted at the Bull's Head in the Market Place and were chaired through the streets. The Bull's Head was destroyed by German bombers in 1940.

17 Richard Watson, bishop of Llandaff, was a Cambridge colleague of their great friend, and host, in Bury St Edmunds, Professor J. Symonds. On their visit to Cambridge at the end of May the previous year, Symonds had introduced them to the bishop, who was Regius Professor of Divinity. Lazowski, something of an unbeliever, was 'ground to powder, though civilly' by the bishop in an argument on the truths of Christianity. François made no reference to the episode in his account of their visit to Cambridge (*A Frenchman's Year in Suffolk, 1784*, p. 95n). It would scarcely explain his failure to mention Dr Percival now.

Richard Watson was the son of a Westmoreland clergyman, master of the local grammar-school. He was Professor of Chemistry at Cambridge from 1764, and elected to the regius chair of divinity in 1771, in which year he published his *Plan of Chemical Lectures*. His first two vols of *Chemical Essays* were translated into German at Leipzig, 1782: in the preface to the fourth, he said he had destroyed all his chemical manuscripts as a sacrifice to other people's notions of a proper occupation of a dignitary of the church. In 1787, Pitt's government consulted him about improvements in gunpowder. He was said to have saved them £100,000 a year (*Dictionary of National Biography*).

Those who wish to, send in papers for new schemes or for inventions, then those papers are read, and everyone discusses them here. This academy examines those things that have been sent to them and judges which should be collected and printed, though this hasn't yet started. One of these meetings is held every week and we were very vexed not to have been here on the right day so as to be better able to understand their transactions.

He persuaded us of the difficulty we should find ourselves in approaching the factory owners, on account of those who have sought out and taken away the drawings of machinery: especially the Marquis de Crillon from whom the constables of the town seized a packet of components of machines. That affair has made the manufacturers afraid to let people see their processing of silk and cotton and various other methods which, luckily for us, we saw at Derby when we were there.

However, we left having seen this large and very beautiful town. It is the manufactures that have made this town so animated.[18]

Alexandre's interest had certainly been aroused by Manchester, and was sustained at once by the Bridgwater Canal. For accuracy of detailed description we return to François, who describes a tour of one Manchester factory. Yet it is left to Alexandre to supply the information that their guide was Dr Percival's son – probably his eldest, Edward, then about nineteen, also training to be a physician, who wrote a treatise on Typhus and edited his father's works.

François: We did go into one factory where we were shown pieces made from a yarn very like those of Rouen: I couldn't see any difference. Their dyes are not perfect, not set any better than ours in the cotton. With some of them, the influence of their damp climate makes a difference, but they showed us a piece of black cotton velvet such as I've never seen in France, lovely and smooth and fine: it costs half a guinea the ell,[19] but truly silk velvet is scarcely better than this. It is dyed in the thread.

This manufacturer employs about 2,000 people daily, some in the country, some in town. One tries to form an idea of the quantity of fabrics they must be turning out. With the number of machines they have at work in this country, 2,000 people is the equivalent of more than 10,000 elsewhere. They all earn between 8 shillings (9 *livres* 12 *sols*) and a guinea (1 *louis*) a week.[20] After this rough estimate of one factory's output, one gets some notion of the scale of the trade of the whole of Manchester.

This same manufacturer complained a good deal about a new tax recently levied on them. It isn't a high charge, but it's the manner by which it's assessed that rankles. It is one English sol (2 sols) per ell of stuff selling at up to 3 shillings (3 livres 12 sols); and two sols (4 sols) on everything selling above that. They are obliged to send

---

18   For some reason Alexandre underlined this last short paragraph.

19   A measure, now archaic, that varied from country to country. The English ell was 45 inches (1.142 metres), a yard and a quarter.

20   These equivalents given by François tally with those given by Arthur Young: see p. xiv above.

their pieces to be stamped when they have paid, and it sometimes happens – going through several processes and especially dying in deep colours – that the stamp gets obliterated. Then the goods are liable to be seized and disputes follow that can only vex the makers and slow down the trade; all in the interests of a very small amount of revenue. Above all, they complain about the trouble they sometimes have in sending the material to be stamped. Mr Pitt, the minister,[21] reckons, after making precise enquiries, that this tax will bring in from this town £80,000 sterling. So, supposing the impost to be at a mean price, it follows that the production at Manchester is between five and six hundred thousand ells every year.[22] I speak only of the cotton trade: it's only on the cotton, or cotton and yarn, that the tax is assessed.

I saw tapes and wool garters made with great dispatch. It's a large workshop, making thirty-two at a time.[23] Between each of the ribbons is a little shuttle, firmly attached to the reed [*peigne*]. Behind, there are four heddles [*marches*] for combining the threads.[24] A man moves a large frame [a swinging 'slay'] to which the reeds are fixed, and also the operating rods with their pegs, to knock the shuttles through their respective warps. The reed 'beats up' the weft but across, so that the little shuttles pass from one side to the other of each ribbon, and the reed, falling at the same instant, finishes the weave. The four heddles move in pairs, alternately, by means of a wooden cam-shaft geared to a cylinder which the two handles rotate. The man works at a prodigious speed.[25]

Each ribbon has twelve threads, striped in different colours, but if you wanted flowered garters, or ribbons for the peasants, you would have to use what they call the *Dutch frame*, made like the one I just described except that, instead of the four heddles moved by the same bar, they have twelve, operated by the workman's feet

---

21   The younger William Pitt, at 23 in 1782, became Chancellor of the Exchequer, a post he combined with being First Lord of the Treasury (prime minister) from December 1783 to 1801, and from 1804 to 1806. He combined with Fox to repeal this troublesome tax seven weeks after the French visit: see footnote 16 above, also p. 235 below.

22   This is between 1,070 and 1,339 miles of cotton fabric a year, about twice the length of Britain itself.

23   They were looking at a ribbon or narrow-fabric-weaving mill. This form of weaving was the first to be mechanised. There was trouble with the weavers when it was introduced to London from Danzig in the 17th century because it could already weave 16 ribbons at a time. Dr Richard Hills explains that he thinks it had an important influence on John Kay's flying shuttle, because on both looms the shuttles were knocked through the warp by being hit by pegs. In the case of the ribbon loom, the shuttles are broader than the ribbons, and there is of course one for each shuttle. They travel on slides and are fixed in so that they cannot be taken out. The shuttle race also forms the structure to which the reeds are fixed for beating up the weft.

24   Four heddles suggests a twill, rather than a plain weave.

25   Attempts to drive these machines by water-power failed, as the weavers still had to be able to watch the looms and stop them quickly if a thread broke, weft ran out, shuttle stuck, etc. etc. Dr Hills has given me this useful summary: cams on one shaft open the appropriate heddles to form the shed through which the shuttles will pass as the slay is moving backwards (probably operated by crank). At its furthest point backwards, the picker rod hits the shuttles through. In the forward movement, the heddles close, and the reeds in the slay beat up the weft against the previously woven ribbon.

and much harder work. Those who know a little about weaving know that without those heddles you can't make flowers. At this frame they make only fifteen ribbons at a time, but they cost a little more. On these two kinds of frame they make all kinds of braid for clothes, shoes, etc.

These workshops occupied us all morning: in the evening we walked a mile out of town to see the entrance to the Duke of Bridgwater's canal.[26] I shall speak at length about this in the following pages; at present I will content myself with describing what I saw at the start of the canal. The river, [27] after passing through the town, enters a vast warehouse, which serves as covered harbour, and passes under it. It is after this warehouse that it begins to widen out and that its banks are made up: it flows over a bed of loose stone or, rather, compact sand. As the river widens and narrows, and as it is important to the navigation that as much water as possible is held at the same height, a hundred yards beyond the warehouse a great reservoir has been built in the form of a clover-leaf, being the form in which the line of circumvallation encompasses most space.[28] It is built of stone exactly set and levelled in relation to the desired height of the canal. The clover-leaf is made to slope so that the water tends to run to the centre and disappear into a vast sump made of freestone, some of it disappearing into the earth, some of it throwing itself into a little stream and going on to lose itself in a river the level of which is very much lower than that of the canal. The level of the waters of the sump is about 30 feet below that of the canal.

5 March 1785   On the 5th we left Manchester rather late[29] intending to reach Worsley in time for lunch and to see the works of the Duke of Bridgwater and his coal mine, and then to go by canal-boat underground. Providence decided otherwise. As there was a very cold wind, Mr de Lazowski's [English] servant was on horseback[30] and my brother drove with Chaveron[31] in the second cabriolet. We noticed a large number of carts heavily loaded with coal on their way to Manchester with no one in charge, but as the road was wide they did us no harm. At about two miles from the town, we found ourselves in a narrow part and further restricted by tall heaps of earth deposited for road-mending. One cart, without driver, approached and, as its wheels were in a deep rut, it couldn't make room for us to pass. We could have stopped, and stopped the cart-horses and got them out of the rut; that would have been the sensible course. But as we should lose time, I hoped that with a crack of the whip I might re-route the cart-horses and thus have enough room to pass. I drove

---

26   Planned by the 1st duke of Bridgwater to carry coal from his mines at Worsley to Manchester, it was constructed 1759–61 by the 3rd duke, with the help of his steward John Gilbert, and the great engineer James Brindley. It runs several miles underground and crosses the Irwell on an aqueduct. See title-page and Pl. 20.
27   The Irwell.
28   See plan from folding map at back of J. Aikin, *Description*, 1795.
29   Alexandre says 'at 9 in the morning'.
30   Alexandre was usually in the saddle.
31   Who had been with them all through 1784 in Bury St Edmunds, as personal servant *homme de confiance de notre famille*.

therefore as much to one side as I could; however, mounting those heaps of earth, which would infallibly turn us over, I whipped the horses to one side, but the cart was so heavy that they couldn't cross out of the rut; heaving still harder, they hooked on to the side of our cabriolet and dragged us backwards over ten yards. My brother was driving the other cabriolet behind us, rather close. He was trying to get out of the way at the moment when, reversing violently, we turned him over and the peasants managed to stop the cart – otherwise I don't know what would have happened. Happily neither he nor Chaveron were injured, and everyone got off with a fright. The second cabriolet had only a bent axle-tree: we had a broken spring and three spokes of a wheel.

We lunched at the nearest inn while the bent axle-tree was re-fitted, and the accident meant that we arrived at Worsley only at one o'clock.

WORSLEY

We found out where the duke's steward lived and went at once to hand him the letter we'd been given for him.[32] He immediately wrote instructing an intelligent man to show us the mine and everything we wanted to see.

It is now about twenty-five years since the duke of Bridgwater, then aged twenty-two, began this immense undertaking. It has cost him, they say, thirty-six millions of our money, but this sum can only be reckoned an exaggeration: anyway it's a secret that the duke has passed on to nobody and that it is even rather to his glory to keep hidden. The object of his enterprise is to exploit an immense coal mine by transporting the coal to Manchester and thence to Derbyshire, Leicestershire, etc., by a large number of canals; and in the other direction to Liverpool and to export from there to Bristol, to Wales, etc., and all the ports round the English coast where coal is dear.

The whole canal, from Manchester to the mine, and from the mine to Liverpool, is about 32 miles long, and it goes for about 28 or 30 of them on the same level.[33] It is 4 feet wide[34] and 4½ deep. The engineer took the greatest care to avoid involving the waters of unreliable streams, and – with frequent reservoirs – the canal is always at the same level. Its principal sources are the little streams that descend the nearby hills, and the waters from the mine itself. The mine is at Worsley.[35] From this place to Manchester the canal, all at one depth and level, is nothing to look at. Its banks are richer than the rest of the countryside: he has taken occasion to build a number of houses which give it an entirely pleasant aspect.

[32] It was John Gilbert: Alexandre noted his name: the duke's right-hand man, in day-to-day charge: really his General Manager.
[33] Worsley eventually became the hub of a 52-mile long maze of canals on *four* levels: they penetrated the Worsley coalfield right through to Walkden and Farnworth. See the Lancashire Mining Museum at Buile Hill Park, Salford, whose curator, Alan Davies, has so kindly gone over these pages and made a great many very valuable observations.
[34] More like 4 metres.
[35] Worsley was where they entered the underground canal system, feeding mines spread over a much wider area.

While our boat was being prepared for entering the mine we went and looked at a very large forge[36] belonging to the duke, for doing all the ironwork needed for the canal or the boats. It is a big brick building, containing two different forges and two tilt-hammers which, as well as the bellows, are worked by water-wheel. I saw six workmen who are employed all the year round. A little further away, another large building is a lime-kiln and mortar mixer.

The lime they get from Wales[37] in exchange for coal. From the boat it is carried up to the kiln in a little cart with iron wheels, then it is winched up to the mouth of the furnace by a long chain: the fire is lit from beneath.

The lime goes into a vast reservoir of water, with which it is mixed, then left until the mortar is needed. When it is, the lime is mixed with the right amount of sand in a great trough in which a great millstone rolls, turned by a water-wheel, and pounding it perfectly. The re-cladding of the canal and of the different vaults in the mine calls for such great quantities of mortar that it is in constant production at this mill.

Worsley   This place is a port belonging to the duke, and lively. It is bordered by the woods destined for use in repairs or in new building; everything comes from these lands. It is the entrepôt, the hub, of everything belonging to him. Here are his boats, his stables[38] for the mules that tow them, a corn-mill he works with the water from a little stream falling down the hillside and passing under the canal: in a word, this port gives you a good idea[39] of the man who was bold enough to undertake so great a scheme, also of the fortune that must have underwritten these expenses, enormous, day-to-day and unremitting. This canal should really be the work of a State, of a province, rather than of an individual – whether from considerations of the cost of the undertaking or of its utility to the whole of this corner of England. However, our boat was waiting.

My brother, feeling unwell and afraid he might be in for a fever, didn't come with us into the mine. Mr de Lazowski and I set out, and his servant came with us.[40] The boat was a peculiar shape: about 45 or 50 feet long and 4 wide, the sides about 3 feet high and curved in slightly at the top. They are built entirely of oak for strength – to carry coal. Each boat usually carries 7 tons (14 thousand-weight) of coal. One built with slightly taller sides, carries 27.[41]

---

36 A forge is shown on the 1786 map of Worsley (Salford Local History Library).
37 This was before the discovery of lime by John Gilbert on the Worsley estate. There are remains of the lime kilns shown beside the dock at Worsley on the 1786 map. Another source found on the duke's estate was at Bedford, near Leigh, 8 miles west of Worsley. (See Hugh Malet, *The Canal Duke*, Manchester, 1977.)
38 The site is marked today by 'Stable Footbridge' off the Barton Road. François seems to be the only observer of the time who names the kind of draught-animal used.
39 It still does, though the activity is merely tourist.
40 Alexandre was naturally upset at being left behind, and referred darkly to Mr de Lazowski's part in it: 'under the pretext, *sous prétexte*, of doubting my health, prevented me, *m'a empêché*, from doing what I cherished'.
41 Alan Davies says 7 to 8 tons was the capacity of the basic 'M' (or mine) boats. The local name for these barges was 'starvationer', possibly on account of the heavily ribbed interior (that's the charitable explanation). A small number of the M boats has been preserved at various sites. By the mid-19th century 150 ten-ton and 100 two-ton (tub-boats) were in use.

20.   *Worsley: the Delph. Narrow boats in the basin at the entrance (right) to the Bridgwater Canal, c.1900.*

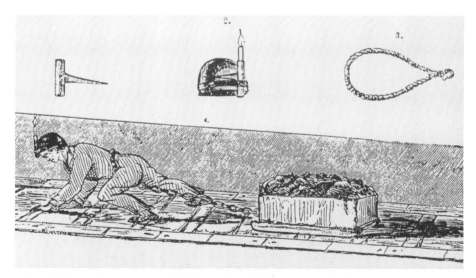

21.   *'The coal is put on small sledges which children drag to the boats . . .'*

We lit several small candles which we stuck along the sides of the boat with clay. The draught of air was so strong that it blew the candles out in our hands.[42] Our guide advised us to sit down in the boat, and we entered a huge rock through a little vault,[43] five feet high by eight in breadth, where it was extremely dark. The canal is four feet deep and all its water comes out of the mine and from what falls into the canal.

We covered about a mile in a straight line.[44] Our man drew the boat forward by catching hold of iron rungs[45] fixed in the top of the vault. In order to do that, you couldn't stand up, but had to be seated, or stand doubled up.

The tunnel is all bricked except in a few small places where a marble rock[46] had been cut through, which avoided any need to make a new tunnel. Only think of the labour involved in cutting this canal through the mine and the rock, and in brick-arching all those parts where the earth wasn't solid!

All the time, we were in sight of our point of entry, which seemed like a mere dot.[47] The further we went, the colder and damper the air became. The vault dripped many filterings of very cold water that made us steadily wetter. The place gave me a headache, and I soon felt very uneasy.[48] The further we advanced, the deeper – so our guide told us – we were going underground, for although the canal remained on the same level the hill climbed steeply above us: he assured us we were a hundred feet beneath the surface. From time to time we came to branches of the canal connected with seams of the mine's coal that we judged either exhausted or too poor to be worth mining; sometimes we came to ventilation shafts which afforded a glimpse of light.[49]

Then the canal changed direction and we lost sight of our entrance:[50] if we had continued straight on we would have been beneath land not belonging to the duke and through which he had no right to go.

---

42 Alan Davies notes that the main horizon canal was fairly well supplied with access, winding and ventilation shafts to the surface: these provided a strong natural ventilation: but see n. 48 below.

43 This probably means that they were entering an area of unlined rock from a narrow brick-lined tunnel (Alan Davies).

44 I'm sure it seemed a mile, but is unlikely to have been as much as 3/8 mile, according to the plans in the NCB Museum (AD).

45 One of these rungs, or rings, may be seen preserved in Salford Mining Museum.

46 Perhaps a mudstone.

47 Alan Davies thinks this probably means that they must have gone in through the more easterly of the two entrances, and so had not yet travelled 3/8 mile.

48 At the Lancashire Mining Museum at Buile Hill Park, Eccles Old Road, Salford, a film of these underground canals is shown. It fairly conveys some deeply alarming sensations: François was not timid by nature, and his 'uneasiness' was genuine. One can only hope the women and small children working down there got accustomed to it. For all the ventilation noted above, a vast area of active workings contains stale air and emitted methane gas, which would account for François' headache.

49 These small-diameter shafts were used to remove waste and give access to workmen: their distribution through Worsley, Walkden and Farnworth provides a nightmare for present-day house-builders and owners.

50 This change of direction, towards the NE, occurs 5/8 mile in.

A little further, we came to a crossways where the vault was slightly higher.[51] This is the branch of another canal going to another part of the mine no longer worked. This is the point to which enquiring strangers are usually brought; but as we had the benefit of a letter from the duke's steward, we continued along the waterway.

Soon we passed two more branch-canals[52] and from time to time we went under vaulting of very fine brickwork. There are something like twelve miles (5 French leagues) of canals like this in the mine.[53]

At last we perceived a light, but from a long way away: we were 150 feet beneath the surface[54] and a good mile and a half from the entrance.

We left the main canal and forked left into one of the branches,[55] to see two workmen who had brought coal in a boat to this place where a bucket was lowered to be filled and then raised. A bucket came down full of water, was emptied and raised full of coal.[56] This whole machine is worked entirely on equilibrium – one bucket is down when the other is up. I don't mean on the surface, but up at the level of a higher-level canal: to understand what I'm saying, you have to know that there are two levels of canals in this mine, one 105 feet lower than the other: ours was the lower one.

At the moment when the lower bucket is filled with coal, a valve opens which fills the upper bucket with water from the higher canal. As the bucket fills, the valve closes and the bucket finding itself heavier than the coal (for the amounts are regulated) it descends, and the coal rises to the surface. It redescends to the level of the top canal, fills as before and descends as before. The bottoms of the two buckets are fitted with a valve. When the water falls into the bucket, its weight shuts the valve, but when the bucket arrives in the water below, equilibrium lifts the bottom and the water runs out.

These machines are very interesting: they are mostly invented by the engineer in charge of all the duke's operations: a man of great talent.[57]

After seeing how this machine works, we returned to the main canal which led us towards the light we had seen. This light was that of the miners working there, and who were loading up a boat. We disembarked to walk along a number of different tunnels, truly very small, four feet wide and only five feet high. We were in one of the seams of coal: excellent, very black and gleaming.

Nothing is more tiring than walking in a stooping position. We walked steadily up a little slope till we reached the place where the miners were working. The working is eight feet all round, which is the thickness of the seam.[58] When the miners start on one, they remove only half, which explains the four-foot width we passed along;

51 Possibly the junction at Edge Fold colliery, a little over a mile into the system (AD).
52 Probably the westerly branches of, first, the Bin Seam, and, second, the Crombouke Seam.
53 This was so in 1785: they were much extended; see footnote 33 on p. 68 above.
54 Probably 200 feet underground here (AD).
55 They had probably just passed Ellesmere Colliery, and so were nearly two miles in.
56 Illustration.
57 James Brindley.
58 At Ellesmere Colliery nearby, the seam was 6 feet 10 inches thick.

and they continue with these dimensions till they reach the present boundary set for their workings. They then return, cutting out the rest that they had left. They cut with sharpened picks and start from the bottom [i.e. undercut] so that the coal falls out with the least trouble. The work is very hard; it is task work and generally earns them two and a half shillings a day: some earn more. All the coal they detach is put on to small sledges which children drag to the boats. For that job they have leather waist-girdles[59] and a small iron chain that hooks on to the sledge. That is very heavy work too, by which they earn between ten (English) sols [fivepence] and a shilling a day (between 20 and 25 sols). I've seen young girls employed in that work, and as skirts would scarcely be suitable, they were dressed entirely like men and they get so hot down there that they are almost naked.[60]

We saw all over the coal-mine. The way led steadily upwards and we arrived at the foot of a dry well, clad in dry brickwork, where we found a ladder, climbed it, and arrived back on earth.[61]

I can't describe the pleasure I felt on emerging from that black hole. There was a little sun: it seemed like the most charming climate, and I relished the pleasure of walking without being bent double.

We saw one of the machines I described that carried the coal in equilibrium with water, and we saw with what precision they are regulated. With each machine there is a supervisor with a graduated lever.

Very soon we returned underground at the place where the boats are brought out for repair.[62] We descended by a very gentle slope till we found a boat. This is on the upper canal: we were scarcely thirty or forty feet underground.

The object of this second navigation was to see one of the shafts which served to lower the coal from the upper mine to the lower mine for transport on that first canal, by which we entered; and from there to go out on the Navigation. This machine consists only of two buckets in equilibrium. They are made very simply. One fills itself with water in the lower canal while the other is filled with coal in the lower mine. This last, being heavier, lifts the other. The mechanism could not be simpler.

---

59 Pl. 21. *Cylindres de cuire* must refer to a leather-bound girdle or belt, encircling the waist: a rope version of it is illustrated in the *Report of the Children's Employment*, Vol. 7, 1842, para. 394. The sub-commissioner admitted he had begun by conceiving the girdle and chain 'unnatural and barbarous' but 'on minute examination . . . found the chain to descend in front quite clear of the pubis, so as to pass freely between the thighs'. Remembering that the child was dragging a sledge full of coal, on all fours, with the chain passing between his or her thighs, this explanation seems extremely specious. I'm very grateful to Alan Davies, Director of the Mining Museum, for showing me this illustration, and the reconstructions in his fine museum.
60 The 1842 children's Employment Commission found 74 girls aged between 13 and 18 working here, and 20 who were under 13.
61 Probably at Burton's Garden Pit: if so, they were 3,377 yards into the system – just under 2 miles.
62 The inclined plane from the surface at Walkden where boats could be repaired (known today at Boatshed Workshops), and then returned below ground to the higher canal (AD).

The canal of the upper mine is entirely like that first one: perhaps there are fewer brick vaults as there is more sound rock. We walked out up the same slope, and in going to see the pump which removes any surplus of water we noticed the tops of several of the air-vents we had passed. This pump is extremely complicated, with a graduated regulator controlled with great attention by a human supervisor. Its object is to lift out of the mine water that obstructs the navigation of the canals by spreading it over the surface of the land from which it drains into the river.

Before starting this canal, the Duke of Bridgwater obtained an Act of Parliament not only to oblige landowners whose property lay on the route of the canal to sell at the current price, but this Act also gave to him alone the right of navigation provided he in return was obliged to take every kind of merchandise and carry it to its destination.

You can imagine what a very large number of boats he needed in daily readiness, and mules to tow them, for he didn't use horses. Mules need less nourishment and work harder. He has four Spanish donkeys from which to breed: I was told he had more than two or three hundred horses or mules working at his mine or his navigation. Manchester and Liverpool are full of a great many of his boats ready to leave. At Worsley there is also a yard where they are built. On top of all this there are passenger-boats plying regularly from Manchester to Liverpool, carrying large numbers of people for very small fares.[63]

The man who took us through the mine told us it produced about 200 tons of coal a day, ce qui fait 400,000 livres which, because there are 5 sols (10 French sols) to the cent, makes 2,000 francs return on the mine every day.[64] That isn't the only profit: that from rights over the canal is very considerable.

The duke employs about 400 workers whom he pays by the day or by task at 2½ shillings (3 livres) a day.

He is a large-scale agriculturalist: he has cleared a lot of low-lying wet lands, no good for any kind of vegetation but which, when drained and well smoke-dried, became excellent farmlands in six or seven years.[65] For all that, it costs almost six pounds sterling per acre, which by its dearness does prevent more rapid progress. He holds, and values himself, all that he has reclaimed in this way, and raised on it a good quantity of bullocks and sheep which he fattens and kills for his workpeople. He sells them the meat at the current price, but they are sure of the best quality at a price they'd have to give for indifferent meat in Manchester.

This is why he is very much liked by his workers. He comes every year and spends a long time visiting his canal and all his works and so much loves all the details that,

---

[63] At Worsley, the boatyard is still to be seen. The last of these canal passenger-boats, *The Duchess Countess* plied between Manchester and Warrington, then served as a houseboat and was photographed high and dry beside the Shropshire Union Canal (British Transport Commission: Historical Relics Department).

[64] If my sums are right (see Notes at p. xiv above), 200 tons of coal a day yielded £17,500, which equalled £175 profit on the mine daily.

[65] Near Chat Moss, later famous for the difficulties it presented to the engineers of the Liverpool-Manchester Railway.

when he is there, it is he who pays them, gives them their orders and, in a word, attends to everything that needs doing.

We shall see in the next volume [in this case, paragraphs] at the very beginning the description of a very beautiful bridge over which the canal passes, above a river.

I forgot to note that, since Stockport, a small town 8 miles before Manchester, we have been in Lancashire.

Sunday 6 March 1785   On the 6th we left Worsley and got to Barton for lunch. It is a small parish[66] and only two miles from Worsley, yet those two miles were long and hard to cover. The road is so bad that it's really dangerous. Only by going with the utmost care did we avoid turning over and wrecking our cabriolets. We covered almost a mile in a half-frozen river which our horses' resolve got us through after a painful struggle.

BARTON AQUEDUCT

Fifty yards from Barton, the Duke of Bridgwater's canal passes on a magnificent aqueduct over the river Mersey,[67] a very considerable valley at this point, almost as wide as the Seine at Paris. The aqueduct is 207 paces long, which I reckon at 640 feet, for their strides are long. It is about fifty feet wide and is carried on three arches. Judging by eye, I reckoned it ran 50 or 60 feet above the river. It is a beautiful freestone building with double arches, keyed in brick, and despite the strength it must have, there is a lightness in its construction. It is a work worthy of the Romans. I rate it higher than the aqueduct bridges of the Languedoc canal, because it is much longer than any of them, and, above all, incomparably taller.

After the canal crosses the river, it continues as far as Runcorn, maintaining its level all the time. It is only there, well above the height of the Mersey where it enters, that eight locks were needed. I am very vexed not to have seen them, but as it would have taken us another day, for there was no means of our continuing that way to Liverpool, Mr de Lazowski wouldn't go.

The Mersey river, which comes down through Stockport, is navigable as far as that town, despite the abundance of buildings all over its banks. As there are so many mills above the river, drawing off water to fill their mill-ponds and each with its little channel and lock, the navigation cost more. Besides, it isn't even practicable in all weathers: flooding sometimes makes it impassable, and so it is almost entirely abandoned: it was possible only for small-scale local business.

---

66 Eccles, the parish containing Barton, or Barton Moss, is a very ancient one.
67 It is still the Irwell, joining the Mersey 4½ miles further on. The aqueduct was replaced, alas, by a swivel bridge. It was sketched by the Rev. Sir John Cullum c.1771 (Suffolk R. O., E2/44/1, see *The Observant Traveller*, ed. Robin Gard, 1989, p. 71). Cullum reckoned it 'a most capital scene: to see ships sailing as it were in the Air, 50 yards [he must have meant feet] above a navigable river cannot fail of striking the Spectator with the most pleasing Astonishment'. In fact, the middle arch of the three was 63 feet wide and 38 feet above the surface of the Irwell: J. Aikin, *A Description of the Country from Thirty to Forty Miles round Manchester*, 1795, p. 113. See our title-page.

Warrington Warrington is where we slept, a fairly large town with a busy weekly market. They say it does a good trade in malt, for the making of all kinds of beer. Its position is advantageous, built as it is beside the Mersey and the canal.[68]

7 March 1785 Warrington to Liverpool, eighteen miles. The road smooth, one of the best in England, is metalled as far as Prescot and beaten flat under the broad wheels of an enormous number of carts provisioning Liverpool. From Prescot to Liverpool is all paved, and very well paved on account of the carts that have to go to collect coal from a mine close beside the high road.[69] The weight and the great number of these vehicles would ruin any but properly paved roads. The coal which is carted seven miles is cheaper than the duke's coal, and as good.

Prescot Prescot is a small town with a very busy atmosphere,[70] built on top of a hill.

[68] See p. 83, footnote 19 below.
[69] A sample of these roads, paved with the local red sandstone, survives in 1991 beside the interesting small museum at Prescot.
[70] In their hurry to get to Liverpool they, surprisingly, overlooked Prescot's main business as a centre of clock and watch-making.

4

The View of Liverpool: Mount Pleasant and the Docks

As the main road sloped down from Mount Pleasant they got an impression of Liverpool as a large and beautiful town enclosing a forest of ships' masts, their pennants all moving at the whim of the breeze. If they overlooked the smog at Manchester, they noted here that 'a dense black and offensive smoke infects the whole atmosphere'; and, later, their view from the cupola above the Exchange was blotted out by a Mersey fog; so, presumably, all those pennants moved pretty limply.

The smog didn't smother their enthusiasm. Nor did the hospitality of the Red Lion. Nor did the sight of the slave-ships, which they roundly deplored: 'this barbarous, most inhuman trade – I saw one due to sail in two days, which would hold 1,500 negroes'. They brought an introduction to a Mr Hatton, a retired merchant, whose 'conversation was very helpful'. A detailed inspection of the various docks was followed by a visit to the town centre and the Exchange. For once, they came away with the feeling that, however good Liverpool's port facilities were, at least at Nantes France had a port with a livelier atmosphere.

At Warrington, the blowing of twist-glass brought them back to the works for a second look. At Northwich, the only way to see the fine white salt in its mine was to stand in a small bucket and drop 180 feet down a shaft. Lazowski descended, forbidding them to follow: there was a scene when they did.

Eggs at a little inn; a talkative old farmer, and a local cheese-making recipe. At Etruria, Mr Wedgwood was away in London: his agent would allow no one to see the making of the black porcelain with figures in low relief. Leaving for Shrewsbury, Lazowski went ahead impatiently, took a wrong turning, and was rather red in the face, with a bottle in his hand, when they caught him up. Arriving late in Shrewsbury, they found the best inns full for the Assizes, and had to manage with a poor supper and narrow bedroom. They were soon off to Ironbridge.

François: The arrival in Liverpool is very beautiful. For the last mile we descended a hill shaped like an amphitheatre above the town, which lies all at your feet. There are few buildings that stand out because there are few that are both beautiful and standing on their own, but what is agreeable is to see a fine large town, in the middle of which springs up a forest of ships' masts with their pennants all moving at the whim of the breeze: at the same time, what a fog, what a dense black and offensive smoke infects the whole atmosphere!

We were (mis)directed to the Red Lion, entered, and had not been there long before we realized that we'd come to the wrong place. We dined, and, soon after, collected our horses, found ourselves in the actual Red Lion, which was hardly any better.[1] It is astonishing that in England, where one finds excellent inns in the smallest villages, one finds such very bad ones in large towns like Norwich, Liverpool, Ipswich and even Sheffield. It is true that in Sheffield the fault is about to be remedied.

As Liverpool has been built mostly in the last hundred years, it is well laid out, the streets large and well built: brick with string-courses of a grey stone brought from some way away: there are regular little freestone porticos with columns. In all these streets there are pavements down each side, and street-lights as in London.[2]

The population is immense. It is rising, we were told, to [blank] thousand.[3] After London it is the most commercial town in England. About 2,000 ships enter and unload in a year, of which over 500 belong here. The chief business is the trade in negroes, which is conducted in very large ships. Liverpool is the English port most engaged in this barbarous, most inhuman, trade. It sends out 300 ships: I saw one, due to sail in two days, which would hold 1,500 negroes. The usual vessels of this port would carry 1,000.

The cod-fishery is a business of some interest: the town sends about six fishing vessels. The whale fishery is bigger; nine large ships every year, and these ships are much bigger, much more strongly timbered, than all the others. It carries five or six small boats intended for the harpooning of the whale and helping to get it on board. These whalers are separated from the others: they are of such superior strength that if any other ship happened to run foul of them it would be damaged.

Liverpool's position makes it master of the whole of Ireland's trade.[4] One can get there generally in 24 hours: all the trade done with that island is immense. Knowing only an elderly merchant retired from business, whom we saw for only a few hours,[5] I can't give many or accurate details about Liverpool. To understand the extent of

---

1   Both the Red Lion and the Golden Lion lay in Dale Street, which may explain their mistake. Alexandre blamed Mr de Lazowski for the mistake. 'He went to the wrong place and we found ourselves at a pub [*dans un petit cabaret*]. We had a fairly awful meal'. He goes on for two extremely illegible pages about the need for good inns in places like Liverpool. The Liverpool Directory for 1787 gives John Potter as landlord of the Red Lion, from which the Warrington Diligence left at 8 o'clock except on Saturdays.

2   Rodney Street is a well-known surviving example of these good features.

3   By a coincidence, three of their acquaintances at Bury St Edmunds, Mr and Mrs James Oakes and their daughter, travelled in their own coach the 217 miles to Liverpool for a 3-week stay that same year, in August-September. James Oakes wrote: 'It's computed there are upwards of 50,000 inhabitants at Liverpool. It has been a wonderful, flourishing and increasing place, though not by any means reckoned so opulent a place as Manchester' (*The Oakes Diaries*, I, 1990, p. 238, ed. Jane Fiske). See also footnote 6 below.

4   The advantages were political as well as geographical, but we needn't go into that here. The Irish trade certainly got Liverpool started, in the late 17th century, on its phenomenal career as a port. Its first dock was built 1709–15.

5   Alexandre wrote: '*8 March*: As the Bishop Llandaff gave us such a good letter for Manchester, the one he gave us for Liverpool we made haste to deliver. It was for Mr Hatton, an elderly retired merchant. His conversation was very helpful to us'. In 1774 and 1777, the Liverpool *Directory* showed James Hatton, merchant, living at 27, Water Street, the main street leading

Liverpool's trade it may help to know that it's the English town that does most trade after London.[6] A hundred years ago, it was only a little fishing port, but its position at the junction of seven canals has in a short time given it superiority over Bristol and all its rivals: the number of its houses and of its vessels increased daily. I saw a large number of new streets which are still being marked out in the ground, and the site intended for two new dock-basins which will be built next year.[7]

The port has a fairly easy entrance, but they insist that vessels entering take a pilot on board, and to enforce this the vessels pay for the pilot on arrival in port, whether they used him or not.

I have never seen a port so convenient for merchant ships. They enter the river through a long but fairly straight channel into a first basin, more or less square, and from there, according to the amount of time they have to be at berth, the quality of the merchandise and the nature of their business, they enter one of six locked basins by paying the proper dues to the corporation. The dues are light. The water is always kept high in the docks by means of gates which, unlike all those I ever saw in France, are curved. The French harbour-locks have gates straight across: these, when closed, form half a circle. Several of these basins communicate with each other through gates above which are drawbridges to allow carts to cross. All of which is convenient and expedient for business, and is operated with care. The warehouses are built round the edge of all these docks, so that costs of transport are small. We were told that the difference in the cost of transport and loading as between London and Liverpool is almost equal to the merchant's profit.

Of these six basins the first is the port, properly speaking, where the smaller boats berth and those that are not grounded by the fall of the tide: but all six are filled with ships the great majority of which are of the finest construction. There is something very satisfying in walking through the middle of the whole port and seeing the active way everyone works and the great variety of their activities. I mentioned that they plan to build two new docks next year. They are not enough: one dry dock is reserved for the whaling ships, the other for the ships belonging to the town.

The ship-yard is very large. There I saw several fine slave-ships for the negro trade being built at present. During wartime[8] they built a fairly large number of ships for the King [the Royal Navy] for which the town of Liverpool undertook the construction by subscription.

---

down to George's Dock from the Exchange. James Hatton, merchant, was listed in Wilkinson's *Advertiser* on Friday 17 November 1775, as subscribing one guinea to the American War Widows' Fund. James Hatton, merchant, ceased to appear in the 1780s *Directories*, presumably because, as Alexandre noted, he was elderly and retired.

6   This may well have been true. In the first population census, 1801, Manchester came first (84,020) to Liverpool's second (77,653). In 1861 Liverpool had overtaken Manchester: 441,171 to Liverpool's 443,938. Neither had ranked anywhere among the first forty English towns as late as 1662.

7   In 1785, two new docks were proposed to the south of Salthouse Dock: King's Dock opened in 1788 and Queen's Dock was completed in 1796 (and greatly enlarged in 1816): *Building of Liverpool*, City Planning Department, Liverpool, 1978, p. 3.

8   The American War of Independence, 1775–83.

22. *Liverpool from the Bowling Green (detail). Michael Angelo Rooker, 1769.*
     'A fine large town, in the middle of which springs up a forest of ships masts . . .'

23. *'They passed the remains of an old wall, very impressive (still) at Wroxeter,*
     Viroconium . . .'

Beyond the ship-yard there are three [dry] docks, the first two of which can take four ships, the last, three. They are the width of a vessel: they are made dry by opening gates which connect with what I call the port. When the tide falls, the port is fairly dry and the three docks drain into it, close their gates, and the ship-repairers work in the dry. It all works perfectly. Only when the ship that entered first needs to get out is there any complication.

The Duke of Bridgwater owns a small part of the port for warehousing the goods being carried on his canal. He has built an enormous warehouse, occupying one part for his own business and letting off the rest.

There are few places levying as little public tax as Liverpool. I don't know if this is accidental or owing to its late arrival on the scene; it pays only 6 sols [9] Land Tax for one pound of revenue, and land-tax is assessed at 2 shillings, more or less, throughout England. The poor-rate which is so high in some parts of this kingdom is only 6 sols in Liverpool. The reason is simple. The manufacture of ship's cordage and all the necessaries of rigging a ship employs a great number of women and children who earn their living: as for the sailors, they pay-in six sols of their month's pay for the hospital where they find with this money a retreat when they're infirm or old.

The infirmary is a very considerable establishment, and the building is fine. The poor-house, which they call the work-house, is even bigger, containing generally a thousand people as well as giving help to a great many in the town.[10]

One of the great misfortunes of Liverpool's situation is the lack of a supply of drinking water. A large number of women go about leading a horse harnessed to a little cart carrying a barrel which they fill up two miles away. This makes a living for many sailors' wives. A lot of the stone for house-building comes from Mount Pleasant[11] very near. On the top of this rise they have laid out a promenade or terrace, with some trees and seats. It is the most charming position they could have chosen. Walking here, you see the whole town, the river, sea, the ships sailing on it, the countryside and the other side of the Mersey. It's the favourite promenade of beautiful women.

Almost in the middle of the town there is a fine public building I must not forget to describe. It is square, stone built, rich architecturally but heavy. The ground floor is an arcade serving as promenade for the merchants: when it rains, it serves as the

---

[9]   3d: see Notes on p. xiv. At 'not more than 2s in the pound upon an average', Liverpool's poor rates were still thought 'extremely moderate' in 1790 when Professor Symonds was here on his own tour of the north. See fn. 68 on p. 30 above.

[10]   Alexandre adds: 'It is even astonishing that the poor-house was in such a good state'. In 1790, Symonds described this Workhouse enthusiastically, as Liancourt himself would certainly have done. 'As soon as children can spin well, they quit the house, being sure of finding employment in Manchester. Everyone who is able to work is obliged to follow his respective trade . . . so that it is a little republic within itself'.

[11]   On the E side: they must have come past it on the way in along the London road from Prescot and Warrington, and were clearly enchanted by it. Its best building now dates from 1815, the Wellington Rooms, lately renamed the Rodney Rooms, which seems hard on the victor of Waterloo, though understandable.

Exchange.[12] I say when it rains because habits have prevailed over convenience, and the merchants prefer to transact their business in the street outside rather than in the building intended for them. The departure and arrival of vessels are announced here. Upstairs is the card-room:[13] the other wings are occupied by the assize courts, sessions, and justices of the peace. Above, a small turret gives a perfect view over the whole town in fine weather. (There was so much fog that I saw nothing.) St Paul's church is rather fine architecturally, but enormously heavy.[14]

Facing Liverpool on the far bank of the Mersey are several signalling towers enabling people in town to know what ships are ready to come in.

The dearness of land, in the centre and all round, is proof both of the wealth of the inhabitants and the future expansion of Liverpool. The gentleman [Mr Hatton] with whom we walked told us that English cloth, of three feet only, sold for fifteen guineas in the town and ten in the suburbs; and, despite that, building is cheap.

In looking at this beautiful town, its port and its walks, I certainly saw all the signs of great wealth. And yet I often found myself reflecting that if a stranger disembarked at Liverpool, and one told him that this was the second commercial town in England, he wouldn't form a fine idea of this nation – however commodious the port is, almost to the point of luxury, with all its docks full of shipping, and with so many people hard at work there, one wasn't looking at activity on a prodigious scale. I'm not thinking so much of Bordeaux or Marseilles; but Nantes has an altogether livelier atmosphere than Liverpool's, its port is even more populous than the English one, and in the rest of the town one sees a whole society.[15] At Liverpool, although there aren't any factories, I didn't even see a cat in all the innumerable streets we walked through in the course of the day. What is the explanation? Liverpool is without contradiction a very rich town and a great trading town.

The price of farm-land as far as 15 miles out is greatly increased by the closeness of Liverpool. All the lands I saw were in pasture. I suppose they leave them alone so long as the grass grows well, and that they plough and grow grain for a year or two only to improve the pasture afterwards. An acre lets at ten pounds sterling: it is beyond all reason. I record it because I asked two different people and both gave the same answer. The general pasture is of course for milk-cows; the milk, butter and cheese for sale in the town.

---

[12] It was designed in 1749–54 as the Exchange by John Wood, the elder, of Bath, and is now one of the finest town halls in the kingdom. It was burnt in 1795 and exquisitely remodelled by James Wyatt and John Foster, the Liverpool Dock Engineer. They moved the portico forward and replaced the look-out turret by a domed lantern. François and Alexandre missed the new interior which I think would have bowled them over, for they were enchanted by Wyatt's rooms at Heveningham. But this wasn't ready until 1820.

[13] In 1779, the Mayor had the Card and Assembly Rooms in the Town Hall furnished at a cost of £230: George Chandler, *Liverpool* 1957, p. 203.

[14] Alexandre was cool about Liverpool's churches with the exception of St George's in Derby Square, which he thought 'very pretty, the interior in mahogany, very elegant'. It was by Thomas Steers, in the manner of Hawksmoor, and replaced in 1819.

[15] François had visited all three towns at slightly greater length in 1783: respectively 20 March – 1 April, 17–27 January and 25 April – 1 May: see *Voyages en France*, vol. II, p. 110, vol. I, pp. 159 and 182.

WARRINGTON

Wednesday 9 March 1785   On the 9th we were back in Warrington. The weather prevented us from going further: it was icy cold, and the fog got right into one's bone-marrow. Mr de Lazowski was afraid my brother might have a fever.[16]

We saw a glass factory at Warrington, making good drinking glasses. I saw about 30 workmen blowing the white, clear glasses.[17] For the rest, we learnt nothing of processes and details: we had entered without speaking to a living soul.

The method of making twist-glasses, those with spirals within the stems, which I hadn't known up to now, made me curious. Before, I couldn't begin to think how it was done, and now it seems so simple. Things that have taken centuries to develop look simple enough to those who don't see all the difficulties. I thought I should find out: as though no one had ever done it before me!

So back we went to the glass-turning.

The workman puts a piece of the fused material at the end of his blow-pipe, then lets it cool off a little, then blows a little till it grows like an egg. Then he sticks on it two, three or four pin-shaped pieces of white but opaque glass, rendered thus by mixing in litharge,[18] puts it back in the heat in order to stick them together: now, holding with pincers the end further from the blow-pipe, he lengthens and binds it at will, and cuts off everything botched or too long, keeping only a small piece about 3 or 4 inches long. You feel it is the precision of the workman's hand that produces that quality in the work. There is no mould: the work depends on the excellence of the craftsman. The upper part of the glass, from which one drinks, is fused to the stem: the foot of the glass is added after. All this is done with astonishing speed. The men get about 8 shillings a day.

Nearby is a copper-foundry about which I am not well informed, for the same reason: we had no introduction, and could only question some workmen who could scarcely turn away from their task.

The copper is brought from a nearby mine:[19] it is cast in six different furnaces:

---

[16] Alexandre admitted: 'Chaveron and I were embarrassed at becoming unwell. Mr de Lazowski re-arranged the day to prevent our getting cold.'

[17] At a Liverpool banquet for the Prince Regent in the autumn of 1806, the glass at the Prince's table had been made in this manufactory of Perrin, Geddes & Co., of Bank Quay, Warrington. The Prince admired it so much that the Liverpool corporation ordered as a gift to him several decanters, coolers, carafes, jugs and glasses. Some of this, heavily cut and splendid, some of it bearing his crest, survives at Windsor and elsewhere. The Bank Quay glass-works had been started in 1757 by Robert Patten and Peter Seaman of Warrington, and Edward Deane and Thomas Falkner of Liverpool. By 1797, Josiah Perrin and Edward Falkner had each the largest share in the firm. François supplies useful notes as to their activity in 1785, a blank period in their records. Cherry and Richard Gray, 'The Prince's Glasses, 1806–1811', *Journal of the Glass Association*, vol. 2, 1987, pp. 11–18.

[18] Monoxide of lead.

[19] Thomas Patten senior had the Mersey made navigable to Bank Quay, Warrington, so that copper could be brought from Ireland, Anglesey and Cornwall to his smelting works at Bank Quay. In 1750, his son Thomas built Bank Hall (designed by James Gibbs, and now the Town Hall).

the fusion in each takes eight hours before it's purified: then it's sent by boat to Liverpool, either to be exported or to be laminated as sheathing for vessels. The dross, all the impurities that form clinker, is excellent as building material. Walls all round here are built of them and they will last to eternity. It would be extremely good for roads.[20]

10 March 1785   On the 10th, we entered Cheshire, divided from Lancashire by the Mersey. Its aspect is a little different, rather hillier and also very green; and much divided by hedgerows.

The whole of the road we covered that day was paved, but with small round cobbles, intolerable for walking or riding, and anyway so broken up that we could only hop. Every mile cost us over ten thousand jolts. We came through several charming places and saw two very fine houses.[21] Some parts of the road were of a deep powdery sand, very restraining: these were the only parts not cobbled, the only parts, perhaps, that the horses wished were cobbled.

NORTHWICH

As soon as we reached Northwich we lunched (it was eleven o'clock) in order to have time to see the salt-works of which there are many all around the town. We provided ourselves with a guide whom we were told was intelligent but who turned out to be little more than a blockhead.

He began by conducting us to one of the establishments of the mine, one of the shafts from which the rock-salt is drawn. The shaft is about 180 feet deep and ten in diameter. By means of a capstan, turned by a horse, two buckets are raised and lowered. The machine is simple, the horse is very feeble. That's how the mine was worked.

It's about sixty years since a quarry of salt was discovered here. First they found salt springs, that I'll come to later. But it is only about twenty years since they found the rock-salt which is richer than any source one might find, for the usual sources come from filterings of water through this rock in the quarry. All the local landowners made trial bores, and those who struck rock-salt established shafts and extracted as much as they could, for there is no 'Master of Salts', with rights over its extraction. Those who own the land-surface own what's under it. The King alone has a right accorded him by the House of Commons: the salt duty is dear, but levied only on

---

[20] Unfortunately, they make no mention of Warrington Academy, so formative in the intellectual life of industrial England: of Dr Percival whom they met at Manchester, and Dr Priestley they were about to meet in Birmingham: its buildings, from 1764, finally eroded in our time. Its precursor survives as offices, having been moved and rebuilt, brick by brick, to make way for a Ring Road.

[21] One of them, Belmont Hall, at Gt Budworth, still stands in its park beside the road. In their admirable book, *Cheshire Country Houses* (Chichester, 1988), de Figueiredo and Treuherz show that this was the house designed by James Gibbs for John Smith Barry and built in 1755, and note its awkwardness. In 1787, the Smith Barrys also came to own Marbury, opposite, the second 'fine house' noted by François. It was Frenchified in the 1850s and demolished in the 1960s.

salt consumed in the kingdom: when it is exported, you pay the merchants what they paid at the mine, which is 5 shillings a bushel (a bushel is 4 pecks, and there are 40 bushels to a ton, 2,000 pounds weight: I can't give French equivalents). The King levies this tax by collectors who go about in pairs in all the places where salt is extracted, and measure it on the spot: by a process of approximation they allow so much for errors in the weighing, and so much for loss through the presence of rock in the salt, and then the proprietor pays.[22] This salt is the best to be found in England. It is of a superb whiteness, but not very salty.

Where we were, we saw the rock-salt brought out of the quarry. We saw it weighed. We thought the mine was a rich one, but the interest lay in seeing down below, and it was necessary to descend in a bucket of modest size, its sides coming up no higher than our calves, in a shaft *180 feet deep*. So we found a shaft of 105 feet where we could descend in a different bucket. I wanted to go down, but Mr de Lazowski did not want me to: he wanted to make sure if there was any danger. As for himself, *he* wanted to descend and, putting on workman's clothes, he bade me not to follow. He descended, and was no sooner down than I went down also, holding on to the rope, and thinking that if anything broke I was lost forever. After me came my brother. Mr de Lazowski thought it not funny at all. He had not gone on down the second shaft when we arrived, and he refused to budge until we went back up. For some time we tried to persuade him to let us go down, but as he wouldn't let us, we had to go up, while he went to the bottom alone.[23] He told me it was like a quarry of a very dazzling substance where strong pillars are left and the rest is extracted by frequent use of explosives. The smell of gunpowder and the shortage of air in the mine made it very unwholesome. Mr de Lazowski was none the worse for it. A little water gets into the mine but only a little: it's collected and sent up in the bucket by which we descended. The second shaft isn't as good as the first for making the descent: the bucket isn't raised by a horse but by man-power, which sometimes fails.

We saw another salt-mine, deeper, belonging to the Duke of Bridgwater who has made a branch canal to take the salt on his great canal to Liverpool. This salt is the best quality of all, and entirely for export: despite that, it pays dues at Liverpool.

The duke has two mines which are joined together underground, beneath the canal which is between the two. The air in the two mines is connected underground, which makes for better ventilation. The two mines are of immense depth, perhaps over 320 feet. They are at the second bed of rock-salt. Between the two is a bed or ordinary stone about 1½ feet thick. The miners think they've found yet another bed of salt under the one they're working at present, and which they are far from finishing. There are two horses working underground in different parts of the quarry. They

22 In 1771, Luttrell Wynne, in his diary in the Cornwall Record Office (PD 465, quoted in *The Observant Traveller*, ed. Robin Gard, HMSO, 1989, p. 72) noted that in Northwich at that time the salt brought in £100,000 yearly to the government. A Treasury survey in 1796 described Northwich as 'easily the most important collection in the land'. In 1817 there seem to have been no fewer than 60 resident excisemen in Northwich, a tenth of the national total ('The Salt Tax', a Salt Museum Publication, Salt Museum, 162 London Road, Northwich, CW9 8AB).
23 Alexandre refers, briefly, to '*la prudence extrême de Mr Lazowski*'.

are lowered in a very big bucket. I think there's a danger of the rope breaking, but the workmen are confident that that will never happen.

There are eighteen places where rock-salt is mined. A multitude of workmen are there, earning between two shillings and half-a-crown [2 shillings and 6 pence] an hour.

There is also in this little town a cotton mill. The ground where the salt lies is gently hilly, and would be pleasant for walking.

Beyond the Duke of Bridgwater's branch-canal are two others going through the middle of the salt-mining country: they transport salt to Liverpool and other parts of England very cheap.

11 March 1785   On the 11th we left Northwich at a very early hour with the intention of making two stops, if necessary, in villages, to get some detailed knowledge of the agriculture of the countryside, their régime, and the way they make their famous [Cheshire] cheese.

We went through Middlewich, a fairly populous little town, apparently prosperous. The weather was charming. We had sunshine and a breeze, fresh but not strong: in a word, one of the finest days we've had since we left Bury.

Leaving Middlewich, we came to a fine, large navigation canal,[24] laid out in a good straight line but I wondered about the function of one of the locks, the level was the same on both sides of the lock-gates and I couldn't imagine its purpose. I saw several little coal barges, each drawn by a horse.

A LITTLE INN AND A FRIENDLY OLD FARMER

We covered about twelve miles with no sign of an inn until we came to three houses, one of which did bear a sign and we asked if it was an inn. The mistress assured us it was, so we pulled up and entered the house. There was only a small kitchen, which could scarcely contain the five of us, and then a carter arrived: we were like herrings crammed into a barrel. We ate two kinds of eggs: eggs fried in lard and boiled fresh eggs, then some very good cheese. Our host didn't wait on us, for he was one-armed. We engaged in conversation with him on the loss of his left arm, and when we explained our plan to see a farm, he proposed a walk over the farm of one of his friends, which we immediately accepted.

Our honest one-armed acquaintance lived close to the friend: we were soon there, for our host's conversation did not delay us; we quickly saw that he said 'yes' to everything we said, and made no further response. His farmer friend is old, good-humoured and talkative, just what we wanted. He led us over his fields and made us admire his twenty cows, and scratched their behinds to show them to better advantage. A good breed, they give 2 gallons of milk (8 bottles) twice a day: he actually has 21. His rent is 145 pounds sterling. Last year he killed a bull weighing twelve hundred [?pounds]. I give this as an idea of the kind of cattle here.

---

[24]   The Grand Trunk Canal, which they saw at the Trent as they left Leicestershire for Derbyshire see p. 36 above.

We crossed a field of pasture over which he had spread a very thick bed of earth. We asked him why, and he replied that it was a local custom; they generally keep their lands in pasturage as long as possible – three or four years, until the grasses that grow in too great abundance oblige them to plough. However, they put down this bed of clayey earth and plough, then sow without any rule, following only their whim; wheat, barley or oats for three years. The last year, they sow seed of red clover with the grain so that when the grain is cut the clover remains and forms, the following year, a fine meadow. They don't let the cattle in the first year, but make excellent hay. This method of cultivation is not in accordance with all the rules, but, as it works, I think it's good. Their land is excellent, and lets, generally, at 20 shillings an acre.

When we returned to the farmer's house, he showed us a young calf born that morning, with which he was particularly taken: he suckled it by hand, for fear of upsetting the mother. It's their general rule that cows and bullocks never work between Christmas and Easter. They are shut in a byre and fed on straw with a little hay. He says the straw of oats is best; then that of barley, and that of wheat is worst for the cattle.

He made us look at his barn, which isn't walled but merely made of pieces of timber, so that the air can get in on all sides and avoid fermenting, which encourages mice and rats. We saw everything, including his oats, which are superb and which he boasted about.

A RECIPE FOR CHESHIRE CHEESE

He took us indoors and asked his wife to tell us how she made cheese. She wouldn't say at first, but her husband egged her on and she opened up a little and told some of her secrets.

She said that to make cheeses you must take at midday milk drawn in the morning, just as it is, put it under pressure, and drain it for some minutes. After the milk has turned, you add three handfuls of white salt and tip the cheese into a mould, the proportions and shape of which are those you want for the cheese. The cheese is bigger than the mould, so that it can't all go in. One puts the mould in the press, where it stays fifteen days, being turned twice a day, re-salting with as much salt as it will take, and putting it back in the press.

After that time, you release it from the press and lay it out in a loft or a room, on some straw, and let it dry for a month. Then it is sold or eaten.

There is what I remember of the information the farmer's wife gave me. The method is so simple that the goodness of the cheeses must depend solely on the goodness of the pastures.

A good cow should give 200 pounds of cheese a year. A pound of cheese is the product of 7 gallons of milk (28 bottles).

The farmer offered us apples, cheese, etc. We accepted nothing, but before we went he wanted to show us two things: one was a goose that had laid 13 eggs, the other was a sow that had had seven little sucking piglets that morning: they were very pretty.

One sees with what simplicity these good people tell one all they know, without fearing to give away the secrets of their livelihood. The intelligent way they talk always astonishes me: it's as though they have some theory.

The farmer is an old man of perhaps 50 or 60; his wife is, I should think, 40. However, he is her fourth husband, and I can well believe she will have a fifth and – if she changes husbands every ten years – she could have eight, for she enjoys very good health.

After seeing the farm and learning how to make cheese, we collected our horses and set off quickly for Newcastle,[25] still twelve miles off. The road is sandy and hilly. We saw two more navigable canals. The country is full of coal mines.

ETRURIA

Newcastle-under-Lyme, 12 March 1785   We came to Newcastle solely to see the porcelain-factory of Mr Wedgwood[26] which is in the neighbourhood of this little town.[27] We had a letter of introduction from one of his friends. We went on the morning of the twelfth. Mr Wedgwood was in London. His agent proposed to show us the workshops, and we followed him. The earth is from the neighbourhood, grey and very fine.

To get a paste of the greatest beauty, you put this earth into the water, pass it through a very fine silk sieve; then, to dry it out, tip it into a copper under which a fire is kept burning. You remove the earth when you think it sufficiently dry. The remaining processes are precisely those of all other porcelain manufacturers in the world. I saw here only one thing I hadn't already seen: a wheel[28] made of brass with different segments of a circle which form very varied patterns. The wheel works with precision; so must the potter's hand.

Here they make the common porcelain we call 'English earthenware': it is a pale yellowish colour, painted with green or with gold, which doesn't have at all a good

---

25 Alexandre's note seems to say something of their own working-methods. One had wondered at their recollection of so much detail back in their hotel at the end of a tiring day. What he says here is: 'After finishing our description of – *après avoir fini décrire* – our farm, we went back to our inn, fed our horses and left for Newcastle': Newcastle-under-Lyme, a reference to the great medieval forest of Lyme. If they really were about twelve miles short of Newcastle, the farm must have been somewhere near Sandbach.

26 Josiah Wedgwood, 1730–95, 'le Palissy de l'Angleterre'; Wedgwood's influence was felt as far afield as Russia and America. (Bernard Palissy, two centuries earlier, was celebrated for his lead-glazed 'rustic wares'.)

27 Newcastle is an ancient borough and market-town. In 1785 the potteries were all in neighbouring villages like Burslem and Stoke, which amalgamated in 1910 as Stoke-on-Trent, now the 14th biggest English city, rudely contiguous with Newcastle. Gilbert Wedgwood, the first Wedgwood master-potter, was established at Burslem in 1640. Josiah was so successful that he had to enlarge the Burslem factory in 1764 and five years later opened the new factory, called, after the Etruscan vases, Etruria, with model village, to the SW of Hanley. Etruria Hall was built for him in 1770. The Wedgwood factory moved to Barlaston in 1939.

28 *un tour.*

effect.[29] What makes Mr Wedgwood famous is the black porcelain, smooth and fine, with perfect figures in low relief.[30] I asked if we could see them but was told the proprietor kept these processes an extremely close secret, allowing no one to show them. No stranger was admitted except by him. We saw various pieces in the warehouse, but were no further forward than we had been in London where their principal warehouse is.

All I was able to learn is that this black earth is red before being baked, and is local. His factory employs 200 people.[31]

A canal passes close to the factory and leads into the interior of the kingdom, or to Liverpool: extremely convenient for transporting these wares to London.[32]

Mr Wedgwood has a superb house beyond the canal, lacking neither gardens nor any attribute of magnificence: there is even a very elegant Chinese bridge communicating with his factories.

This is not the only porcelain factory in the district: they are on all sides and in enormous numbers. But the others are nowhere near this in perfection: they make only tea-pots without any relief, and the cups are smooth.

It is a smiling countryside: prodigiously peopled and everyone looks prosperous: the fields are well cultivated, the towns busy. Newcastle is well built: only one main street, but large and straight, with tall houses and good shops.

Sunday 13 March 1785   The 13th we left Newcastle before seven o'clock in order to lunch at Drayton[33] and sleep in Shrewsbury. It was fine weather but frosty, and the wind very cold. As it was a Sunday, we saw no one on the road: it seemed sad. Drayton isn't much of a town. However, we saw two or three pretty houses after lunch. While the horses were being harnessed, Mr de Lazowski rode off, saying we would catch him up on the road. But instead of taking the road to Shrewsbury he went off along another one. As soon as the cabriolets were ready I mounted, and, as the stable-boy showed me the road, I made no mistake and we covered three miles pretty quickly without seeing Mr de Lazowski. We asked those we met whether they'd seen the person we were looking for. Persuaded that he'd taken the wrong road and that he couldn't have gone far in so short a time, we waited more than an hour for him. My inclination was to wait longer because it was possible that he might discover – rather

---

29 These cream-coloured earthenware designs were mostly elegant and very popular in the 1780s, becoming as sociably acceptable as porcelain: a famous service sent to Catherine of Russia in 1774 is in the Hermitage.

30 Here he is referring to the black basalt ware, 'Etruscan'.

31 Alexandre's account illustrates his more straightforward reaction: 'His pottery is more beautiful than any I've ever seen. It is yellow and beautifully smooth, but simple and elegant.' He uses the words *faience* and *porcelaine* indifferently: I suppose *faience* more accurately describes earthenware than *porcelaine*, which François uses. Alexandre adds: 'We spent the evening at Newcastle and wrote a little.'

32 It was Josiah Wedgwood who encouraged Brindly to undertake the Trent-Mersey 'Grand Junction' in 1766: he dug the first sod.

33 Known as Market Drayton, as there are others.

late – that he'd made a mistake, would not want to venture into cross-roads and would be coming back up the same road to Drayton and then on to where we were waiting. But Chaveron's advice was for us to go on further, at least for a mile, to the first turnpike, to make sure that he hadn't gone a little further; and I took M. Chaveron's advice, We had no sooner arrived just short of the turnpike than we found him: he had taken a cross-road and ridden more than eight miles: he was waiting for us with a bottle in his hand, and even a little red-faced.

SHREWSBURY

We arrived late at Shrewsbury, for it was a hard journey, and was indeed our furthest day's travel since we left Bury: 33 miles is a long journey for horses working regularly.

As we coincided exactly with the period of the Assizes, the town was so full of people that we were turned away at three of the better inns and were reduced to staying at a cheap little eating-house[34] where we found decent people but a pretty poor supper and a little narrow bedroom.

Shrewsbury is the capital of Shropshire, a small county in England but very near Wales. It's odd that the town is surnamed Salop but no one can tell me where this jolly name comes from.[35] It isn't just a popular form, but is written on maps and road-signs.

Its position is picturesque: built on a steep, craggy hill, it faces south. The river Severn, fine and wide, runs at the foot of the town and brings its provisions, for I don't believe it's a very big trading town. There are two parishes with stone spires of prodigious height.[36] The streets are fair enough, in which I saw several flourishing shops: it must be the place of residence of several gentry of comfortable fortune, for not only are public balls held here regularly, but there is also a theatre four months in the year. The assizes bring life to the little town which, I'm told, is rather empty at other times.

[?*14 March*]   Next day we left to see an iron bridge thirteen miles away. You cross the Severn several times on bridges beautifully built by the county and paid for by the travellers.[37] *Alexander spotted the remains of* Viroconium, *a view he thought a painter might desire.* One of the bridges is magnificently embellished by Lord Berwick who

---

34 Alexandre called it a '*gargotte*', and added 'We were a long time finding it. It had to refuse several late-comers. What was worse was that our horses, who had worked so well, scarcely had room to lie down.'

35 It's good to see that François approved 'Salop'-shire, for it was an early Norman-French 'improvement' on Scriopesberie-shire (Domesday Book), the shire based on Scriopesberie, what we now pronounce 'Shrosebery'.

36 St Alkmund's 184 feet, St Mary's 138$\frac{1}{3}$ feet. (There were two other medieval parishes, St Chad's and St Julian's.) It is odd that Shrewbury's thriving markets and business activities didn't make an impression on François, but he does mention '*plusieurs riches*' shops, and he wasn't here long.

37 One of them, Atcham Bridge, is designed by the Shrewsbury-born architect John Gwynne in 1769 and survives alongside a modern one. (He was the architect of Magdalen Bridge at

has a very beautiful house nearby. We saw it from a distance: not yet completely finished but it has a grand and noble appearance. The turf of the park is of a fine quality surprising at this time of year.

Coalbrookdale is the name of the place where the iron bridge was built: it is a large village built on both sides of the Severn and spreading over the hillsides.[38] The two sides are remarkably steep, almost equally thickly wooded, and yield a great amount of iron ore, which I will talk about later.

On arrival, we had a truly superb view of the iron bridge. As it is unique in the world, I want to ponder a little on the details, and that is how I shall start the next volume [here chapter]: then I will describe the furnaces in which it was founded.

Oxford.) Noel Hill, MP for Shrewsbury and Salop, 1768–84, was created Lord Berwick of Attingham in 1784. Attingham Park is indeed a noble house by George Steuart, 1783–85, and was, as they wrote, almost finished. Nash later (1807) did entrance-gates near Atcham Bridge. Humphry Repton designed the park. A mile east, still in view of the house, William Hayward had bridged (1774) a tributary of the Severn which they presumably crossed, to follow the east bank of the Severn. François gives no hint as to which bank they followed, but Alexandre speaks of 'the remains of an old wall', which suggests the east bank and the great bath-house of the fourth biggest town in Roman Britain, the remains of Viroconium at Wroxeter. A little further on, Alexandre records, I think, the Wrekin: 'a hill from the top of which you find, *vous trouvez*, the Severn crossing the countryside': it doesn't sound to me as though they found time to climb it and see for themselves, or he'd have written 'j'ai trouvé', or, since his spelling was idiosyncratic, 'j'ai trouvez'.

[38] In fact, Coalbrookdale was the name of a small dale north of the Severn gorge, on the road towards Wellington: the name already spread to include the Iron Bridge settlement along the north bank. But south of the bridge, the village was Broseley, as they discovered.

5

Coalbrookdale: The Iron Bridge

After Robert Bakewell's extraordinary stock-breeding farm at Dishley, and the water-powered machinery of Mr Swift's cotton-mill at Derby, and after their testing experiences in the network of the Duke of Bridgwater's underground canals and his coalmines around Worsley, the iron bridge, spanning the gorge at Coalbrookdale like a palpable black rainbow, naturally moved François to some of his most vivid and committed description: it was unique in the world, and he enquired more keenly than most of the early visitors to those Vesuvial scenes. His young brother even attempted a careful, but wobbly, annotated ink-drawing (Pl. 25). There can be few visitors today who are not roused to admiration by their first sight of this bridge: to see it so soon after its erection must have been marvellous.

They had the luck to fall in immediately with 'two superior workmen' who offered to show them over these active furnaces and forges. They dived back into the new inn at the bridge-foot, and had hardly swallowed their dinner when 'our man called for us: he seemed wonderfully honest and intelligent'. He showed them, with proper pride, the intricate scale-model in mahogany he had made to guide the bridge's construction, for he is now identifiable with Tom Gregory, foreman pattern-maker to Abraham Darby III, of the great iron-founding dynasty. The Frenchmen could thus feel almost personally 'in on' the creation of this new wonder of the world.

They began at the 'Old Blast Furnace' – the very one in which the iron for the bridge had been made. Like the bridge, and the hotel, and Gregory's 7-foot wide mahogany model, this old fiery furnace with its cast-iron beams, dated 1777 above the tapping hole, still survives to be seen. It is now a major feature of the Ironbridge Gorge Museum, which is one of Europe's finest museums, as befits the nursery of its iron and steel industry. There the French visitors were proudly shown the specialized coke-smelting of iron – reckoned among the greatest advances in technology in the history of the modern world – in the place where the first Abraham Darby had pioneered it.

They spent the rest of that first day in Abraham Darby's works. François quickly learned that 'the hill to the north' (?Lincoln Hill) produced 'the most plentiful as well as the best iron ore' – serious evidence against the current view that only Swedish ore was used. At the same time he learnt, presumably from their expert guide, that the skill of the iron-founder really rested on his stoking the blast-furnace with the right balance of ingredients (coke, mined coal, and limestone) for the particular kind of iron required. He described the working of furnace-bellows by steam-engine (occasionally, when the bellows were working perfectly, you could manage two castings in 24 hours). He described *the 'splendid' teeming of the molten iron, and the pounding by the great hammer (that was still worked here by water-wheel), and the 'potting' stage in producing wrought iron, and how the more elaborate products – from pumps to flat-irons – were moulded. 'Is it not shameful that we cannot do as much in France?'*

Next day, along the gorge from the hotel to neighbouring Broseley. The great ironmaster John Wilkinson, to whom they had a letter of introduction, had returned from London with a very bad cold and couldn't see them. His representative showed them everything the firm was doing – all furnaces and forges grouped round one fuel-supply yard – and where the water that drove all the power-wheels was carefully recycled so as to be able to continue working through times of drought. That day, they saw another iron-works, and a not very successful tar and coke works. As at Sheffield, François was horrified by the working conditions he witnessed at Coalbrookdale: 'What a price our luxury costs!' After two days of almost continual exhilaration, they thought they'd seen everything they could take in, and set off for Birmingham, noting as they rode much nail-making.

Ironbridge, Coalbrookdale, 14–15 March, 1785   *François:* The iron bridge over the river Severn in Coalbrookdale is a work unique of its kind: not only is the arch entirely made of iron, but so are all the parts of the bridge and even the abutments.[1]

As the Severn is a river of some size, especially in those times of the year when the waters increase suddenly, the bridge spanning it with a single arch must be large: its height takes account of the boats passing under it very often, bringing coal to the local forges.

The arch is composed of five iron semicircular hoops: they are 100 feet 6 inches long and are made in two pieces: they stand on a large iron plate seated horizontally on a bed of hard freestone, the bridge's abutment. The two pieces are joined together in the keystone of the arch. The five circles are identical, perhaps 5 inches square in section. Above, iron girders are supported by the iron curves, and slope up to meet above the keystones of the five arches. The road is metalled with clinker and earth and the delicate guard-rails on either side are also of ironwork, and tall enough so that one can't lean over. The two bars in the middle of each balustrade carry a lantern which is sometimes lit.

The bridge is 24 feet wide, and 40 feet high above the level of the abutments: I can't take the level above the water, as that varies so often.

As the five long curves of iron that support the girders would not be adequately strengthened if there were only uprights rising perpendicularly from the horizontal abutments, and the key being too long, they would inevitably bend, and perhaps break; it has been necessary to add two more concentric circles of iron hoops rising from the abutments to take some of the strain at two intermediate points.

These two arches of what I call their secondary order are each made in one piece. They are all tied to the leading arch by arms perhaps four feet long.[2]

---

[1]   The great arching hoops of iron certainly spring up from near river-level, but the abutments are of stone, as he says a few lines further on. They were evidently laid after the iron structure was built into position.

[2]   The three concentric iron circles are firmly braced together by regularly-spaced perforated iron stays or struts.

24. *The Severn at Coalbrookdale. Michael Angelo Rooker, 1780. A well-known engraving was based on this drawing.*

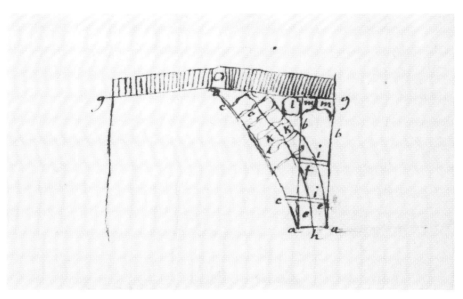

25. *Alexandre's ink-sketch of the Iron Bridge.*

One sees that the whole bridge is made in the simplest way: nothing has been done by way of embellishment, and it is noble and handsome. The iron used in it weighs 756,000 pounds:[3] each of the five arches, 10,000 pounds. The bridge was abutted and erected in three months without one of the builders getting hurt, and without any component having to be remade.

It was begun in 1779 and finished in 1780[4] without the navigation being delayed for an instant. I believe it was necessary to take the measurements several times before making the moulds.

This unique bridge – for neither the ancients nor the moderns have ever made one entirely of iron – was built by subscription. The promoter, Mr Darby,[5] a young man who, between himself and his business associates runs a great many ironworks in this district, undertook the work for £3,000 sterling, which was paid to him by fifty people on the speculation that the right to collect tolls would bring in a fat interest on their outlay. They obtained an Act of Parliament to build the bridge and establish the bridge-toll. They needed sixty subscriptions of £50 sterling, and no one was allowed more than eight shares. Mr Darby and his friends took a large number, thinking they would make fortunes; and finding that they have lost a lot of money. The building of the bridge cost much more than the £3,000, and the interest on their money has been poor, so that Mr Darby has been on the point of bankruptcy.

While we were admiring the bridge, its lightness and the nobility of its construction, two men came up who looked like superior workmen, and were very willing to reply to many of our questions: and when we admitted to them that we had come with the idea of seeing the processes of the foundries that this area was so full of, one of them proposed to conduct us, and to come and collect us after we had dined.

We returned to our inn so as not to lose time. It's a small square building, newly built, at the end of the bridge.[6] It is scrupulously clean and very good, although Coalbrookdale is only a village: but I suppose that the number of people coming to see the bridge out of curiosity often brings them custom.

We had no sooner dined than our man arrived: he seems wonderfully honest and intelligent for a workman.[7] We went first to the foundry where the iron bridge was made.

---

3   The fact that the French party met Thomas Gregory, Darby's foreman pattern-maker, and were shown the foundry by one of his inspectors (see below) gives authority to these figures recorded by François. They are rather less than the weights given to Richard Gough in 1789 and used in his revised edition of Camden's Britannia. (Gough's figures were accepted in Singer, Holmyard, Hall and Williams, *A History of Technology*, IV, 1958, p. 102.) Gough gave the overall weight as 378½ tons, i.e. nearly 848,000 lbs. See also A. Raistrick, *Dynasty of Ironfounders*, 1953, pp. 198–99.
4   It bears the date *MDCCLXXIX*, 1779, on the lower of the three semicircular arches. In fact, begun in 1777 and opened on New Year's Day, 1781.
5   Abraham Darby III, 1750–91. See A. Raistrick, *Dynasty of Ironfounders*, etc.
6   It is the Tontine Hotel, named after the scheme by which it was built: the subscribers getting an annuity which increases as their numbers are reduced by death. It was opened only four months before their visit, and is still in business in the 1990s, standing up to greet the visitor at the southern end of the bridge.
7   Alexandre, too, found the judgment and intelligence of the old workman '*étonnant*'. Alexandre made a rather sketchy drawing of the bridge and described it at some length.

At this place the Severn runs through a deep gorge, the hills on both banks are prodigiously tall and wooded right up to the summit. They produce the iron ore, the limestone and the coal, three things very precious to find together. The hill to the north produces the most plentiful as well as the best ore;[8] limestone is there in great quantity, the different folds of this ridge of hills are covered with forges and furnaces.

The first man we'd spoken to is the one who worked first on the iron bridge: he had made a model of it in mahogany, which he showed us.[9] After a brief conversation, being unable to accompany us, he procured for us one of the supervisors who could explain to us the working of the foundry.

The ore extracted from the hill is entirely in the form of ironstone: it varies in quantity and richness. To cast it, they mix several qualities together to make the iron soft and more easily fused.

The first procedure is to mix the ironstone broken in small pieces with the coal, and to fire them in order to calcine them a little and through that to develop the ferruginous parts. The fire reddens them. They burn for about six hours.

The coal, for its part, is burnt for six hours, too, in the open air: it is thrown in large heaps with straw and the bark of trees and fired: the coal sheds its superfluities and some of the sulphur it contains.[10]

After these preparations, the blast furnace is stoked with purified coal [i.e. coke], mined coal and limestone to assist the fusion. The proportion of the three ingredients depends on the quality of the iron required, and on the ore used: so the skill of the founder lies in getting the balance right.[11]

The furnace is made to reverberate the heat so that the flame, covering all sides of the furnace, puts ore in fusion more quickly: it is continually stoked up by two great bellows worked by a steam-pump.[12] I know how it works but won't describe

---

8   Lincoln Hill. At Sheffield (p. 55) François clearly had the impression that local iron was used, *not* Swedish. Here his testimony is more circumstantial and seems incontrovertible.

9   This gives the clue to the man's identity: he was Thomas Gregory, foreman pattern-maker, associated with Abraham Darby in the final details of the design (Raistrick, *op. cit.*, p. 198). His mahogany model of the bridge was given to the Society of Arts, and later to its present home, the Science Museum in South Kensington.

10   It was now coke. Here at Coalbrookdale, coke was first used to smelt iron by Abraham Darby I in 1709. 'This was one of the greatest advances in the history of technology, on which subsequent ferrous metal production in the modern world has been, and still is, based': J.R. Harris, *The British Iron Industry, 1700–1850*, 1988, p. 30.

11   It is, as Raistrick said (*Dynasty of Ironfounders*, 1953, p. 120) surprising that the workman responsible for the proportions in which the furnace charge was made up was only the *second* highest paid. François' testimony as to the methods of the iron-making of the Coalbrookdale Co. may help resolve some of the arguments aired by C.K. Hyde (*Technological Change and the British Iron Industry, 1700–1870*, Princeton, 1977).

12   The blowing apparatus was first produced by John Smeaton c.1762; the improved steam-engine by John Wilkinson c.1776, when it was used in his furnace at Willey (just south of Broseley): Singer *et al*, *Hist. Technology*, IV, p. 104. See below, pp. 100–04, for their visit to Broseley. John Harris (*The British Iron Industry, 1700–1850*, 1988, p. 35) says 'only a fraction of coke iron-furnaces used Watt engines when they became available after 1775'.

26.   *Inside the Smelting-House at Broseley (detail), c.1788: G. Robertson, engraved W. Lowry.*

it now: there is a great number of them in these workshops. The bellows are made like iron tubs; the rise and fall of pistons expels and compresses the air: the draught is so strong that if you put your hand in front of the mouth of the bellows it is instantly blown out of the way. In France, bellows are worked by wheels: they don't produce much wind-blast, nor is it so continuous.

In the same way that the proportions of the baskets from the mine, of limestone and of coal, vary on account of their qualities, and of the iron one hopes to obtain, so will the length of the fusion. However, generally they bring 8 baskets of ironstone, 5 of coal and 3 of lime, which serve to aid the fusion by separating the iron. I can form no idea of the weight of the baskets: they're all the same size but must differ considerably in weight.

Generally the fusion takes sixteen hours: sometimes, when the bellows are working perfectly, it is possible to manage the casting process twice in 24 hours, but that is rare.

The casting is done exactly as I've seen it done in France. The sand needed for the moulds is brought from 2 or 3 miles around: it is of the finest quality of its kind. I was extremely pleased to see the rolling (teeming) of this molten iron: what a splendid sight! A stream of red, burning metal, boiling and filling all the moulds put in front of it: all the workmen with iron implements which they wield, sweating, straining: the flickering of the light in the whole workshop: what a spectacle!

The iron is cooled in *saumons* that they call 'pigs': they are triangular and three feet long.[13]

They go back into a forge fanned continually by two bellows; sometimes the wind is brought by iron conduits from those that blow in the foundry. The fire is so fierce that the metal melts almost, or at least amalgamates with the coal: the smith recovers it in pieces with pincers and puts it on an anvil made in the shape of a trough, where it is beaten by an immense hammer and smoothed out and refined.

The hammer is worked by a water-wheel[14] with extraordinary power and speed. The mechanism is simple. The water-wheel turns the axle of a solid wheel, of small diameter, armed with cams.[15] When they meet the hammer, they lift it, and it falls just as the next cam lifts it again.

---

[13] In 1958, H.R. Schubert, in his chapter on 'Iron and Steel' in Singer *et al.*, *op. cit.*, IV, p. 106, said: 'The problem of producing pig iron suitable for conversion into wrought iron seems to have been solved about 1749–50 by Abraham Darby II, but, unfortunately nothing is known about the technique he applied.' François was presumably watching and describing this technique, refined after 35 years. The iron was teemed into a channel made in the sand, which has a number of shorter channels running laterally from it: the long one is the sow the shorter ones the pigs. The Broseley engraving (Pl. 26) shows the pigs like the white and black keys on a piano.

[14] The first forge-hammer driven by steam had been built at John Wilkinson's forge at Bradley (near Bilston, Staffs.) in 1782: it struck ?30 blows a minute: the head (7½ cwt) was raised 2 feet 3 inches between blows. Clearly the Darbys had not yet got a steam hammer, but were doing very well with water-power.

[15] *dents.*

After the iron has been beaten in this way, it is thrown on one side to cool. Then a workman breaks with a great hammer[16] the kind of plates that have formed: he breaks them into little pieces. Women put these into pots[17] in such a way as not to lose the place between each lot of iron plates: they insert one of coal all broken up into small pieces.[18] These pots are made in the neighbourhood: they cost 1 English sol (2 sols) each: any clay that will bake is suitable for making them: they are about a foot high and 10 inches in diameter.

Once the pots are full they are placed in order in a [reverberatory] furnace in which the fire has been heated up to full blast: twenty usually go in at a time: they stay there two and a half hours, while the action of the fire raises the iron to fusion point though it remains solid all the time. The coal has vanished: so have the pots, entirely.

The workman inspects it from time to time to see whether the iron is ready: his judgment is the only rule. When it is, he takes a long shovel (peel) and removes the iron (which has retained the shape of the pot) to the very edge of the furnace. There, another workman grabs it with great pincers and lets it fall on to an iron plate placed to receive it. This makes a noise like cannon-fire. Then he drags it, still with the same pincers, to another workshop, close by, dumps it on to an anvil, and a hammer even bigger than the first beats it to compress it:[19] it is founded on an iron bar already made to manage the job more easily, and it is under this great hammer that the iron, which arrived in the form of the pot in which it was baked, takes the form of a straight bar about ten feet long. The bar is cooled down gradually. This is the state in which it is mostly sold, either for export or to Birmingham merchants for conversion into steel.

Sometimes, though, they make steam-pumps or chimney-pieces,[20] flat-irons, or grenades, cannon-balls, etc. etc. They model and mould them: that's how it's done. If there is anything one wants to have cast, then it is necessary to have an exact model the same size and proportions. It is set in a frame filled with sand, well beaten and pressed. This mould is made in two pieces. The model is pressed into the sand: the mould is opened, the model removed, and the space for the piece one requires lies empty.

There is a space for a little drain, sometimes several, according to the size of the piece, leading through the mould so that metal can run out. The sand is firm enough not to be displaced by its contact with the molten iron: the result in metal is exactly the shape of what you had in the wooden model.

The models of chimney-pieces are in wood, ornamental flowers in copper applied on top. One sees how many of all these processes are quick.

---

16 In Cumbria, the workman and hammer were already being replaced by a mechanical stamp and the process was known as 'potting and stamping': J.R. Harris, *op. cit.*, p. 38.

17 Or clay crucibles.

18 The object of the coal was to remove silicon from the coke pigs, but it added sulphur. François didn't notice the addition of some lime in the pots to absorb the sulphur. This 'potting' process was the fore-runner of the revolutionary 'puddling and rolling' process that Henry Cort was developing in the 1780s. François vividly depicts Coalbrookdale going its own way in 1785.

19 If this bigger hammer had been steam-operated he would probably have noted it.

20 *pièces de cheminées* seems very imprecise, but see eleven lines lower.

Modelling the steam-pumps and drain-pipes is a longer and more difficult operation: the models are made with scrupulous accuracy, and as some pieces are large, they are difficult to mould. The best workmen are put on to make them: the difficulty comes with matching them up when they are finished. However, they work with such precision that they even cast the great cogwheels, with teeth fitting exactly into those of another wheel made alongside it, and there is never a shortage of such products. When they want to give to the cast iron that good black colour which preserves it from rust, they throw into the sand of the mould a very finely powdered charcoal. We saw many steam-pumps of considerable size that they have lately produced. We admired them as things simply unknown in our country: they smiled, and when I asked them which piece they found the most difficult to cast, they replied that nothing they did was difficult.

Is it not shameful to us that we cannot do as much in any foundry in France and that Messrs Periers who set up a steam-pump in Paris[21] were obliged to bring there all the parts from this country? They were cast in Coalbrookdale.

I have said that all the wheels necessary in ironworking are water-wheels; I must note here how well they manage the water by larger wheels fitted with little canisters that don't lose the weight of a single drop of water. To add to which, the same company working the forges, the water that turned the first descends, in stages, over the two others and at the moment when it looks like being lost, there is a steam-pump which drives it back to where it came from, so that the three forges have been fed by the same water in all 20 years since they were established, if one discounts the water lost in evaporation.[22]

BROSELEY: MR WILKINSON'S WORKS

We spent the whole time after a hurried early dinner visiting the ironworks, and next day (15th) left our inn to go to Mr Wilkinson's house, who lives at the other end of the village. We had a letter for him.[23] Mr Wilkinson is one of the greatest ironmasters in the world. It is he who invented the art of boring cannon, which hitherto had

---

21   This was for the Paris water-works. A French observer in 1775, Marchant de la Houlière, in a Report to the French government on British methods of casting naval cannon, reckoned there were already 14 blast furnaces in Shropshire. Barrie Trinder, *The Industrial Revolution in Shropshire*, 1973, p. 55.

22   John Harris, *op. cit.*, p. 35, noted that the use of Newcomen engines for re-cycling the water supply to provide power to bellows was pioneered in Coalbrookdale from 1742. Unusual drought in 1733–34 had caused serious production-failure (Raistrick, *op. cit.*, p. 110). François shows how well the Coalbrookdale Co. had secured itself against dependence on the natural water supply: so had John Wilkinson on the other side of the gorge at Broseley: see third para below.

23   They had the impression that Coalbrookdale was the name of one large village on both banks of the gorge. John Wilkinson (1728–1808) lived in Broseley, which is a separate village to the south of the river. At Broseley he established his ironworks, installing the first Boulton and Watt steam-engine from Soho (Handsworth, Birmingham) in 1776. His house, The Lawns, still stands in Church Street, Broseley, rather neglected in 1992.

been cast together with the breach. He established near Nantes the boring-mill I mentioned in my journals of travels in France;[24] it is he who sold a steam-pump to Paris, indeed several others, and who still sends daily several thousand pieces of mechanism we cannot cast.[25] He has acquired immense wealth, mostly by his genius. We are assured that at times he is not only casting pieces for export to France, he is doing it in all his forges – an enormous number – and even in all the forges of Coalbrookdale.[26] I suppose he must employ about ten thousand workpeople every day. One may judge how much business he is doing with foreign countries!

We didn't find Mr Wilkinson: he was in bed with a heavy cold he had caught in London. He read the letter we had brought him and sent us to his nearest ironworks where his agent [*commis*] showed us everything they were doing. The works are very fine and convenient in the sense that all the workshops employing fire are together: they are all ranged round a big empty space into which horses bring the coal and all else necessary: it is all under one roof.

As the processes are the same as those I have described I won't repeat myself, but just report what is different. Here it is only that the multiplicity of wheels in the forge is turned simply by rain-water: it is collected in a large pond or conduit that can be opened or shut off at will. The conduit is near a very large steam-engine, which raises the water and drives it under the wheels [i.e. they were undershot]; and there you see the junction of several conduits (all of cast iron) that carry water to the wheels working the forge. The water's distributed with great economy. When it falls to the bottom, a slope carried it to the pump which recycles it: any surplus water needing to be removed from the conduit is negligible.

---

24 See *Voyages en France*; also Arthur Young, *Travels in France*, Cambridge, 1929, ed. C. Maxwell, pp. 117, 199, 310, 396. In fact it was John Wilkinson's brother, William (whom he could not get on with) who went to France. 'Until he arrived', Young wrote, in 1788, 'the French knew nothing of the art of casting cannon solid, then boring them.' He went on: 'Mr Wilkinson's machinery for boring four cannons is now at work, moved by tide-wheels; but they have erected a steam-engine with a new apparatus for boring seven more.' (Young went on to say that Nantes was inflamed in the cause of liberty . . . The American Revolution has laid the foundation of another in France if the government does not take care of itself.) This tide-mill, where Wilkinson seems to have worked 1777–80, installing two small cupola furnaces, was on the isle of Indret, in easy reach of Nantes. At Montcenis in Burgundy (3 August 1789) Young found 'one of Mr Weelkainsong's establishments for casting and boring cannon: the French say this active Englishman is brother-in-law of Dr Priestley and therefore a friend of mankind, and that he taught them to bore cannon in order to give liberty to America'. These works were at Le Creusot, where Wilkinson worked 1781–85, helping the French establish their first coke-furnace for iron-smelting. Joseph Priestley *had* married the sister of John and William Wilkinson. It is doubtful if the Wilkinsons' improvements of French armaments had any but commercial motives. In 1788, the company made parts of the first iron bridge projected in France; it also controlled glass works and by 1787 was employing nearly 1,400 workmen. François seems not actually to have caught sight of the boring-mills of Coalbrookdale.

25 François is referring to John, here in Broseley, not realizing that it was William who was established in France. 'Several thousand pieces daily' sounds like an exaggeration, but so he wrote and seems to have been informed.

26 By May 1780 the Coalbrookdale Co. were 'putting up a mill at the Dale to bore cylinders in the manner J. Wilkinson bores his', probably under licence.

A second of Mr Wilkinson's inventions, no less useful, is a bellows which, by itself, supplies all the workshops of the forge: it is worked by a steam-engine: but here the difference is that there is only one immense iron vat and the valve is double. The wind is blown into a large cast tube, not very long, which carries it to a reservoir of water: in the middle is a kind of brick tank which the water can enter. The air received puts the water into equilibrium without losing any. In the result, several cast tubes that meet here distribute the wind-blast to all parts of the ironworks – always equally and continuously, because the interrupted breathing of the bellows is condensed and smoothed by the water, steadying and strengthening the blast. It is the best kind of bellows that could be devised, as he assured us.

The agent tells me that Mr Wilkinson employs between 200–300 workmen in this forge alone. He has many others in Coalbrookdale and the neighbourhood, and even in other parts of England: he told me he thought Mr Wilkinson employed two thousand men. They earn more or less according to their job, but at a rough reckoning they earn as much as 2 shillings or 2 shillings and sixpence a day. Every day they have to work three hours then sleep three hours,[27] and so on, for their whole lives, except on Sundays. They scarcely ever live to old age: they eat and drink everything they earn and are miserable all their days. We were told not one in a hundred puts anything aside against old age. This is as much because they work hard and need to eat well as because they don't believe they will live to old age. They have the best food the countryside can provide, and never eat poor quality meat.[28]

Seeing them at work, I reflected as I very often have before: how lucky I am to be born into a position in which I don't have to work in order to live; and how unhappy I'd be if I had to work as hard as I could for three hours, then sleep for as long,[29] and scarcely close my eyes before I had to wear myself out again! What a miserable fate! What a price our luxury costs!

The ore is found very near the works:[30] it is brought in trucks on four small iron wheels made for the job, and to enable them to be drawn more easily they are set on tracks over which two parallel iron rails are laid for the wheels to roll along. These

[27] Barrie Trinder thinks this may be a linguistic misunderstanding. He says that twelve hours on and twelve off would make more sense; that François may have nodded and translated the English word 'twelve' as *trois*, sounding very similar. And see note 29 below.

[28] Nine years earlier, 13 June 1776, their friend Arthur Young described Coalbrookdale vividly, and his enthusiasm presumably helped to determine their visit: 'One immense steep of hanging wood has the finest effect imaginable: that wood thickly scattered with cottages, the inhabitants busily employed in the vast works of various kinds carried on in this neighbourhood. One circumstance gave me much pleasure. There was not a single cottage in which a fine hog did not seem to make a part of every family; not a door without a stone trough with the pig eating his supper, in company with the children at the same business, playful about the threshold.' A. Young, *Tours in England and Wales*, 1932 reprint, pp. 145–53. This is pleasantly perpetuated at one of the museum's cottages.

[29] He clearly *believed* three hours was the stint, but he would if he had mistranslated 'twelve'. Neither Alexandre nor Lazowski supplies a check.

[30] This unambiguous statement is matched by one François made the previous day and another at Sheffield, and conflicts with received teaching on the subject: see p. 96 above, and immediately below.

kinds of track make themselves indispensable: our workman reckoned that Mr Wilkinson used about twelve miles of them, and he assured us that there were over a hundred in the country.

The agent told us that about forty steam-engines a year were made at Coalbrookdale, mostly for the English but a few for export: of these forty, Mr Wilkinson made about eighteen.[31]

Leaving the works, we went to another that didn't belong to the same ironmaster and where they worked only with iron from Cumberland.[32] The ore arrives in boats in stone broken very small: it is blood-red: it is cast with charcoal and very little limestone. They cast twice in 24 hours. They make bars, but they don't leave the iron in pots. They find it very profitable because it fuses more quickly, and they use less coal and less charcoal.

The rest of our day was not so well spent: we wanted to see pitch being made with the smoke of coal. We crossed over the water to the only establishment in the business, for all those which have begun have failed. The makers don't make enough profit, and these assured us they were losing money and that they would probably be giving up soon.[33]

Eight or ten furnaces in a row are lit, the air can get in only through a small hole which creates the effect of bellows, and a great quantity of smoke is driven into a gallery that serves as reservoir. From there it is led by a tin pipe into a stone-built lead-lined covered cistern in which the smoke, condensing, produces a black moist substance. Once the smoke has entirely gone, the workman takes some of the liquid stuff and pours it into casks, where it settles. Two-thirds are pitch, a kind of inflammable water, like spirits. The last stage is boiling down the very thick material, which becomes excellent pitch.

Near Coalbrookdale there are several tin-mines[34] which are profitable: the tin isn't refined in the area.

There is a great abundance of coal-mines. the coal is good and mined in large lumps. Some mines are already worked out; others reach a prodigious depth; others are on the slopes of the river, and their galleries leave the river-banks horizontally and continue to a great depth underground in a short distance: there one often sees tumbrels, specially built, drawn by three horses, and the men leading them with little

---

31 These were probably steam-engines of the old Newcomen kind, designed to pump water for a wheel (Raistrick, *Dynasty of Iron Founders*, 1953, p. 150): the kind of 'very large' engine used to work the wheels of Wilkinson's own forge as noticed above.

32 This, too, contradicts the notion that only iron-ore from Sweden was used.

33 This was the tar and coke works run by the inventive 9th earl of Dundonald (1749–1831), adjoining the Calcutts ironworks. It was still producing in 1803, when a Swedish industrial spy wrote off the tar refinery as an invention 'on the whole of little value'. M.W. Flinn, *Svedenstierna's Tour in Great Britain, 1802–03*, and Barrie Trinder, *The Most Extraordinary District in the World*, Ironbridge Gorge Museum Trust, 1988, pp. 78–81.

34 *Mines d'étain* certainly means tin-mines, but there are none near Coalbrookdale. François may have been confused by the fact that Richard Reynolds, brother-in-law of Abraham Darby II, was connected with the tin-plate industry of South Wales (Raistrick, *Dynasty of Iron Founders*, 1953, p. 87). But he was presumably referring to lead-mines.

candles in their hats. Accidents are very frequent in the mines: they are often worked by poor people who, to save trouble, don't erect sound props, and the gallery collapses.

I've explained that the owners of the land-surface in England are the owners of what's beneath. These richly productive hills belong to gentlemen to whom companies of smiths pay so much a year for mining rights. This sum doesn't exceed fifty or sixty guineas for the entire hillside.

The prodigious consumption of meat by the work-people is a tremendous advantage to the agriculture of the area. The lands in the bottom are enclosed and are pastures. A little higher up, the lands are not so much enclosed, and grow more corn and turnips with which to nourish and fatten the cattle. The price of land on average is 35 shillings an acre. The farmers are excessively attentive to the careful fattening of their cattle to produce good meat, because the workmen who eat such a great quantity of it would want none of it if it were not the best possible. Anyone spending eight or ten days at Coalbrookdale would certainly find a great many things worth enquiring into, particularly if he was well informed in natural history, chemistry or music.[35] For us who know nothing of those things, we would consider all that with the pleasure that the arts give to the observer; and when after two days we thought we had seen everything we could, we set out for Birmingham.

As we left [16 March], I looked again at the iron bridge. Its elegance and simplicity pleased me extremely.

We climbed a very steep hill, down which a great quantity of coal was being hauled from mines two or three miles away, and the roads were frightful. Soon after, we took the turnpike road, but were no better off: we paid more, but had equally bad roads. We arrived at

Wolverhampton. Wednesday 16 March 1785   It's a fairly large town built on a hill, the streets well paved and the houses well built: all in all, not a bad town. Its population is immense: they reckon ten to twelve thousand people. They make a great many steel objects, but the majority are instruments for agriculture: very few intricate things.

Everything manufactured here is sold as Birmingham steel-ware, for far from being made in the town, this manufacture extends almost twenty miles into the neighbouring countryside.

We were at Wolverhampton on a market-day. I have to say it was more like a fair than a market. The market-place was full of people, the streets were full, you could walk nowhere, and the confusion lasted all day: they sold every kind of produce and cattle.

---

35   This is a surprising remark. What music was to be heard in Coalbrookdale in the course of eight or ten days? At adjacent Madeley, the evangelical John Fletcher, 1729–85, listed song-singing as one of the sins to be avoided: Barrie Trinder, *The Industrial Revolution in Shropshire*, 1973, p. 277. If they'd been at Cromford near Matlock Bath two months later, they'd have heard the bagpipes and reels celebrating the arrival of 40 or 50 'North Britons' from Perth for training at the mill: R.S. Fitton, *The Arkwrights*, 1989, p. 77. One wonders if Lord Dundonald brought pipers to stir the work force in his tar-works (p. 103 above): he certainly employed several Scots at the works from about 1784 (Barrie Trinder, *op. cit.*).

Our idea in going via Wolverhampton to Birmingham was to see an ironworks belonging to Mr Wilkinson; for although it turned out the shorter route, we wouldn't have taken it otherwise.

17 March 1785   We left before lunch on the 17th and went to the iron-works,[36] three miles along the road to Birmingham. To our disappointment, the furnace wasn't working. We found Mr Wilkinson's agent who told us that one of the main components of the steam-pump had broken: they had had to suspend all work. We could see only the mill.

This machine is notable because it works where there is absolutely no natural water-supply: the hammers and bellows have to be worked solely by the steam-pump. Working bellows by steam-pump is a process I've described and know well, but no one before has worked the hammers without any water. This discovery belongs entirely to Mr Wilkinson, and it is so much more useful because in dry countries one could never extract and cast iron because the cost of transport would be too great.

The mechanics of the machine is simple, but by reason of the economy of the pieces and the wheels; the more immediately the force is applied, the less there is need to present more resistance. They are mostly of cast iron, each of the toothed-wheels is cast in one piece of iron: the enormous axle of these wheels is also of iron, as is the fly-wheel,[37] a wheel twenty feet in diameter, which must have a weight equal to all the parts, for it is meant only to augment the strength by its weight.

The steam-pump is very large, the air is greatly rarefied to add strength to its action, the piston is about five feet long. To the fly-wheel is attached not another piston to work a pump, but a long iron beam[38] which carries at its other extremity an iron lantern-wheel.[39] This lantern-wheel, as one might imagine, goes up and down, but its teeth engage in the long iron teeth of a wheel so that instead of a simple vertical movement, the lantern-wheel makes a slight turn and the fly-wheel falls back, the movement begins again.

To this wheel which is worked by the lantern an axle is attached which, at the other extremity, carries a solid wheel with four cams[40] with which it lifts up the great hammer that beats the iron.

This axle I mentioned is very big, a good three feet in diameter, and solid iron. It's another steam-pump that works the bellows, although it would be possible for the same one to work the two hammers and the bellows. But they find it more convenient to keep the two workshops separate.

---

36 This was the historic 'Bradley Furnace' at Bilston (Staffordshire), where John Wilkinson set up on his own about 1748 and, 'after many failures, finally succeeded in substituting mineral coal for wood-charcoal in the smelting and puddling of iron-ore'. He set up on a much bigger scale at Broseley in Coalbrookdale in the 1760s.

37 *balancier*.

38 Beam. OED says: 'a heavy iron lever, having a reciprocating motion on a central axis, one end of which is connected with the piston rod from which it receives its motion, and the other with the crank or wheel-shaft'.

39 *la lanterne*, a kind of cog-wheel.

40 *dents*.

Almost all the iron made at this forge is shipped by canal to Birmingham to be converted into steel.

The agent showed us two shafts going down to one of Mr Wilkinson's coalmines: it is nearly 300 feet down, and here the same steam-pump that lowers and raises the buckets full of coal also extracts all the water in the mine – a double operation that makes a great saving.

Near the coalmine, one of Mr Wilkinson's new establishments is not yet finished: it consists of a steam-pump of the most enormous size, which, by itself, will work four hammers, two bellows and two iron refineries: the power, precision and scale of the machinery are astonishing. All is made of cast iron by Mr Wilkinson. I asked his agent how many pounds weight of iron had gone into this machine: he didn't know, but I imagine it must weigh thousands and thousands of pounds.

All these machines are under the same roof, which is like that of a shed. The main pillar, that supports most of the timber-work, is an iron column. We were assured that the whole machine would be ready in a month. I doubt it, for there are still many parts to make.

It's extremely convenient for Mr Wilkinson that two canals pass close by, one either side of his works: carriage of his goods doesn't cost a great deal.

In all this neighbourhood a great number of nails is made and sent to America. At this particular time the demand is much greater than can be met. I had never seen them being made. The process was amusing to watch. The majority are made by women, who are perhaps more suitable, being more adroit than men. The iron has been split into thin rods, one end of which, about two or three inches, is made red-hot. Then, taking the rod in the left hand, they make a point with a hammer on an anvil which is shaped so that there is a little slit, over which the pointed end is laid: a smart blow of the hammer cuts the nail to whatever length is required. It is put into a mould with the blunt end sticking up: a hammer turns it into the nail-head. The mould is nothing but a piece of iron like a coat-sleeve in which is a little hole the size of the nail being made. The women generally turn out two thousand a day, earning a shilling. The smallest nails are the most difficult.

Along the canal that we followed a short way back to the village where we'd left our horses, we saw several brick kilns: one for pottery and one for porcelain. The whole country is singularly industrious. These kilns are notable for being conical, and rising to sixty or eighty feet, all brick, no place for timber. This shape, like a pointed head-dress, is part of an enormous site in the middle of which is the furnace and the workmen conveniently at work all around. *Bilston* is the name of the place where we left our horses.[41] It's a large village, with many steelworks. We're still in Staffordshire, but Birmingham's in Warwickshire, a very short distance over the frontier of the county.

From Wolverhampton to Birmingham we saw nothing but houses and factories. For fourteen miles we are really in one continuous town – a town in Flanders, with countless houses and some gardens.

---

41 See note 36 above.

6

Birmingham; Coventry; Leaving the Industrial Midlands

For their first day in Birmingham they hired a carriage, and all three climbed in to visit the famous experimental scientist Joseph Priestley at Fair Hill, near Spark Brook. He spoke good French, showed them his laboratory (set away from the house), spoke of much jealousy between the manufacturers and said that if they hadn't been French they would never be shown any of the industrial processes. 'A small thin man in a large wig', he made a vivid impression on Alexandre, and gave them letters of introduction to Matthew Boulton and Henry Clay.

They crossed Birmingham from south-east to Hockley Brook, Handsworth in the north-west, the site of Boulton's Soho Manufactory, 'the largest factory in Britain'. There they described the Sheffield plate being made, and a new steam-pump for mines, a powerful new oil-lamp, and Watts' duplicating machine, which mystified them (and was a long way short of xeroxing). It was the workers' dinner-time, but they saw button-making and contrasted it with the methods they'd seen at Sheffield. They were severely disappointed to miss Matthew Boulton, notoriously hospitable but away in London. Presenting themselves at his house, they at least saw his (then) very grand gardens.

They had more luck back in Newhall Street with Henry Clay, one of the four great pioneers of modern production in Birmingham. He himself took them all over his workshops, specializing in very attractive paper-board goods and in buttons. Birmingham itself – 'vast, handsome and well-peopled . . . you can hardly walk the pavements without being obliged to step off' – was nevertheless 'sombre' with the smoke of the steel and plate factories.

After Palm Sunday mass (they walked out to the Mass House still at Edgbaston), François had his white breeches and new frock coat covered in mud in a slight accident in the harnessing up of one of the gigs, but they were soon picking their way painfully over the appalling road to Coventry.

There they described how ribbons were being made at phenomenal speed and were bemused by the profusion of children: 'they must be born two or three at a time'. After listening to a wretchedly debased version of the Lady Godiva episode, they found themselves careering along the excellent road to Warwick. There, as at Shrewsbury, they coincided with the Assizes, and were reduced to lodgings in two middle-class homes. For compensation, they saw a great deal of society thronging the town; and saw the Shire Hall, the gaol, the 'Priory' and the Castle, where they were particularly struck by the views over the surrounding country from the windows of the noble apartments. Their thoughts were turning to Shakespeare and Stratford.

BIRMINGHAM

Friday 18 March¹ 1785   *François:* We had three letters for Dr Priestley, took them on the morning of the 18th, and found him in his little house,[2] busy with a great pile of papers, His reputation is too great for there to be anyone in the world who hasn't heard of him. His discoveries in chemistry, especially about Air,[3] they say will make him, after his death, as famous as Newton. He has discovered things that up to now have been entirely unknown, and of the greatest use to manufacturers.[4] Although I'm a long way from being able to appreciate his work, I entered his house with veneration. I thought that perhaps one day I'd be very glad to be able to say I saw Dr Priestley.

He led us into his laboratory where we saw numbers of different tubes with which he has lately been making experiments. For some time he has been neglecting chemistry in favour of theology, which leads everybody to regret the waste of his time. He speaks French well. Dr Priestley is small and very slim.[5] He has a rather common appearance, yet his eyes are lively, and there is something about his face that conveys his genius. He told us we could equally well see the Birmingham factories with or without letters of recommendation: however, he gave us two. He warned us of the extreme jealousy that prevails between various manufacturers of the town; and that if we were not French there would be no question of their showing

---

1   Their first full day in Birmingham, where they arrived on the 17th. Alexandre comes into his own, as he did at Manchester, where he 'scooped' François by naming Dr Percival. At Birmingham it is Alexandre who says who supplied them with letters for Joseph Priestley, who gives the more vivid account of Dr Priestley and names Henry Clay, the owner of the second of the celebrated pioneering factories they visited. Alexandre's account follows his brother's, below.
2   Not large, but three storeys, and five bays wide: it stood at Fair Hill, on the south-east edge of the town near the hamlet of Spark Brook: see Pl. 60, also Alexandre's account.
3   He first read a paper 'On different Kinds of Air' in 1772.
4   He showed Wedgwood the application of electricity to the decoration of pottery: his discovery of 'dephlogisticated air' (oxygen) could be used in a blow torch to melt platinum, not to mention its medical uses: when Wedgwood found one clay would vitrify and another wouldn't, he sent samples to Priestley for analysis, and when Boulton and Watt met problems relating to 'air', they went to Priestley.
5   5 feet 9 inches, standing very upright. The boys were presumably taller. The distinguished French geologist, Saint-Fond, had been shown Dr Priestley's laboratory, 'standing at the end of a court', the previous year. He said it consisted of several ground-floor rooms, and described in detail the apparatus for making inflammable gas. For him it was 'a great pleasure to see this estimable philosopher in the midst of his books, his furnaces, his physical instruments, surrounded by his family, a well-informed wife and an amiable daughter, and in a delightful house where everything breathed peace and goodness'. (B. Faujas de Saint-Fond, *A Journey through England and Scotland to the Hebrides in 1784*, 2 vols, ed. Sir A. Geikie, Glasgow, 1907: cf. p. 62, footnote 13 above, and below, p. 247).

us all their processes; certain things they hid from everybody, but nevertheless we should see quite enough to satisfy our curiosity.[6]

Alexandre: On the 18th we took a carriage[7] in the morning, and arrived to see Dr Priestley, for whom we had three letters: from Mr Young, our Suffolk friend, another from the bishop of Llandaff, and a third from my uncle Larochefoucauld.[8] The letters were most useful. He doesn't live in town, but two miles out, in a small house: the country round him is agreeable; there's a pretty little garden, and some fields that belong to him. Over his mantelpiece the portrait medallion is a copy of the one made for Mr Wedgwood, who is his friend, and who after having had his portrait done a different way, finally had it enlarged and sent it to him (Pl. 27).

Dr Priestley did not match the idea I had formed of a great man: I saw a small thin man in a large wig. What I have read so far does not make me curious to read my journal, but in my old age I shall be able to re-paint the picture of a man so famous that I shall pride myself on having seen him. On arriving at his house we were taken through two work-rooms where a young man arrived and they discussed, I suppose, things to be marked for conservation. He spoke of the difference and of the great difficulty of the two languages, French and English. He seemed to me to have ideas about an exchange [*bourse*] in methods of speaking one's language. A moment later, he suggested that we go and see his physics laboratory which has made his great reputation.

After leaving his laboratory, which is only a short way from the house, and in a place where it is isolated, we re-entered his manor and he produced two letters: one for the manufacturer of plating;[9] the other was for Mr Clay,[10] a manufacturer of paper-board of whom I'll speak later.

---

6   On so short an acquaintance it is quite possible that Priestley underestimated their supplies of this commodity. He had certainly made an impression on Alexandre.

7   They couldn't all three have got into one of their cabriolets; and their horses and cabriolets needed rest and maintenance.

8   The 6th duc was actually the *cousin* of their father Liancourt, who succeeded him in the dukedom of La Rochefoucauld when he was murdered by the mob in Gisors on 4 September 1792. In 1776–77, Dr Benjamin Franklin, smoothest of American diplomats, initiated France's alliance with America against Britain, associating himself with the 6th duc and with Lafayette. In June 1782, Priestley had a long letter from Franklin, with news of his own and Lavoisier's chemical experiments and good wishes from the duc (J.G. Gillam, *The Crucible*, 1954, p. 152). That year, the duc was elected member of the academy of sciences. He published studies in geology and mineralogy and observations on agronomy, and a translation of the constitutions of the 13 united states of America (1783). In 1785 he became president of the *Société de médecine* and a citizen of the town of New York. With Lauzun, Talleyrand, Lafayette and Noailles, he formed the Society of Thirty, meeting at Adrièn Duport's house, rue du Grant Chantier. He presented to the Assembly the address of the Friends of Liberty of London. He became president of the administration of the Départment of Paris and represented it in the Legislative Assembly. He signed the suspension of Pétion and Manuel for their responsibilities in the invasion of the Tuileries on 20 June 1792. His own arrest was signed on 16 August: his murder in Gisors followed on 4 September. He was more suited to experiments in the laboratory than in the political arena.

9   Matthew Boulton.

10   Henry Clay.

27. *Dr Joseph Priestley, the Wedgwood portrait.*

28. *Von Breda's portrait of Matthew Boulton, examining geological specimens: through the window, his factory at work.*

Thereupon Alexandre got into the coach and went off with François and Mr de Lazowski (whom neither of them mentioned) to Soho in Handsworth, then on the north-western outskirts of Birmingham. Here, on a heath, Matthew Boulton had built his Soho Manufactory in 1761–66, and transformed the heath into a landscape garden. He seems to have been the first to apply the silver plating methods to household ware – coffee-pots, tea-pots and so on – and he called in the best designers, Adam, Chambers, Flaxman, etc. The site of this factory, one of the most famous in England, is at present derelict once more, but Boulton's Soho House, in poor condition, survived remarkably intact and, since 1993 has been carefully restored, and in 1995 opened to the public.

François: We went to Soho to see Mr Boulton's manufactory, the biggest factory in the whole of Britain. It is outside the town.[11] There we saw steel being worked as at Sheffield, except that here it is finished by hand-polishing. It is done by women with their hands, puttying the pieces on to a board, within a frame. Between five and six hundred workpeople are employed here. Mr Boulton has made many machines that do great honour to his inventiveness, and have made him a great fortune. I will mention only three.

He has managed to make a particular steam-pump work on two-thirds of the coal that would ordinarily be used, and this he has achieved by a special construction. Parliament has awarded him the exclusive right to make it and market it for 21 years, which gives some idea of the usefulness of the discovery: normally such patents are awarded for only ten years.[12] The discovery is chiefly valuable to Cornwall, where the scarcity of water-power makes its use imperative. Mr Boulton charges the Cornish as his profit for this steam-pump the one-third of the coal that this pump saves. This amounts to a large annual sum.

Another of his inventions is a lamp giving as much light as four candles and which, through the intensity of its flame, makes no smoke, even when burning poor quality oil.

The third but by no means the least useful invention is a machine with two cylinders which makes an instant copy of a letter.[13] It is especially valuable to those at the head of a great retail-business, who need to keep copies of their correspondence. One notes that to obtain a copy, the original has to be written on paper, and with ink, both supplied by Mr Boulton: the paper receiving the copy is very fine.

I can't say how this is done: the mechanism is a complete mystery to me. Certainly, it produces only a faded copy of the original. However, as those who know about printing know, the characters that go into the press one way come out printed in reverse: here, the copy comes out the same way as the original. The operation is done by two cylindrical presses between which the paper passes. I suppose there may be

11 François omits, but Alexandre records, the information that they brought a letter from Dr Priestley for Mr Boulton, but that 'Mr Boulton was in London, which prevented us from seeing what we wanted to see'.

12 Originally developed by James Watt for his own convenience, but taken over with characteristic enthusiasm by Boulton, as François describes.

13 This is presumably a reference to Watt's duplicating machine.

a double operation, or that the ink penetrates through the copy-paper. However, there isn't really enough for that, and you can take two copies from the same original.

This machine sells in Birmingham and London at twelve, ten, six and five guineas.[14] I wish I could see one again, to try to puzzle out its mechanism.

François ends a chapter here, a good place for Alexandre, who remembered to explain their disappointment at Mr Boulton's absence in London, to take over for two paragraphs.

Alexandre: We saw little, but I will describe the little we saw. The Soho factory is situated in a bottom [Hockley Brook, with what Boulton called 'the most convenient water-mill in England']. The factory is a very impressive building, in brick, very simple but beautiful. We arrived at the worst possible moment, when all the workers had gone off to dinner. We were two miles from the town – too far for us to go away and come back. So we went into the shop,[15] where my brother opened his poor and slender purse, wanting to buy everything; and as soon as we had left, wanting to return, and so we wasted the morning.

After a long time the workpeople returned and we saw them at work. The thing we were able to see was the making of buttons, which we had seen in great detail at Sheffield. However, there is a great difference in the perfection of the machines and in the way they are used.

We return to François, but then come back to Alexandre, who gets well into his stride at Mr Clay's factory in Birmingham itself.

François: Mr Boulton has rather a pretty house near the factory: its position is pleasant with a view of the town across a little valley.[16] His grand gardens are terraced and

---

14 The larger ones were designed for offices, the smaller ones for travellers.
15 Boulton had an agent in London, a Mr Matthews in 1769, and presumably a showroom. Miss Philippa Bassett, Senior Archivist in Birmingham Central Library, has kindly shown me a letter in the Boulton Collection there, in which Col. G. Kendall, apparently an attaché at the French embassy in London, tells Boulton he had twice desired Mr Matthews 'to hasten the goods the Dukes de La Rochefoucauld and de Liancourt had ordered, as they propose setting off next week for France'. The letter is dated 4 March 1769, and gives a rough time for the ending of Liancourt's early visit to England with his cousin: see *A Frenchman's Year in Suffolk, 1784*, 1988, p. xxiv and Pl. 3. It would be pleasant to know what goods they had ordered: Kendall ordered for himself coffee-pots, candlesticks and watch-chains. The French ambassador ordered toss-pans for cooking. The journal Liancourt almost certainly kept is assumed to have been lost during the Revolution. We can only guess whether the two Dukes visited Soho or whether they were content to order via Col. Kendall.
16 They may have brought their letter from Dr Priestley to Soho House itself, only to learn that Matthew Boulton was away in London. It must have been a severe disappointment. Robert E. Schofield, in his fine book *The Lunar Society of Birmingham* (Oxford 1963, p. 27) wrote this of the house: 'Ambassadors, princes, even Catherine of Russia were among his guests, but these were not the most special of his visitors . . . The people for whom he names his home *l'Hôtel de l'Amitié sur Handsworth Heath* were manufacturers like himself or scientists from whom he could

planted, tastefully, with evergreen trees. There is no lack of ornamental water: three strips of it have been created, at great expense.

19 March 1785   Dr Priestley's second letter was addressed to a maker of trays, paper-board,[17] buttons etc. We met the man himself, and he had the kindness to show us over all his workshops.[18] We saw the making of paper-board, which is composed of several sheets of brown paper. The paper is made so as to take the paste evenly spread over the whole of both sides; the paste is made so as to take colour without blotching it. The paper-board is made on frames of whatever thickness is required for the finished article. For buttons it isn't very thick. They are all black when made for the clergy. They are painted and varnished in the board, then heated. With a cutting-out machine they are cut to shape, then a tin button the same size is made and embodied with the little piece of paper-board by heating them. To finish the button, it is turned and polished with a stone mounted on the end of a small instrument.

This kind of button has the advantage of being light and solid, and its colour never fades. I mustn't give the impression that they make only smooth, flat buttons. I've seen them being figured and even embossed, by pounding the hollow parts [*en pilant les échancrures*] of the paper-board, and obtaining a paste with which they fill moulds: the paste, as it dries, assumes the same body as the paper-board itself.

Trays, so much in demand for tea in England, are more difficult to make. The paper-board is thicker and it is worked like wood, with saw, file, etc. They are of such perfection that it's impossible to tell where the pieces are joined. Their paintings and varnishings [i.e. japan-varnishing, or japanning] are truly superior to everything I have so far seen. One can imagine nothing more beautiful. They are water-proof: the last stage in production is to rub them with soft-soap and pieces of cloth and dry them in drying-stoves.

In this factory I have seen being made every kind of thing that could possibly be made of paper-board: tea-caddies,[19] ladies' work-boxes, little coffers, snuff-boxes,

learn. The Lunar Society, which first met regularly at his home, grew from this kind of entertainment.' Johanna Schopenhauer (*A Lady Travels*, 1988), here with her husband in 1805, was delightfully received by Boulton, then 77 and carried by two sturdy servants indoors, but pushing himself about outdoors in a comfortable little carriage. By then he'd had to turn away strangers who came without introduction.

17   This material, originally known as paper-board, was later, incorrectly, known as papier mâché.

18   Alexandre luckily identified him as Henry Clay, whose works were in Newhall Street. He patented his paper-board in 1772, and it stayed in fashion for over a century (Conrad Gill, *History of Birmingham*, I, 1952, p. 102). He was one of the four great pioneers of modern production in Birmingham 'who carried on at the same time the old traditions of craftsmanship' (Gill, p. 99): the other three were John Taylor (gilder, plater, japanner, and a founder of Lloyds Bank), John Baskerville (printer, japanner, trainer and backer of Henry Clay) and the great Boulton.

19   Alexandre came away with a tray and a tea-caddy 'for all kinds of tea', *élégant, et d'un charmant carton avec un grand goût*. (He makes *carton* and *goût* feminine; makes his own genders, grammar and spelling: perhaps his illegible scrawl is an attempt at concealment.) In his next paragraph he says he saw 'these pictures of nymphs singing, made with great taste and elegance and doing honour to Mr Clay'. He adds, 'the painter is called Mr   ' [and leaves space for it (Pl. 28a)].

breadbaskets, buttons, etc. and even paintings of the greatest perfection. As to design and colour, they always represent a small group of women, or of children, or an antique vase, all executed with the most exquisite taste.

This same manufacturer [Mr Clay] has the secret of painting on marble to more convincing effect than is done generally: he showed us a white marble chimney-piece painted in medallions with garlands of laurels and roses which are utterly charming; it costs 250 guineas.

He makes a number of very expensive wall-papers; he has made several of them for the Empress [Catherine of Russia], and she has lately ordered from him a superb chimney-piece painted with the noblest furnishings any sovereign ever had: her very words, so the manufacturer told us.[20]

The town of Birmingham is vast, handsome and well-peopled, its roads broad and straight, with a number of regular small squares:[21] it would be a very fine town if the houses were not so low, and the windows larger. But the great smoke created by the steel and plate manufacturers makes the whole town sombre. It's impossible to keep the windows clean for a single week. I find that that alone is enough to destroy the appearance of the most beautiful town in the world. For the pavements to be regularly paved is something too common in England for me to mention it. There are hackney-carriages, something one doesn't see all that often in big towns.

You can have little idea of the crowds of people going by in the streets all the time: there is as much life as in Paris or in London. You can hardly walk on the pavements without being obliged to step off. Dr Priestley told us there are 32,000 inhabitants. Almost all of them are workers, for the women and the children find employment in making buttons and in the polishing of steel.

---

[20] Alexandre quotes the words of the imperial letter: *'Envoyez moi ce qu'aucune tête couronné ne put de vanter d'avoir.'* The Hon. John Byng was in Birmingham on 4 July 1781: his interest in the manufactories was confined to three amusing sentences: (*Torrington Diaries*, I, 1934, p. 49) 'We spent this morning in visiting Clay's and Boulton's factories; the latter at Soho, 2 miles from the town: the works are common in every hand, but an inspection of their different professions affords great pleasure, and an happy idea of the improvements of my countrymen. Boulton employs 500 workmen; before the war he had 700: women and children contribute to the wonderful cheapness of his wares. At Clays I am most tempted, but at Boulton's most amused: the button is now the most flourishing trade at both.'

Sylas Neville visits Boulton's factory on 30 October that same year, 1781. Mustering none of Byng's pleasure in what he saw of the results, he noted, in four brief paragraphs, that some things shown in Boulton's showroom were not of Boulton's manufacture, 'which is wrong'; that the number of persons employed in making a single button was a chief safeguard against artificers being lured abroad; and that a silver tureen was then being 'chased' for the Empress of Russia. He also noted Watt's duplicating machine, and devoted a sentence to Henry Clay's 'factory of Baked paper, as one may say'. B. Cozens-Hardy, *The Diary of Sylas Neville, 1767–1788*, Oxford, 1950, p. 280.

[21] He uses the word *places*, which in Birmingham could be translated as small squares. Byng noted that St Philip's church formed the centre of 'a new square'. And Alexandre noted that they went to see the canal, *'le plus commode que j'ai vue*: a branch comes from London here and enters *une large place, bien grande et large*'. He does a crude sketch of it, looking very square!

In Birmingham we made the same reflexion we have so often made, how extraordinary it is that in England, where we've noticed hundreds of times their continual attention to the common good, that they persist in the custom of burying the dead among the living, which contributes, I'm sure, to putting the second group among the first. All those we've spoken to on this subject have expressed their dissatisfaction with the state of affairs, but a start has to be made and nobody makes one.[22]

The taxes aren't heavy in Birmingham or in this area. The Land Tax is very low in its effect on poor people: not more than 8 English *sols*.

Alexandre: 20 March was Palm Sunday, too great a feast of the church for us not to go to mass. So we went in search of a chapel 2 good miles out of the town, and we went on foot. This chapel is surrounded by fields and in an isolated farm.[23] There was formerly a chapel at Birmingham, but since the time of Cromwell the Catholics were rejected, being poor and unimportant. They say there are perhaps about 400.

We attended mass in this chapel, and now we are back in Birmingham. We left after lunch.

28a. *Japanned tea-tray from Henry Clay, possibly of the kind Alexandre bought.*

22 They had noticed the large central burial ground alongside Park Street and St Bartholomew's chapel. It took another half-century, with Edwin Chadwick and the Health of Towns movement.
23 The Rev. Peter Dennison, of Oscott College, directed me to the Franciscan Mass-house, a handsome early 18th-century brick farmhouse, still called Mass-house, at number 6, Pritchatts Road, Edgbaston, near the University. There was a school and chapel here from c.1727 to 1786, with the school continuing till 1789. (He cites Thaddeus, *The Franciscans in England*.)

François: We stayed two days [18–19 March] in this town. On the third, at the very moment of our departure, I nearly had a nasty accident.[24] I was in our cabriolet; Mr de Lazowski was about to enter when I noticed that my horse's collar had been changed. One knows that in England the horses are most frequently harnessed with collars. I told the stable-lad to go and find mine and bring it to me. To put it on the horse you have to take off his bridle and, to save time, instead of beginning by completely unharnessing the horse, he removed the bridle. The bit was no sooner out of his mouth than the horse moved off, with no bridle, harnessed to the cabriolet with me in it, and throwing the poor lad to one side. I'd been talking to someone and hadn't noticed what had happened, and when I felt us move forward I was at first rather frightened. Luckily for me the lad had unhooked the traces; so the horse dragged me no more than ten yards before the harness fell off him and he bolted. The cabriolet, being perched high up on its springs, threw me some fifteen or twenty feet forward and I fell on my hands and knees, nothing broken, neither my legs nor the cabriolet. Someone stopped the horse, and soon afterwards we got away. But I can't help lamenting a pair of lovely white breeches and a brand-new frock coat which were covered in mud.

From Birmingham to Coventry the roads were so bad that we could scarcely trot. The badly laid pebbles and the ruts, constantly intersecting, made me frequently lose patience.[25] I had hoped to arrive in time to save staying there, but the roads were against us.

COVENTRY

20 March 1785   Coventry is built along two roads, one of them at least a mile and a half long.[26] The buildings are by no means elegant, and the ground by no means level, but is paved. The church is worth seeing: grand, noble and containing several extremely old monuments of white marble already almost black.[27] The town hall is alongside: singular for its great antiquity and its gothic form.[28] The prisons are newly built, and

---

[24] It clearly put the recollection of their Palm Sunday morning walk to mass from his mind. More curiously, Alexandre makes no mention of the accident: merely that they left towards 2 o'clock for Coventry: 18 miles.

[25] This verdict on the road is modified by Alexandre, who recognized that, 8 miles from Birmingham, at Stone Bridge, they joined the London–Holyhead turnpike for the rest of their way to Coventry. (Later, under Telford and the Parliamentary Commissioners, it took in the rough 8 miles they had just covered from Birmingham.) At Stone Cross Alexandre recognized 'a beautiful farm and château belonging to a Mr Brown'. He is surely referring to Packington Hall, its 'landskip' park one of Capability Brown's striking early works (1751): it belonged not to him but to the earl of Aylesford. It is dismal that François was in so much of a hurry that he failed to notice Packington.

[26] It is now completely dislocated by a formidable Ringway for motor-traffic.

[27] Alexandre, too, was impressed by St Michael's: 'worthy to be a monastery, and with several tombs well carved in marble'. He reckoned the marvellous spire was '108 toises' (see Notes, p. xiv): anyway, it rises to 295 feet.

[28] St Mary's Hall, in Bayley Lane, south of St Michael's church, was built in the 1340s and enlarged in 1400 for Coventry's merchant guild, at the time when this was the fourth town in England. Alexandre said it was 'well furnished'.

of rather a noble order, though heavy, as befits such building.[29] The town is lived in by quite a number of gentry, comfortably off. But the great mass of the inhabitants make gauze and ribbons: almost all have a frame at home. The silk comes mostly from Derby and Derbyshire, where it is spun as I described when we passed through. Their biggest output of gauze is of the common variety: the better quality they make in competition with us and claim that we can't do it as cheaply as them. A worker reckons to make twelve ells[30] a day, and earns a shilling (24 *sols*) or a shilling and a half.

They work the greater part of their silk undyed[31] because it's cheaper, and when the pieces are manufactured they are all boiled in soapy water and become white. They are packed off to London to be measured, stamped, and assessed for the new tax at, I think, one English sol per ell. This tax is harmful to them and makes it more difficult to compete with foreign trade.

The gauzes are made as they are in France. The frames seem to me to be mounted in the same way: there's just one kind of frame that I've never seen before. It makes a gauze of three threads, one over the other, all twilled together and with the wool, which produces kinds of small lozenge or diamond-shapes, pleasant to look at. For this frame there are three warps stretched by the weights: the rollers over which the warps are folded are not fixed, because the folded line being longer than the straight line, one feels that to make the lozenge-shapes the warps need to be lengthened a little. This gauze fetches a good price, and is bought almost entirely within the Kingdom.

The ribbons are made at incredible speed. An ordinary workman turns out dozens every day, but he doesn't earn more than a shilling or 15 English sols.[32] The flowered ribbons are made by a man who makes only one at a time; but a hundred are made on a frame like those I described when we were in Manchester. The workman makes 21 of them at once, and without great effort. They are all mounted on the same line, and the reed moves a shuttle beside each warp, which all hold together by an iron rod which passes through the thickness of the reed and to which is fixed a little sleeve coming out of the middle of it. The workman with just one hand on the little sleeve draws the reed towards him and pushes it back again, and weaves the ribbon by throwing the sleeve so far to the right and so far to the left: he rests the other hand.

A word, in passing, about the usefulness of machines. How is it possible to sustain competition with other countries without machines? If, for example, a man earning only a shilling a day could make twenty-one ribbons at a time, it is clear that with the same machines we could easily eclipse English ribbons in foreign markets.[33] For

29 He is presumably referring to the County Hall, just round the corner from Bayley Lane, in Cuckoo Lane. It was done the previous year by Samuel Eglinton, a Birmingham architect: rusticated, blank-arched, fort-like ground floor: Tuscan portico.

30 The English ell was 45 inches, a yard and a quarter.

31 *en jaune*, literally yellow, though François uses *jaune* for cream-coloured, and here the second part of the sentence seems to demand 'undyed'.

32 See Notes on p. xiv.

33 Alexandre, too, was much exercised at the disadvantages the French were under in relation to Coventry's ribbons and gauzes, and devoted some particularly indecipherable pages to the theme.

one of our workmen could live well on 15 sols a day, while an English worker lives wretchedly on 24. Once the ribbons are made, they are glazed, brushed and dried at the fire.

I saw a large number of women making ribbons, although the frames can be rather tiring for them, on account of the treadles. Infants and little girls clean the ribbons and spin silk for darning. I have even seen them ten or twelve years old, working small frames very quickly, though in truth they scarcely had the strength to move the reed.

Here I must record that in my experience I never saw so many children as there are in this town. Dozens of them come into the houses. They must be born two or three at a time. What is sure is that everywhere that there is work to be done, arms are soon there to do it, especially if it is profitable.

They complain that their trade is not so flourishing as it was a dozen years ago: that they can find a sale only for low-priced goods and that gauzes, above all, are not so sought after as they were. I suppose, if there is a falling off, that it is their fault, and that a little inventiveness in fashions would restore their fortunes. Besides, a sign that their commerce is favourable is that several of them have told us that they couldn't find enough hands. It is a contradiction that springs from the desire that manufacturers have to amass quick fortunes: they persuade themselves that it was easier in former times.

There is a canal that brings cheap coal to Coventry: not more than seven or eight miles long, it was built at the expense of the town:[34] it soon joins another main canal which links up with the rest of England and London. The water-circulation in England is as abundant as the blood-circulation in the human body.

There's a market twice a week. Some porcelain is made here.

In Coventry there is a tradition as ridiculous as it's old. Everyone affects to believe that the town, which was then a village, was about to be created a city (the precise period is already forgotten). The occasion was celebrated with public feasting, and a young woman got drunk, mounted a horse and rode naked through the town. Everyone was so horrified that nobody went to look out of the window except one man, who looked out and was struck blind. In virtue of this miracle, a wooden copy of the head of the voyeur is preserved, an exact copy it is said, and it is kept in the very window. It is painted every year, and on the first of June a girl, dressed in flesh-coloured linen, sits on horseback, rides right through the town, and in front of the wooden head makes every kind of grimace.[35]

---

34 The Coventry canal links the town with the nearest coalfields on the north-east edge of Warwickshire, towards Nuneaton and Atherstone. It joins the Oxford canal three miles out of Coventry.

35 It is sad that the story of the Lady Godiva had become so much debased by the time François heard it. Godiva, a considerable benefactress of religious foundations, flourished c.1040–80, and in 1043 persuaded her husband, Earl Leofric of Mercia, to found Coventry's great Benedictine abbey. (It was founded on 4 October, not 1 June!) Her fame as a benefactress of religion was displaced by the story of her ride, recorded by Roger of Wendover in the 1230s, but basing himself on an earlier writer. In this version, Godiva asks her husband to release

From Coventry we went to Warwick, Warwickshire's capital. The road is excellent, very agreeable to drive over. The countryside is beautiful, the fields all made ready for the spring, and there are frequent houses of gentry.

WARWICK

21 March 1785   Our arrival exactly coincided with the Assizes so that all the inns were full.[36] However, we wanted to see the castle, and needed to stay in Warwick, which meant lodging in middle-class homes. Our living-room was in one house, one bedroom was in another, and one room with two beds in the inn: our horses lodged at the other end of the town, but that was the best we could do.

For compensation, we saw a great deal of society thronging this little town. The judge went by several times in his coach, accompanied by over forty persons in livery and with trumpets: but the judgment-trumps that accompanied the dignitaries and announced the sitting were dismal, beating the ears in the way cowherds in France summon their cattle.

Warwick stands high up, dominating the country round. It is built on two crossing roads, along fine, wide and straight streets. I wasn't able to discover the precise population, but about ten thousand at a guess.

The houses are very pleasant, though there wasn't one real beauty.

First we went to look at the place where justice is done: it is newly built.[37] Its architecture is fine, noble, suited to its job, with columns of the Corinthian order. On entering, you find yourself in a great room of perhaps 150 feet by 50 feet. Behind that, to right and left, the room opens into two round courtrooms divided from this front hall only by wainscot up to sill-level and in one of which the justices of the peace hold their quarter-sessions; the other is where the judge holds the assizes. The two courts are ornamented by smooth round columns of white freestone.[38]

Next door is the prison built five years ago by subscription, prompted by charity for the prisoners. The architecture is suited to its function: heavy and solid, with exactly the right effect: a fine cage in which one's liberty is lost. The walls are thick, the windows hardly open. The building is dignified by round columns, though they are attached, only half free of the walls.[39]

Coventry from heavy tolls. Leofric agrees, on condition that she rides naked through the town. To his surprise she does so, covered in her long hair, and he grants the charter.

    It is interesting that the story of 'Peeping Tom' first appears only in the 18th century (c.1732): the city accounts record 'a new wig and fresh paint' for his effigy on 11 June 1773.

36 As at Shrewsbury, they had bad luck with the assizes.

37 The Shire Hall seems to have been designed by Sanderson Miller and by the brothers William and David Hiorn, masons and architects at Warwick: 1753–58. They made a memorably good building.

38 The two courts are octagons with pretty plaster ceilings: the smooth columns have Corinthian capitals.

39 Nikolaus Pevsner (Buildings of England, *Warwickshire*) was tremendously moved by this building, 1777–83, by Thomas Johnson, a Warwick architect and builder: 'An astonishingly early date for a building decidedly in the Ledoux style. Elephant grey stone . . . The columns

29.   *Warwick Town and Castle from Warwick Priory's gardens. Pen and ink drawing by Canaletto.*

30.   *Warwick Priory from the gardens. William Oliver.*

Encouraged by the desire for a walk and by the fine weather, we went into a garden that we found open, looking beautiful. In the middle stands a house called the Priory, because, I suppose, it was one. It belongs nowadays to a private family. The park is something like 200 acres: we walked in the pleasure garden, which is small but well looked after: the kitchen gardens and hot-houses too. The whole property is in the most agreeable situation: the house is part of the town, the park part of the country, on the slope of the hill on which Warwick stands, from which one discovers a charming valley, extensive but not vast; not exactly exciting, but interesting in detail.[40]

In the park, a pump turns a water-wheel which gives an abundant supply of water to several fountains in the town, in this way compensating for such a high situation.

Our walk ended at the castle, which belongs to Lord Warwick and has long been owned by the earls of this name. It was founded on a rock that rises 300 feet sheer above the surrounding country and the river Orwell[41] which runs at its feet. It is fortified by a large number of very tall towers which give it dominance over the town, for the site it is built on is no higher than that of the town. The towers are built of large blocks of stone and crenellated. The moats dug on the side towards the town were immensely deep: they are mostly filled up. Towards the country, there was no need of them. The entrance is protected by a first gate armed with two towers. The surrounding wall isn't very high. As you go on, you reach another gate with very thick walls: an enormous portcullis closed the entrance. There it still is. I can't imagine what purpose it serves now. The courtyard is very large.

The whole place, once heavily fortified, is now entirely given over to gardens, and so agreeable that one can scarcely believe.[42] They are maintained with the utmost care. All is immensely picturesque: sandy walks, carefully laid out in a natural way, and clumps of trees; all the court with the moats, all the first court and the garden. In the middle of the fine lawn that adorns the courtyard is a great urn of white marble carved in low relief: it is cracked and pieces are missing but that seems right for an old castle.[43]

---

were meant to be fluted and they would have been among the earliest revived Greek Doric columns in England and indeed in Europe.' H.M. Colvin, *Biographical Dictionary of English Architects, 1660–1840*, 1954, was content to say: 'It is remarkable as one of the earliest attempts to adapt Greek Doric to the purposes of an English public building.' François got it right enough.

[40] The quadrangular fabric of the medieval priory became first an Elizabethan mansion and was then Georgianized. In 1927 it was removed to a site near Richmond, Virginia and belongs to the Virginia Historical Society. The garden was laid out by the royal gardener, Henry Wise (1653–1738), whose work survives only at Melbourne, Derbyshire. The County Record Office now occupies the site, still a pleasant public park.

[41] It is the Avon.

[42] Laid out by Capability Brown, 1749–59, one of his earliest works, and then 'out-Browned' by William Gilpin, in terms of the Picturesque, in the 1770s (Mavis Batey and David Lambert, *The English Garden tour*, 1990, p. 218).

[43] 'The Warwick Vase' was acquired by Glasgow Museum and Art Galleries in 1979. It was found in 1770 in the bottom of a lake at Hadrian's Villa in Tivoli, and bought by Sir William Hamilton who gave it to the Warwicks in 1774. Byng (*Torrington Diaries*, I, p. 230) called it 'a vulgar overgrown Roman basin in the centre of the court; which I would toss into the centre of the river or give to a church for a font'. He too admired the apartments and the way they were kept up.

The apartments are of the noblest, the rooms large and elegant: it's easy to see this is the house of a very great lord, and that you'd need to keep up a very big establishment in order to live here. The hall, dining-room and drawing-room are enormous – incomparably grand, right through from beginning to end. The living quarters consist of a fine suite of rooms. All the rooms are hung with priceless pictures and portraits by the great masters. And what a surprise one gets on looking out of the window: the most stunningly beautiful view. At one's feet, below a sheer, perpendicular rock cut as if by man, flows the river, forming a fine cascade and turning several mills. An ancient bridge of fifteen arches crosses, a little further on, carrying the road to Stratford. Looking left, one sees the river approaching through meadows at the foot of rich slopes; and to the right it snakes away into the far distance, in flatter country. Immediately in front, the most beautiful hillside rises gently, furnished with a prodigious number of houses, several villages, gardens and carefully cultivated fields. You need to have seen this view to appreciate it. Descriptions are nothing. How can I convey the effect of the shadows, the diversity of the objects, the elegance of the shapes, etc. etc. The best pen could never recreate it, and mine . . .

We climbed to the top of one of the towers, the tallest, from which we could see the whole of the town. Its aspect is pleasant, it is all very carefully looked after with, I suppose, the greatest expense. The castle is a glorious thing to have in your family, and very agreeable to live in. The place has withstood several sieges.[44]

Lord Warwick usually spends eight months of the year here: it gives him infinite pleasure. He was in London when we were here.

When we wanted to retire to bed, there was another inconvenience. We found everyone at the inn so busy that we could only with difficulty make ourselves heard, and to reach our room we had to cross a vast hall where the sheriff was giving a supper party. These gentlemen did nothing but drink, laugh and sing all night long: sleep was impossible. From time to time, one of them would come into our room looking for a great-coat: they had forgotten where they'd put them, for there certainly weren't any in our room.

---

[44] It was taken over in 1978 by the Tussauds Group, which tends it well: it now has hundreds of thousands of visitors every year.

7

Shakespeare and Stratford; Oxfordshire; the Bath Road

They were shocked at the crude colouring of Shakespeare's monument in the church, pleased by the White Lion, and not much moved by the birthplace. They were much more pleased by the recently established Chapel House inn standing alone near Chipping Norton and a junction of turnpikes. Though an English traveller here in 1781 wished the cooking were up to French standards, François declared the luxury of the rooms beyond anything in France: 'England is charming!' A short walk away, they admired the magnificent baroque décor of Heythrop House. They were eager to reach Woodstock and Blenheim, 'the most beautiful house in England'. There they started with Capability Brown's breathtaking park and found the house 'of great splendour', though they were much vexed to find Louis XIV's bust stuck up on the south front like a trophy. They were especially stunned by the library, and by glimpses of the park through the windows.

At Oxford, they were among the first to appreciate the gradual unfolding of the curve in 'the High', culminating in Magdalen's new bridge. They saw the Radcliffe observatory and its new telescope, and the Radcliffe Camera. But promised letters of recommendation failed to arrive, and the weather was wet, turning to snow.

Nearby, Lord Harcourt's prospect house and gardens at Nuneham were 'everything one could desire': they listed a dozen of his pictures by various masters, and described 'what is called a flower-garden'. Then Wallingford and the river-side road to Reading (another commendable inn), and they had reached the Bath Road. At the Bear at Hungerford, the Recorder of London, with his very pretty daughter and a friend, beat them to the roast beef. They had 'one of the most beautiful inns in England' – the Castle at Marlborough – entirely to themselves, and set out on foot to inspect and speculate about the mysterious sarsons in a nearby valley, and the ubiquitous tumuli.

March 1785   *First, Alexandre contributes some personal details*: On 22 March, as our journal had been neglected and we needed to catch up to be ready for several important places ahead of us, we left Warwick early in order to spend the night at Stratford, where we intended to spend the whole of the following day.

After a restless night, we decided to leave towards 7 in the morning. We could see that there'd been a very sharp overnight frost: the air was biting and I was afraid I had a bit of a chill. The road to Stratford was beautiful, the fields enclosed and well cultivated.

Stratford-on-Avon   *He enquired into the rotation of the crops, and noted down the five courses: his chill seems to have come to nothing. François resumes*: We left for Stratford-on-Avon, a very small town, with no trade and few people, but which will forever be famous as Shakespeare's birthplace. We stayed at an inn built by subscription at the time of the Garrick Jubilee,[1] an inn the more astonishing for being in a hole like Stratford[2] it has beautiful stables and a pleasant garden.

We went to see a monument someone had erected to Shakespeare in the church: I don't know who did it, but it is a most scandalous thing. His effigy, recessed some six feet up on the wall, shows him holding a book and a pen, in marble painted and re-painted in red and green paint by a dauber.[3] Beneath the monument is his grave, with those of his wife and daughter. (All this is in the choir.) On his tombstone, these words are engraved as he ordered:

> Good friend, for Jesus' sake forebear
> To move the dust that resteth here.[4]
> Blest be the man that spares these stones
> And curst be he that moves my bones.

François transcribed it with slight inaccuracies: Alexandre got it right and gave François a good French version of it. François continues: Beside the wretched tomb of Shakespeare is a white marble monument, well sculpted, to someone whose name would never be noticed if one hadn't gone to see his neighbour's monument.[5]

---

[1]   It was the White Lion; standing where the Birmingham road entered Henley Street, which continued on to the Clopton Bridge. It ceased to be an inn in 1857, and was demolished in 1979. Its site is occupied by the inevitable 'Visitors Centre', leading into the Birthplace. Byng stayed there later in 1785 and described there 'a head of Shakespeare, and under written:

"Here sweetest Shakespere, fancys child,
Warbled his native wood notes wild." '

(*Torrington Diaries*, I, 1934, p. 224). In September 1769, Garrick inaugurated the new Town Hall with a dramatic entertainment – a sort of pageant – written by himself (and not improved by torrents of rain). He also presented the Town Hall's chief feature, John Cheere's lead statue of Shakespeare. That was the real start of Stratford as centre of pilgrimage, complete with holy places.

[2]   *un trou*. This is an odd way of describing a town in a valley-bottom at a river-crossing, surely a natural site for a good inn?

[3]   Alexandre described it as '*vilain et indigne d'un tel homme*', and a shame on the town. It was perhaps the 'daubing' that offended the Frenchmen: the red and green paint has given way to a more seemly red and black. John Plumptre in 1790 complained of the paint (*Plumptre's Britain*, p. 27). The church monument lacks the romanticism of Cheere's statue, which is the popular image. Yet the figure looking out over his grave in church shows the mature genius, prosperous and still at work with plume and paper. It is thought to be based on his death-mask, taken by his son-in-law: it was carved by Gerard Johnson, whose workshop was near the Globe in Southwark where Shakespeare was a familiar enough figure. It is the most credible of all the likenesses.

[4]   In fact the words are: 'To digg the dust encloased heare'.

[5]   Presumably Rysbrack's monument, against the east wall south of the altar, to James Kendall, 1756. Alexandre noted the old scutcheons of the Clopton family, who in the late 15th century built the long stone bridge over the wide Avon: they crowd the Clopton chapel.

31.   *Stratford-on-Avon. Shakespeare's monument by Gerard Johnson, in the parish church.*

Returning from the church, we saw on one façade of the building in which justice is done and which they call the Town Hall, a statue of Shakespeare put up by Mr Garrick, with this inscription:

> Take him for all in all,
> We ne'er shall look upon his like again.

That is difficult to translate but I think it may be rendered by: 'Regardez-le comme tout dans quelque chose que ce soit, nous ne verrons plus personne qui lui soit égal.' In the English, this is very elegantly expressed: my grasp of it is confused, and I can't translate it very well.[6]

The house near our hotel is the one where the great poet was born. It is a poor little cottage: one knows he was the son of a shoemaker,[7] and the house is exactly as it was in his day. We were shown an old three-legged chair sealed up in a wall in a corner of the fireplace: there, it is said, he used to sit. [Later] he lived in a house that has now fallen into the hands of a stranger: it is there that he planted mulberry-trees that he refers to in several of his works. This stranger, having received unfriendly treatment from the townspeople, got his own back by pulling down the house, cutting down the mulberries, selling up and departing: just to be revenged, they say.[8]

---

[6]   Their evident admiration of Shakespeare was unusual among Frenchmen – largely owing to these difficulties of translation. Alexandre, noting the inscription, adds: 'With which a Frenchman agrees', and also tries to translate it. It is a classic example, like Othello's 'Put out the light, and then put out the light', of the extreme difficulty of conveying the simplicities of poetry, from one tongue into another. 'Take him for all in all' would certainly test the ablest translator. What is curious is that neither Frenchman *transcribed* the second line accurately; but even the sculptor was taking liberties with it: he carved 'We shall not look upon his like again', to make sense of it as a public tribute to Shakespeare himself. Neither they nor, presumably, Lazowski noticed that it was Hamlet, to Horatio, after they'd seen the ghost of Hamlet's father, who said, of his father:

> Take him for all in all
> I shall not look upon his like again.

The ghost was one of Garrick's earliest London roles and so successful that, next year, 1742, he was playing Hamlet, the Prince himself, in Drury Lane.

[7]   In fact, a glove-maker, and a prosperous one: when Shakespeare was four, his father was bailiff (mayor) and the Queen's Players came to perform in the town. The house had come down in the world by 1785. It is now restored to something like its 1564 proportions but is so thronged by visitors and so 'cared for' that it never seems 'lived in', in the way Elgar's birthplace does. The three-legged chair has gone: Byng eyed it eagerly that summer but Mrs Hart was not tempted to sell. It is said to have been sold by Thomas Hart to Princess Czartoryska: *Torrington Diaries*, I, p. 224 and p. 240.

[8]   This was New Place, the town house of the Cloptons, that Shakespeare bought in prosperous middle age: it was a handsome brick and timber house with 5 attic gables to the front. In 1756, its owner got into trouble for felling an old mulberry tree that Shakespeare *might have planted*. He was tired of people clamouring to see it. A cantankerous fellow, he went further and pulled down the house itself, as François says. The site remains, with a modern 'knott' garden.

Alexandre, too, quoted this story. Then he grew unusually philosophical and observed, rather drily: Wine is poured out for people content to drink water . . . The English, in general jealous of what they have, and believing themselves the best people in the world, boast more than anything about the great men they have produced, and Shakespeare in particular . . . they will suffer no comparison to be made with him.

Wednesday 23 March 1785   On the 23rd we left Stratford and dined at Shipston-on-Stour. Leaving Stratford, you cross the bridge, with its inscription recording that it was built by one of the Clopton family. The country is well peopled and more charming than one can say; the fields, and the gardens. Shipston is a nice town, where we dined.[9] The road to Chapel House is busy.

François resumes: To go from Stratford to Chapel House we went through very pleasant country, but there were fewer enclosed fields: in spring they often plant thick hedges which they remove in the autumn and burn in winter. Their fields are excellent, ploughed with four horses, yet lacking in something I believe to be essential: there is little variation in the order of their cropping; which is oats or barley, wheat, turnips or beans and oats with which clover is sown; and the land is sown with grass or clover for two years, sometimes three.

This part of England is more like France than any I have seen. Fairly rich villages stand amid open fields: the houses are not scattered across the countryside. This regime seems less good when you look at it closely. It is certain that enclosed fields work better than open ones, and it is natural that fields that lie around the house are better farmed than those at a distance.

CHAPEL HOUSE

Chapel House is a considerable inn standing on its own in the countryside. It is a most convenient house, built less than ten years ago.[10] The parlours and bedrooms are of a luxury and comfort that can't be compared with anything in France.[11] The

---

9   At the George or the White Horse. Chapel House, in Over Norton, is ten miles beyond Shipston on the Oxford road, close to its junction with the road from Worcester.

10   Part of the inn still stands as a private house (Mr Nigel Curry) in beautiful Cotswold stone. (A wing was removed, and the stone used to convert the stables opposite into cottages.) Johnson and Boswell stayed in 1776 when, perhaps, Mr Kerby had extended it, which would explain François' statement about the rebuilding. Here, Johnson gave his judgment that 'There is no private house in which people can enjoy themselves so well as a capital tavern . . . the more noise you make . . . the welcomer you are'. Its position near the junction of the Stratford–Oxford and Worcester–Oxford turnpike explains its success.

11   The Hon. John Byng was here in 1781 and again four months after the Rochefoucauld visit, when, of nearby Chipping Norton, he wrote: 'All the inns are eclipsed by that of Chapel House, which is quite a principality . . . is apart from village noises, an excellent station for hunters and I should suppose for convalescents, from the dryness of the soil and purity of the air . . . The outside of this inn and the bedrooms seem excellent, but the menage is poor work: commend me in this last particular to the French inns, where for 30 or 40 sous per head the cook serves

stable-block is immense: we were assured that they have fifty-two post horses. It is true that I saw them arriving and departing every minute of the day, for the road is a very busy one.

The house is surrounded by a very pretty garden of an acre or more. There is an abundance of evergreens, flower-beds are already planted and the lawn – at the heart of it – is as fine as can be: it is cut once a fortnight. In summer, the game of bowls is played on it: it is called '*le bowlingreen*'.[12]

We were amazed to find so good an inn in the middle of fields: everything one could desire is provided. England is a charming country: if you have money, you want for nothing.

24 March 1785   We stayed in this house as much to write up our journal, which was two or three days behind, as to go to see Lord Shrewsbury's house, only three miles away.[13]

HEYTHROP HOUSE

We arrived by an avenue about three miles long (over a league) and perhaps 200 feet wide, formed of clumps of tall trees, mostly oaks, and interspersed between them always another clump of evergreen trees. Through the effect of perspective, the two sides of the avenue seemed from the house to be a continuous alley of trees.

The house is designed with four fronts, and built in the most elegant manner about sixty years ago. The main building is joined to the offices (forming two wings) by two open arcades, creating a highly agreeable effect. A flight of steps leads up to the hall beneath a large portico supported by four fine Corinthian columns.

The interior of the house is not nearly as magnificent as the outside. I won't describe all the rooms I entered: the Library and the saloon alone were remarkable.

The first is 83 feet by 20. Its decoration is magnificent, mostly in a beautiful stucco, extremely refined. The ornaments are in bas relief over-doors, representing

---

up an excellent repast without the plague of want of invention in English inns; with the same dull round of "mutton and beef for steaks, sr, fowls and ducks, sr, and veal for cutletts, sr".' (*Torrington Diaries*, I, 1934, pp. 52 and 220–21). François obviously felt less critical of the cuisine: he was by now used to the English fare.

12 Byng noted, *ibid*, 'Here we came at ½ past six o'clock; after tea we endeavoured to play at bowls in the garden: and laugh'd at the crouded fantastic follies of a Ranelagh or a Vauxhall; whilst Mr R. [his friend, Reynolds] played on his flute, to the delight of the house company, who came forth to hear his melody; to which eccho likewise gave her assent'.

13 Heythrop House, a Baroque palace, much influenced by Bernini, and with a front doorway after Borromini (Sherwood and Pevsner, *Oxfordshire*), built in a great four-mile park in the early years of the 18th century by Thomas Archer for the 12th earl and first duke of Shrewsbury: it was gutted by fire in 1831, restored by Waterhouse in 1871 in a Vanbrugh idiom, with fine chimney-stacks. It was used as a Jesuit College 1922–69; now (1991) as National Westminster Bank's Staff College. Part of the great avenue approach from the north-west has become the fairway of a golf-course: the house is now approached by a long winding drive from the south-east.

plaques of Europe, and several medallions and trophies of instruments relating to the sciences and arts. The ceiling, smooth plastered, is supported on Corinthian columns: the cornice is Ionic. The background of the stucco is green, the low-relief decoration white. Two white marble chimney-pieces are carved with the greatest possible delicacy.

From the Library one enters the saloon, 47 feet by 25, by 20 in height. The furnishing is four great panels of superb Brussels tapestry, each representing a quarter of the globe with the fruits and the animals particularly associated with it. Europe alone was in masquerade. Above the four doors are the seasons painted in chiaroscuro, in such perfect imitation of the bas-reliefs that I was taken in by them.[14]

The chimney-piece is the most beautiful I ever saw in my life: it is in Egyptian marble of very great value and marble statuary sculpted by Carter.[15] The ceiling is painted with the greatest perfection, representing several subjects from the fables.[16]

What constitutes the principal beauty of this room is its regularity, its proportions combined with its magnificence: I put it above all the others that I've seen in other houses.

The park has no more than 200 acres, the pleasure garden a dozen: the landscape is excessively melancholy. From the windows of the house one sees much uncultivated land: from this point of view, I do not believe living in this house to be at all agreeable.

Lord Shrewsbury is a catholic. He has a chapel to which we went, but when we arrived, mass had been said: it was Holy Week.

25 March 1785   Alexandre implies that they returned from Heythrop to the comforts of Chapel House. He says: After returning from Ethrop, we had the same reason as at Stratford for staying: our journals were badly behind. If we could remain for the day and write, we would soon catch up. The 25th was Good Friday. Before we left we went to look for a man from our host's farm, who turned out to be very large: he soon came, and Mr de L began to interrogate him.

Six pages of prices and crop rotations followed, and comparisons with East Anglian muck-making. François said nothing of this, and got on with describing the journey.

---

[14] In his description of the saloon, François seems to differ widely from Jones's *Views of Seats, Mansions and Castles*, 1829, quoted by Sherwood and Pevsner, *Oxfordshire* (Buildings of England, 1974). Jones described 'a *stucco ceiling* representing the four quarters of the globe'. There may well have been alterations between 1785 and 1829. This gives particular value to François' account, and one wishes he had described more of the ill-fated interior. Unluckily Alexandre limited himself to the same two rooms. The palatial proportions François recorded show that the 'saloon' was what Archer designed in 1705 as the larger of two drawing-rooms; and that the prodigious Library had originally been the 'gallery'. From the Library one passed through what was originally a bedroom in order to enter the saloon (cf. Marcus Whiffen, *Thomas Archer*, Los Angeles, 1973), pp. 22, 52.

[15] Presumably Benjamin Carter (d.1766) who 'worked chiefly as a maker and carver of marble chimney-pieces' in Rupert Gunnis, *Dictionary of British Sculptors, sub* Carter.

[16] '*de Lafontaine*', Alexandre adds.

François: On the 25th we set out on the road for Blenheim, the country unremark-able, neither beautiful nor depressing. The fields are not enclosed. We arrived in good time at Woodstock, the name of the little town: the duke of Marlborough's house is called Blenheim.[17]

BLENHEIM

I was so pleased to be about to see the most beautiful house in England. We lunched and, at about eleven o'clock, it was time to start on the gardens. So we did.

The pleasure grounds, the garden proper, cover two hundred acres: the grass is cut every fortnight and the plants maintained in the finest order. Fifty people are employed solely in this garden[18] and often they are obliged to call on the help of additional day-workers. The garden was laid out by M. Brun, the very famous architect. The winding gravel walks are maintained with such care that not only does it appear that each grain of sand is arranged by hand, but gutters have been placed at certain distances apart, to prevent the rainwater from standing about on the walks.

If the garden [park] is vast, it is – even more – varied. To the south[19] of the house, the abundance and beauty of the water, the far bank which rises like an amphitheatre, the cascade, the new bridge and the piece of water immediately below, all together form such a grouping of charming objects and so grand an effect that it is impossible that there is a comparable array anywhere else.

To the east,[20] the lie of the land is quite different, in contrast with the south:[21] the garden seems to melt into the park amid a great many old and superb oak-trees, with their grotesque shapes and their natural grouping producing a very agreeable effect. Finally the level [to the south-east of the house] and the picturesque view of Bladon village which stands out among a group of trees and makes a very pleasant view.

The gardens have been greatly enlarged by the present duke[22] who has made some of the best features: the second piece of water is entirely his. It is the water coming from the first lake:[23] it falls down a cascade eighteen feet high into a cutting which imitates the natural stream[24] so perfectly that it is impossible not to be deceived.

17 Originally Blenheim Castle, but when people saw what it was, Blenheim Palace.
18 He uses *jardin* to describe the carefully designed park 'landskip' round the house. This was originally planned by Vanbrugh and Henry Wise when the house was built. It was largely remodelled by Capability Brown in the decade 1764–74, keeping Vanbrugh's unfinished bridge but creating the unforgettable serpentine lakes, the 'great cascade' about ¾ mile to the west and bringing the park right up to the house. (Watery formal gardens were delightfully created against the west front of the house by Achille Duchêne in the 1910s and '20s).
19 François has somehow got the cardinal points wrong. Here he means to the north, or north-west.
20 Here he is thinking of the east and the south-east (where Bladon lies).
21 He means north.
22 George, 4th duke, great-grandson of the great duke, succeeded in 1758, died 1817.
23 He clearly thinks of the water on either side of the bridge as one piece – the Queen Pool to the east, with its marvellous island of poplars, and The Lake to the west, running ¾ mile to the Great Cascade.
24 The river Glyme.

32. *Blenheim Palace south front, Louis XIV's bust on centrepiece, brought from Tournai's city-gate, 1709.*

33. *Oxford. The Radcliffe Observatory. T. Rowlandson, c.1810.*

Although the cascade isn't supplied by a large abundance of water, the arrangement of rocks enables it to make a very delightful effect.

The first piece of water, with its higher level, which was made at the same time as the house,[25] is indisputably the most beautiful piece of artificial water in England and perhaps the world. It is immensely wide and long and forms a semi-circle in front of the house. It is more than a mile long. The water curving round these artificial bays has an air of being naturally led towards the cascade. The bank opposite the house is covered with a great many trees, which deposit the objects that collect round the bow of the boat. This water one crosses, in front of the castle, on a magnificent bridge built of large blocks of freestone. It is supported by three arches, the middle one modelled, it is said, on that over the Rialto at Venice.[26]

The park is eleven miles in circumference, enclosing a great many charming places such as one might expect in a collection of valleys, hills, waters and woods.

The exterior of the house is of a great splendour, though prodigiously heavy and loaded with ornament. The buildings could scarcely be more considerable, but unluckily their architect, named Van Brugh, was a man of wretched taste.[27]

In the middle of the east front[28] is a bust of Louis XIV that the great duke of Marlborough took at Tournai: it bears an insulting inscription: *Europae haec vindex genio decora alta britanno.*[29]

François was so upset that he skipped from the Great Hall quickly right through to the Library. Once again, Alexandre, calmer, though with a sense of hurt French pride, comes into his own with interesting personal observations.

Alexandre: The width of the house is 328 feet, and within that span are great, great, noble and beautiful buildings by Sir John Vanbrugh. On the south front is the bust of Louis XIV taken from Tournai. This is very vexatious [*très fâcheux*] to the eye of a Frenchman who has some love for his nation, and who is rather jealous of the proud glory of a nation.

We entered through the east gate, built in the style of a fortress, in the top of which is the reservoir that supplies water to the whole house.[30] The [Great] Hall is a

---

25 No: there was only a rather insignificant stream to start with, making the splendid Italian Bridge look out of scale. The bridge contained rooms for picnics and pleasure, but Brown submerged the lower ones when he made his fine lake.

26 It resembles rather one of those aqueducts of classical antiquity that one sees in a landscape by Claude.

27 One can see how this great, gifted virtuoso, Sir John Vanbrugh, dramatist and architect, offended a patriotic young Frenchman by the very success of his monumental tribute to Marlborough. Soane called Vanbrugh 'the Shakespeare of Architects'.

28 It is the south-east front, above the saloon.

29 A possible rendering is 'Thus the liberation of Europe, by the high and honourable British genius'. The 30-ton bust was taken from the gates of Tournai after its sack in 1709: it stands on the centre-piece over the saloon 'like a head on a stake'.

30 This is exactly right. This is still the main entrance and still gives the feeling of entering a fortress. The cistern above was filled from a pump within the bridge over the lake. Mercifully

beautiful room, high and supported on Corinthian columns. The ceiling was painted by Mr Thornhill and shows the plan of Malplaquet where the duke was the victor.[31] We entered the Saloon under a bust of the duke. This room has the most beautiful proportions, like the other rooms in the house. For this reason it is decorated in stucco, so as to seem more open to fresh air. The different compartments[32] represent the different nations [in fact the four continents] with their different fashions and dress. The ceiling represents him in the midst of his victories, arrested only by peace, and showing well how he made use of speed in achieving his success.[33]

François, who says nothing of the Saloon, nevertheless makes some sympathetic comments: Several rooms are furnished with tapestries representing several victories of the great Marlborough, and among others that of Blenheim.[34] Of the rest, I found nothing very remarkable: when one is expecting to see a magnificent house at close quarters, one isn't astonished by it. The Library is, of all the apartments, the one worthy of note.

One is stunned on entering: 183 feet by 31. Doric marble pilasters and doric columns support a rich cornice, the entablature of white marble and the different compartments of the ceiling[35] are of the best taste and finest elegance. This room was designed as a picture gallery. It was the late duke who turned it into a library and filled it with 24,000 volumes, valued at at least £30,000, the finest collection of a private individual.[36] At one end of the room is a statue of Queen Anne by Rysbrack in white marble, the most perfectly finished sculpture in the world. Beneath is an inscription: To the Memory of Queen Anne, under whose, etc.

they seem not to have noticed, as they went on under the clock tower, two lions of England savaging two cocks of France, carved by Grinling Gibbons and set for all to see above that gate. Nor did they comment on the four prominent tufts on each of the four corner-towers: they look vaguely like thistles but represent ducal coronets crowning the inverted fleur-de-lys of France!

31 In fact Thornhill's famous ceiling shows Marlborough kneeling before Britannia and offering her his clearly marked plan of the battle at Blenheim. But Alexandre's observation is nearer the mark than François, who grunted: 'The ceiling represents subjects from fable'. He described the Hall as 'elegant stucco': it was stone, 'Cutt Extrordingry rich and sunk very deep' by Grinling Gibbons and his team working in the west court.

32 He means the different scenes, through the 'colonnades': he has neglected to explain that the walls of the saloon are painted to represent a trompe l'oeil colonnade open to the air of the outside world, from which different people (two of them portraits of the painter himself and the duke's chaplain, Dean Jones) look admiringly into the room: there are late echoes of classical wall-paintings and of Veronese's frescoes in the Villa Barbaro at Maser.

33 It is a great oval showing the duke's Apotheosis. It is a pity that François and Alexandre seem not to have known that these painted walls and the ceilings were by their countryman, Louis Laguerre (1663–1721), suitably named.

34 It hangs in what is now the Green Writing-room, and shows Marlborough accepting Tallard's surrender: still apparently as fresh as when it was woven.

35 These were by the great plasterer, Isaac Mansfield.

36 It was created between 1710 and 1728 by the earl of Sunderland and housed here until it was sold in 1872.

He translates it into French: 'A la mémoire de la Reine Anne, sous les auspices de laquelle, Jean, duc de Marlborough fait ses conquêtes, et à la libéralité de laquelle lui et ses descendants doivent avec reconnaissance sa possession de Blenheim'.

Before leaving the Library, the traveller should, at least for a brief moment, look out through the window: the view is truly delightful: the beautiful 'canal', and several detailed glimpses of the natural scenery of the far side of the valley.

The chapel is in one of the wings. It houses the mausoleum of the duke of Marlborough and his duchess and their two sons who died young. They are attended by History (with quill) and Fame (with trumpet). Below, in low relief, is the capture of the Marshal de Tallard.

The house was built and the gardens and park created by order of Queen Anne in the 4th year of her reign, and paid for by the State.[37] These she gave, with the royal lordship of Woodstock and its dependencies, to this John duke of Marlborough, 'in recompense for all the victories he brought us', and principally for the battle of Malplaquet, of which he was given the name.[38]

This gift by the crown and the services of the duke are expressed in stately verse on the pedestal of a column 130 feet high, which carries a statue of the duke: it stands beyond the bridge, facing the house.

The whole park is given over to deer and some sheep: the beef necessary for the household is fattened, but nothing more.

By sending one's name to whoever is in charge, one may ride through the park on horseback or by carriage: one may see it and the gardens every day except Sunday at any hour one pleases.

The town is small. They make the most polished steel in England, and gloves and excellent leather breeches. Everyone in the village assures you you must buy something to safeguard the house against witchcraft.

Alexandre noted that it sent two members to Parliament, and had a corporation and a market.[39]

From Woodstock we went to Oxford on the morning of the 26th. It is only 8 miles, and the finest smoothest road you could wish for.

OXFORD

26 March 1785   We arrived at Oxford on 26 March. This town is of great antiquity: it was consecrated to the muses by the Britons long before the Romans came, who called it Bellositum.[40] It is confirmed that the walls, of which several sections remain,

---

[37] Blenheim Palace cost £300,000, of which the Marlboroughs found £60,000.

[38] No: principally for the victory of Blenheim. After that battle he was made a Prince of the Empire, but the name of his principality was Mindelheim. Malplaquet was five years later.

[39] Unfortunately his cahier XV is lost: we have nothing from him until 2 April, where XVI opens at Calne with Chaveron's toothache.

[40] This is fabulous indeed: evidently, he had been reading *The New Oxford Guide, or Companion through the University*. There was no significant settlement here in Roman times: the district was

were built since the Norman conquest on Roman foundations: this proves that the town was important from the earliest times.[41]

Times of trouble didn't prevent there being scholars in the University. Authors worthy of trust assert that there have always been three centuries since its origin, and so it has been at all periods. One must observe, however, that Cambridge disputes with Oxford over their respective antiquity.

The origin of this town isn't clearly known: it is safest to reject all the stories made up about that, and to begin since Christianity was propagated in the kingdom. Alfred is thought by some to be the founder, but it seems more probable that he was only a re-founder in a period of confusion and ignorance, and that established order and safety which – except for some interludes of turmoil – have been maintained ever since. Alfred founded several colleges and assigned them revenues and students too.[42]

The town is situated on a very slight eminence, with slopes spreading imperceptibly down into a plain covered with the most beautiful meadows. The sun shines on them and the river Cherwell waters them, flowing past the walls of the town to join the Isis below it.[43] On all sides, the landscapes are crowded with wooded slopes, and cultivated like gardens: their aspect is charming, wherever you look. The valley lies wide open to the north, which fills the town with a cool wind, very healthy for the inhabitants.[44]

The main road runs from east to west; it is magnificently paved and clean and of great width. Its chief beauty derives from the fronts of three colleges.[45] It runs on a slight curve which makes it, I find, more beautiful, because at several stages one is surprised to find it continuing, with no sign of the end. At the end, one comes to the bridge, newly built.[46] It crosses two branches of the river. In the middle is a platform clad in masonry, to very fine effect. The bridge has eleven arches and bears the arms of the town and the university.

The University of Oxford consists of twenty colleges and five halls. The difference between colleges and halls is that the former are immensely wealthy, the latter have only the rent of their houses to pay the masters, professors, fellows etc. All these

administered from Cirencester and Verulamium. As he says a few lines later: 'the origin of this town isn't clearly known'.

[41] In Domesday Book, 1086, there were houses inside and outside 'the wall', of which nothing survives: but there are remains of the 11th-century castle and large sections of the 13th-century town wall, notably at New College.

[42] François doesn't often purvey so much popular nonsense. Is it a coincidence that he acquired it at our oldest university (where the beginnings of the university go back only to the early 13th century)?

[43] He is describing Christ Church meadows. His 'walls of the town' are those of the old colleges, Merton, Christ Church, etc. The Isis is Oxford's name for the stripling Thames.

[44] Cool it often is, but Oxford's climate is not reckoned healthy: see, e.g., James Morris, *Oxford*, 1965, ch. 7.

[45] All Souls, Queen's and ? University College. Magdalen is really a view *stopper*, and Lincoln and Brasenose show only flanks.

[46] Magdalen Bridge, 1772–82, designed by John Gwynne of Shrewsbury. They had admired his Atcham Bridge on March 14th, the day they left Shrewsbury.

colleges were founded either by kings and queens or by individual endowments: they are extremely rich and their buildings vast and magnificent. To describe them would, I think, be wasting my time. The architecture is always rich, and sometimes heavy but if, on the one hand, such an abundance of fine buildings encourages an art as important as architecture, isn't it slightly ridiculous that three-quarters of a town so large – twenty-five colleges, each of them little villages – serves only fifteen hundred young men, of whom only a thousand are resident at one time?

Among the most generous benefactors who have enriched the University of Oxford we distinguish Doctor Radcliffe,[47] whose liberality has surpassed everyone's. He was a doctor who left Oxford his principal beneficiary. From his estate an important hospital was built in freestone: it is at present maintained by the subscription of gentlemen and of neighbouring parishes. Then there is the observatory, an elegant building,[48] well sited to give a view of the whole horizon: the duke of Marlborough has contributed a 12-foot telescope that cost him over a thousand pounds sterling. On top of all that, there is the library that bears his name: it is intended for medical men who belong to the public society.[49] The building itself is well worth attention.

It occupies a square space. It is composed of various orders of architecture with all possible elegance and magnificence. The building is supported on a circular arcade, a rotunda[50] carrying a vast dome which is lightened by its height. The interior is equally beautiful and majestic. The books are housed on a circular gallery supported on Ionic columns, and the middle is ornamented by everything that is most perfect in stucco, variously coloured. The Librarian is a Ministerial appointment. This doctor has also made donations to colleges. His legacy was immense. Each college has its own library. The university has a general library.[51] Several colleges are endowed by collections of excellent pictures given by various individuals.

The University of Oxford has not produced as many illustrious men as its rival: luck hasn't served it well. Locke[52] is the only very celebrated man from Oxford. I don't believe that anywhere in the entire world you will find a university so magnificent as this: and rarely will you come across a town so beautiful.

[47] 1650–1714. John Radcliffe, physician, was at Wakefield Grammar School, University College, Oxford, and became a Fellow of Lincoln College before becoming a hugely successful 'fashionable' doctor, in great demand at the Stuart court from 1686. He clearly combined remarkable medical understanding with great experience.
[48] More: it is a large copy of the Tower of the Winds at Athens on which the first of all weather-cocks was raised: no longer an observatory but a medical laboratory. 'Architecturally the finest observatory in Europe' (Sherwood and Pevsner, *Oxfordshire*, 1974). It is mainly by James Wyatt. (Pl. 33).
[49] ? The College of Physicians. Dr Radcliffe left £40,000 for the building. Built 1737–49 to the design of James Gibbs, crowned by drum and dome: as distinctive an element in Oxford's skyline as St Paul's is in London's.
[50] The eight large pedimented bays at ground level stood open till 1863.
[51] This seems an inadequate reference to the Bodleian Library!
[52] John Locke, 1632–1704, the philosopher, was at Christ Church. Lazowski would probably have included Edward Gibbon, 1739–94, the historian (see p. 198 below), though Gibbon's fourteen months at Magdalen were unrewarding.

We were expecting letters of recommendation for Oxford that a friend was due to send to us here at Oxford, but either they were lost in the post or our friend forgot about them. They didn't come, and so we had to leave without having come near to satisfying our curiosity as to the precise way young men study in the universities.

27 March 1785   We stayed at Oxford on the 27th, which was Easter Day. The weather was bad: it rained so hard that we couldn't emerge from our inn.[53] Next day was finer: we had some snow in the morning, but not much, and soon afterwards the sun appeared.

NUNEHAM COURTNEY

28 March 1785   We went to Nuneham,[54] the country house of Lord Harcourt; only six miles out along the main London road. We left our horses in the village, which was all built by the late Lord Harcourt: it's made up of about two dozen houses, twelve on each side of the road, with gardens round them. They are uniform, and of brick.[55] I doubt if they are let out very dear.

The house is a short mile away: you have to cross the whole park, which we did on foot. The ground is agreeably uneven, the grass covered with sheep and deer, which presented a pleasant landscape. We couldn't see the house till we were on top of it: it presents itself badly, its situation didn't appear to me to be the best. We arrived right up to it; for the slope of the hill, just over the top of which it stands, is too steep; and all one sees on arrival is the mass of stone, unembellished, looking like a very ordinary house.[56]

From the other side, the position is altogether different: the house stands high up above the river Thames as it flows past from Oxford. (It has changed its name here, from Isis, to the one by which it is famous). It runs two hundred paces below the foot of the house, its waters are clear, it winds through meadows and the valley renders the whole view delectable. To the right, in the distance, one sees the whole

---

53 On Palm Sunday, in Birmingham, they had walked two miles to mass.

54 Nuneham Courtney (originally Newnham, as François spelt it).

55 When lord Harcourt decided to build himself a new house on the ridge, the old village stood too near for his liking, so he re-housed the villagers down beside the main road. (Their cottages seem to have been again replaced in 1832).

56 The first earl (1714–77) employed as architect Stiff Leadbetter of Eton, who designed a rather 'ordinary' villa in 1756, suitable as a retreat rather than a family house. It had a *piano nobile*, approached up a double flight of steps. But Athenian Stuart provided it with fine friezes and chimney-pieces (much of which is destroyed). The 1st earl fell down a well in 1777, and for the 2nd earl, Capability Brown in 1779–82 transformed the grounds into what Horace Walpole described as 'one of the most beautiful landscapes in the world'. With help from Henry Holland, Brown altered the house into the one the Rochefoucauld party visited in 1785. He raised the original wings to 3 storeys and created a new top-lit staircase at the centre of the house. (Robert Smirke made major alterations in 1832). The landscape was marred by the Army in World War II and by electricity pylons, but views of the villa from the river survive.

of Oxford, its outlines easily distinguishable.[57] One can even make out some of the duke of Marlborough's plantations at Blenheim, eight miles beyond. To the left the river widens: it forms a crescent as it follows the line of a range of wooded hills which, by the sombreness of its colour, contrasts well with the cheerfulness of the view to the right. Immediately opposite, almost face to face, is a very good village[58] amid a most fertile landscape.

Two sides of the house are wings, joined by a covered gallery: these are offices, servants' quarters, etc.

You enter the house by a very small door and climb a little staircase, which bears no relationship at all to the magnificence of the rooms above. There all the rooms are distributed in the most convenient way: they are elegant and opulent.[59] You see a great many pictures, and all by the best painters, mostly of the Italian school. Among so many rooms, all furnished with distinguished taste, and which would take a lot of describing, I would choose two above all that are more beautiful than the others: these are the *salon* that they call the Octagon, and the room they call the Saloon.

The Octagon is the place where the company spends most time: it is in the middle of the house, and the view from its windows is everything one could desire: it would be even more so if it weren't for a clump of great old elms bang in front and not ten paces away that allow no view of the countryside except to either side. My opinion is that it would be better if they weren't there, but Mr de Lazowski thinks it better that they remain.

The dimensions of the Octagon are 30 feet by 20 and 18 in elevation; the furnishing is green damask. What constitutes the principal splendour of this room is the collection of pictures: *Magdalen* [?Madonna and Child: see 1825 *Oxford Guide*] by Guido; a *Holy Family* by Barocci;[60] a *Venus and Mars with Cupid*[61] by Poussin; a *Moses purifying the waters of Marah*,[62] also by Poussin [*Exodus* 15, 23–5]; and finally a famous Rubens landscape, representing *A Wagon overturning, in moonlight*. Each eclipses the previous one. What can I say? That wasn't all, though I don't remember the names of the other masters. These alone were a complete knock-out.

The Saloon is the next room. The dimensions are 49 by 24 and 18 feet high; the furnishing is crimson damask, the frames moulded gilt. The chimney-piece is a masterpiece: white marble.[63]

---

57 Paul Sandby painted the house and its view 25 years earlier, c.1760 (see Frank Emery, *The Oxfordshire Landscape*, 1974, Pl. 16); also from the Lock Cottages on the Thames (Luke Herrmann, *Paul and Thomas Sandby*, 1986, Fig. 7).

58 Radley.

59 'I wish for a library, and could spare some of the gilding and French taste' (Byng, in 1781: *Torrington Diaries*, I, p. 5).

60 Guido Reni (1575–1642). Federigo Barocci, or Baroccio, of Urbino (1526–1612): see his *Holy Family* in the National Gallery.

61 Sold in 1940 to the Boston Museum of Fine Arts.

62 Bought in 1958 by the Baltimore Museum of Art. The famous Rubens is in the Hermitage.

63 This is known as the Red Drawing Room. The painter Paul Sandby designed the marble fireplace. Athenian Stuart did the rest.

The pictures are two large landscapes by Van Artois, the figures done by Teniers; a *Saint Margaret*, of the greatest value and in beautiful condition, by Titian; *Joseph and Potiphar's Wife*, by Cignani; a *Holy Family* by Le Sueur;[64] *Louis XIV mounted and with his Court* by a great master whose name I've forgotten;[65] and, for complement, there's a valuable *Fête on the Texel* by Van de Velde;[66] and a landscape by Claude Lorraine which is truly admirable.[67]

It mustn't be thought that I've mentioned all lord Harcourt's pictures: I've named only a small number of them because – apart from having no intention of making a list – I can't recollect all the names. It does seem to me a private collection of the greatest quality and value. One that's the most valuable of all is a *Ulysses and Nausicaa* by Salvador Rosa, which was given to lord Harcourt by the duc d'Harcourt.[68]

From the house we went into the garden: not more than 30 acres, but they are so arranged in terraces as to leave nothing to be desired. Walking there, one has the delicious[69] view I mentioned earlier, varying all the time. The present lord Harcourt has extended the garden by a walk that follows the river's edge and prolongs the terrace: it isn't very wide but it's a mile long.[70]

In the middle of these gardens is a small garden – no more than an acre and a half, and separated from the rest by palings and trellis-work: it is called a flower-garden.[71] To anyone walking there it seems much bigger than it is, on account of the arrangement of the groups of trees and irregularities of the terrain. A sandy path goes all round it and rare, exotic trees are to be seen everywhere. Mounds with verses and inscriptions in all languages[72] are not wanting. There is a grotto covered in a great many shells and fossils – more a museum of natural history than a grotto.

---

64 Carlo Cignani (1628–1719). Eustache Le Sueur (1616–55).

65 Van der Meulen. The 1825 *Oxford Guide* adds: 'The Prince de Condé on a dark grey horse, Vicomte de Turenne on a dun one, between him and the King'.

66 Perhaps this is the Embarkation of Charles II at Scheveningen in 1660, with English and Dutch yachts. 'Vandevelt' in the Great Drawing Room in the 1825 *Oxford Guide*.

67 The 1825 *Oxford Guide* has 'a very fine landscape by N. Poussin', but no Claude.

68 In the 1825 *Oxford Guide*, this hung at the upper end of the Eating Room. François-Henri, Comte de Lilleborne, 5th duc d'Harcourt (1706–1802), Governor-General of Normandy, Governor of the Dauphin, member of the Académie Française.

69 He was not alone in using this adjective: see Mavis Batey and David Lambert, 'Nuneham Park' in their book *The English Garden Tour*, 1990, p. 231.

70 Joseph Faringdon depicted this walk, in Boydell's *History of the River Thames*, see Batey and Lambert, *op. cit.*, fig. 181. They note that, in Boydell's book, Nuneham is given more coverage than Windsor Castle.

71 Made in 1772 by the poet-gardener William Mason, a pleasant character who declined to join in the earl's teasing of Capability Brown. A charming engraving of it by W. Watts, in 1777, after Paul Sandby, clearly shows its novel character. (Pl. 34).

72 Sir Brooke Boothby wrote the inscriptions to Rousseau in this flower-garden: *loc cit*, p. 232. The layout was influenced by the description of Julie's garden in *La Nouvelle Héloïse*, and a statue of Rousseau stood in the shrubbery. Odd that François didn't mention it. I expect Lazowski did, but his surviving letter-book deals only with the latter part of the tour.

34.   *Nuneham Courtney Flower-garden. Watts' engraving of P. Sandby's painting,*
      1777.

35.   *Fyfield, nr. Marlborough: the Devil's Den. 'A druid temple unfininshed': see p. 114.*

The parish church stands in the garden – a very elegant building, like a Roman temple. The architect of the house did the church as well: the entrance is away from the house.[73]

Spending a great part of the year in this country house, lord Harcourt farms 200 acres and makes it pay, fattening a good many bullocks for the London market. He buys them young, lets them graze in his park and generally fattens them at five years on a mixture of oil-cake, bran and chopped hay: they fatten well on this feed, which they're given three times a day. As well, they have as much hay as they need. They fatten in six or eight weeks, and sustain the journey to London without getting thin. Each has a stall with running water and without being tethered.

Lord Harcourt's park is 200 acres. Nuneham is in Oxfordshire. We went almost as far as Wallingford along the main Oxford-London road. Wallingford[74] lay two miles off our route. It isn't much of a place today, though it sends two members to Parliament. Formerly (I speak even of the time of William the Confessor),[75] it sustained two major sieges. It was fortified by a castle, though nowadays one sees only its platform and ditches, partly filled in. There are two markets a week. Here we enter Berkshire. Land cultivation is different here from the rest of England – few enclosures, rights of commoning general: no turnips, crops so valuable for cattle feeding. And yet the land is so good that the rent for an acre is generally between twenty and thirty shillings. The land is never fallow:

> 1st year   : wheat
> 2nd year : oats or barley
> 3rd year : peas, and so on.

Their lands must have clear bounds to be so close together without being enclosed. In the summer, they put dry hedging along the paths to separate the ownerships. In winter the sticks can be burnt in the oven, so nothing is wasted.

29 March 1785   On the 29th we slept at Reading. The road followed the Thames all the way, passing through little clumps of trees, with frequent pleasant views. We often saw the very pretty houses of gentry. This landscape, no more than 40 miles from London, is full of very beautiful little places.[76]

READING

Reading is a considerable town, both in size and in its trade. It is situated on a tributary at no distance from the Thames,[77] and is reached by a great number of

---

73 The designer of the church was not Leadbetter but lord Harcourt himself with the assistance of James 'Athenian' Stuart, 1764. Stuart, with Nicholas Revett, was a pioneer of ancient Greek architectural studies. But François is right, this is essentially a 'Roman temple'.

74 Where they presumably spent the night of the 28th; it is 7 miles from Nuneham.

75 A pardonable, if fundamental, confusion

76 Cholsey, Moulsford, Streatley, Pangbourne, Purley: one still sees how picturesque they must have been along this beautiful stretch of river.

77 The Kennet.

shallow boats carrying its merchandise to London: these are mainly oil, soap, charcoal, salt etc. and all sorts of heavy goods which they make or refine; some cloths, although this branch of trade may have fallen slightly. At one time, they say, there were 140 cloth-manufacturers: today there are hardly ten. They make some of this serge that the working-women turn into petticoats. Work that employs many able-bodied men is bringing in from the country the superb timber, for joinery and carpentry, with which Berkshire is well supplied. It is brought to Reading and there embarked to London.

Reading sustained sieges in the Civil Wars: it was encircled by a wall of which there is now very little to see.

This town abounds in inns and I daresay that the worst would be found excellent in other parts of the country. We weren't staying in the best, but it was one of the best we have ever stayed in. The house is large and clean, the stables likewise: a garden of 2½ acres, full of canals for keeping fish alive in two garden-rooms used for taking tea in the summer; a small kitchen-garden, hot-houses and a waterfall. I haven't mentioned that we were served by two men with powdered hair. The nearer one gets to London, the better one finds the inns: as we weren't in the best in the town, one could judge what that must be like.[78]

THE BATH ROAD

Newbury, Wednesday 30 March 1785   We left on the 30th, planning to dine at Newbury. We had left the road towards London that we had followed from Oxford, and were now heading for Bristol. We covered seventeen miles, almost all the time in a plain and along the most beautiful road I've ever seen: you couldn't wish for a better. Admittedly, the soil in these parts is sandy and gravelly, but the road is exactly like a garden driveway. The gravel on the roads is broken down extremely fine by the quantity of passing carriages, and you don't see the tracks of a single carriage. These roads are better than paved ones, but it is hard to find roads as good as this. It doesn't happen in England as often as some people think. I've now travelled enough in England to know that one more often finds bad roads than good ones. The badly metalled roads are worse than all the others; the well metalled are the best of all.

The country is becoming slightly more enclosed, though not yet very much: commoning is abolished here. We followed all along a valley formed to the south by a chain of pleasantly shaped hills: the houses of rich people here could hardly be more numerous: some of them very grand. Not that the country to the right, the north, is deprived; but, as the hills are less high, they don't look so well and anyway they aren't so grand.

---

[78] The two principal inns at Reading in *Paterson's Roads*, 1826, were the Bear and the Crown. They must have been at the Bear. The Crown was nowhere near a stream. On 2 Sept. 1774, Gilbert White at the Bear wrote of 'a stream or canal running under its stables; in it many carp lie rolling about in sight, being fed by travellers'. Byng found it too crowded in July 1784. It stood in Bridge Street. (Information from Margaret Smith, Reading County Reference Library.)

We stopped at Newbury only for dinner. It was in one of the largest inns, although it didn't immediately create such an impression as some others.[79] I don't know how many rooms there are, but we were shown into a small room that was extremely well furnished, with engravings, and so on. I asked how many post-horses, post-chaises, etc., there were and was told eight horses, ten chaises; and two diligences – for four people – leaving regularly, one every day.

Hungerford   We went on to spend the night at Hungerford, a village of no importance where, however, the inn is very good.[80] We found ourselves there with Lord B, travelling tête-à-tête with Lady B: other companions at the inn were the Recorder of London with two of his daughters, very pretty. From his office, the Recorder is clearly a man of importance: rich, I imagine. He ate good roast beef, and we didn't.[81]

Marlborough, 31 March 1785   On the 31st we left for Marlborough, ten miles on. We came through a forest, the estate of the ancient dukes of Somerset. It maintains a great deal of game, much of which is reared for shooting. Marlborough, in Wiltshire, consists of only one broad and fine street, not well built: at the top stands the house built for the last duke of Somerset,[82] which is now an inn, perhaps one of the most beautiful inns in England. I counted 23 bays' width in front[83] and five from front to back, all with two storeys as well as the basement floor.[84] The senior staff tell us that their master pays in rent for this house and outbuildings between three and four hundred pounds a year. There are between 130 and 140 beds available, and the most beautiful apartments and furnishings. The service is magnificent – the porcelain, the silver tea-pots, canteens, bread-baskets, beer-tankards, flagons, a beautiful tea-urn – in a word, everything one could wish for in the house of a great lord: in truth it seemed almost as if we were staying with the duke of Somerset.

The garden, about four or five acres, is well maintained: one part is a kitchen garden with a canal: they have even gone to the length of building a fish-tank with several sections, each for a different kind of fish. At one end of the garden is what is

---

79   At Newbury, the Globe was the inn that supplied post-horses (*Paterson*).

80   The Black Bear was the inn that supplied post-horses (*Paterson*). It is now well known as 'The Bear'.

81   James Adair was Recorder 1779–89: a Whig, but his horror of the French Revolution led him to join a force of London volunteers in 1798 – the discipline hastening his death that year. He had one son and one daughter, who perhaps had a pretty cousin or friend for travelling companion. (I owe this note to Mr R.M. Harvey of the Guildhall Library.)

82   It was built for the 6th duke (1678–1748), 'in whom the pride of rank and birth amounted almost to a disease' (Macaulay). 1½ million bricks were ordered in 1699, and the west half of the house was built by 1706. It was prettily gardened, with requisite cascade and grotto, by his daughter-in-law, but when her husband, the 7th duke, died in 1750 it was sold and became the Castle Inn, stayed in by a great many distinguished people. It became part of Marlborough College in 1843.

83   The main house is 15 bays wide, composed of two blocks each of 6 bays, and a recessed middle block of 3 bays. It is certainly very grand indeed.

84   He might have added the dormered attic floor.

called the Marlborough Mound, perhaps a hundred feet high, a truncated cone.[85] It is an immense heap of earth that served when there was a strong castle here: a place from which to observe the enemy. Now a spiral walk runs round its sides, very pleasant for walking, the slope so gradual that you hardly know you're climbing. There is a small quincunx of young trees on the top, where there's a lovely view of the town and the countryside.

In size and magnificence, the stables correspond to the house: well built, and with room for fifty visiting horses on top of the 105 post-horses kept by the inn.

They assured us that almost every week the house is as full of visitors as it will hold. However, when we were there we were on our own. Lord Chatham, Mr Pitt's father, a most remarkable man, often travelled from Bath to London and stayed here. When he was attacked by the gout he hired the entire house, so that no one else could stay, and these attacks sometimes lasted a fortnight.[86] He would have liked to hire all the post-horses, so that no one could go past.

A DRUID TEMPLE UNFINISHED

We had hardly arrived at Marlborough when, ignoring the heat which was already quite strong, we set out on foot for three miles to see some very extraordinary stones: they followed the line of a little valley, which is waterless, and they are so large that it would be impossible to move any one of them. It is a kind of very hard marble.[87] They are distributed over the ground and have clearly been brought there, for not only is there no quarry of a comparable material for twenty miles around, nor of any kind of stone, but, in excavating around them, one finds them unconnected with any stone. Some are upright, others half-buried. We even saw several of them one upon another; one on top was very irregular in shape, but we reckoned it about 20 feet in diameter and 5 to 6 feet thick: it is 10 feet from the ground, held up by others.[88] We climbed up on to it and admired the strength that had managed to lift

---

[85] Now 60 feet high, it is all that remains of a Norman royal castle.

[86] Chatham's 'gout' seems to have been a very severe manic-depressive illness.

[87] In fact a formidably tough sandstone; sand formed into a natural concrete over perhaps 70 million years and left lying in these great blocks on, and near, the top of the chalk bed as the softer sand washed away and left them. Their strange appearance led to their being called sarsens ('Saracens', strangers), but sometimes greywethers, from their resemblance to flocks of sheep. They may still be seen near Fyfield, along the Kennett stream in the dry chalk valley just west of Marlborough. This may be where the Rochefoucauld party saw them, though their numbers have since been much reduced by housebuilders and roadmakers. It is sarsens like these, but much grander specimens, superbly moulded, that form the most impressive monoliths and trilithons at Stonehenge, and which may have come from this Marlborough area. (The Frenchmen visited Stonehenge on their way back from Plymouth.)

[88] If they were three miles from Marlborough, most of the stones were as nature left them. However, these dimensions suggest that someone had directed them from Clatford Farmhouse, beside the Kennett, about a mile up the 'little waterless valley' to 'The Devil's Den' (at OS 152696, just east of Fyfield): these sarsens seem to have formed the 'false entrance' to a long barrow that had already been removed by ploughing. (Pl. 35).

it. There is a great many of these stones, grouped together in different ways. Some stand upright, kept up solely on their most pointed edge.

The moving of these stones is generally attributed to the Gauls: it is thought that they wanted to raise a Druid temple[89] or some public building and that they transported these stones for a distance that cannot be less than thirty miles, for we have been told that there is a similar kind of stone in the hills round Bath. If that is true, then these stones have been in this place for about two thousand years: they were hewn from the rock at a time before the use of metal was known,[90] and brought here when there weren't any machines. Even now we would be hard put to it to move any of them. People have broken up a large number of them to build houses and walls, and to repair roads. When I say that it is thought that the Gauls were the transporters of these massive lumps, I am not referring to popular opinion but to the perception of the most learned people who have written on this subject.[91]

[89] Apart from 'The Devil's Den', if that was what they had seen, the majority of sarsens they had so far seen had never been moved. Renaissance writers associated Druids with Gaul as well as Britain, and there was a tradition of heroic Druids as Gaulish law-givers. François perhaps naturally thought of Druids as Gaulish rather than British: law-givers or not, he referred next day to 'their barbarous religion'.

[90] This was more perceptive than the observation of so distinguished an antiquary as Thomas Tanner (1674–1735) who thought these (at least at Stonehenge) were works of the Britons, but 'after the Romans came in' (Stuart Piggott, *Ancient Britons and the Antiquarian Imagination*, 1989, p. 115).

[91] How helpful it would have been if he had named any of them!

8

Avebury in the Snow

At Reading they had turned happily westward along the Bath Road, heading for Bristol, Bath and ultimately Plymouth. They were naturally eager to see Bristol and Bath, but at Plymouth the great excitement for young Frenchmen was the chance to see the harbour and naval base, and to see men-of-war at close quarters. Captain Symonds, on duty here as commander of a 64-gun battleship, was the brother of the professor of history who had been their host during much of their time in Suffolk. There they had become 'best friends in the world' with the Captain's son, Jermyn, spending his shore-leave that year in Bury.

They arrived in Bristol without the usual letters of introduction, but admired the architecture of the Exchange, and Queen Square with its noble equestrian statue of William III, and found a Suffolk friend, Mr Moseley, who was taking the waters at Clifton. His friend, M. Crispin, knew France and spoke French well. At Clifton they saw Goldney House, with its very remarkable grotto, and were taken to see the (then) 'incomparable' view at Kings Weston and the nearby Roman camp.

At Bath, too, a Bury acquaintance showed them the whole town. They were much impressed and wrote enthusiastic descriptions. Another Bury friend, Miss Gage, staying with her mother at Bath, asked them out for the evening: a small party, 15 or 16 ladies, 10 or 12 men: François had hoped the food would be more substantial. He was vexed with his young brother who declined to share with him the Bath Guidebook he'd bought, but he recorded a disturbing accident to one of the new mail coaches. It happened just outside their door, and caused his comment on the incredible speed of these new coaches: only 15 hours from London to Bath – 117 miles. More than 9 miles an hour on average, and in practice 10 or 12 mph. He unwittingly creates an image of the traffic that year on the Bath road, and of the relentless pressure thereby created for the structural improvement of the main coach roads.

At Emburrow, near Wells, they must have thought of their friend and mentor Arthur Young: they found the local farmers gathered for a ploughing wager. As they exchanged the Mendips for the Quantocks and came to Glastonbury, they reached the point at which Lazowski's letter-book begins – in mid-sentence. Presumably there was at least one earlier volume of these copies of his letters home to the duke, but it appears to be lost. By very good fortune it covers the last part of the tour, right up to their embarkation at Dover: for François gave up his journal at Salisbury, and Alexandre at Windsor.

In Exeter, they are impressed by the public promenade on the site of the castle, within the city walls. Also by the great cathedral organ set up on the screen between nave and choir (they were in Exeter on successive Sundays). Beyond Brent, Alexandre got involved

in a discussion about farming practice with a farm labourer, and at Saltram Lazowski
particularly admired Robert Adam's saloon, despite the pictures by Reynolds and Angelica
Kauffman. But the weather was lovely, they were impatient to get to Plymouth, where
they arrived hot and very tired – especially their horses – late one evening. Almost as soon
as they arrived, there was Jermyn to welcome them. He spent all four days with them and
accompanied them back as far as Exeter.

A WELL-PRESERVED DRUID TEMPLE

1 April 1785   *François, thinking of yesterday's sarsens, exclaimed*: All this is nothing! Next
day, some five miles from Marlborough, we saw the well-preserved remains of a
Druid temple: it is about a mile from the main road, and joined to it by an avenue
of these great stones set down at some distance from one another, but in the same
alignment.[1] The place in which the temple stands is oval and surrounded by a broad
and deep ditch. The oval is perhaps 300 *toises*[2] at its greater diameter, 200 at its
smaller. At the entrance on the side of the avenue I mentioned, two great stones are
placed as though to provide, between them, a gateway. They are 20 feet high, 18 feet
long, and between 5 and 8 feet thick: they stand rather like a high wall.

In the interior, there is a large number of others, some of them as large, others
smaller, placed without obvious order. Most of the houses of a little village are built
within the temple enclosure, which nevertheless survives intact. One knows that the
Druids, careful to hide the mysteries of their barbarous religion,[3] fortified, so to say,
their temples: probably the stones in the interior were lines of circumvallation,
which, with the aid of the ditch, protected them from any insult.

I'll say nothing about a great many small mounds which are to be seen all over
the countryside: they have the air of being burial-places, but no one has given us any
light on this subject.

While we were walking about in the temple, the snow descended on us so thickly
that it completely blotted out the daylight: it fell in great flakes and we had to beat
a swift retreat to the place on the main road where we left our horses: we couldn't
help remarking that it was the 1st of April, and that the day before had been stiflingly
hot.

We waited some time to see if the snow stopped, but seeing that it continued to
fall, we moved on into the little town of Calne, where we stayed.[4]

---

[1]   It is odd that they didn't refer to its name, Avebury, or Abury. Tanner had remarked that
Avebury is 'a monument more considerable in itself than known to the world' (S. Piggott, *op.
cit.*, p. 115). Pevsner, in The Buildings of England, *Wiltshire*, 1963, wrote that 'in scale and
conception it ranks among the foremost works of prehistoric man in Europe'.
[2]   A *toise* seems to have been reckoned at rather over 2 yards: 6.395 feet.
[3]   Their reading of 'the learned people who have written on this subject' had evidently not
embraced the works of the antiquary William Stukeley, who came to believe the Druids were
'of Abraham's religion entirely', and so, respectable as a kind of Old Testament Christians! (S.
Piggott, *op. cit.*, p. 145).
[4]   Lansdowne Arms or White Cross? The former was the grander-built, 13 bays wide, replacing
the Catherine Wheel, and now called the Lansdowne Strand.

Calne, 2 April 1785   On the 2nd, Chaveron had to have a tooth pulled out, on account of a violent inflammation in his cheek, so we stayed on. There was little to satisfy our curiosity in so small a place. Cloth-making kept it alive, but of a very common kind, all brown-coloured! They are sent from Bristol to the Indies. They are made of the local wool; combed, never carded. All kinds of long-haired coarse serge bed-covers are made at Calne.[5]

Among the processes of cloth-making, fulling is one of the most interesting. Usually, the mechanism of the mill is complicated, but here it is quite simple, and so much the better for that. You have to imagine two trip-hammers beating down into the troughs; a wooden shaft, holding two cams opposite each trip-hammer, raises them and lets them fall on to the cloth which is in the trough. The shaft is turned by a water-wheel, and the whole machine costs no more than 20 pounds sterling. The trip-hammers are not equipped with iron cams; the cloths are coarse because there is a need for them.

Alexandre noted that, as they had to spend the day in Calne, we took the opportunity to write up our journal and those letters that were pressing.

Sunday 3 April 1785   *François*: On the 3rd, the tooth drawn and the inflammation gone, we set out for Bristol in the finest weather one could wish for: it was even quite warm, and the snow vanished in an instant. We went through a large place called Chippenham, doing a considerable trade in the same type of cloths as they make in Calne, and these are also sent to the Indies.

The road was extremely hilly, which provided us with several fine views, the land is for the most part dry and the farmers wretched. All the enclosures on these hillsides are made with drystone walls. They sow a great deal of lucerne (sainfoin), calling it 'French grass'. They reckon it grows very well on hills, badly in the valleys, which is why they like it in these parts.

BRISTOL

After London, Bristol is the largest town in England, and the richest: Liverpool disputes this last claim, but the people I've discussed it with acknowledge Bristol's superiority.

The antiquity of the town goes back into the thickest mists of time. The Britons, about 180 years and more BC, gave it its name, which means 'delightful place'.[6] It sits in a very deep valley on two rivers, the Avon and the Froome [*sic*] both navigable. They enter the Severn three miles away, an estuary six miles wide combining the advantages of the open sea with shelter from dangerous winds. To the north of Bristol, several tall hills protect it from the cold winds.

---

5   The bacon business, for which it is now widely known, had already been established some 15 years.
6   In fact, its earliest (11th-century) spellings, *Bricg-stow*, are credibly Anglo-Saxon and mean appropriately enough 'Bridge-place' or perhaps even 'Bridge holy-place'. The Frome is pronounced Froome.

The town is old, the roads narrow, not clean, the houses tight-packed and ill-built; yet, as one walks about, one gets the impression of a highly commercial town and a very rich one. Its situation is so favourable to shipping that it ought to be the first town in England for the number of its ships. However, for some years that trade has fallen a bit: all bemoan the fact, but competition extinguished does not rekindle.

Bristol trades with the whole world: with the north, trade in negroes, the Guinea coast, the West Indies; though little with the Levant. Indeed, where does she not send ships? The number is the only variable, but I can give no details of their trade. Having no formal recommendations to anyone in business here, I've been unable to go into any detail.

Some parts of the town, being more modern, are better built. A new bridge over the Avon is newly and pleasantly done:[7] its stone balustrades and three arches are all of ashlar. The quays are numerous and convenient, facing the warehouses so that unloading is easy. There's a square, called Queen Square, truly square, large and dignified by a bronze equestrian statue.[8]

The Exchange is a superb building, built according to the rules of the most beautiful architecture: the interior is in the form of a square peristyle [an arrangement of columns round an open court] where the merchants gather: it is perhaps 80 feet in each direction: they say it is the most perfect building of this kind in England.[9] Bristol was strongly fortified and withstood several sieges. The castle was formidable, but Cromwell took it in battle and then destroyed it entirely, so that nothing of it remains today.[10]

They reckon the population of Bristol is sixty thousand people.

Although we had no letters we were not entirely without acquaintance: we found a Suffolk friend and went to see him. He is M. Mansley,[11] rector of a small parish near Bury, and he came here to take the waters.

We climbed the hill to the north to go and visit him: the parish where he is staying is called Clifton, and from it one enjoys the most beautiful view. One sees the town in the bottom of its valley, the sides all covered with an immense number of houses.

---

7   The 1769 replacement of the medieval bridge is now much Victorianised.

8   Rysbrack's statue (1732–36) celebrated William III (as Alexandre noted): the noblest equestrian statue in England, it regained its dignity in 1994 when the flood of motor-traffic was diverted. Queen Square was planned in William's reign and named after Queen Anne's visit in 1702.

9   It was built 1740–43 to the design of John Wood the Elder, and Pevsner regarded it as 'his outstanding public building' (*North Somerset and Bristol*, p. 415). Here it now stands beside a pedestrianized Corn Street, and provides offices for the Borough Treasurer. The interior courtyard, much degraded, serves as some kind of market.

10   The mound is now part of Castle Park: two medieval vaults survive in Tower Lane.

11   Alexandre called him M. Marley and M. Morley, and they clearly had difficulty with the word Moseley: Rev. Richard Moseley was rector of Drinkstone 1763–1803: Rev. Maurice Moseley was rector of Tostock 1775–96. Either could have gone to Bristol Hotwells to take the waters, and both are likely to have known the La Rochefoucauld brothers. Rev. Maurice d. at Tostock, aged 49, after 'a very bad Paralittic stroke' (*Oakes Diaries*, I, p. 332). Rev. Richard d.1803 after suffering a stroke while out coursing at Hengrave.

It is a nuisance that the glassworks and pottery and other factories dispense a great deal of smoke, which prevents one from making out clearly what one is looking at.

Our friend took us to the house of someone he knew, an old friend who had long travelled in France and England, and speaks the two languages well. He is intelligent and agreeable, and his house wonderfully well situated. His name is M. Crispin.[12]

The mineral waters are below Clifton Hill and to the west of Bristol: they emerge from an immense rock where the pumps draw them up from a fair depth. The waters have the reputation of being the purest in the world: they are clear, slightly warm, and tasteless, and taken chiefly for chest ailments.[13]

I've heard it said that they have scarcely any effect. I asked the gentleman from Suffolk what he thought, and he assured me that they have the same effect on him as if he had drunk too much, going straight to his head like wine and making him drowsy for some time. The assemblies here are not lively: it isn't really a place for pleasure, since those who come here take the waters from necessity, and nobody finds that diverting.

Goldney House   On Clifton hill there is a house with a very remarkable garden,[14] just opposite the church. It is terraced and from it one enjoys a glimpse of the whole valley and the town. A steam pump supplies the water, so that there is no shortage. Under one of the terraces there is a curious grotto, representing a den of lions: one sees two of them, sculptured life-size, at the far entrance to the den. The grotto itself is more a museum of natural history than simply a grotto; and I'm bound to say I think it is a pity to have sacrificed such a fine collection of shells and coral polyps:

---

12 Alexandre called him M. Crespin and said he had travelled everywhere in France and Italy and was '*rempli d'esprit*'.

13 Addison, Pope, Sheridan and Cowper came at various times to try the waters which – as François reported – were believed to cure tuberculosis, and the other lung troubles. But faith in them, and the fashion for them, faded early in the 19th century. Bottling them helped Bristol's glass industry. Today only the 'Colonnade', a fine crescent-terrace, survives, despite heavy motor-traffic down by the river. From 1620, sensible people, like Dr Tobias Venner, saw the danger of drinking such water except under reliable medical advice (*Via Recta ad Vitam Longam*: it reached a 3rd edn in 1650): L.M. Griffiths, 'The Reputation of the Hotwells, Bristol, as a Health Resort', *British Medical Chirurgical Journal*, 1902. To Mr Moseley, the Frenchmen's Bury friend, it seems to have done no good at all.

14 This is Goldney House, then the home of the long-established merchant family of that name. From the early 18th century the Goldneys were the company bankers of the Darbys of Coalbrookdale. In their house a magnificent mahogany panelled parlour with spectacularly carved overmantel survives from about 1723, within a depressing rebuilding of the 1860s: now part of the university women's hostels. The garden supplies the main attraction, with extensively tunnelled and superbly shell-and-coral-clad grotto. It was probably suggested by the great silk-miller Van Moollon's grotto, now gone, at Zijebalen, near Utrecht, and took from 1727 to 1764 to construct. It has been completely restored in 1985. See P.K. Stembridge, *Goldney, a House and a Family*, Bristol 1969 and Mavis Batey and David Lambert, *The English Garden Tour*, 1990, pp. 195–99. Back in 1756, Mrs Delany was begrudging such a sacrifice of the shells, much as François does in 1785. They are professionally examined by R.G.J. Savage, 'The Natural History of the Goldney Garden Grotto' in the *Journal of the Garden History Society*, Vol. 17, No. 1.

they are plastered on the wall, and the water cascades into the grotto. It makes it cool there in summer.

Three miles away, we came to a place called *the point*.[15] It is a hill rising above the plateau, and from which one sees the Severn, Wales and a great part of Somersetshire; the town of Bristol and the Avon banks are at your feet; nothing equals the beauty of this view, and to report all the details would be a long business and fail to create the picture; I decline the attempt. *Whoever is curious will go there*: I can only affirm that here is one of the most beautiful prospects in Europe.[16]

To reach it, we crossed one of Caesar's camps where they daily find Roman medals and coins.[17] This camp is round, large and surrounded by an even greater ditch: it stands up on the edge of a prodigiously steep rock. One notices a cliff-path they fashioned for getting to the river.[18]

Bristol is in Somersetshire: a part of its suburbs and its waterways are in Gloucestershire.

5 April 1785   On the evening of the 5th we left for Bath, only twelve miles from Bristol.

BATH

Alexandre explained that, on the 5th, they had lunched with M. Morley (i.e. Moseley) and gone on to the bank, as their purses were empty. At Bath they spent Wednesday 6th April sightseeing. Alexandre explained that at Bath they had two acquaintances from Bury. They went to the home of one of them, a Mr Laquet (or ? Lagret: François never referred to him by name, and Alexandre only once) 'whom we had seen in Suffolk: he is very polite (honnête) *to us, said he would be very happy to be of use to us . . . and so* (enfin) *we went with him and we saw the whole town'. Curious that François never so much as mentioned him. On the other hand, he does name their other Suffolk friend, Miss Gage, who was here with her mother (see below). It is equally curious that Alexandre says nothing about her. When they were in Bury, they visited the Gages at Stanningfield, and François thought of them as 'one of the most intimate acquaintances we have'. They were Catholics. Miss Gage's mother was a Fergus, of Montserrat in the West Indies, who evidently had a house in Bath (see* A Frenchman's Year in Suffolk, 1784, *p. 27 and note).*

François: Bath is certainly the pleasantest town in England; even, as some think, in Europe. It is all built in freestone, commonly available here, though what is less common is the general nobility and elegance of all the houses and the number of delightful squares one sees.

---

[15] Alexandre named the spot, which was Kings Weston: the ineffable Mrs Elton 'explored twice to it last summer, most delightfully', in her brother-in-law's new barouche-landau (Jane Austen's *Emma*).

[16] The view over Avonmouth is now grimly industrial.

[17] The camp, occupied by St Blaise's chapel, stands just south-west of Henbury.

[18] The path running south-west down Kings Weston Hill, or a briefer path to the Hen Brook?

The old town is built down in the valley bottom and against the slope of a long hill, exposed to the north. Its streets are narrow and not aligned, its buildings individually don't merit a mention: in this it is poor; but, since it has become fashionable to visit Bath, the old town is full of fine shops and rich merchants. And the town itself has extended higher on the slopes of the hill: there all the houses are new, built, I suppose, in the last twenty years, over a considerable area; the roads well paved, and the pavements made of large flat stones, very good for walking on. For so charming a town it's a nuisance to have to be perpetually climbing and descending: this steady slope is a disadvantage, breaking the uniformity of the street fronts.

Among a large number of superb streets and delightful squares, the Crescent holds first place.[19] It is built on a circular plan, two storeys above the ground floor, and clad in columns and with urns[20] above the stone balustrade around the roof, which is almost flat, in the Italian manner. The architecture is of the Corinthian order. The wide arc on which the crescent is planned is very grand. It contains 27 houses, all large and capacious. One individual[21] has built the whole crescent and has sold most of its houses: a few are only let.

The Crescent looks out over a great gentle grass slope down, over a fair distance, to the bottom of the valley. This slope serves as promenade to all the beautiful women. The morning is the time when they are generally there.

From the Crescent, returning down its approach road you arrive in an enclosed circular space called the Circus. It is complete,[22] with three roads leading into it. The houses have two storeys above the ground floor, very stately. A singular feature is the combination of the orders of architecture in this design: against the rules, yet producing a very pleasing effect. The first storey is in the Ionic order, the second in the Corinthian and the third, with the cornice, in the Composite order.[23] All is supported on coupled columns, small, but light and very elegant.

Descending from here, one arrives in Queen Square, a proper square, built along all four sides.[24] Its architecture is noble, grander than that of the Circus. In the middle

[19] He is describing the Royal Crescent, 1767–74, designed by John Wood the Younger. (Lansdown and Cavendish Crescents were added after the Rochefoucauld visit.)

[20] Urns now gone. Were they perhaps acorns, as in the circus?

[21] John Wood.

[22] Built 1754–58, and reckoned 'the most monumental' of the elder Wood's works, especially when you remember that the centre was stone-paved: the great plane-trees were the romantic contribution of the early 19th century. In 1740, John Wood the Elder and Younger worked three days surveying Stonehenge, and published it, with incomparable plans, in 1747. They believed it 'the remains of a Druid temple' and it may have been in the back of the Elder John's mind as he planned the Circus (S. Piggott, *Ancient Britons and the Antiquarian Imagination*, 1989, p. 146. Christopher Chippindale, *Stonehenge Complete*, 1983, who gives illustrations, pp. 92–3, figs 63 and 64).

[23] François has confused the orders – perhaps through making too hurried notes, or none. The first is Tuscan (with antelope frieze), the second Ionic and the third Corinthian.

[24] 1729–36, illustrating, according to Pevsner, the style and mind of the Elder John Wood 'at his best', treating a whole side of a square 'as a palatial composition'. (The middle of Wood's west side was unluckily altered in 1830.) Pevsner judged that the sequence Queen Square – Circus – Royal Crescent was the ideal urban illustration of Uvedale Price's principles: 'that deposition of objects which partial and uncertain concealment excites and nourishes curiosity . . .'.

is a square lawn with a triangular stone pyramid at its centre, erected on the occasion of the accession of the present king,[25] who took the waters at Bath while still Prince of Wales.

There's no shortage of ballrooms: there are two, the old and the new. They are in two different buildings: the old assembly rooms include a ballroom of considerable grandeur, furnished magnificently; a cardroom, also very large; and a tea-room. I can't record the dimensions of these rooms because I didn't make a positive note of them. My brother bought the book that gives a precise description of them and of everything in Bath.[26] I didn't buy it, thinking that he would lend it to me; and I can't forbear to say that, not being in the nicest humour in the world, he declines to let me have the use of it. Perhaps it's wrong of me to say this: it will pass, with a lot of other things.

So I shall not report the precise dimensions of the rooms.[27] In any case, that sort of exactitude is scarcely in the plan I've adopted for these journals: I am content to give an idea of the assembly rooms, very spacious, very convenient, where the rank and fashion of England comes together for part of the year.

The new rooms[28] are a model of magnificence, elegance and taste: all are very much larger than the old ones, and in addition there is an octagonal room[29] where the ladies assemble for a time before going into the ballroom, either to warm themselves or to get together so as to enter in company. I think the ballroom must be 118 feet long by 40 feet wide.[30] The orchestra is in the middle on a kind of dais. The window-shutters are made so that, when they are shut, they give exactly the illusion that they are pictures representing figures from the mosaics of Raphael.[31] The room is lit by a large number of crystal chandeliers, each with as many as forty candles: there is even one with forty-eight. The keeper of the assembly-rooms assured

---

[25] In fact erected in 1738 by Beau Nash in honour of George III's father. The inscription reads: 'In memory of honours conferr'd / And in gratitude for benefits bestow'd / In this city by His Royal Highness, Frederick Prince of Wales / And his royal consort'. 'Poor Fred' died in 1751: his son succeeded as George III in 1760.

[26] The famous *Bath Guide* of 1772 proudly gives every detail.

[27] Needless to say, Alexandre does just that: *'salle où on joue aux cartes, 60 pieds de long'*, etc.: he was at that rather boring age. He also grangerized his notebook by pasting in J. Collyer's engravings of the front of the new Guildhall and the Royal Crescent: they fitted neatly into his notebooks' page-size, 7 inches wide by 4 inches tall, and are remarkably handsome. (Pl. 36)

[28] Known as the Upper Rooms, standing just east behind the Circus, and designed by the Younger Wood, 1769. The original furniture was sold in 1920. A restoration was completed in 1938, but German incendiary bombs gutted the rooms in 1942. The rooms were successfully restored again under Sir Albert Richardson after 1956. A new redecoration has been completed in 1991 for the National Trust.

[29] The chief use of the Octagon was as card room. A 'Card Room' was added in 1777; now equipped as bar and refreshment room.

[30] François has already forgotten that his 'plan' was supposed to be *not* to give these dimensions. The 1772 *Guide* gave them as 106 feet 6 inches by 43 feet 6 inches.

[31] The idea was for the shuttered windows on the outside wall to echo the figures in their niches on the inside wall of the building. These *trompe l'oeil* sliding canvas blinds, painted by Edmund Garvey, were destroyed in 1942.

me that nothing so grand of this kind was to be seen in England. They haven't forgotten to add two billiard-rooms.[32]

Very strict agreed rules of behaviour are maintained in the public assemblies of Bath. A master of ceremonies, chosen by the majority of those who come for the waters, is at the head of each of the rooms, by which I mean the old and the new assembly rooms. It is always a gentleman who has served in the army: he is the despot, the absolute master, during the balls. He places the wives and daughters of the lords on the benches at the top of the room; then those of the baronets, gentlemen and merchants. He decides what time the assembly shall begin, and at 11 o'clock brings the dancing to an end, even if a particular dance has barely begun, because it is felt that the fundamental reason for coming to Bath is to take the waters and to take care of one's health.

The Master of Ceremonies decides the way the ladies are to dress, have their hair dressed, if they are to wear robes, come in hats or bonnets, which is a frequent cause of quarrels; for, if a lady arrives with a hat when she shouldn't have one, whether from ignorance or contempt for the Master of Ceremonies' edict, it is customary for him to send them away to change, which has not always pleased several husbands and fathers. However, his authority is to be respected, for in this way the general good and peace prevail at the expense of a little individual annoyance. At the beginning of the ball, it is the Master of Ceremonies who organizes the minuets and chooses the dancers for them, taking careful account of their social rank, which is generally observed in England in all public assemblies.

In return for going to so much trouble, the proceeds from two balls each go to the Master of Ceremonies. Everyone pays five shillings but a great many people give one or two guineas. This job is worth about fifteen hundred pounds sterling a year, but it is hard earned through all the disagreements to which the master is exposed. In view of the arrogance and pride of the English, I even find it very surprising that any gentleman can be found to undertake an office which necessarily places him at everyone's disposal, makes him no friends but assures him enemies and disgruntled people. Everyone thinks he has a right to go first, and if one is placed beneath one's rank, one only hopes that whoever has affronted one did it by mistake.

On arriving at Bath, if you want to take part in the assemblies, you forward your name to the masters of ceremonies. In both the new rooms and the old rooms are several forms printed with the rules devised by the respective masters: these rules are neither more nor less than tomfoolery. They are rules for polite behaviour and prescribe forms that no one can fail to know. One could read them only to laugh at them.

In each assembly room there are two balls a week: one where one has to be entirely *dressed*, the other where one goes informally [*en négligé*],[33] as in all other English

---

[32] A game close to the hearts of the two brothers: during the severe weather early in 1784, 'our greatest pleasure all this time was to play billiards' (*A Frenchman's Year in Suffolk, 1784*, 1988, pp. 98–9). They coincided with the brief existence, in the early 1780s, of a very good billiard-room, run by subscription, in Angel Lane, behind the Angel Inn in Bury: information from Dr Pat Murrell.

[33] Mark Girouard says he thinks this may be what was called the Cotillon Ball at the time.

36. *Bath. New Guildhall engraved by J. Collyer, grangerised copy in Alexandre's notebook.*

37. *Glastonbury Abbey, drawn and signed by T. Gainsborough, perhaps when he was here in 1782.*

towns; and there one dances one dance *à l'anglaise*, another *à la française*.[34] During 'the Season' the balls are very numerous.

I doubt if there is anywhere in the whole country where the assemblies cost so little as at Bath. One subscribes for a whole season of three months (there are two seasons a year), two guineas for the balls at which one is formally dressed, and half a guinea for those at which one is casually dressed: for that sum one is entitled to go to all the balls. On top of that, each time one goes, one pays at the door six shillings for the tea, coffee and cream. If one doesn't want a season's subscription, one pays two or three shillings a time. A small additional expense is a voluntary contribution which it is usual to put into a hollowed-out book near the door for the benefit of the master of ceremonies: it is part of his stipend.

The only picture in the card-room is the portrait of the old master of ceremonies, not a very interesting bequest for the company.[35]

Bath owes its adornments to several mineral springs, which have become increasingly fashionable and above all in these last ten years: they bring here from all sides rich people who come for diversion. Each year there are two seasons: April to June and October to January. There are scarcely any London families or comfortably-off provincial families who don't feel obliged to spend at least a month every year at Bath.

It's a very long time since the properties of Bath waters were discovered and appreciated. They claim that King Bladud was the first to make this discovery: he is of very ancient date, about 863 years BC. It's he who gave one of the springs the name of Royal Bath, and his statue is preserved in it. However, they were found to be little frequented, for there was no practicable road, even up to the reign of Queen Mary, for she came here for her health and expected to perish on the way: the hills were so steep that on one of them the carriage lost its horses and descended backwards.

There are four springs: *The King's Bath, Queen's Bath, cross bath* and *hot bath*. The first three differ little as to quality and temperature; the fourth is very much warmer. The waters of the first three are warmer than tepid, slightly yellowish in colour; they have, very slightly, a taste of bitumen. The water from the hot bath is so hot that one can hardly drink it straight from the spring: the smell is stronger. If you let the waters cool in a stoppered vase they lose some of their colour and deposit a sediment, which diminishes the taste.

They are all pumped up from no great depth. Below the room where the drinkers assemble every morning is a bath open to the sky, and where one bathes: the bottom is paved with large stones and the sediment from the waters makes it very slippery. The springs replenish the bath all the time and there is an overflow arrangement to

---

34 *à l'anglaise* and *à la française* may have been 'country dances' and 'minuets'.
35 I think he is referring to the Octagon, originally a card-room, and to which 'the Card Room' had to be added in 1777 as cards were so much the rage. He is not very discerning about Gainsborough's portrait, itself wonderfully discerning, of Captain William Wade, the first Master of Ceremonies, 1771.

stop the level getting too high. One bathes in a large flannel dressing-gown. Men and women unused to the experience go in on the arm of a guide. You choose the depth of water you want to be in according to the various parts of the bath. There are separate hours for men and women, but spectators can converse all the time from the windows of the pump-room above.

One pays half-a-crown[36] for each bath one takes, and is furnished with everything necessary. The site of the King's Bath is the most beautiful. The four springs are in the old town. All around are lovely shops, richer even than London's. There are several booksellers who lend all kinds of books to take home for as long as one likes for a half-guinea[37] a season.

Around Bath there are some agreeable walks, although the country is very hilly; for on all sides there are nothing but hills scooped out like amphitheatres (mostly dry), woods covering one part of the landscape, the rocks, the fields, the hills and streams make this countryside very picturesque. It is not good country for shooting or coursing.

On all sides and close to the town are the quarries furnishing an abundance of the beautiful stone of which Bath is built. To bring down the stone from the quarries and the hills they have very ingenious machines; they are a sort of tumbrel, and they slide over pieces of wood purposely laid parallel. A single horse can bring down an enormous weight, and so that the load doesn't go too fast it is followed by a man with the means to apply a brake when necessary.

As Bath attracts three-quarters of the men and women of fortune in England, so a great many marriages take place there every year: many young men and young women come here with this idea,[38] and it is generally held that a girl who has been for two or three seasons to Bath without having found a husband will remain unmarried all her life; at least that the odds are against her ever marrying.

It is one of the dearest places in the kingdom: everything here is the same price as in London, and there is the same luxury as in the capital.

We found here a friend from Suffolk, Miss Gage whom we often visited in the Bury neighbourhood. She was at her mother's home: they asked us home to spend the evening with them.[39] It is the same life that I've been told is lived in London: with numerous assemblies. We had to be a small party, and our dress was excused as we were travelling. There were fifteen or sixteen ladies and ten or twelve men. We were together from 6 o'clock until eleven: we had tea, coffee, punch, biscuits etc., but no supper: that really took me in: I was hoping to eat rather more substantially. I didn't notice much luxury in their furnishings.

While we were at Bath there was an unhappy accident that is apparently not uncommon, but which gives one the chance to mention this new postal arrangement.

---

36 Two shillings and sixpence, now 12½ pence.
37 Ten shillings and sixpence, now 52½ pence.
38 As the egregious Mrs Elton put it, in Jane Austen's *Emma* thirty years later: 'The advantages of Bath to the young are pretty generally understood.'
39 See p. 151 above. It isn't entirely clear whether they spent the evening at home with Miss Gage and her mother or, possibly, went on to the Assembly.

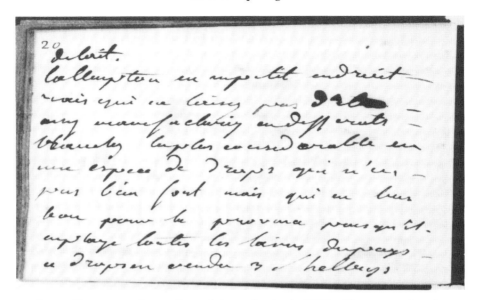

38/39. *Two pages from Alexandre's pocket-book XVII. His manuscript, from 'Cullompton' to '3 shillings', is translated at the foot of p. 162, towards which these two plates could be moved only by disorganizing the whole neighbouring text.*

One of these carriages was overturned at our door, the driver thrown from his seat and a horse badly hurt. This type of carriage is for the letter-post: it takes four passengers, accommodated in a kind of Berlin, very tall and harnessed to two horses. These carriages travel at an incredible speed: they take only 16½ hours to travel from London to Bristol, which is 117 miles; and fifteen hours from London to Bath, 107 miles. This is more than 9 miles an hour and as they are obliged to stop for some time in all the towns they go through, the overall average speed is 10 or 12 mph. They often turn over and very often the horses have to be killed.[40]

Three things François omitted but Alexandre mentioned in passing: 'une très belle infirmerie, la cathédrale' [the abbey] and a riding academy.

[40] These were the new mail coaches adopted by Pitt the previous year from John Palmer's proposals. The speed of letter-delivery from Bath to London was instantly cut from 40 hours to 15. The coaches were exempt from turnpike tolls, and carried an armed guard to some purpose: apparently no mail coach was robbed between 1784 and 1792, and highwaymen found themselves redundant. François' first-hand evidence of a driver thrown and a horse badly hurt is interesting, for it is sometimes said that no serious increase in accidents followed the greatly increased speed. A rapid improvement in the structure of the main roads became imperative.

38/39.   *Two pages from Alexandre's pocket-book XVII. This interleaved page of blotting-paper reveals an artistic talent in some ways almost modern.*

A PLOUGHING WAGER

7 April 1785   From Bath we went, on 7 April, to Wells over hills and valleys. We lunched at an inn[41] in the middle of fields where a great farmers' dinner was taking place, occasioned by a bet: a farmer had wagered that it was impossible for one man alone, with two horses, to plough two acres with a simple plough (one with a single ploughshare) in less than eight hours – or less than six hours with a plough with two shares. The man who had won the bet had ploughed the acres in 5 hours 30 minutes with the single share, and in 3 hours and 50 minutes[42] with the double. Their soil isn't heavy. You can see how well agriculture prospers in this part of the country: the hills are cultivated to their very crowns: the valleys are all in fine meadows, covered with cattle.

The weather is excessively hot and the sun shines as if it were the end of May. Wells is a very small town, to be recommended only for its church, the remains of an abbey destroyed by Henry VIII: it is grand and beautiful. The portico is a work of immensely detailed architecture: the stone is carved intricately, like paper. It is a superb Gothic work.[43]

---

41   The Old Down Inn: see *Paterson's Roads*, 1826, p. 102. 12 miles from Bath, 6½ miles from Wells, near Emburrow. Established in 1640, it still serves as a small inn at a crossroads.

42   Alexandre gives different times: the differences are immaterial.

43   The great church at Wells was always a cathedral, the seat of a bishop, never that of an

GLASTONBURY

8 April 1785   On the 8th, continuing on our way in fine weather, we went first to Glastonbury, passing a chain of hills higher than the others in these parts.[44] There was a very rich abbey in Glastonbury.[45] Henry VIII destroyed it and appropriated its possessions. With his usual clemency, this prince had the abbot hanged, his head stuck up on the gate of his abbey. Several monks received the same treatment,[46] the rest were driven out. The ill-preserved remains of the monastic buildings still show what a considerable abbey it was: there are several arches, and together with foundations represent the vestiges of a superb church: the ground it occupied is immense (Pl. 37). Every day, they find in the orchards that occupy the site the heads, bones, and so on, of monks; and sometimes coins. The belief round here is that they buried large sums immediately beneath the convent. On a plateau formed by two of the tallest of the hills I mentioned, a kind of earth mound has been constructed in the form of a sugar-loaf, of considerable size and height, and on top of which are the remains of a tower. The mound is man-made, and serves as a beacon for shipping.[47]

Here, mid-sentence, on a soiled, crumpled first page, Lazowski's letter-book starts – copies of the letters he sent home to the boys' father (BL, Add. MSS, 42095). Among his first observations were six oxen and one horse having a hard time working one plough in the grey clay at the foot of Glastonbury Tor. A local began to tell him the familiar story of Joseph of Arimathea's visit to Glastonbury, and of the growth of the thorn where his stick touched the ground. Lazowski couldn't comment 'as I didn't have the patience to listen to the end'.

abbot. Church history was *not* one of the La Rochefoucauld boys' interests, but the joint diocese of Wells with Bath (which *was* originally monastic) is confusing. We tend to think of the whole west front as an entity: it is certainly so in architectural conception. François saw the centrepiece, beneath its great gable, as the 'portico': correctly, for it does mark the main western entrance. (In the Middle Ages the whole front was gaudily painted and looked like an Italian church in coloured marbles: *Country Life*, 6 December 1990.)

[44]   The Mendips do rise to just above 1,000 feet above sea-level.

[45]   It is generally reckoned to have been the richest abbey in the kingdom, and one of the most beautiful. Even Henry VIII's odious officials described it as 'the goodliest house of the sort we ever saw'.

[46]   No: they were just driven out. The abbot had failed to hand over a gold chalice to the King's commissioners, and so was dealt with as a thief.

[47]   This is Glastonbury Tor. Abbot Whiting, the last abbot, was dragged on a hurdle up to the very top of it and hanged there for all the country people to see. From the north-east, the tor appears as a dramatically conical natural hill (518 feet): it tails back 1,000 feet to the south-west, a strange whale-back ridge impressively moulded in a series of terraces. One sees why the Frenchmen were so sure these were man-made. The geologists assert that they are merely the result of differential erosion of strata of differing hardness. Archaeologists have wondered whether they were made for defence, or for agriculture – even for a gigantic and very ancient 3-dimensional maze for pre-Christian functions. These questions remain unresolved: P. Rahtz, *Archaeological Journal*, CXXVII, 1970, pp. 6–7, and Nick Mann, *Glastonbury Tor*, 1986. The great tower of a medieval chapel of St Michael still stands strikingly aloft on the summit.

François continues: In the past, according to unquestionable evidence, the sea came up round the foot of these hills in the levels that are cultivated now. It withdrew and is now more than 4 miles away.[48] One can see it from the top of the mound, where the valley at ones feet shows authentic signs of having been an inlet of the sea.

There is a silk mill at Glastonbury but it is worked by hand: it could stand up to the competition of silk spun by big machines only because manual labour is so cheap.

Returning to our horses, we went on – in very hot weather – as far as Bridgewater. This little town is quite convenient for trade, for a deep navigable river carries stout vessels to the sea: there are six, and we rode past them.[49]

FARMING AT THE FOOT OF THE QUANTOCKS

Bridgewater isn't on the most direct road from Bath to Plymouth. We deviated by about ten miles in order to come this way. Our object was to find out what we could of the agriculture of the district, which is generally admired and above all in connection with the fattening of beef. Beef from the neighbourhood of this town ranks in the London markets as the best.

The farms between Bridgewater and Taunton are mostly large, their houses are built up on the hills, and all one sees down below are the barns. A farm amounts to 700 or 800 acres, with a rent of 30 to 40 shillings. All the land in the lower levels is for grazing, and nothing else. The arable is on the slopes. The rotation is: 1. Wheat 2. Turnips 3. Barley, or oats sown with clover 4. Clover on its own. Before sowing the wheat, they manure the land and spread lime over it. The turnips serve solely as fodder for the sheep, of which the numbers equal the number of acres of the farm: they look pretty well.

The ploughlands run down to the pastures and provide the fodder for a great many cows and bullocks. There are several small farmers who live off the butter and cheese their cows produce. There are few horses, for the land is ploughed by a pair of oxen, which are sturdy and not too fat: they have short legs and flat backs (see our visit to Mr Bakewell early in our Tour); and they work for from three up to five years, spend a year recovering in the meadows, and being fattened: that continues for another year. They are fattened up with hay alone – just ordinary hay: they find that clover, lucerne, and artificial meadows aren't as good, though they're better for horses.

---

48   Like the fens of East Anglia, these Somerset levels were swamps and lagoons, the marshland abbeys taking a lead in draining them in the Middle Ages. The sugar-loaf tors would, like Ely, have been islands. Remarkable remains of two famous nearby Iron Age lake-villages are shown in the museums of Glastonbury and Taunton. Now the sea has 'withdrawn' a distance more like sixteen miles than four.

49   The Parrett estuary leads into Bridgewater Bay and the Bristol Channel. Lazowski wrote: 'It makes the wealth of the little town, importing salt, coal and consumer goods for the district, and exporting its farm products and manufactures'. He, too, refers to their famous beef, also their pottery and brick-kilns. 'Their ovens and driers are built under a brick pyramid of the kind I think I described to you back at Warrington . . . more economic, more durable, roomier, a bigger air-passage than the ordinary kilns: the bricks are excellent'.

They take particular care to water their meadows, and even to lay on a network of running water, which doubles the crop.

TAUNTON

9 April 1785   We dined at Taunton, a small and very pretty town, though inhabited by very few gentlefolk. But, as it has a considerable trade in woollen stuffs, there are people who are comfortably off. We saw very good shops and a very lively market: we could hardly get across the market-place, and what surprised me was that I saw three horses for sale at between 20 and 30 guineas.

Lazowski mentioned 'different sorts of cloth, ribbons and silk mills', and many children employed. He also gave a detailed account of local brickmaking methods, mixing the local red clay with a finer blue clay and extremely fine sand: he devoted two whole pages to the firing methods resulting in a fine red-brown brick. Reflecting generally on Somersetshire, Lazowski asserted: All the ploughteams were of oxen, with one or two horses harnessed in front to lead the way. The oxen are generally harnessed with a wooden collar and pull from the shoulder – as bad a system as that of harnessing them by their horns. The great objection to ploughing by oxen is their slowness. The barns are always built by a running stream.

He made a rough sketch to show the kind of wooden bar devised to hold the collars, and therefore the horns, of the oxen apart as they ploughed, two by two. François adds: We went to Wellington, and from there on to Cullompton, which made a journey of 34 miles in very hot and very dusty weather.

At Cullompton, Alexandre demonstrates the value of his notes as well as his natural limitations, which included his sketching abilities, as we saw at Ironbridge. He was 17½, remember, and his brother and tutor kept up a fairly relentless pace. About Cullompton, though, François mentioned only the heat and dust. Alexandre found time for a sketch on the blotter (with which his notebook was interleaved), possibly inspired by some suggestive blots (Pl. 39, p. 159). He is perhaps sketching himself or his brother (spurred), and Chaveron (? with pipe), and the two dogs (? pigs). From the 16th century to the 18th, Cullompton was one of the most important little woollen manufacturing towns in Devon, and had a lively market. Alexandre was moved to say: Cullompton is a small place but it doesn't let [go of: two blots lend imprecision to his message] different branches of manufacture: the most considerable is a kind of cloth, not very strong, but good for the district because it makes use of all the wools of the neighbourhood. This cloth sells at 3 shillings. The wool is beautiful and – more often for its beauty – fetches a good price. I think we have told you they make use of some wools from Spain, though I don't know which part.

'We have told you' is a clue that Alexandre, like the others, really was writing his journals with his father in mind.

40. *Exeter Castle, the fashionable promenade. Engraved R.White, 1744.*

SUNDAY AT EXETER

Sunday 10 April 1785   *François continues*: Next day we went to Exeter, the capital of Devonshire, rich and large, built on the side of a hill. The long, broad, main street ends at a modern bridge, carried on three arches over a considerable river coming up inland. There is a large port, and the stoutest merchant vessels can reach it, for it is only three or four miles from the sea.[50] They bring coal, sugar and all goods from foreign parts, exporting the products of this part of Devonshire. Exeter has a big trade in woollens, but knowing no one in the town, I can give no details.

The cathedral is beautiful. Its organ deserves the attention of lovers of church music.[51] The town's site and strong encircling wall have made it very impregnable

---

[50] In fact Topsham, 4 miles downstream, stands at the head of the Exe estuary and is its main port. Since the construction in the 1560s of the Exeter ship canal, merchantmen were able to come up to Exeter, but Topsham remained the main outport. Richard Polwhele recorded that the canal-banks down to Topsham were a favourite summer's evening stroll from Exeter in the 1780s.

[51] Lazowski notes: 'Not only is it the largest we have ever seen, but excellent.' He adds that they were in Exeter on two Sundays, on their way to and from Plymouth. The great case of John Loosemore's organ of 1665, standing up above the choir-screen, still strikes every visitor to Exeter cathedral. At that time, his brother Henry was organist at King's College, Cambridge, which may explain the similarity between these fine instruments. Exeter's organ was largely rebuilt by Henry Willis in 1891: John Norman, *The Organs of Britain*, 1984, p. 168.

in the days before firearms: it has withstood several sieges, and was taken only in Oliver Cromwell's time. The castle is in one of the angles of the wall. It dominated the whole town, but its fortifications have all been destroyed and transformed into a promenade where the fashionable folk of the town assemble. (Pl. 40).

Alexandre was particularly impressed by the view from this promenade: 'before you, a beautiful countryside, hills well covered with woods, villages just above them, and everywhere very fertile'. *He also liked the broad, well-built High Street*, 'full of shops where you can find everything; and the people industrious and polite, the women very pleasing – better looking even than in the rest of England. Very recently, the town has been much augmented. Its situation makes it naturally clean, the air good'.

Lazowski adds that the course of the river had lately been altered through the lower town to increase the current, and that all the factories had been built on the land thereby gained. Alexandre went on: In this county there are a great many gentry and, for many of them, the custom is to drink cider, and to cover their land with lime-phosphate.[52] One can only hope that that's good: one can't be certain.

11 April 1785   *Alexandre says they left Exeter on 11th and dined at Chudleigh, and that the road was very hilly* – good, if we could climb the hills with our horses, which begin to need a rest. *They were flanking Dartmoor. He liked Ashburton, in its valley, selling stockings, mostly linen, and dearer than those of Wells: a good pair fetching not less than 3 shillings. A considerable Saturday market in woollens and horses. They stayed the night at Ashburton.*

12 April 1785   *On the 12th, after going through Brent, the others got ahead: Alexandre fell in with a workman and had a long lesson on local farming practice. His English was so 'singular' that Alexandre was hard put to it to understand a word, but in the end 'we got on pretty well'. They dined at Ivybridge, and after dinner went on towards Plymouth. The road led past Lord Boringdon's house, Saltram, with its remarkable view over Plymouth. Alexandre clearly enjoyed the 43 miles from Exeter: François was having a break from his journal, saving his detailed notes for Plymouth. Only from Lazowski do we learn that they actually called on the Parkers at Saltram. He described the saloon as 'superb and very elegantly furnished, though the pictures are almost all by modern English painters'. They perhaps didn't see the dining-room, equally superb. It and the saloon had been designed in 1768 by Robert Adam (the dining-room originally designed as the library). John Parker, for whom Adam worked, became Lord Boringdon in 1784. He was a lifelong friend of Sir Joshua Reynolds, ten of whose pictures are still in the house, including delightful family portraits. A set of Angelica Kauffman's large history paintings (now in the staircase hall) were originally acquired for the saloon, probably at Reynolds' instance. At that time she certainly would have counted as 'a modern English painter'.*

---

[52] *claire*, which means burnt bones, which is lime phosphate.

We can now turn to the rather slender notes François bestowed on their approach to Plymouth. He was not a great one for the picturesque.

I have nothing particular to note between Exeter and Plymouth. The road is extremely hilly, the farming average: ploughing is everywhere done with oxen, and the soil is a deep red. The irrigation of some small meadows, and some picturesque views, are all there is to beguile the traveller. Few houses, and no farm-houses, stand in the fields. We slept at Ashburton, halfway. The weather continued delicious.

9

Plymouth and Mount Edgcumbe

Jermyn Symonds accompanied them for the whole of their four days in Plymouth, showing them 'as much as possible'. Apart from the pleasures of reunion, it was a terrific advantage for three Frenchmen – on the 'enemy' side till the American War ended two years earlier – to be accompanied all over the Plymouth naval base by a young naval officer, whose father was commanding a 64-gun warship on guard duty here, and ready for action. They dined with the captain ashore at his home, and were dined by his officers aboard the Diadem. *They were quite shocked by the scrupulous cleanliness of everything aboard. Their glasses were filled with 'extreme politeness' and they went 'very merry' ashore.*

As usual, they observed a great deal – battery-emplacements, docks, Royal Marines Barracks, relative depth and treacherousness of channels. They weren't allowed into the shipyards: the authorities 'pride themselves that in this way they will keep secret matters that we actually know in Versailles as well as they do in London'. And Captain Symonds kindly whetted their appetites by 'steering right past the front of the yards'. He took them over to see Mount Edgcumbe, where they also got a view of the shipyard. One can't help imagining, with some amusement, these three patriots adjusting their borrowed telescopes on to these interesting details. They were spared the knowledge that, nowadays, the Mount Edgcumbe gun platform is manned by captured French guns manufactured in the year II (1793–94), and stamped with the Cap of Liberty.

They parted company with Jermyn at Exeter, but were going to see him again in France. It rained heavily at Honiton, and François said he thought it was the first time the skies were overcast since they left Cambridge – a tribute to their enjoyment. He had clearly forgotten that freezing fog in the Peak District. At Axminster, he was in his own element, watching, not uncritically, the carpet-making. It is curious that he skipped the rope, twine and net-making at Bridport: but Lazowski didn't. Dorchester's antiquities impressed them, especially Lazowski: Maiden Castle, Poundbury Camp and Maumbury Rings. François found the tree-lined walk round the town agreeable: 'rather a French feel, for one sees little of this kind of thing in England'. Then Bryanston and Blandford charmed them: 'the town serves as a kind of eye-catcher or garden ornament' to Mr Portman. Another isolated coaching inn – Woodyates – before Salisbury, Stonehenge and Wilton, and François' final commentary.

PLYMOUTH

François: We arrived at Plymouth Dock very late, for the high and extremely steep hills we were constantly climbing or descending were very troublesome to our horses.

Plymouth and Plymouth Dock[1] are two very different towns two miles apart. Plymouth itself is an old town poorly built and paved, higgledy-piggledy, one of the dirtiest towns I've seen: but it is large and busy.

Dock, taking its name from the royal navy's base, is a very new town, in large part built since the last war, quite big, well laid out but not well built or peopled: it is the home of everyone employed in the building of warships.

What decided us to come to Plymouth and so spend a fortnight longer than we ought to have done in England, was that we wanted to meet Mr Symonds's brother, captain of the *Diadem*, a 74-gun battleship,[2] here on guard duty. We also hoped to find his son Jermyn [François always spells him Germain] whom we had got to know very well in Bury St Edmunds last year.

The moment we arrived, we enquired whether anyone knew our friends and how we might see them. We discovered that the captain lived 8 miles away, and wasn't in town. We had made up our minds to go and see him next day when, almost at once, there *was* Jermyn, who, by good luck, had come to find out if we had arrived. He most kindly never left us the whole time we were at Plymouth, and showed us as much as possible.[3]

Wednesday 13 April 1785   Next day, we saw all over the town and its fortifications, which are simple, and solely to guard against surprise attack.[4] Beside the entrance to the harbour there are three batteries; one of twelve, one of eight, and one of four guns. The last has been installed since the expedition of M. d'Orvilliers;[5] they claim that as it is placed so high up, it can't be destroyed by enemy fire. We saw the high walls surrounding the shipyards of the royal dock, which were established about fourteen years ago and dominate the whole scene. The walls are all over 20 feet high and sometimes over 30; they not only protect the entrance on the landward side, but are continued along the shore out to about 6 fathoms. There is only one gate that's guarded by soldiers. No one is allowed in but the workmen and those in charge

---

1   Dock was begun by William III as royal dockyard and naval base in 1691. In 1824 it was given the name Devonport: Alexandre agreed about Plymouth being filthy, but thought Dock *très joli*

2   Lazowski says '64-gun battleship': one of several minor discrepancies between him and François. Lazowski was right: David Erskine, referring to J.J. Colledge, *Ships of the Royal Navy*, I, p. 162, says *Diadem* was a 64-gun 3rd-rater.

3   Lazowski noted his amiability: 'he is a naturally happy and kind young man, *plein d'honneur*, who, in spite of having been at sea at the age of ten, and remaining at sea eight years, until the Peace, had acquired none of the vices of sailors, nor any of the roughness of that life'.

4   Lazowski told the duc de Liancourt he believed the place 'perfectly shielded from attack'.

5   Admiral d'Orvilliers (1708–91) engaged the English fleet in the indecisive battle off Ushant (Ouessant), 27 July 1778. (The English admirals Keppel and Palliser were court-martialled and acquitted.) The expedition referred to by François was a menacing cruise off Plymouth by the French fleet in August 1779: it withdrew through bad weather, bad provisioning and disease.

of the work; foreigners and even Englishmen with no business there are stopped at the gate.[6] They take all these precautions because these shipyards have several times been on the point of being set on fire: besides, they pride themselves that in this way they will keep secret matters that we actually know in Versailles as well as they do in London. The officers enforcing these orders told us how useless they found them.[7]

We saw the Royal Marine Barracks, newly built,[8] large and well ventilated: the barrack-rooms are large and clean, with one window on one side and two on the other so that the air crosses the room, dispersing any smells. The soldiers sleep fourteen in a room, two to a bed. The beds are large and remarkably good for servicemen's beds. They aren't allowed to do their laundry in their rooms: they do that below, in little outhouses for the purpose. Each barrack-room has the wife of one of the soldiers to keep it in order, clean it, and look after their clothes, etc. They have a complete new outfit every year, but I find that they are not so well equipped as our soldiers.

The officers lodge in two wings, with large or small apartments according to their rank. Captains have two rooms, with more rooms above for the servants of those who have any. They have the right to choose from their companies a soldier-servant, for whose pay they are not responsible. All officers have the same right; discipline is not severe; they do as they please except for half-an-hour's drill in the yard. They are not obliged to answer the summons to the cook-house: if a soldier doesn't come to the mess, the others eat his share. It is understood that he is elsewhere. They are supposed to attend evening roll-call, but most of them come in later, over the wall. The officers shut their eyes to this offence, which would be punished very severely. A captain told us all these details: he very courteously conducted us everywhere.

Marines have the advantage of being fed on board ship when they are at sea, and when they disembark they receive their pay as though their food was still owed them. They have that in common with the sailors.

From there, we went to see the place where they keep the guns belonging to ships-of-the-line, all those belonging to each ship being grouped together: one of them bears the name of the ship, and they are mounted in splendid order in covered ordnance-parks. At this place [9] we embarked in the captain's barge Captain Symonds sent for our sight-seeing. We went up-river[10] and passed through the middle of the English squadron at anchor here. This stretch of the river, which is above the Royal Naval Dockyard, is a continuation of the harbour, and perfectly sheltered. It is two

6 In 1954, W.G. Hoskins could write: 'Visitors of British nationality may be conducted around, on application at the main (Keyham) gate, at any time during ordinary working hours.' Forty years on, they are not much encouraged.

7 Lazowski's picture is slightly comic: 'I would describe the dockyards to you, but it would be based only on what we could see from our boat in the harbour, and with our spy-glasses from the high ground opposite the yards . . . Although the commandant of the yard was a friend of captain Symonds, he could not allow us in.'

8 Begun the previous year, and much extended in the 19th century: fiercely guarded, 1994, presumably on account of the IRA.

9 This was presumably the Gun-Wharf built by Vanbrugh, 1718–25.

10 This stretch of the Tamar river is called the Hamoaze.

miles wide and extends about four miles upstream; the battleships and frigates are at anchor in three lines; each has dropped two anchors; they are totally unarmed and unready. Passing them, we counted 36 with two gun-decks and seven with three.[11] We also noticed a group of our own ships: the *Caton*, the *Terrible*, the *Bienfaisant*, the *Japon*, the *Glorieux*, the *Vaillant* and several others lie alongside the *Gibraltar*, the huge ship on which they captured the Spanish admiral. They rate our ships extremely highly when they are sail-rigged the English way. According to the English, their construction is better than the English construction. But theirs are faster when ours are sailed by us. Two ships of the same power are not to be compared for nobility of structure; the French vessel wins hands down; it looks more powerful, and those who don't really understand are easily deceived.

We went ashore at Captain Symond's house, where we dined. The rest of the day we spent with him. He has a large family and is happy in its midst. His command not requiring his very assiduous presence, he lives here in this little house.

14 April 1785   Next day he wanted to come with us to Plymouth. We re-embarked and went down-river with the tide. Again we passed through the middle of the squadron and it seemed not to take long. Then we took our bearings. The port of Plymouth lies open to the south-west winds: vessels arriving in the roadstead have to watch out for three rocks which lie only ten feet under the surface at low tide. This entrance is protected from due west by the hill called Mount Edgcumbe, but, to get into the harbour, ships can't pass between this hill and a small island, Drake's Island,[12] that would be the natural channel and the same wind serves, but there is a chain of rocks eighteen feet deep that they call The Bridge. There's a very narrow way through it which is so dangerous to attempt that they cite the example of an armed frigate which crossed The Bridge during a storm: the captain himself was reduced to taking over the wheel.

So ships are obliged to reconnoitre the bottom of the bay, to double past Drake's Island, then, backing to the west, enter a channel for no more than a quarter of a mile; then they head upstream and reach harbour. But the great inconvenience of such a channel is that, to enter easily, you need either two different winds, or one from due east. If the east wind doesn't prevail, ships have to wait alongside Drake's Island for a favourable wind, sometimes for a very long time. It's true that, once past Drake's Island, ships enter a vast river: there's good anchorage some three miles wide from the port as far as the place where the beer is brewed for provisioning the fleets, and some four or five miles in length from the narrow entrance to the bottom where the river divides in two. This is where the warships are at present. Part of the shore is edged with rocks, but in the water they aren't dangerous, being too deep down to do any mischief. In all this river there are 26 feet of water at low tide.

---

11 Lazowski made it 35 and six: compared with François, his description of Plymouth is disappointing, curiously unanimated.

12 Drake's Island they called 'Gray Island': they must have mis-heard or mis-remembered. I have corrected.

We went to the hospital. It is on a peninsula between Plymouth and Plymouth Dock [Devonport], near the Royal Marine Barracks, and is solely for the soldiers and sailors. After they've been admitted some time, their pay is withheld. They can be brought by water from ship to hospital. The negroes, a small number of whom are serving on the vessels, are treated like the whites: the hospital is in the best possible order, and there is running water on all sides. The sailors' wives are allowed only short and infrequent visits.

From the hospital, Captain Symonds very kindly took us to see Mount Edgcumbe, which is on the other side of the channel. It belongs to Lord Edgcumbe, an admiral of no great note.[13] There is nothing special about the lay-out of the place. Nature did all of it, art nothing.[14] As this mount stands above the port and is a good height, on one side you get the most beautiful view possible of the two Plymouths, the shipyard, the river, and the warships at anchor, a great many houses all round and tall hills and rocky escarpments producing a very picturesque effect; then, turning from the east to the south, one sees only the main ocean, the view that raises the hope of seeing France but cannot satisfy it.[15] There are several beautiful plantations of hot-house varieties, very little damaged by the sea-winds. I saw many tulip trees of great maturity.[16] In

[13] George Edgcumbe, born 1720, served in the Royal Navy under Hawke and Boscawen, succeeded his brother as Lord Edgcumbe 1761, was Commander-in-Chief at Plymouth 1765–71, and was created Viscount Mount-Edgcumbe in 1781, Admiral of the White in 1782, and Earl of Mount-Edgcumbe in 1789. So he was Lord Mount-Edgcumbe at the time of the Rochefoucauld visit, but perhaps Captain Symonds still thought of him as Lord Edgcumbe.

[14] This is a quite natural failure of appreciation. Back in 1750, a visitor had marvelled at the way the side of the hill to the east had been planted right down to the water, 'but also to the south in the face of the very main ocean, where firs, pines, arbutus, laurustinus and cypress thrive exceedingly, and there is a terrace on the side of the hill through this wood'. The first stage had to be evergreen protection for the gardens, and the great thing, always, was the views: in 1778, Lady Harcourt of Nuneham, where the Frenchmen had lately been, heard from her friend Lady Edgcumbe, 'you have no idea what an amazing sight it is, thirty sail of the line now lying under a terrace of shrubs, as if only to ornament our park'. Today it is mostly the white sails of pleasure-craft that decorate the bright blue ocean. The Edgcumbes went on to create a flower garden on the model of the Harcourts at Nuneham (Mavis Batey and David Lambert, *The English Garden Tour*, 1988, pp. 236–41). These young Frenchmen were characteristically more drawn to the details of the naval establishment.

[15] You cross to Mount Edgcumbe Park on a pleasant ferry from Stonehouse Pool near the Royal Marine Barracks. Keeping left through very fine formal gardens including, now, the French Garden, you come up to the Mount Edgcumbe Battery, a gun platform with commanding views east across Plymouth Hoe and the Citadel. The guns were not there at the time of the Frenchmen's visit in 1785. One wonders if Wilkinson had a part in their manufacture? They are captured French guns, cast with initials of the Republic (RF), and with the Cap of Liberty, in the terrible year II, i.e. 1793–4.

[16] Great grandiflora magnolias now stand and flower magnificently, even after the destruction of nearly a thousand trees in the gale of January 1990.

41.   *Plymouth Dock, seen from Mt. Edgcumbe. J.M.W. Turner, engraved W.B. Cooke, 1816, the French Wars over.*

42.   *Dorchester. Maumbury Rings, 1786. Engraved J. Newton.*

one part of the park I saw seven different conservatories. The house is very old, crenellated and flanked by four round towers.[17]

As I said, we were not allowed in the shipyards, and everyone not involved in construction was kept out; which is why Captain Symonds, understanding our natural curiosity, steered us on our return trip right past the front of the yards.

We saw four basins,[18] two single basins and one double at high tide: as the tide begins to fall the dock-gates are shut and more water can be pumped in. The workmen work in the dry as long as necessary, then they give way to the water at high tide. We saw three basins in which two new ships were being built. These basins were without gates, the slipways were high up, and the new ships need to be more or less thrown into the water at their launching, which has great disadvantages. There are several canals for keeping the timber, and the storehouses are arranged in front of the canals so that the ships can come close in to be rigged and equipped. There are enormous storehouses in these shipyards, and a room for the officers. More than eighteen hundred workmen are employed daily: they earn two shillings an hour, on average, and have permission to take away every evening as much wood as they can carry on their shoulders. One can't help thinking that they cut well into the timbers so as to have plenty of scrap.

We went to dine on the *Diadem*, which was in battle order to guard the port, as I noted earlier. Six ships are in similar readiness,[19] whose officers serve three years consecutively. These gentlemen were kind enough to show us over their ship. It is kept in such scrupulous cleanliness that we were astonished: I saw nothing like it on a frigate in Toulon. They blame the uncleanliness of the French, and say it causes more casualties than the English. They wash the entire ship every day. We dined with them on board, and the politeness of these gentlemen was taken to extremes: we drank well and were very merry indeed.[20] We withdrew during the evening and returned to Captain Symonds's house.

---

[17] It was a house of c.1550, on an unusual square plan with a round tower at each corner, all of a pinkish sandstone. In 1749 the four round towers were replaced by more elegant octagonal ones that still looked 'round' to François. In April 1941 the house was hit by incendiary bombs intended for poor Plymouth, and completely gutted. Rebuilt 1958–64, it is now owned by the Cornwall County and Plymouth City Councils, open to the public and very well shown.

[18] A basin is a dock made in a tidal river, normally with flood-gates to keep the water at a constant level.

[19] Here is another minor discrepancy: Lazowski says 'there are nine, of 74 and 64 guns, not including the frigates and cutters that often sail out to prevent smuggling, which, I tell you in passing, has sustained a terrific blow (*un terrible échec*), having much increased since before the last war'.

[20] Lazowski noted two major differences between British naval custom and theirs. The first concerned the lowly position of English midshipmen – 'including the king's son, Prince William [later William IV]: they didn't mess with the officers, they had to climb up to the top-sails and carry orders, like ordinary sailors, under the 1st Mate. Secondly, women lived openly on board for the refreshment of the sailors. Captain Symonds, one of the most respectable family men I know, reckons thirty women a day are needed [among a reduced crew of perhaps 200–300 men doing guard-duties]: the men themselves regulated matters without any trouble . . . But that isn't all: two lieutenants had a woman each in their cabin, who dined with them every day:

15 April 1785   Next day we went ashore at the place where the beer is brewed for the Royal Navy, on the shore opposite the port; then, climbing the hill on foot, we saw the places where they are proposing to build some fortifications against possible enemy landings: this is along Whitesand Bay, in parts where there are no rocks.[21] But we regarded these fortifications as useless because these are unimpressive sites and bordered by rocks: if the wind was strong or the sea rough, one would never dare to land, and anyway one would need a wind from the south-west. The anchorage is good all along this bay.

During our stay in Plymouth we made enquiries about several new English inventions, some for conserving ships and timber, some concerning the nails with which the copper sheathing was fixed – iron nails gnawing into the planking: but as I don't remember the details clearly, I won't say any more.[22]

Chaveron, whom we left behind in Dock [Devonport], went into the shipyards: not knowing that it was expressly forbidden, he went in several times. Nobody said anything to him, and what he told us added nothing to what we saw from our boat as we passed close by the shore.

That is about all that we were told we should see at Plymouth. We were there three days. On the fourth [16 April] we returned by the same road to Exeter. Our friend Jermyn came with us as far as that town.

18 April 1785   On the 18th we left Exeter in rather cloudy weather and reached Honiton for dinner. This part of Devonshire is very fertile and pleasant, more level, more enclosed and well farmed. Soon the rain started, and came down hard. In casting my mind back over the narrative of my entire journey, I don't believe I've once made mention of rain. We had a little on leaving Cambridge, but that was more of a mist; and since that time the skies have never been overcast. This is the first time.[23] Honiton is a very small town.[24] We got to Axminster as fast as possible, to

though not with us, out of consideration. But they made the tea . . . It is a bad example, but must be tolerated as English sailors endure an austere discipline'. Old Admiral Jervis wrote to Nelson in June 1797, the year of the great mutiny: 'I perfectly agree with you: the overflow of Honourables has been the ruin of the service. I never permitted a woman to go to sea in the ship' (H. Nicolas, *Dispatches and Letters of Lord Nelson*, 7 vols, 1846, II, p. 398).

21 Whitesand Bay is the rather bleak stretch of shore west of Rame Head, all now part of the Mount Edgcumbe Country Park, and looking towards Looe and Polperro. A successful enemy landing here might indeed have been a nuisance to Plymouth, but François' observations are sound. Lazowski mentioned Cawsand village and bay, immediately west of Mount Edgcumbe: 'its easy landing made it the general resort of smugglers before the recent legislation'. He rehearses at some length the unwisdom of an enemy landing west of Plymouth.

22 Lazowski noted one new peacetime experiment in preserving men-of-war. A 3-decker was de-masted and covered with a good, but light, roofing from bow to stern, to protect it from rain and sun. It wasn't possible to judge the success of the experiment, but it was expensive, costing £600 sterling.

23 He seems to have forgotten about all that snow and ice! Alexandre says how wet it was at Axminster after being good all the month.

24 The rain distracted them from its pleasant appearance, its weaving and lace-making activities.

spend the night. It stands exactly on the boundary of Devonshire and Dorsetshire.[25]
It is quite famous for the making of carpets that bear its name and are sold all over
the world.

AXMINSTER

This business is in the hands of a single merchant and its increase is very considerable,
for more than 300 persons are employed in it, not counting a great many spinners
spread out into the countryside. The wool they use is coarse and only combed: they
dye it at Axminster. The carpets are made exactly like those of the Savonnerie;[26] the
warp is stretched perpendicularly and double, and the carpets are woven by making
a double knot with the two threads of the woof, and the wool is cut like a velvet with
a little knife, on the round handle of which the knot is formed. These carpets are
thick and solid. The colours are beautiful, but not very varied; the designs rather
commonplace. The carpets are made by women, earning about two shillings a day,
and completing about a foot in height by three in width every day. They are sold at
13 shillings a square yard. The most beautiful fetch as much as 24 shillings: they
make about a hundred of them in a year.[27]

The weather looked much better next day. The sky was a shade black, but it wasn't
raining and to the east there was a hope, however uncertain, of a fine day. Leaving
Axminster,[28] we found we were in hillier country: across the county boundary the
soil is less red and sandier. The hills, prodigiously frequent, grow crops right up to
their crowns and good agriculture seems to be the fashion.

Wanting to enquire about some details of the farming routine, we stopped a
labourer on his way from the fields and asked him several hundred questions.[29]

The farms are extremely large: one of six hundred acres is nothing out of the
ordinary: land lets at between thirty and forty shillings an acre, meadows are farmed
at as much as fifty, and on such a farm the farmer has up to eighteen hundred sheep.
Each sheep yields eight pounds of wool: the wool sells at eight shillings a tod: the
tod is 28 pounds. A herd of cows, twelve or fourteen, returns about five guineas a
year profit. As for horses, eight are enough, for the land is light, requiring only one
ploughing for the sowing of wheat.

[25] Well, a couple of miles on the Devon side of the border.

[26] The ancient French carpet-factory established in 1627 in the Savonnerie (soapworks) de
Chaillot: in 1826 it joined with the Gobelins works in l'avenue des Gobelins (XIII[e]), where a
separate *atelier* de la Savonnerie continues.

[27] The carpet manufacture started here in 1755, but failed in 1835. (The original building
stands north-east of the parish church: the manufacture has been revived since World War II.)
Of the Axminster designs, Lazowski noted that they included 'neither figures nor landscapes'
and in that regard there was 'no comparison' between Axminster and the Savonnerie: but they
plainly did not see the carpet made here 'c.1780' for the state bedroom at Blickling, Norfolk,
nor one made 'during the 1780s' for Harewood House with a powerful circular design reflecting
Rose's ceiling plasterwork: *Temple Newsam Country House Studies, No. 3*, Leeds City Art
Galleries, 1987, colour Pl. 5B and Pl. 73.

[28] Alexander notes the date, the 19th.

[29] There is no exclamation mark in the text. Thomas Hardy would have marvelled!

The valley bottoms grow only grass: from time to time they are enriched by bringing sheep in for one, or several, nights: they are neither artificially watered nor drained. The grass is fine and lush. The arable is on the slopes and tops of hills: the general rotation is:

1. wheat
2. flax
3. turnips
4. barley and clover for four years.

Before sowing wheat, they manure the land, either liming it or bringing in sheep over several nights before clearing last year's clover. Flax is grown generally round here: an acre with a good crop is worth four guineas. The turnips are sheep fodder: without turnips, and all winter, they give them hay. They fatten them on hay, from time to time, and sparingly. I don't remember how much hay they reckon to harvest from an acre, but prodigious quantities, their soil is so good. The labourers' wages are not dear: no more than a shilling.

I forgot to say that most of the flax is for local use: they don't ret it, they merely dry it in the sun, and beat it. It is made into linen cloths and great quantities of stockings.

BRIDPORT

Climbing and descending, and keeping near the edge of the sea, we arrived at Bridport,[30] only a little place with one huge street. They have a market twice a week. The sea is only a mile and a half away, with a little harbour where coal is unloaded and the local produce shipped out.[31]

The way the sea encroaches on this coast is surprising: daily it brings down some part of the high cliffs confronting it, and there are notable advances, every year.

DORCHESTER

Wednesday 20 April 1785   On the 20th we came to Dorchester, the capital of Dorsetshire. As we left Bridport, we found a countryside quite different from that of the previous

[30] Alexandre says they dined and slept here. He hadn't enjoyed the nearness of the sea and the sound of the wind.

[31] He gathered all those innumerable agricultural details but surprisingly failed to notice that the breadth of Bridport's main street was for making fish-nets from the local flax, and that there were rope-walks. Bridport's new Town Hall was building that year. Perhaps his mind was turning to home after sixteen months in England. Lazowski didn't fail to notice that 'you couldn't take a step without coming upon a rope-walk or rope-yard. In this trade, the women do the work . . . The hemp comes in from abroad'. Lazowski also describes the timbered structure of the harbour: 'a row of piles revetted with timbers to form a quay all round the basin. The harbour-mouth is simply a timber scaffolding with stones in the bottom: the sea finds less resistance, and destroys less. There is room for vessels of 150 or 200 tons: big enough'. A farm of £600 has a flock of 1,800 sheep: detailed description of the sheep. Flax-growing is the distinctive activity of the area. An admirable booklet by Anthony Sancturay, *Rope, Twine and Net Making*, 1988, describes these historic Bridport activities.

day: it is as profitable, but the land is unenclosed. As a great deal of it is uncultivated, there are many sheep: the wool not notably superior.

Near Dorchester there are several monuments to Roman greatness. There was a camp almost three-quarters of a league in circumference and supported by six entrenchments: in form it is very nearly round.[32] The amphitheatre is nearer the town. It is made entirely of earth: the glacis (sloping banks) are perhaps thirty to fifty feet high. It is oval in shape and the middle has been scooped out.[33] You can still see the remains of a Roman road, several miles of it, paved with great flat stones like those we have on the continent.[34] These stones have been removed in places, and serve as field-walls in nearby fields.

Although the town of Dorchester is near the sea, it has no sea-trade. Serving the needs of a large number of gentry and two hundred soldiers is the main business of the place. There is a tree-lined walk round the town, very agreeable: it has rather a French feel, for one sees little of this kind of thing in England.[35]

[32] From its six entrenchments, it seems clear that he means Maiden Castle. Lazowski described it much more carefully, saying 'There is very little of this kind that is so complete. It stands a clear 3 miles south-west of the town [in fact 1½ miles] and occupies the entire platform of a hill. It is irregular and forms a half-circle, elongated on the side towards the town. But in the middle, to enclose the whole of the platform, it describes a second almost perfect semi-circle, in diameter scarcely two-thirds of the first. Along the parapet of the interior, the camp must be about 2 miles round judging by the time it took me to walk round. There are three circumvallations separated by two very deep ditches. The height of these circumvallations, measured from the bottom of the ditch, must be at least 50 feet. To create such steep slopes it was necessary to stabilize the soil with turf as they raised the walls. There are two entrances, one towards the town, one towards the sea 4 miles away.' Lazowski shows that they also visited *Pomery, or Poundbury, Camp* 'immediately west of the town beside the main road, contained within one earth rampart but so much criss-crossed with trenches and works of Romans, Britons and Saxons, that it was hard to make anything out'.

[33] This is *Maumbury Rings*, just south of the town. The Romans adapted a Neolithic henge by scooping out 12 feet from the interior to form the floor of the area. There was a pen for the wild animals, and possibly boxes for the chief spectators (Pl. 42).

[34] Four main Roman roads converge on Dorchester, *Durnovaria*, from the four cardinal points: Axminster, Ilchester, Badbury Rings and Weymouth. None has exposed Roman paving any more: they are busy roads still and were presumably soon being macadamised and so on. Lazowski noted that, as at Nîmes, the inhabitants had destroyed the roads to make use of the flat stones. He added, 'If we'd been on horseback, or if my companions had been as keen on walking as I am, we would have followed these tracks for about 6 miles.'

[35] Mr R.N.R. Peers, Curator of the Dorset County Museum, kindly informs me that the western part of the Walks (Colliton Walk, West Walk and Bowling Alley Walk) were planted between 1702 and 1712. The South and East Walks date from 1743. Then, by stages, avenues were planted along various approaches to the town – those along the Weymouth Road from 1755 to 1795; along the Bridport Road, by which the French probably arrived, up to 1795. In his Guidebook to Dorset, Michael Pitt-Rivers described elm avenues approaching the town 'to look French', and 'done by Napoleonic prisoners grateful to the kindness of the inhabitants'. It is pleasant that, in 1785, François already thought the Walks had 'rather a French feel'.

BLANDFORD

21 April 1785   Next day we got to Blandford for dinner: a pretty little town with many gentlefolk and beautiful shops. The entrance to the town is especially charming: one sees the house and the park of Henry William . . .,[36] a gentleman of great wealth, who has spent lavishly. Dissatisfied with the convenient, but old, house he had, he demolished it, and has built in the course of the past year an entirely new one, very beautiful but not all that large. Through his park a superb river flows, its course re-shaped to his fancy.[37] The town serves him as a kind of eye-catcher, or garden-ornament.

A gardener told us that in this valley the meadows are let out at between 3 and 3½ pounds sterling an acre: on the high ground the soil is poor, and in all this part of Dorsetshire doesn't let at more than ten or twelve shillings an acre. The fields are not generally enclosed: some are, but only a few: fifty or sixty acres made into only one field. We passed an immense amount of land lying waste that, I believe, could quite well be cultivated. We thought that many battles had been seen on these plains, perhaps very long ago: there is a great number of small earthen mounds, places where the dead were buried. We also saw, across an extremely ancient earthwork, entrenchments certainly made to some plan, but we came to no conclusion about them.

Woodyates   We slept at Woodyates, a place that now consists solely of a coaching inn.[38]

I must no longer omit to say how much all the country people long for rain. I've already remarked that during our whole journey we've had rain on only two brief occasions, and it has always been very warm: since 2 April the warmth has sometimes been excessive.[39] despite that, the vegetation is scarcely beginning to move: you can see hardly a sign of the small green buds on the branches, and the grass is rather grey than green; the corn comes through very slowly and nature hasn't yet put on spring clothes.

36 Neither he nor Alexandre could recall the name of Henry William Portman, of Bryanston Park, grandfather of the 1st Viscount Portman. Luckily the two Christian names fix which house and park they specially liked: there's much to admire in and about Blandford.

37 Michael Pitt-Rivers, noting the rebuilding of the house in 1890 (Norman Shaw) and its translation into a well-known school in 1927, writes of its debts to the Portman family 'for the woodlands and landscape gardening of this ordinary chalk ridge, and for straightening, widening and deepening the Stour to make a magnificent prospect now suitable for rowing eights' (*Dorset: A Shell Guide*, 1966).

38 Even that has now gone. Unlike that other solitary coaching inn, Chapel House, Woodyates elicits no comments from the French travellers. In 1782, Byng found 'the bedrooms miserable and the beds shocking': *Torrington Diaries*, I, p. 105. Michael Pitt-Rivers says it was once owned by Robert Browning, a great-grandfather of the poet. He also notes Woodyates as 'the centre of a maze of pre-historic sites': Long Barrow, Grim's Ditch, Bokerley Dyke, etc. It isn't surprising the Frenchmen were so bemused: archaeologists are still 'coming to no conclusion' on much of what they saw – the great Dorset cursus, for instance.

39 It says something for this recent spell of nice weather that it seems totally to have effaced the memory of the frigid conditions in which they began.

22 April 1785   From Woodyates[40] our road as far as Salisbury was one of the most boring we ever travelled: the whole road was through country that was not being cultivated, and not even cleared, where we saw only the remains of two ancient camps; very few trees and no houses. However, I ought to mention a little valley, extremely narrow, that we crossed.[41] It was quite well populated, and the fields, carefully irrigated, are very green. The higher slopes on both sides of the valley are farmed but not enclosed and the soil looks pretty poor.

[40] They left Woodyates on 22 April and drove 10 miles into Salisbury, presumably arriving early: that same day, they seem to have seen the cathedral, the cutlery and the cloth works, and Old Sarum, three miles out of town.

[41] Coombe Bissett has an old packhorse bridge as well as a Georgian one.

10

Salisbury, Stonehenge and Wilton; Windsor

Salisbury made a very good impression: clear water running in brick channels through the streets, fine textiles, and grand cutlers 'to their Majesties': Alexandre longed for a superb knife but the price, 4 guineas, frightened him. The cathedral commanded all their admiration. François thought it 'One of the most beautiful churches I've seen in my life: what distinguishes it is its extreme lightness of construction'. They went to visit Salisbury's original site up at Old Sarum. There, Lazowski can't resist philosophizing and inviting cuts: 'ideas more than reality are the chief principle of our pleasure and pain'. He was trying to explain to the Duke why we enjoy ruins. The French soon had increased opportunity for such enjoyment.

The three of them hired horses and rode to Stonehenge, 'perhaps the best preserved Druid temple in the whole world'. François set down with care the arrangement of the mysterious stones. Then he stopped. His journals have been the lifeblood of the narrative of this tour. Probably that day's round trip – Salisbury, Stonehenge, Wilton, Salisbury – was too richly indigestible. Any sightseer, guide, travel-writer can sympathize. It's wonderful that he kept going so far, that his journals survived the Revolution, and that Lazowski can provide a continuation, however different the tone.

The Wilton marbles, a striking collection – 'all the great men of the republic and the empire' – they thought the richest outside Italy, and 'so vast that it spread all over the house and even in the main courtyards' – probably looked better then, grouped in the grand apartments, than they do spaced out along an alien cloister. In the garden, Lazowski saw his first cedars of Lebanon, and made a puzzling remark about their being grafted. He wished they could have gone on to see Clarendon House (he was knowledgeable about the rare whereabouts of English baroque houses), and to have had time to see the prodigious grass-crops at Orcheston.

They dutifully headed for London. At Whitchurch, two boarding schools they noticed, one with an attractive garden. Then, making their midday break at Hook for dinner, they were persuaded by the elegance and hospitality of the inn to break off and spend the rest of the day in that neighbourhood. It was everything that Lazowski admired, and he described it lyrically: houses sit in well-kept parks and gardens, the little Whitewater river decoratively diverted to provide water-gardens and a mill-stream for the freshly-painted and proudly maintained paper-mill – 'one of the gayest of landscapes, one of the most varied, that I've seen in all my life'.

Neither Alexandre nor Lazowski gives any details of the trip from Hook to Windsor: Alexandre mentioned a heath – presumably Bagshot – not the gayest of landscapes; a few

179

of Lazowski's pages are lost. Alexandre's brief account of Windsor Castle is moving because simple and candid, as usual; and with a touch of boyish patriotism. This is the point where he drops out; immune from criticism by his brother, having kept going longer. His last word on Windsor was: 'But it's the view one remembers, the horsemen, and the avenues of elms since they were established'.

We are left with Lazowski, whose book of letters home to the Duke shows that they could hardly have crammed more into their eight days in London before setting out for Dover.

François: Salisbury is a large town, well built and extremely agreeable: the streets are aligned in grid-pattern,[1] and all have a stream of clear water running in a brick channel.[2] The market-place is very large, its houses look clean and elegant; I saw some superb shops. The town is situated in a valley at the junction of two rivers, the Avon and the Wylye,[3] both considerable: three miles from the town they receive a third,[4] and become one fine river.

There is nothing to see in Salisbury but the cathedral, which is one of the most beautiful churches I have seen in my life; it was built in the thirteenth century by several bishops who succeeded one another in less than 42 years;[5] its plan is a double cross, it is richly decorated and what distinguishes it from all the others is the extreme lightness of its construction:[6] it is built of no more stone than is needed to support it. The piers are slender to a surprising degree and they divide into many small branches that support the vault on all sides; they give the illusion of being designed for elegance rather than as mainstays. This church is 480 feet long[7] from the west portal to the end of the choir: the nave occupies 235 feet and from the ground to the top of the vault is 84 feet. The nave aisles on either side are spacious, and surmounted by two more arcades,[8] one above the other, to support the nave roof. This is rather flat.[9] The tower is built in the middle of the great crossing: in consequence it stands on only four piers, aligned with the nave and about forty feet apart. The tower is square, 207 feet high, and supports a spire reckoned to be the

---

1   The old built-up area round these streets is still known as the Chequers.
2   See Peter Saunders, *Channels to the Past: the Salisbury Drainage Collection*, Salisbury and South Wiltshire Museum, 1986, pp. 2–4.
3   François may be forgiven for calling this river, from Wilton, le Willy.
4   The Nadder. One of the reasons for moving cathedral and town, lock, stock and barrel from Old Sarum, its ancient defensible site, to its present one in the 1220s was the absence of water there and its abundance at the new site.
5   The foundations were laid in 1220. The main work took sixty years: the contract for the spire was made in 1334.
6   François saw the architect's main aim: the Norman cathedral they abandoned at Old Sarum, a mile away, was presumably relatively ponderous, and here they had a chance to build in the latest light Gothic form on a virgin site.
7   In reality (they liked statistical precision) 473 feet, but a great and striking length, six times greater than the width.
8   Tribune and clerestory.
9   He may have had Notre Dame and Beauvais and Amiens in mind: French cathedral roofs tend not to be flat!

Of Sheffield's steel, François wrote: 'One can admire here the same desire for perfection that the English show in all their work: the steel is finer and better than ours . . .' At Salisbury, Lazowski mentioned 'steel, perfectly polished, mostly made into cutlery', while Alexandre coveted a very elaborate knife as 'an example of the beautiful way they work steel'. Inevitably most of this has vanished, but when the open channels gave way to drains in the 1850s, a collection of finds (basis of the present Salisbury Museum) included a few items of Salisbury steel: Nick Griffiths' scale drawing of a knife and fork is reproduced slightly over half-size.

43. *Salisbury cutlery.*

tallest in England,[10] for the cross which is placed there (I don't know why)[11] is a little over 400 feet from the ground.

What is very astonishing in the construction of this spire is that its walls are as thin as can be and that when they were erected they had nothing to support them:[12] but, after a great storm in 1660 disturbed the balance of the spire, the great architect Wren inspected it and had it braced towards the top with the iron which gave it, they say, as much stability as when it was first built.[13]

The Bishop's Palace stands to one side of the church, its garden surrounded by an old crenellated wall.[14]

Salisbury has two considerable manufactures: steel, perfectly polished, mostly made into cutlery;[15] and a rather fine cloth.[16] They also make a great many serges, flannels, etc. Before England lost her Levant trade, the bulk of the cloth she exported there was made in Salisbury. This branch of the trade has been replaced by the fine cloths they didn't make before.

Three miles from Salisbury is Old Sarum, the old town of Salisbury. It was a hill-town, standing high in the middle of a valley: it is round, and commands the whole countryside. It is fortified by a very deep double ditch. They say it was a Roman station. It was abandoned in the reign of Henry III because they couldn't procure water, and so the inhabitants established themselves down in Salisbury. Old

---

10   At 404 feet, it is the tallest, by nearly 100 feet.

11   Perhaps he meant that, at that height, it was very hard to see. In fact the iron cross had an important function in supporting the truly astonishing internal wooden scaffold, which survives, and one stage of which has been reasonably described as 'one of the most remarkable works of carpentry known' (Cecil A. Hewett, *English Historic Carpentry*, 1980, pp. 144–45: here, and in his Plate V, he gives a most brilliant account of this great structure.)

12   Lazowski, too, commented on the thinness of the freestone supporting this 'immense stone needle'. They hadn't the advantage of Cecil Hewett's analysis of the way the weight of these walls was both self-supporting and steadied by the timber-frame. The walls of the spire are a regular 8 inches thick: the total weight of its Chilmark stone has been reckoned about 4,500 tons. The timber scaffolding weighs a mere 45 tons. But what a breathtaking feat of engineering. In his letter from Salisbury, Lazowski referred to the 'pestilential' custom of establishing family vaults and tombs in churches and he added: 'to have a true idea of the ancient customs in Europe, you must travel in England: you find them at every step . . . I don't think England has an equal in the world for the great importance it assigns to epitaphs, or where funeral monuments are so multiplied, and carved at such expense. When the merest gentleman dies, he is carried at great cost to the tomb of his ancestors. The Reformation has changed nothing, unless it is that the body is never accompanied by priests'.

13   Wren reported in 1668.

14   Alexandre's contribution was to note at once that the cathedral stood in the middle of a beautiful lawn, of which a part served as cemetery. In the town, he also lost his heart to 'a superb knife of fifteen pieces', which I take to be an elaborate pocket-knife. 'The price, 4 louis [presumably he meant the *louis d'or*, which equalled our guinea: see Notes on p. xiv] frightened me or I would have bought it as an example of the beautiful way they work steel.'

15   P. Saunders, *op. cit.*, pp. 7–9; VCH *Wiltshire*, VI, p. 130. In his poem 'A Journey to Exeter', in 1715, John Gay asked Salisbury: 'What sempstress has not proved thy scissors good?'.

16   VCH *Wiltshire*, VI, p. 129: in 1784 a *Directory* refers to the making of flannels, cloths, serges, blanketings, linseys, cottons and yard-wide fancy cloths.

Sarum was in origin a fortress of the Britons but more recently, since the Conquest, a considerable town was built there. One is shown the place where the church stood, and the palace of the British and then the Saxon kings. Several synods and parliaments were held here, and the estates of the realm assembled here to swear allegiance to William I. Near this fortress is a farm, the sole survivor of the ancient town. However, the place keeps the name Old Sarum, and sends two members to Parliament, chosen by the owners of certain lands. Those elected to Parliament would be very much embarrassed to say who it is they represent.[17]

STONEHENGE

Though it is nine miles from Salisbury, we didn't forget to visit the temple of the druids, the best preserved perhaps in the whole world: it is called Stonehenge.[18]

The stones of which this monument of antiquity is built are not factitious.[19] They are of almost the same kind of jasper as those of Marlborough,[20] but much larger. One supposes they have been transported some sixteen miles from a quarry where this same stone is found. The stones are generally 20 to 30 feet high, 12 or 15 feet wide and 4 or 5 feet thick: all are dressed. Several able calculators have reckoned their weight to be 40 tons (80,000 pounds), and they imagine it would take 140 oxen to drag them: one may judge from that what the work cost, bringing them

[17] Lazowski went into greater detail about Old Sarum – beginning with the guess, from the name-ending, that it was a Roman town, that 'the emperor Sevin resided here in the 2nd century, later the Normans, who built their cathedral here'. (He believed the cathedral stood, with the castle, in the inner bailey: very little ruined masonry was visible in 1785, a bit of vaulting beside the entrance, not much else.) Lazowski's response to Old Sarum is interesting mainly for the light it throws on his personality, his tendency to resort to philosophy, a tendency not discernible in his young companions. 'This description of Old Sarum', he says to their father, 'will be of small interest to you, but it isn't the same for the traveller: one likes to be carried back in imagination to a remote period, and although the feelings that these remains give rise to may only be feelings of sadness – as one views the habitations of a Roman emperor – ideas, more than reality, are the chief principle of our pleasures and pains. One is greedy to feed these ideas, and one travels the world to find the remains of antiquity, which often have no other merit than to knock down modern illusions.'

[18] Alexandre explains that, next day, the 23rd, the three of them hired horses and rode 9 miles from Salisbury to see Stonehenge, taking in Wilton on their return to Salisbury; on the 24th they drove to Whitchurch. François' pen dries up after describing Stonehenge. One sees how daunting Wilton is to describe but it is frustrating to have no further word from him on this journey. On their return to Salisbury that evening Alexandre saw 'the hospital, a fine building outside the town, but I learnt nothing of how it was run'. It had been built on the west bank of the Avon, 1767–71, to the design of John Wood of Bath. 'After that we returned home and we wrote. We were very much behind.'

[19] In the 1720s the antiquary William Stukeley complained of the detestable practice of breaking off pieces of stone with great hammers, which 'arose from the silly notion of the stones being factitious', i.e. artificial (Christopher Chippindale, *Stonehenge Complete*, 1983, p. 72). Chippindale's chapter, 'A Delusion of Druids', pp. 82–95, is masterly, saying all that needs to be said.

[20] i.e. an immensely hard sandstone formation over perhaps 70 million years.

44.   *Visitors to Stonehenge, December 1790.*

45.   *Wilton, the Palladian Bridge, with cedar beyond.*

sixteen miles and dressing them as they are. It is a pity the machines have been lost that moved these great masses. The temple stands near the top of a rise. It is enclosed within a circular ditch, very nearly filled in, and about 210 feet in diameter. The monument consists of a triple ring of stones; the first two are of these most massive stones, all placed two by two and almost joined: they support a third, of the same dimensions, and held by a kind of tenon, fitting into a mortice. The tenon is in the form of a nipple.

The most central row of stones is the least massive: they are conical, pointed and the size of a man. It is claimed that there was an altar of black marble, and that with the aid of the book that gives a detailed account of the ceremonies of the Druids, one can place them exactly: as I haven't read it I cannot judge. I can say that I've seen a work so impressive and so ancient, that it inspires a curious degree of respect.

The entire landscape is uncultivated excepting only the valleys. The temple stands in the middle of a wasteland, and around it all one sees are several little mounds, clearly artificial. There are a great many of these mounds, and they seem to be aligned in one direction. They say these are the places where Saxon and British chiefs were buried: those deserving particular honour were encircled by a ditch: *ceux à qui on a voulu faire honneur étaient entouré d'un fossé.*

François' manuscript stopped, abruptly, with those words. His brother continued his briefer notes in the eighteenth of his small 'pocket-sized' diaries. At 17½, he lacked the valuable descriptive abilities of his older brother. Lazowski's letter-book, carefully copied from his letters home to their father, was presented to the British Museum in 1930:[21] *fortunately it covers the last stages, from Glastonbury onwards, of their tour, and we now become largely dependent on it. I began to read it with high hope: I remembered the general rules Lazowski prescribed for his letters home to the duc de Liancourt during their short July tour in Suffolk the previous year: 'I want to take note only of what we in France haven't got – either at all, or in the same forms and the same condition – and which we could introduce at home with advantage; also those things which will really enable you to know a nation justly celebrated both by its power abroad and by the happiness and comfort it enjoys at home'. I also remembered his succinct injunction: 'We need details, not general reflections'. Poor Lazowski seems by nature to have been some kind of political philosopher: he fell naturally under Arthur Young's spell in 'political arithmetic'. I have done what seemed necessary to reduce on the one hand too many unusable details of 'crop rotation' and on the other general reflections on national characteristics, their relationship to the theatre, fine arts, etc. However, the younger brother and the tutor together enable us to complete the tour that François has described so conscientiously so far.*

Alexandre found the long approach to Stonehenge: the saddest view in the world, but at last you arrive and the stones easily make up for the awful countryside. *Lazowski agreed: like Avebury,* the temple is situated in *un lieu triste,* and even today everywhere is uncultivated as far as the eye can see: nothing in the world could be sadder: not a

---

[21] By M. Charles Dollfus, 5 rue Eugène Manuel, Paris 16, according to a letter from the Keeper of the BM Manuscripts to M. Jean Marchand, 23 November 1939.

tree, not a bush; a thin turf on a bed of chalk almost up to the surface; no water; a sad monotony, dry, arid and interrupted only by a number of Barrows, or ancient tombs of earth and turf, apparently arranged in a square, and either single or double, containing one or two skeletons or quantities of bones. One supposes that chiefs were buried in tombs close to the temple, and this is borne out by the ornaments found. They are made entirely of turfs which have been stripped from around them, and which were placed one on top of the other in the form which they still have today, of a bell: it is impossible to doubt this.[22]

Lazowski noticed the cursus, un course de chevaux ou un hippodrome running between two ditches: *Stukeley had found and described it in August 1723. It runs for two miles. Lazowski decided that it must be an ancient trackway leading beyond the provincial boundary. He concluded, of Stonehenge in general, that* whatever they are, these remains are astonishing, and it is impossible to give you any true idea. I am bringing you two engravings, which say infinitely more than twenty pages of description. However, I must give you the dimensions, as the engravings are not provided with any scale. *Lazowski's description of the henge monuments followed, much like François'.*

WILTON

From Stonehenge we went to Wilton, the estate of the earls of Pembroke where you should go if you haven't been to Italy to see a superb collection of antiques – antiques of a very different kind from Stonehenge: here your eyes are exposed to the arts of Greece and Rome.

This collection is the richest in all England, and doubtless in all Europe with the sole exception of Italy.[23] Apart from the busts and statues of anonymous people, here are the busts of all the great men of the republic and the empire, carved in blue or black marble, or in porphyry. The principal room, that I would prefer to call a gallery, is vast,[24] and is furnished with a collection of arms and armour, beginning with the time of the cavalry and right down to the present. Here in this gallery are assembled their most precious pieces, but the collection is so vast that it is spread all over the house and even to the main courtyards. In front of the main entrance someone has placed a column of blue Egyptian granite on which is the beautiful Venus Julius set

---

[22] The term Bell Barrow is still in use. In outline it is more like a broad-brimmed hat, and so distinguished from Disc Barrows, Cone Barrows, Long Barrows, Twin Barrows, etc.

[23] It was largely formed by Thomas, 8th earl of Pembroke (1656–1733) from the Arundel, Mazarin and Giustiniani collections.

[24] A fire in 1647 gave the Pembrokes the chance to have a magnificent suite of state rooms designed by Inigo Jones along the garden front. One of these great rooms, almost a perfect cube, leads into another, nearly a double cube, which must be the vast room Lazowski refers to: these rooms, in sequence, do give the impression of a gallery. The exact measurements, which would have pleased Alexandre, are given by John Heward in his recent article on Wilton in *Architectural History*, Vol. 35, 1992, p. 100.

in the temple of Venus Genetrix in Rome.[25] I can't give you the details of all the statues, busts, reliefs, vases, tables, etc., here in such profusion, nor of the pictures which are so numerous. You know the engraving of *The Pembroke Family*: Van Dyck's lifesize original is in this house.[26]

The building, not in itself beautiful, was begun under Henry VIII. The gardens, without being extremely extensive are extremely pleasing, and if the water is not on the grand scale, which the landscape would not permit, it does have the greatest effect. It is like a river near the house,[27] and it develops into a large lake of water that is always clear because always running. One can go across it almost in front of the house on a covered bridge, of beautiful architecture, the plan taken entirely from the antique.[28] But it is too near the house, and instead of serving as an eye-catcher, it interrupts the most beautiful part of the garden. In this garden I saw some fine cedars of Lebanon. (There are fine ones at Blenheim, but inferior to these). For the rest, all those that I've seen are grafted, like apple trees.[29]

There I saw also for the first time a superb quincunx of silver-firs,[30] very straight and rising to a considerable height. These are the most handsome firs I have yet seen in a garden, outside the *pleasure ground* in the park.

Here you overlook the Salisbury valley, and it is difficult to imagine a soil richer, more smiling and more peopled. I would have liked to spend another day in

---

25   According to John Bold, *Wilton House*, RCHM, 1988, p. 88, the column with the statue of Venus was shown by Knyff to be standing in the east forecourt in the late 17th century, taken down when Wyatt was here, and eventually stood in its present position, east of the house, in front of Westmacott's 3-bay loggia. 'The antique column of Egyptian granite from the temple of Venus Genetrix was bought by Evelyn for the Arundel collection', then bought by the 5th earl of Pembroke. Capital and base were fitted in the late 17th century. 'The Renaissance bronze statue of Venus which surmounts the column was also acquired by Evelyn'. (Caesar claimed to be descended from Venus. He covered the breast of the statue of her in his temple with British pearls.)

26   Alexandre characteristically noted its size: 12 feet high by 18 broad on one wall of the double cube. Alexandre also noted Inigo Jones's famous staircase, 'very large and beautiful and painted in fresco'. (Wyatt replaced it!) It was recently argued that Isaac de Caus was the designer of Wilton, but more recently still Inigo Jones has been re-established as the great British Vitruvius, with Wilton as one of his latest mature works (T. Mowl and B. Earnshaw, 'Inigo Jones Restored', *Country Life*, 30 January 1992).

27   It *is* a river, the Nadder.

28   Alexandre thought it pretty but 'rather Chinese'. It was built in 1737 from designs of the 9th earl and Roger Morris. (Pl. 45)

29   It is now thought that the cedars planted here c.1621 may be the first grown in England. Despite the gale of January 1990, which completely uprooted one 300-year-old, several noble cedars still distinguish the park south and south-east of the house, Lazowski's testimony about grafting is very interesting. It is nowadays thought that only *variegated* cedars are grafted, which these were probably not. Could pruning and/or gale damage have left an impression of grafting? See note on the Chelsea Physic Garden, p. 226 below.

30   *Sapins argentes*: does he mean *Abies nobilis glauca*, or just 'blue conifers'? I am grateful to Thomas Hutton for his advice on this. What caught Alexandre's eye in the garden were 'elm-trees of the greatest beauty'; and, in one part of the garden, 'a very large number of hares'. (A quincunx is a cluster, or group, of five trees.)

Salisbury, to visit Clarendon House, charming and an extraordinary building belonging to the lord of that name.[31] Also to see Orcheston village where the tithe of a particular meadow is farmed out at four pounds sterling an acre.[32] I know of no comparable valuation, but I cannot doubt this. The permanent secretary of the Society of Agriculture of Bath was sent to report on it, and his report was as I said. This means that the produce of that meadow must fetch at least £30 an acre. This enormous yield is due entirely to irrigation. It is the same chalky Wiltshire soil I've already described to you: the valley is muddy and sour: without irrigation it would produce little hay and of a very poor quality.

There followed a renewed reflection on the extreme need to introduce turnips for winter-keep.

In that valley there is no aftermath, as there is in the part of the county we have seen. They have a fair number of cows to put out to pasture after mowing-time. An acre of these meadows lets at three or four pounds sterling, and I doubt if they'd be worth ten shillings without the irrigation. It is a means we often have, and as often neglect, in France as in the majority of English counties.

Yours &c.[33]

23 April 1785   *Alexandre*: Back in Salisbury that same evening from our excursion, I saw the hospital, a fine building, just outside the town.[34] I learnt nothing of its management. In the hotel we got on with our writing. We were well behind with it.

Sunday 24 April 1785   Left Salisbury on the 24th and had our dinner at Andover after 17 miles.[35] It lies in a very agreeable valley: a pretty enough town but unremarkable. We continued to Whitchurch, 7 miles further on, the road pleasant, not very hilly. Three miles before arriving, we saw the park of [he left a blank for the name: the earl of Portsmouth], very large, and you follow the pallisade almost into Whitchurch. The house, which you see away to the left, is new, large and beautifully sited.[36] It is on the English plan of one large unified range not intended to be very tall.

---

31 Thomas Villiers, 5th earl of Clarendon; the male line of Edward Hyde died out with the 4th earl in 1753. Villiers, ambassador to Poland, Vienna and Berlin in the 1740s, died in 1786. Horace Walpole described him as 'a very silly fellow'. David Verey thought the house might, like Heythrop which the French had lately seen, have been designed by that most baroque of English architects, Thomas Archer (c.1668–1743).

32 'Orcheston grass' was famous in Aubrey's day: he reckoned it grew twelve or thirteen feet high. One sees why Lazowski was so disappointed at not seeing it. Nowadays, it lies out in the army-training area of Salisbury Plain, beyond Stonehenge, but St Mary's church and the beautiful flint-and-limestone-and-old-red-brick houses ignore the sound of gunfire, as they bask in their lush, tree-shaded valley.

33 A reminder that this is from a letter-book copy of the original letter to the duc de Liancourt.

34 1767–71, by John Wood of Bath, now much extended.

35 He wrote 'Overton', but from the mileage meant Andover. Overton lies further on beyond Whitchurch.

36 Hurstbourne Park was rebuilt for the earl of Portsmouth by James Wyatt c.1780–85 (and again in 1894 after a fire). Demolished 1965.

Whitchurch is large for a village, but small if you think of it as a town: no great population, but the church, in the middle, struck me as being big and very beautiful. There are two boarding-schools, one for girls and one for boys: the girls' house stands in what seemed to me a very attractive garden.[37]

25 April 1785   We left Whitchurch very early on the 25th, planning to get to Wokingham[38] for the night. After 17 miles we stopped for dinner at Hook.[39] We had left Wiltshire[40] . . . where we found only a great number of antiquities; above all, over the whole land, the earthworks of the Romans, all in different forms. Coming into Hampshire, you find a difference in the landscape more marked than any I've seen since I've been in England: charming, with many towns and villages and country houses.

HOOK AND THE WHITEWATER MILL VALLEY

At Hook, the inn seemed so good that we decided to go no further, but stay here. We hope this evening to gather some information on the agriculture of the district, and so I'm leaving my journal and waiting for the farm-worker whom we've sent to look for. As he never came, I was reduced, to my great disappointment, to learning nothing about this countryside. We set out on the 26th and dined and slept at Windsor.

We begin to depend heavily on Lazowski's letter-book. His next letter was written in Windsor on 28th April. They had arrived there on 26th, after travelling from Whitchurch to Hook on the 25th. He begins: We have had two days of travelling since I last wrote, crossing Hampshire, the favourite residence of William the Conqueror. There he established the New Forest, still so called, expelling the people from it to make way for game. This awful devastation he paid for in the end.[41] It is in the middle of the county, the New Forest, that one finds the kind of little horses they call ponies. Instead of going round by Southampton and Portsmouth, we took the direct route to Windsor, so I can't give you much of an idea of Hampshire. One needs only to think of the 80,000 acres of poor woodland to detest William the Conqueror's barbaric passion for hunting. Nevertheless I'm glad to have had before the eyes of my young people so striking an example of the ease with which dreadful things can be done and the slowness with which they are undone.[42] I'd have liked us also to see Winchester, an ancient seat of William the Conqueror, but, as I've often said, circumstances have shortened our journey cruelly.

---

37 What must have impressed him about the church was its massive spire, rising to 120 feet. I have discovered nothing of these boarding schools.

38 Spelt Oakingham, as was then usual.

39 Alexandre calls it Odiham, but Lazowski says specifically that they were at Hook, which is a hamlet of Odiham, lying on the main road. The attractive inn was presumably the White Hart, its exterior still much as it was in 1785.

40 Indeed they had, 8 miles east of Salisbury.

41 Was he thinking of the arrow that killed the Conqueror's son, William Rufus, in the New Forest?

42 This is the first reference, in what we have of his letter-book, to the edifying of his 'young people', but that they can have had the New Forest actually before their eyes is impossible: it

Anyway from Whitchurch for about 28 miles and as far as the seacoast, according to what we were told, the soil is dry and chalky, and they have done little or nothing to improve it. Their lands, with the aid of large flocks of sheep, are worth about half a guinea an acre . . . Turnips, barley, hay, clover (for 2 or 3 acres): this system's no good.

After that [in north-east Hampshire], the aspect of the countryside changes, small valleys multiply, most of them watered by streams and all forming good fields. The subsoil is often chalk, but you see it only in the (frequent) ditches from which the chalk has been extracted to spread over the soil and make rich pasture.

It would be difficult to form an idea of more beautiful country, all enclosed, sparkling, animated.[43] The farmhouses are in perfect order, numbers of them belonging to individual gentry, with their parks or *lawns*[44] planted with trees and dotted with lakes, the houses placed half-way up a slope or on a plateau (natural or artificial), a truly delicious part of the county.

How I wish I'd learnt to draw: I'd have brought you a drawing of a little valley with a sizeable stream flowing through it, in which various cuts and diversions have been made. These different streams, maintained either at the same level, or made so that the owner can lower or raise the level at will, arrive after irrigating the fields and supplying water to the *lawn* of a pretty house: it reunites to form a large stream on which a paper-mill has been built.[45] This paper-mill itself is built and kept so beautifully; its drying-houses and its fencing are so well painted, indeed the paintwork is so often renewed, that it almost looks as if the mill was built solely to serve as eye-catcher to the house. It stands in a superb setting of trees through which the stream descends, forming a pool behind the mill. This paper-mill adds further to the enchantment by closing the view, shutting out some of the distractions of one of the gayest of landscapes, one of the most varied, that I've seen in all my life.

I can give you no particular details of the farming: we could get none, though we stayed on for that purpose, more or less.

Enchanted by the picture of this countryside, we found an inn [the White Hart at Hook] standing by itself, with a handsome farm nearby: the inn very clean, and the gardens surrounding it strikingly elegant. We went in, and had a good meal. The

---

lies south of Salisbury and west of Southampton, and their route was due north-east from Salisbury. It is just possible that they mistook Harewood Forest, between Andover and Whitchurch, as an outlying fragment of the New Forest, but it lies twenty miles north of the New Forest, and Alexandre made no reference to it. Lazowski's young people would have been well enough aware of his hatred of uncultivated land: indeed, in a modest way, they had come to share it.

43 Lazowski is describing the countryside round Hook.

44 He uses the English word.

45 This is Hook's watermill, a paper-mill on the Whitewater river, making paper from c.1739 to 1826. John Evelyn, 24 August 1678, had written in his wonderfully vivid and vigorous diary an account of the working of a paper-mill near Byfleet, only 20 miles east of Hook: linen rags for white paper, woollen for brown, etc. It's a pity François had abandoned his journal before they came to Hook. One wonders if he ever read Evelyn's journal, first published in 1818. They were near the centre of comparable national dramas. The old mill is now the home of Mr Just Betzer, and office of his film company.

extraordinary elegance, and even more the cheerfulness, of this house and its gardens proved irresistible, and the strong desire to obtain some information about the land-use of the district decided us to stay.

We asked if there was a chance of our having any conversation with a well-informed farmer in the neighbourhood. We were told that, at present, they were extremely involved in the pressing business of sowing, but that someone could be procured that evening or early next morning. Thus we were lured into deciding to spend the rest of the day at Hook. It is the name of this hamlet. We never managed to get our information. The farmers were too busy and we had to be content with what we could see with our own eyes.

No fields are left fallow, but none have been irrigated. Generally speaking, their arable is not so extensive as in other counties. They employ too many horses and their wheeled ploughs assist neither speedy ploughing nor the regular cut of the Norfolk furrows.

But I noticed a farmer using a machine which should prove very useful, and which I must describe to you.

It is made for the final working of the soil, to level and dress it, by breaking down the clods. It operates just as well as the plough for tillage, but has two great advantages: it breaks up the soil better and trebles, at least, the work done on a given area.

It is made like a long harrow, but the wooden upright is made to a much sturdier specification. You will see why the teeth of this harrow are shaped like arrow-tips, 5 or 6 inches to the tip, where they are bent.

This page is smudgy and looks crumpled, as though it was once one of the last pages of an unbound notebook. A gap follows in the text, of one or – more probably – several pages. Lazowski's next page begins mid-sentence, and one finds the party already sight-seeing in

WINDSOR CASTLE

... is nothing worth the attention of strangers beyond a few pictures, and the painted ceilings, and the Dining Room, and the Chapter of the Order, executed by an Italian at the time of Charles I[46] and under his direction.

Alexandre was more appreciative: The castle stands upon an eminence above the whole surrounding country and derived its strength from its position: but it is ugly. The State Apartments are beautiful and grand, and one finds in them lovely paintings. I

---

46 He must, I think, be referring to the ceilings of the Queen's Audience Chamber, the Queen's Presence Chamber and the King's Dining Room, all done by Verrio at the time of Charles II, not Charles I. The reference to the Chapter of the Order must be to the Chapel of the Order [of the Garter], which was painted by Verrio but which Queen Victoria transformed into the extraordinary Albert Memorial Chapel.

46. *Windsor Castle. Henry VIII's Gateway and St George's Chapel, c.1780.
P. Sandby.*

won't describe the interior: it would take too long. The only modern work I saw was the Queen's Chamber, with just one bed very well embroidered. From the terrace one sees marvellous country – trees and fields and – at one's feet – Windsor and Eton, separated only by a superb wooden bridge. The river, fairly large, provides charming views. Near the castle stands a tower in which the State Prisoners were put. M. de [blank] was the last, to our great shame . . .[47] The Queen's House, below the castle, is where the King and Queen live: it is simple, and one isn't shown it. The children's house is nearby. The chapel is a most beautiful building. I can't give its proportions, not having taken them. I will say only that the vault is extremely broad. But it's the view that one remembers, the horsemen and the avenues of elms since they were established.

That, on Wednesday 27 April, was Alexandre's last entry: not so natural a writer as his brother, nor of course so mature, at least he managed to keep going at his diary-notes four

---

[47] M. de Belleisle. Prisoners of State were usually confined in the Norman Tower, but the Maréchal-Duc de Belleisle, captured early in 1745 on a mission from Louis XV to the King of Prussia, seems to have been kept, according to Horace Walpole, 'magnificently close' in the Round Tower. He was said to be costing more than £100 a day, and was exchanged, after Fontenoy, a few months later. The damage to his pride led him to boast that he could conquer Britain with 5,000 scullions of the French army: T.E. Harwood, *Windsor Old and New*, 1929, p. 278. I owe the reference to Mrs Jill Kelsey of the Royal Archives at Windsor Castle.

days longer than François. If he was inclined to brevity, their mentor, Lazowski, more than compensated. But without Lazowski we should have no idea how or when their long tour through England ended. Lazowski continues for the rest of the tour.

What is most famous at Windsor is its Terrace, and its Parks, and the beauty of the country round, and beside the river. Beyond the Park lies an immense landscape *into the abstruse geology of which, the mosses of Lapland, and the great costs cultivation would entail, we needn't follow him.* I was saying that the Terrace of the Castle was famous: it is elevated as if by nature above the most beautiful turf. One side displays a land rich and astonishingly peopled; the other a countryside and its pleasures. This last receives its life and movement from the herds of fallow-deer, and from the horses and cows grazing in the middle of the park.

Outside the castle walls the Queen has had a house built: the house of an individual person, quite large, very neatly built, with enough room but nothing of grandeur or magnificence, nor even of elegance, which is remarked upon. Here the King and Queen live, as in London, as two people with their children, on their own. Their officials do not live with them: only a small number of servants. The house looks first onto a garden-lawn, not large, surrounded by a walk planted with evergreen trees: then the view falls to the great, ancient park. At the bottom of the garden is built the house where the children are, and where they have been brought up during the winter; sometimes they are brought up to Kew, when Parliament is in session, to be near London.

This great park contains an enormous number of deer. Here the King occasionally hunts, but generally the deer are taken for two or three days away from the park before the hunting. The stags were brought over from Hanover.

I saw nothing of the inside of the house: no one is admitted. Anyway, it would be useless to offer you any details of the King's private life. All that seems to me a sterile curiosity, and I promise you I've made scarcely any enquiry into it. *'Scarcely' is good, and like most modern journalists, Lazowski cannot resist speculation.*

That the King is or might be wrong, or right, to have adopted, and persisted in, this kind of domestic life is a question judged here generally against him; one on which, however, I find I have no opinion; though there is something on which I could well have one: it is on the means by which one might make of Windsor a place superb and charming. Without any more expense than there has been, one could buy the houses that separate the castle from the park, throw down the first wall and these sad crenellations and – preserving everything masculine and picturesque about the castle – make a truly beautiful place, a truly royal seat.

Lazowski saw the possible difficulty, since the Revolution (meaning of course 1688), of 'resuming' houses on the royal demesne without paying the regular price, and thought that the word 'Property' was the general banner under which the whole nation had ranged itself since the Revolution.

The College of Eton, certainly the first in England, has risen in imitation of the university. It is a royal foundation, and the appointment of its masters, officials, etc., rests with the Crown. The college has considerable endowments administered by the corporate body of the college.

The buildings are ancient, forming two great quadrangles, in one of which stands the statue of the founder. Fellowships at Cambridge are appropriated to this college: free places for students in some colleges are reserved to students at Eton who go on to the university. Moreover, it is the school of the young nobility, who board there, but notice that Eton has become the school of the wealthy only because the teaching and study there is excellent. However, the same religious bias prevails here as in the universities. You have to be an Anglican to be admitted.

We leave tomorrow [28 April] for London. As we pass through we shall see Kew and perhaps Richmond.

Yours &c.

London 6 May 1785   We've been here several days,[48] but we have so filled the time that it would have been very difficult for me to write to you. In my last letter I mentioned Kew and Richmond. These are two country houses of the King of England.

At Kew the house is nothing extraordinary: a large square house,[49] without columns or porticos, very simple, quite undistinguished. But what makes it famous is its Botanic garden, perhaps the most comprehensive in Europe in both plants and trees. There is nothing I am less well informed in than Botany, so all I can tell you about is the arrangement. All the plants are listed by family; all are numbered on lead plaques, the numbers corresponding to a catalogue. The hot-houses match the magnificence of the collection. They are heated variously, according to the original climates of the plants: the heat ranges from that needed by the Moluccan spices to that of Malta. The aquatic plants are kept damp in lead containers, or in a stream, or totally immersed, according to their needs. The trees are distributed by family, but with obvious arrangements, so that dwarf trees and shrubs are in front and large trees and forest trees in the background. Each family is arranged in a sort of amphitheatre so that you can see the whole family at a glance.

We were unable to see the garden. It is open only once a week, starting at midsummer, as the King's children are here till then.

Richmond is only about a mile from Kew as the crow flies, but as the Thames separates them we had to find the bridge. We were so anxious to arrive in London and see our mail that we didn't want to lose a day in Richmond. So we were content to see it from the river. The land from the palace down to the water's edge is flat, which is why it pleased William [III], who came here often, as he was able

---

48 When he wrote, on 6 May, they had been in London eight days, leaving on their ninth. They had presumably arrived on Thursday 28 April: Lazowski, and probably all three, attended a routine, but classic, exchange between Pitt and Fox in the Commons on the 29th. They left for Dover on Saturday 7 May, and sailed on the 10th.

49 The White House, Kew, was simple, but it was hardly square: it was Palladian. The Botanic Garden was one of the passionate creations of Frederick, Prince of Wales, whose children, including George III, were brought up here. It is strange that Lazowski seems not even to have noticed Sir William Chambers' 10-storey Chinese pagoda, from which the gardens could be surveyed.

to lay it out in the Dutch way.[50] They say the view from the top of the hill behind the house is superb, and well it may be: it overlooks the Thames and a broad plain bounded by London, but we didn't see it. I mention it in case you ever come to England.

---

[50] Richmond and Kew are contiguous on the south bank, and Henry VII's splendid palace of Richmond was demolished during the Commonwealth. Plans for a partial restoration, for James II, by Wren, were interrupted by the king's flight into exile in 1688. Lazowski seems to be confusing Richmond with Hampton Court, which certainly did lie across the river, and had been a favourite retreat of William and Mary. 'It is due to William III and his gardeners George London and Henry Wise that the Home Park and Bushy Park are now the best places in England to remember the grandeur of Versailles' (Pevsner and Cherry, *The Buildings of England, London 2: South*, 1983, p. 498). But the Frenchmen allowed themselves no time for seeing Hampton Court, either. Their approach to Kew from Windsor was presumably through Hounslow and Brentford.

11

Lazowski's Views of London

This chapter is based on the long letter Lazowski wrote to the boys' father, the duc de Liancourt, on 6 May, after eight early summer days at large in the capital. Lazowski's letters were nothing if not organized, and this one is grouped into subjects where possible, and in a sequence – until he got carried away on some impulse to theorize. With François I have found it undesirable to cut out even a word – unless it is an occasional irrelevant (to us) list of the local rotation of arable crops that Arthur Young had taught them to record. With Lazowski in London, dependent on him though we are, it has not been painful to prune entire paragraphs.

Already Alexandre is consciously missed, for he would have said where they stayed in London, which of their friends they met, and so on. The nearest Lazowski came to such domestic detail was when he said they were so anxious to arrive in London to see their mail that they declined to linger in Richmond. Naturally, he would be unlikely to name the poste restante, for the duke would have been addressing letters to it. Was it their acquaintance Thomas Walpole in Lincoln's Inn Fields? More likely Thomas Coutts, the banker, in the Strand. When poor François arrived in London seven years later, in August 1792, having narrowly cheated the lanterne's noose, he made straight for 'M. Couth', and was very warmly welcomed. He wrote, perhaps not too precisely, that he had then known Thomas Coutts and his wife and three very eligible daughters 'for five or six years', seeing 'a good deal of them in France'. Coutts' bank could well have been their poste restante in 1785. And Bates' Adelphi Hotel, also in the Strand, could well be where they stayed. For in that dejected visit in August 1792, François certainly lodged with 'the honest and particularly obliging Bates: he has always shown me all kinds of small attentions'. 'Always' does suggest an earlier visit, probably this in 1785. If they were staying in the Strand, they would have been sure to notice the Frenchman Mazzinghi's Guide to London, published in French and English that year by P. Elmsley in the Strand.

Lazowski saw that a detailed chronological account of the eight days would produce a very long letter. So one sees him sitting down to make a list of the subjects he wanted to cover. It began with the streets and squares supplied with abundant water for the fire-pumps (still with the Great Fire of 1666 in mind). The highly utilitarian architecture of the 'Area', unknown in Paris, street-lighting, which led him irresistibly to a hobby-horse, police and their unobtrusive role in London, as distinct from Paris. Then the theme to which he gave most space – the Arts: Royal Society, Opera, Royal Academy, and so on. I have added headings to each of his topics so that readers can see at a glance the list he *obviously jotted down before starting. An unfortunate deviation on national theatrical characteristics is redeemed by a recollection of Mrs Siddons.*

Then, what should have been his most passionate group of subjects – the City's trade, and Westminster – may have received less space than he intended. Not that he neglected them. This letter occupies 96 of the 384 pages of the letter-book. The alarming total is misleading, for he – very uneconomically – wrote only down the left-hand half of each page. To apply his own habits of measurement to his London letter, he devoted 15 of those 96 pages to the town's physical make-up, 45 to the Arts, 36 to the City's trade and Westminster's politics – approximately an eighth, a half, and three-eighths to each of those main themes. The final three-eighths contains a first-hand account of a Commons set-piece on the State of the Revenue, between Pitt and Fox. It must have been a deeply exciting experience for him, more spell-binding even than Mrs Siddons.

It took place on their very first day back in London, 29 April, and may have lost a little of its reality when he came to write his letter seven days later, though he would certainly have made copious notes during the debate. He says, merely, 'I was present', not 'we were present'. Could it be that only one MP would sponsor the permitted one 'stranger'? He may have thought the boys would be writing their own accounts. If only they had been! Any Frenchman present who later saw the disastrous Assemblies at the outset of the Revolution would have been dismayed by the total contrast. Arthur Young didn't even wait to see how they went, in Paris, but set out on his farming survey along the Marne.

Lazowski is in his element observing one of the great London breweries: 'the cellars testify to the grandeur of this establishment . . . it pays the state in excise duty £54,000 sterling'. He doesn't bother to name it, but on balance it must have been Whitbread's. He rapidly describes the Chelsea Physic Garden and the Chelsea Royal Hospital, and ends by promising to begin his next letter with his observations on Greenwich. When you consider that this very long letter had to be copied out by him for the letter-book before it could go to the post, you see that Lazowski had severely reduced his time for sightseeing on his last day in London. One can't help wondering what the boys were doing.

You mustn't expect me to write of London in great detail: it would be an endless job; and, anyway, there are Directories and Guides; even a book by a Frenchman entitled *London*. So I'd be spending much time to no purpose. I'll tell you nothing that's to be found in print: or at least I believe so.[1]

When I say London I mean Westminster rather than the City, the old London of the Bankers and merchants. All over England, as in the ancient Roman empire, when you refer to 'London' you say 'Town' or 'the City' and when you speak of the

---

1   The 'book by a Frenchman', admirably serious and full of useful information, in English and French on facing pages, and dedicated to the Hon. C.J. Fox, was published in 1785 by P. Elmsley in the Strand, and written by Jean Mazzinghi. It includes a very good account of the contents of the British Museum. When Lazowski says he'll say 'nothing that's to be found in print', it's certainly true that he borrows nothing from this excellent compatriot. Mazzinghi's title is *Le Guide nouveau et universel dans les villes de Londres et de Westminster, le bourg de Southwark et leurs environs.* I was greatly helped by the staff of the British Library in tracking it down.

47.   *London. Bloomsbury Square in morning sun, 1787. Edward Dayes.*
Engraved Pollard and Jukes.

kingdom of England you never say 'the kingdom' but 'the Empire'. In monarchies one naturally speaks of the Majesty of the throne, but here one speaks of the majesty of the people; and of ministers as 'servants of the people': all the delegated powers are reckoned to 'emanate' from the people. The English haven't deliberately copied the ancients, but they are so much brought up on them that they use their expressions involuntarily. You would be as amazed as I have been by the astonishing erudition of M. Gibbon in his work on the causes of the greatness and the decline of the Romans, yet people are not astonished by it here.

STREETS

But back to London: it is a superb town built along the Thames, its streets broad, well-paved and straight, their length sometimes amazing. As much as possible they have been crossed at right angles, and they have arranged running water in all these streets in such a way as to prevent the water stagnating in times of drought. One opens a stop-cock of the water-conduits that supply the fire-pumps, and lets out enough to water the streets and form a current in the gutters to clean them down.[2] Added to this the number of large and beautiful squares, looked-after and everywhere, and you will see that there are unrestricted air-currents in all directions, and

---

2   Cf. Salisbury, p. 180 above.

understand how it is that there is infinitely less mortality in London now than there was before the Fire [of 1666]. For cleanliness and convenience, Paris is not to be compared with it.

I'm well aware that for people who have carriages, these things don't much matter, but they are not the majority, and in truth it's hardly just that seven hundred thousand should be sacrificed to the remaining twenty thousand . . . London is infinitely superior to Paris: there are pavements for pedestrians on both sides of every street, paved in stone, level, and along which you can walk comfortably without getting covered in filth. The town is very well watered and supplied with cheap water from the river, beside the extreme advantage of the conduits which can supply a great quantity in the streets in the case of fire.[3]

SQUARES

There are several squares, each with a pond, enormous in proportion to the size of the square, each serving at once as an ornament and a reservoir of water for the neighbourhood.[4] They reckon there are more carriages in London than in Paris, and knowing the state of the nation as I do, I cannot doubt it. But here one doesn't see Wiskis,[5] gigs, Cabriolets that are such a nuisance to the pedestrians in Paris. Here, clean and convenient carriages – without being as showy as ours – don't go at the same rate and have no excuse for a coachman failing to see pedestrians who have to cross the street. The pleasure and satisfaction of going fast can never counter-balance the danger.[6]

AREAS

. . . beneath the ground floor, so that the house is cleared of the kitchen smells, and all the refuse that food preparations involve; and that, above all, people come there only when the bell summons them. You see that this arrangement has created another architectural form: an excavation of the pavement in front of the house about 4 feet in width for the length of the house-front, to a depth of about 8 or 10 feet. This

---

3 Back in 1724, Defoe asserted that 'no city in the world was so well furnished for the extinguishing of fires: by the great convenience of water, which being everywhere laid in the streets in large timber pipes, as well as from the Thames as from the New River. The pipes are furnished with a fire plug and when opened let out not a pipe but a river of water into the streets . . . The New River, brought by an aqueduct or artificial stream from Ware, continues to supply the greater part of the city with water.'

4 It is odd that in 1782 Pastor Moritz didn't notice the 'static water' occupying some of the principal squares (see p. 59 above): on 17 June he wrote: 'These squares contain the best and most beautiful buildings of London: a spacious street, next to the houses, goes all round them and within that there is generally a round grass plot, railed in with iron rails, in the centre of which, in many of them, there is a statue.'

5 Cabriolets, light and high up from the ground, based on an American model of the 1760s: also called Timwhiskys.

6 A page seems to be missing here, between fols 106v and 107 (BL pagination): the subject has jumped from the streets to the design of London houses and the creation of 'the Area'.

space forms a sort of forecourt giving light and air to the offices. Into one of the corners of this court they generally insert stone steps for the servants' entrance and the tradesmen's deliveries, so that the house never gets messed up. These forecourts on to the street are protected by iron railings 6 feet high.

With these paved footpaths and sunken forecourts you will easily see that there are no carriage-entrances.[7] The stables and coach-house are at the back or in cul-de-sacs, or in little unfrequented streets, parallel to the main ones.

The result is a kind of uniformity which strikes me as being not bad, though I know that our town houses,[8] with their different design and ornament, and our way of buildings, have something more imposing; and without looking generally at Paris, here is the same wealth and, above all, the same comfort, which is striking, in both the outside and the inside of the buildings. In all this ant-hill of people, there is much to cheer your spirits, yet I feel that if Paris had been burnt down like London – there's more than *one* Sicily[9] – we would have made a regular plan: then Paris would be, without question, the first town in the world.

STREET LIGHTING

All the streets and the very many roads leading into London, for over two miles, are lit by lantern: but although there are many times more than there are in Paris, although the expense is enormous, yet the roads are not as clearly lit; they are not reflecting lamps [*en réverbère*]. They are mounted on iron posts all along the pavements on both sides of the road. The cost of maintenance is enormous: £300,000 sterling, they say – over 7,200,000 French livres. Private individuals supply the upkeep in each place.

PLEASING ABSENCE OF POLICE

The name of the police is unknown in London as in all other towns of the kingdom[10] . . . which results doubtless in inconvenience, but what are such inconveniences in comparison with the monstrous abuses, continual activities and audacities against liberty? Do you suppose there are no rogues in Paris where the police inquisition is exercised in all its forms? Is it not a shameful, fertile spring of corruption, so much more monstrous because it bears on the violation of deeply respected rights, the

---

7 *porte-cochères.*
8 *hôtels.*
9 He's clearly thinking of the burning fiery catastrophes wrought by Etna, most terribly in 1669 (fourteen towns and villages overwhelmed before the cascade of fiery lava curled over the top of the 60-foot walls of Catania and ran a mile and a half out into the sea) and 1693 when an explosive earthquake destroyed Catania and buried 18,000 of its inhabitants. The most recent calamity that would still have been in their minds occurred on 5 February 1783, wrecking in two minutes most of the houses in all the cities, towns and villages from Messina to the western slopes of the Apennines in Calabria Ultra.
10 François went into this fairly thoroughly, *A Frenchman's Year in Suffolk, 1784*, 1988, pp. 80–91.

sanctity of the home? Doesn't it perpetuate villainy, by encouraging and rewarding informers? There are certainly rogues who don't fear the police anymore: the people of London often deal them justice by ducking them in the pond in the King's stables.

As for our provincial constabulary [*maréchaussée*], as actually composed, it is more an arm of the administration than a protection for the people.[11] What occupies them is what concerns the Minister: the capture of deserters (yet the deserters are not arrested), and, above all, except for the district round Paris and the royal palaces, the safety of the roads; which happily don't suffer from this and scarcely enter into their operations.

But whether there is any more theft in England than France I very much doubt, and I dare say there isn't.

We pass over a page of speculation on cause and effect and hypothetical national customs.

HIGHWAYMEN

There are certainly more highwaymen around London than around Paris: we must guard against confusing the effect of particular causes with that of general ones. London is the centre of immense trade, an immense affluence in every kind of people who depend on their talents and industry to live. Near London are sailors back from long voyages, knowing only the curb of ship's discipline to which they submit by habit from infancy, and now are let loose in a town where luxury and debauchery soon relieve them of their pay . . . Last year, for the first time, there were two assassinations. One worries little about robbers here, they are not cruel: in France they are interested in killing you, for whether they kill you or not, they have the same punishment. It isn't the same here. *More speculation.*

This town is the centre of all the tribunals of justice, of an immense navigation, a prodigious internal trade and a foreign trade so great that it absorbs more than a third of that of the whole kingdom. All the English are more in the habit of coming to London than we are to Paris: it isn't surprising that so much of the fashionable world is here.

I haven't the time nor the desire to write to you of London's public buildings. Apart from St Paul's and Somerset House, I haven't seen anything worth a foreigner's coming to see. St Paul's is the first monument in Europe after St Peter's Rome, yet it was built by the subscription of individuals.[12] No people has more of magnificence in their buildings, but they are buildings belonging to individuals. You have more beautiful buildings in Italy, but I wouldn't want to suggest what you wouldn't find elsewhere than here.

---

[11] On the eve of the Revolution, several liberal *cahiers* (manifestoes) urged the strengthening of the maréchaussée constabulary: Simon Schama, *Citizens*, 1989, p. 322.

[12] What François thought about London on their brief stay, 28 December 1783 to 8 January 1784, at the beginning of their English visit, may be seen in *A Frenchman's Year in Suffolk, 1784*, 1988, pp. 6–15.

ROYAL SOCIETY

I think I must begin with the Royal Society, famous for its members and its Philosophical Transactions. The members meet in Somerset House, where the King has given them rooms: that is the government's only contribution. You know its origins. *Summary of Constitution, subscription &c.* The Society of Medals is next door, its usefulness not so general.

SOCIETY FOR THE ENCOURAGEMENT OF THE ARTS AND AGRICULTURE

The Society for the Encouragement of the Arts and Agriculture is voluntary, existing by subscription, renting a house to hold meetings, preserving machines of all kinds, and new implements of husbandry submitted to the Society; and awarding prizes. We saw the collection and I promise you it is precious. They admit only those models judged capable of general use, either in manufacture or in agriculture.[13] The new improvements in ancient farming-practice, practical methods for the large-scale growing of new plants, corn-crops or fruit are naturally admitted as contributions. The Society has already produced two volumes of Transactions, proof of its usefulness.

The Arts

THE THEATRES AND THE OPERA

London has three places of entertainment, properly speaking: the two national theatres – Covent Garden and Drury Lane – and the Opera. These two theatres have their plays, which are mounted for them: that is to say that the managers, or directors, having bought the plays from the authors, have the full rights over them; which of course doesn't apply to Shakespeare, nor to the other old authors.

These plays are the singular concern of the Press, anxious about being subjected to a sort of censorship: they developed into a war of Party, and according to whether the manager was of the opposition or the Court party he played the one or the other, but it isn't that which introduced this sort of policing. You know it's forbidden, even in Parliamentary debate, to refer to the King by name. According to English law he can do no wrong. He is part of the Constitution and as for the exercise of government, in accordance with the Constitution, he has represented it entirely: in consequence, one can speak of him only with respect. But he was played in the theatre; his absurdities, his vices, his personal and political shortcomings were enacted.[14] All that

---

13 The mahogany construction-model of the Iron Bridge at Coalbrookdale they were shown at Coalbrookdale by its maker, Thomas Gregory, was given by him to the Royal Society for the Encouragement of the Arts and Agriculture, and by them to the Science Museum, where it is proudly displayed in the main transport galleries.

14 Lazowski was referring to the time, half a century earlier, when Walpole's grasp was loosening and George II's government found itself under frequent attack in the theatres. In 1736, Henry Fielding had opened fire in the Haymarket, with *Pasquin; a Dramatick Satire on the Times*. He

was laughed at eagerly, but it could have led to trouble; it could have gone to people's heads; the emotion, the passion roused by this portrayal – above all, the effect of almost daily meeting in the assemblies – could upset the peace. It was therefore judged that, before being performed, the plays had to have been read by one of the lords [of the] bedchamber, or Lord Chamberlain. But notice that there is no question of proceedings against anyone: the shafts of criticism, sarcasm even, in these causes are not forbidden, and I have seen these shafts. The tribunals hold the balance fairly.

You will not excuse me for going on so long about their theatre, yet it is one of the subjects that I know must please you; and today it is a kind of thermometer to judge the civilisation of a nation.[15] Passions are the same in all nations, for all men are built the same: so the death of Caesar on the stage in Rome and in London would have more or less the same effect as in Paris. But in Paris I am, and would be, touched: the noble republican pride of a Cassius and Brutus would have for me an impressive majesty. I would be fired by Cicero, with his sacred love of country; and if I don't become a Roman in the theatre it is the fault of the tragedy or the actors. I now find I am more at ease in judging the actors, but generally I find them to be without talents, often they are no more than declaimers, without nobility, without dignity, with no more merit than to be articulate, pronouncing their language perfectly, but what would provide great pleasure if one were reading the play is ruined by their acting, their ineptness. This is a phenomenon on which I've racked my brains to no purpose. This nation has thought everything out, and consequently perfected everything; it is perceptive, it has faith in its customs, as in its work; it is generally eloquent and certainly it is in the great national assemblies that its orators are formed; it is much travelled; it is more knowledgeable about Antiquity than we are; it spares neither trouble nor expense in its arts, which it cultivates with success; it is enthusiastic about the fine arts, and it discusses them, as I think, with taste; in a word, it is a free nation and a rich one. And yet – its theatres are less widespread than in France, and, by comparison with ours, their actors are strikingly inferior; and these actors have had, and have, a great example. Can you help me resolve this paradox, for I give up.

The great model I wish I could have spoken of is Garrick. Their present model is Mrs Siddons. She is Irish,[16] but speaks perfect English, with precision and inimitable

---

apparently followed it up with *The Golden Rump,* a robust satire directed at the King and royal family; but a prospective manager showed Walpole the script. The 1737 Licensing Act followed, restricting the number of playhouses, and authorizing censorship by the Lord Chamberlain. To the applause of Walpole's son Horace, of Pope, Smollett, &c., Chesterfield denounced it as an encroachment not merely on liberty, but on property, 'wit being the property of those who have it'. Similar arguments are exchanged today.

15 I have cut 2½ paragraphs of philosophizing about a Frenchman's national reactions to English comedy and tragedy. It is easy to see how tedious Lazowski must sometimes have seemed to his young companions. If only he could bring himself to describe performances he had actually seen.

16 She was not Irish, but English, a member of the great Kemble family of actors who came from the West Country. In November 1783, Horace Walpole allowed that her voice was 'clear and good', her acting 'proper' but with little variety. Later he was more captivated, but Lazowski was captivated first; so was most of London.

48. *London. Mrs Siddons as Lady Randolph in* Douglas. *J.R. Cruikshank. Engraved Roberts.*

grace, so inimitable that foreigners are at once aware of it. It is nearly eighteen months since I was in London on my arrival, and saw Mrs Siddons.[17] I spoke and understood only a few words of English: true, I could read it, but that does nothing for speaking and comprehending speech. Nevertheless, I understood a hundred times more of Mrs Siddons' words than of anyone else's. She and Lord Loughborough have given me the most pleasure in hearing them speak.[18]

Her precision of speech, joined to an excellent and pleasing voice, is not the least of her qualities: she possesses to a remarkable degree the language of the passions. Her exclamations are natural, much more even than our Mlle du Mesnil.[19] She never declaims, but always has the tone for the part. She rises with the action, and often is more sublime than her role would have suggested, but it is as a woman of genius. She seizes and sends forth a crowd of thoughts, of subtleties of fine and strong speech, and often of situation, where one wouldn't have perceived them. She becomes the author as she acts, and in my life I never saw an actor or actress so perfect in the role, combining so well her acting, her attitude, her expression, composing herself round a word in a manner so suited to the scene and plot. She is so astonishingly perfect and sublime in these last accomplishments that a stranger with no knowledge of the language would be moved, touched, uplifted by her acting, so that he would understand, and tears would come to pay the truest tribute to the talents of this sublime actress. She has received from nature more than everything necessary for successful performance on the stage. She is a fine and beautiful woman . . . We have no one with whom she can be compared. (Pl. 48)

The two theatres are run by two managers, or directors.

One can't say that the English have no *Opéra Comique*, yet it would be difficult, after following ours in Paris, to say they have one. They have wretched comic episodes, partly set to music, but with no connection between playwright and

[17] The only night they could have seen Mrs Siddons was that of 2 January 1784, when she appeared at Drury Lane in J. Home's *Douglas*, a romantic tragedy: it ends with Lady Randolph (Mrs Siddons) in despair, hurling herself over the edge of a cliff. (Alas, François thought he was seeing a comedy: I suppose it might have seemed more than slightly comic if you didn't understand a word.) See *A Frenchman's Year in Suffolk, 1784*, p. 14, and see also John Genest, *Some Account of the English Stage, 1660–1830*, 10 vols, 1832, VI, p. 297. In this production she was said to be 'very great in the scene with Glenalvon [the villain who organized the slaying of her son]: particularly when she said "tis open as my speech" '. She was also reckoned especially fine when, in the 5th Act, she said 'Oh spare my son – and Despair – Despair'. It would have been possible for the Frenchmen to have seen Siddons as Rosalind in *As You Like It* on her benefit night at Drury Lane on 30 April 1785 (Genest, VI, 341). Her notices were unfavourable, as she had 'contrived a dress which was neither male nor female'. Mrs Jordan soon became the popular Rosalind. During this season, Siddons played Lady Macbeth ten times, Rosalind only four. It is irritating that Lazowski gives no hint that he knew of this performance.

[18] When he came south from Edinburgh, he took lessons in elocution from the elder Sheridan to modify his Scottish brogue: evidently a sound investment. Lord Loughborough came on Assizes to Bury St Edmunds, and is likely to have been there for the July Assizes in 1784, when François was so much impressed by the judge's patience and compassion: see *A Frenchman's Year in Suffolk, 1784*, 1988, p. 83 and note.

[19] Marie-Françoise Marchand, *dites* Dumesnil, tragic actress, 1711–1803, born in Paris.

musician: above all they are graceless and without the spontaneity that sometimes we push over into silliness. Nor are their pieces like our Vaudeville: I don't know what they are like.[20]

The opera is Italian. There are several music lovers at the head of this enterprise which they created and sustain by subscription. All the actors and actresses are Italian: the leaders are all castrati. They play the works of Metastasio.[21] The opera is bad: I tell you only what I have gathered. The costs are enormous. First and second seats, and the pit, or ground floor, in which you are seated as in all theatres in England, are a half-guinea, and the theatre is always full. There is a craze for the opera. It is the mania of the fashionable set, and the nation's theatre is neglected. They often have the leading singers of Italy, and they procure male and female singers at great expense. But although I found the dances above my expectation, they are infinitely inferior to those of our opera; and in general the opera, as to its stage-machinery, dances, dancers, and everything contributing to the marvellous and the spectacular is very much better done by us.[22] But they hear only Italian music. National pride is obliged to give way to taste, and their music is barbarous. They abandon us and are the first to be frivolous about it. They have adopted the Italian opera and have naturalized it for themselves, and so the others are banned. They put their Handel among the primitives; but they won't hear of you putting into the same class with him our Rameau and our Lully.

It is high time I desisted about the theatre, but I can't without saying how furious I've been almost always when, in one of their little plays, a Frenchman comes on the stage. We are never introduced for our genuine absurdities, but for vices that aren't ours. You never see a Frenchman as he is: often frivolous but often loyal, performing a great and good action to which his precious feeling for nature impels him; as readily as his continual need to please often gives him an air of agreeing with everyone. It's his instinct that this sensibility, and its lightness, its coquetry is only the fashion, or – to be more precise – a matter of sensibility.[23] My enterprising Frenchman, living only for work, leaving home only to make his fortune by however ridiculous means, you would see parodied, portrayed only as French valets and dear French cooks. This is how foreigners introduce them on the stage: 'Here's a macaroni; a fop. Why, here's a pick-pocket. Here's a card-sharper. Here's a coward for you'. &c. It pleases the audience. The image has been built up, characterizing us for a great many people, and aided by feelings of rivalry. But if enlightened people spoke out against the propagation of spite, two peoples who should like and respect each other would come to do so. Happily the free exchange of ideas is strong. And I repeat what you

20 It would help if he named what he had actually seen. Allardyce Nicholl thought rather well of the comic opera of the period.
21 Pietro Metastasio, 1698–1782, Italian poet and librettist: his *Isacco* Charles James Fox thought one of the four finest poems of the century. His libretti were so charming that composers overlooked the absence of such qualities as passion.
22 Above, he says 'I tell you only what I've gathered': here he says 'I found the dances above my expectation.' It looks as if they actually went to the opera during this week.
23 One sees how the French might have found themselves misrepresented on the stage if this is how they thought they were!

must often have noticed in my letters: it would be impossible for anyone to receive, and look after, strangers better than the English generally do.

THE PANTHEON

I can't possibly mention all the various sights to be seen in this town. I will mention two. First, the Pantheon, an enormous room most elegantly decorated, shaped beneath a superb dome, with upper galleries along two sides, supported by columns and pilasters in imitation of the most beautiful marble and of the richest architecture.[24] I have seen nothing so magnificent and so grand. They give concerts here, sparing no expense. There are dances and, generally, the masquerades are held here. The room is lit by an immense crystal-glass chandelier hanging in the middle, and by smaller ones placed in niches round the circumference, and by festoons and branched candelabra of different colours on the cornices, and distributed in festoons on the architrave. I haven't seen it lit: it is said to have a great effect.

The Pantheon was established and is run by a company that puts up the money for the events: overall it makes money. In Paris, it would not survive.

RANELAGH

Ranelagh is another such establishment. It stands a mile and a half out of London, on the Thames beside Chelsea. Its sole aim is to bring together an enormous crowd of people to take tea there, or ices. It is an immense round room. I no longer remember its diameter but at least 130 or 140 feet.[25] The whole circumference was fitted out with boxes, in two tiers, entered from the floor of the great room. Each box is furnished with a table and a bench fixed to the partition on either side of the alcove.[26] In the middle of the room is an enormous chimney with fire-places facing four ways. I found it bizarre rather than tasteful. They keep a good fire going while the nights are cool: one doesn't reckon to go promenading at Ranelagh before midnight or one o'clock. You arrive by a very pleasant road, or by boat along the river. The person who dreamed up the whole idea made an immense fortune out of it.[27] One also finds music there, though that isn't what one goes for.[28] The gardens are mediocre.[29]

24 James Wyatt won the competition and made his name with the building in 1770–72, in Oxford Street: burnt down 1792. Its upper part was entirely of wood. Finally demolished 1937. Sir John Summerson pointed out that, though the dome was based on that of the Pantheon in Rome, the overall composition, remarkably, followed that of Sancta Sophia, both of those, of course, being great works of masonry: *Architecture in Britain, 1530–1830*, 1953.
25 Its diameter was 185 feet.
26 Ranelagh is well illustrated in Robert Carrier and Oliver Lawson Dick's invaluable *Vanished London*, 1957.
27 The rotunda was the work of 'Mr Jones, the furniture designer': John Summerson, *Georgian London*, 1962 edn, p. 118.
28 On 29 June 1764, Mozart, aged 8½, played there in aid of a proposed Lying-in Hospital: he played on the harpsichord, and works of his own composition on the organ: entrance tickets 5 shillings.
29 Moritz, too, found the garden 'mean-looking and ill-lit', by contrast with the illuminated splendour within.

I've said too much about the places of entertainment, but I wanted you to see that, in London as in the provinces, people love assemblies, great gatherings. It is a major trait in the life of the nation.

If I wanted to tell you of the arts and commerce of London I would need to write you an encyclopedia, and a dictionary of commerce, for all the arts are cultivated with prodigious success. It pays magnificently; for a great many people are occupied with matters of taste, and not with mere appearance. However, I must do my best to give you some idea.

MUSIC

Music is cultivated in London as it is throughout the kingdom; that is to say, universally. The harpsichords, the pianofortes, are more commonly seen here than in Italy; and so it isn't only people in fine company who love music, and are brought up in it from childhood, but everybody of middling fortune. There are very few, really very few houses in the country where one doesn't come upon one musical instrument. If you want a fair idea of the manner in which this art is practised in England, remember the concert given last year in Westminster Hall to celebrate Handel's centenary: 500 musicians were all brought together in London and played difficult works.[30]

We have been to see a man, famous in the world of music, whose name you know through his connections with Jean-Jacques: this is Dr Burney, who published *The History of Music*.[31] He has studied his art in the chief countries of Europe, and during these travels he got to know J.-J. [sic]. But we didn't see him: he was ill. However, we desired, and were given, an hour's conversation with *Cecilia*, Miss Burney, his daughter, the author of that charming novel which so delights you when you read it in translation – in which, though, it lost all its warmth.[32] She is not pretty, talks

---

[30] There was more than one concert, and they were certainly ambitious. Handel was born in 1685, but on Roubiliac's memorial to him in the abbey the birthdate was carved as 1684. Plans were made in 1783 for centenary celebrations, which were held on an unprecedented scale in 1784; and others followed in 1785, 1786, 1787, and in 1791. In May and June 1784, performances included the Dettingen Te Deum and Coronation and Chandos Anthems in Westminster Abbey; one concert held at the Pantheon included various songs and choruses, four concertos and an overture (symphony): *Grove*, 5th edn, IV, 1954, *sub* Handel Commemoration.

[31] The familiar form Jean-Jacques was probably fairly usual among the French intelligentsia but *may* suggest a familiarity between the duc de Liancourt and J.-J. Rousseau. At the beginning of Lazowski's description of the little tour they did with Arthur Young 21–26 July 1784, he expressed his admiration of the way Young allied his knowledge of political arithmetic, etc., with sensibility: 'he is enraptured by the beauties of J.-J. and of Voltaire, and he can shed tears over *Clarissa*' (Richardson's novel).

[32] The second novel of Fanny Burney (1752–1840), *Cecilia*, appeared in 1782: 2,000 copies sold out in three months: it was admired by Burke, Mrs (Elizabeth) Montagu (1720–1800), the Queen of the Blue-stockings, and old Mrs Delany (1700–88), another gifted Blue-stocking, whom she was helping to settle into a house in Windsor at this time. If she looked exhausted, the cause might have been helping her old friend to move house.

very little, and is clearly exhausted from overwork. Yet everything about her expresses a rare sensibility: I am certain she's in the thrall of a great passion.

POETRY

Poetry flourishes less generally in England than in France: I mean, fewer people chance their arm at verse-making. Admittedly, they are good at the epigram, but they don't go in for song writing as much as we do. However, they love the poets, and feel as warmly as we do. And it was an Englishman – much praised for it indeed – who put up the best defence I have seen of Voltaire when he was accused of having mis-represented Shakespeare – having translated him badly – and of having curtailed genius by wishing to subject the English to the three unities in their tragedies: an accusation widely felt, but publicly expressed by Lady Montagu.[33] They have great poets of every kind. The reputation enjoyed by Dr Johnson, who lately died,[34] is proof that they make poets: in a word, they cultivate literature in all parts of the kingdom, so how could there not be poets?·

There isn't much point in my writing about eloquence: one makes a reputation only at the Bar or in Parliament. In the provinces, one can do little unless one speaks in public or writes: so there, too, eloquence is found, for there is great interest in the art of persuading.[35]

PAINTING

As for painting, I owe you a retraction of a hurried judgment which I remember making during our first tour in Suffolk, when I accused them of having no painters.[36]

---

33 Voltaire, in the 18th of his *Lettres Philosophiques* (ed. G. Lanson, Paris, 1909, Vol. II, p. 79), described Shakespeare as 'un génie plein de force, sans la moindre étincelle de bon goût, et sans la moindre connaissance des règles'. This was answered magisterially by Dr Johnson in his edition of Shakespeare in 1765: T.S. Eliot reckoned Johnson's judgment of Shakespeare more of an honour than burial in Westminster Abbey. But, as Lazowski indicates, Mrs Elizabeth Montagu (his confusing her with Lady Mary Wortley Montagu is easily understood) took Voltaire thoroughly and unanswerably to task: her *Essay on the Writings and Genius of Shakespeare* appeared in 1769 (and later editions). It is hard to be sure which Englishman 'put up the best defence I have seen of Voltaire', but it seems possible that Lazowski had seen, in the library of one of their English friends, Pope's earlier (1725) edition of Shakespeare. In his introduction, Pope wrote of Shakespeare's contemporaries in Voltaire's superior vein: 'Not only the common audience had no notion of the rules of writing, but few even of the better sort piqued themselves upon any great degree of knowledge or nicety that way.'
34 13 December 1784.
35 See under Parliament, below, p. 218.
36 He was describing the splendid library at Heveningham Hall, and I didn't trouble to add this 'hurried judgment' to several details with which he supplemented the uncluttered account François gave of that house; I should perhaps have printed every word in the light of the wretched condition into which Heveningham was allowed to fall in the 1980s (*A Frenchman's Year in Suffolk, 1784*, 1988, pp. 138–42). This is what Lazowski wrote: 'The library is magnificent, in ornament and in arrangement, though still without its books. At the entrance, a sort of vestibule

49.   *London. The Royal Academy Summer Exhibition, 1787. K. Ramberg. Engraved P. Martini.*

I come away from their salon – called an exhibition – and, moved by all that I saw of their painters during my travels, I am perfectly sure that they are our equals now. I am not referring to this actual moment: I know no one here who equals our Lebrun[37] or Le Sueur;[38] yet, if we have a great poetic painter in Greuze,[39] they have an extraordinary man in Sir Joshua Reynolds. This exhibition [of the Royal Academy] takes place every year, whereas our *exposition* is put on only

has been fashioned by means of two columns of stucco imitating jasper. In the space above the bookcases there are medallions [painted within oval plaster frames] of English poets and some Greek and Roman poets: one sees only two Frenchmen – Voltaire and J.-J. – the medallions are poor. What I've seen so far in England, in sculpture and painting, has not given me an exalted idea of its painters and sculptors in the grand manner. Form, and everything to do with ornament, is charming, often of an exquisite taste; though it belongs a good deal less to the original taste of the nation than to the Antique, borrowed from Italy and imitated and adapted to its own uses with a truth and an elegance that constantly strike me. I've seen some fine pieces of sculpture: Newton, for instance, at Cambridge, but they are by a Frenchman, Roubiliac [1705?–62], carved in Italy and brought here, like many of the monuments at Westminster. [In fact, he worked in England from about 1732]. It's perhaps a risky judgment, but one reinforced by everything I've seen in seven months, and not shaken by the view I heard confidently expressed the other day that their annual exhibition of pictures in London is superior to ours in the Louvre.'

37   Charles Lebrun, 1619–90.
38   Eustache Le Sueur, 1616–55.
39   Jean-Baptiste Greuze, 1725–1805.

every two years: and their standard is as high as ours. It is already a proof that art receives more individual encouragement. And the luxury of their furnishings, decoration and, above all, of their country houses, is infinitely superior to ours; and as the painting is a principal means of decoration, painters have more employment. It is a natural consequence that artists multiply as the arts are cultivated, and the perfection follows in the same degree. Here, where riches are more widespread, the arts must benefit. In France, the King names the subjects of history pictures, in return for which he pays magnificently, and does it only for the encouragement of art. Here they are unaffected by these extraordinary resources which never, by themselves, create good artists: patronage by individuals does everything – more here than in France, for here they are richer and more ostentatious. So the history painters are as numerous, their imagination without being more brilliant seems to me more powerful than with us. Their scenes are truer, more wisely and robustly realized, their lay-out richer and the touch has nothing of the glitter we complain of in our painters; glitter that sometimes cloys, and always detracts from whatever what it touches might have had of robustness and vigour, so that painters who have such qualities lose them.

Whatever the serious pre-occupations of the nation, whatever the political discussions, whatever the shortage of such lively communications as our nation may have on the question of taste in general, is fully recompensed by several circumstances that you can reduce to two. The first is the passion, or perhaps the necessity, of an educated young man for travel, and above all in Italy, of whom at least some bring back a good appreciation of pictures. The second, even more important, is their love, grown into a universal taste, for everything from, or based on, the classical world . . . Don't assume that Renaissance painters are slavish imitators, or that their genius was cooled by the experience: they based themselves on good models . . . If you think you can attack Michaelangelo because it was from the Antique that he studied his art, and on which he based his own, then it's the same with the educated Englishman's profound knowledge of classical authors and the ancient world in general. Even more, perhaps, their political constitution has made them research avidly everything we can recover of our first masters in this art – as they have been, and are, in poetry and eloquence.[40]

ENGRAVING

For the rest, you would very much like their engravings: you have often admired their subjects. I say nothing of their skill with the burin.[41] We have, and we had great masters, but it is a subject you love. Often, a bewitching expression, a Venus of sensuousness, who captivates you at a glance, a touching sensibility suggestive of an abundance of such scenes, holding you like a gripping narrative; and finally a grace which is breathtaking in a people you have been thinking of as republicans: yet here

[40] He returns to the influence of the Ancient World on eloquence and politics when he discusses Parliament (p. 220 below).
[41] engraving-tool.

are all these subjects in their pictures. You don't have to believe my remarks, but judge for yourself from these half-copies.

I've been most of all enchanted by portraits, half-pencil, half in colour in this kind of gouache the name of which I can't tell you: more grace could not be united in one picture.

THE R.A. SUMMER EXHIBITION

I can't finish on pictures without mentioning a new genre exhibited this year for the first time. It's a landscape taken in one of the new-found islands in the South Seas; done by one of the painters who made the last voyage round the world.[42] It opens up the idea of a new nature – trees, landscape, colours, shapes: it is all extraordinary, and done so as to excite curiosity.

Pieces of sculpture are not numerous; but there are enough to be able to judge that here this art is at least as advanced as painting.[43]

Apart from more general reasons for believing it, you can see that in a nation in which public monuments multiply, and in this genre, the artists have an added motive, a powerful incentive, to achieve celebrity: I have seen so many in Westminster Abbey and in different churches I visited on our tour – marble monuments carved with rare perfection.[44] Besides, marble is worked much better, and much more than in France. The chimney-pieces in the saloons of their country houses are objects of luxury on a ruinous scale: so are some halls, decorated in marble. One is bound to succeed with so much practice. In the [Academy] Exhibition I saw the work of an

---

[42] This was John Webber (1752–93), landscape-painter, trained five years in Paris, and appointed draughtsman to Captain Cook's third and last expedition to the South Seas. He witnessed Cook's death and supplied the illustrations to the official account of the expedition, published 1784. The 1785 summer exhibition included his views of Macao, Cracatoa and Otaheite (Tahiti). New subject matter, certainly, but he was no Gauguin. On Wednesday, 4 May, Sylas Neville very much admired Wright of Derby's private exhibition, then went on to the Academy: Lazowski didn't date their visit, but they might have been there that same day. Neville was very dismissive: 'The Exhibition of the R.A. has but few pictures of great merit this year – indeed I did not stay long, the crowd of company and heat of the rooms made it into a Calcutta business' (*The Diary of Sylas Neville, 1767–1788*, ed. B. Cozens-Hardy, Oxford, 1950, pp. 326–27).

[43] Nollekens was exhibiting 'a busto of a gentleman'; and the Irishman, John Hickey, 'a bust of a nobleman in marble' – probably his patron (and Lazowski's favourite speaker) Lord Loughborough. That year, the painter Thomas Proctor turned to sculpture, and exhibited his 'Ixion', highly praised by Benjamin West, and by Horace Walpole, who described it as 'a prodigy of anatomy'. It was bought by Sir Abraham Hume, but I have been unable to trace it, or even a representation of it. Horace Walpole's great chum, the Hon. Mrs Damer, was showing that summer the Portland stone keystones she carved for Henley Bridge, probably her best-known works. She also exhibited two terracotta kittens, destined for Strawberry Hill, but now lost sight of.

[44] This is rare discernment of Lazowski's. It was not until 1953 that a comprehensive and appreciative *Dictionary of British Sculptors, 1660–1851*, compiled by Rupert Gunnis, was published.

able sculptor:[45] the movement, the expression and the life that this piece diffused everywhere were enough to enable me to form a high opinion of the perfection of the art in this country.

As to the other arts, it is useless to speak of them: you need to know or, at least, to have an idea of England, of its riches and luxury.[46] After all that I've written about that, you also have every day in Paris things they have manufactured: of their main works you must have formed a shrewd opinion. The state of the sciences naturally compares closely with that of the arts. You may know it easily through the Philosophical Transactions, as a foreigner may know ours from our *Mémoires* of the Academy of Sciences. But it is of the *depôts* for science, the public establishments that I shall write. In this respect London is very much inferior to Paris. It seems that the nation has decided to concentrate all its resources in its two universities, which as you will recall have very great wealth in their libraries &c. Or, to express it better, it has felt that the exercise of talent, that the study of sciences, like the cultivation of the arts, would always come about through having a stake in the enjoyment of the results. So . . . they have always distributed blindly and maintained with an expense that always exceeded any advantages in return. For the rest, it's by the effects that you have to judge causes, and from this point of view you don't need my observation to form your opinion.

THE BRITISH MUSEUM

Until the period of the present reign, London had no public library nor any repository, either general or specific, related to the arts and sciences, such as that of the *Cabinet Royal* in Paris. It is in this reign that the nation has laid the foundations of the museum which I shall describe.

They bought a house[47] and a very large site, then divided up the house and added to it everything necessary to the foundation of a great library;[48] and to enable it to expand to house a great and beautiful collection of natural history,[49] destined to grow daily; also the superb and astonishing collection of antiquities, of every description, from the chevalier Hamilton,[50] ambassador to Naples, which the nation has bought

45 He may well be referring to Thomas Proctor's 'Ixion'.
46 Again this curious implication. Even if Lazowski didn't know of the duke's stay in England in 1768–69, he must have known e.g. of the duke's visit to his sons (and Lady Blois) in April of 1784 (*A Frenchman's Year in Suffolk, 1784*, 1988, p. 133). Perhaps he merely felt that the duke's 1784 visit wasn't long enough for him to have 'an idea of England'.
47 Old Montague House: finally replaced by Smirke's building of 1847–57.
48 The library was begun in 1753 with the splendid collections of Sir Robert Cotton (1571–1631) and of the Harley family: in 1757, George II handed over the Royal Library, which brought with it the right of compulsory copyright deposit: one copy of every book published in Britain had to be deposited in the BM by the publisher, as it still does.
49 The collection of a fashionable Chelsea doctor, Sir Hans Sloane.
50 Sir William Hamilton. It was a truly fabulous collection of Greek vases (730), terracottas, ancient glass, bronzes, ivories, gems, coins (more than 6,000): bought by the British Museum in 1772 for £8,400. It is the basis of the present department of Greek and Roman antiquities.

50. *London. British Museum, Hall and Staircase, 1808. Pugin and Rowlandson, drawn and engraved.*

to be kept here. Josiah Wedgwood reckoned he himself brought into England, by the sale of his imitations of the Hamilton vases, over three times the amount the nation paid for them.[51]

The Museum, without exterior magnificence, stands well enough, in the depth of a great court. Fronting the road are individual lodgings for the people employed. The Museum itself is occupied entirely with the items described.

The nation has made considerable grants to the library, but they are nothing compared with the bequests, donations and individual presents. They are presented with so much so readily on the understanding that the gifts are used, and that only a positive law, directly framed, can alter the form of this establishment.

Generally, all authors send a signed copy of their works to the Museum:[52] furthermore, the nation has assured an annual fund for the maintenance of the museum and to furnish the library with new works – those by the nation and by foreigners – and for the acquisition of interesting manuscripts as they might become available. For the rest, this library, reckoned at 60,000 volumes, is greatly inferior to the Bibliothèque Royale: there is no comparison.[53]

From the library, arranged in different rooms by subject-matter, you enter the cabinet of natural history. You won't expect details . . . it is furnished almost like ours. They have given the greatest attention to completing the collection of national products, and consequently all have an immediately useful function. Also, the section on the minerals of the three kingdoms is not only rich in specimens of all kinds, arranged in impressive order, but the most complete you could imagine.

Of the antiquities, it's enough to say that it's the Chevalier Hamilton's collection, amassed during fifteen years at Naples with all the facilities presented him by the excavations at Herculaneum and Pompeii: it embraces every object relating to customs, arts, the Roman way of life – starting with their pottery and kitchen vessels and finishing with their dress, their luxury goods and their weapons.

In this collection but not mixed up with it one finds some British antiquities: some part of the ancient stakes driven into the banks of the Thames by the ancient Britons to block and defend the passage of the river against Caesar; stone axes of the wild Britons, &c.

In addition to any idea you are able to form of our *Cabinet d'histoire naturelle*, and when you join to that even the King's collection in Paris, you certainly won't have any idea of the collection belonging to the Chevalier . . . . . . [He has put six dots: can Sir William Hamilton's name have escaped him since he wrote it in the last paragraph but one? It seems more likely to be the failure by a copyist to read the name.] – which he sold by auction with the sanction of a Parliamentary Bill.

The immensity and rich variety of these astonishing collections – from all periods – are inconceivable. They occupy a very large house, and so extensively that the

---

51 See the visit to Etruria at p. 88 above.
52 See footnote 48, p. 213 above.
53 In 1991, the number of printed books in the British Library approached 10 million, to say nothing of the western and oriental manuscripts.

staircase-well, up which you climb to the different storeys, itself forms a gallery stocked from ground-floor to roof.[54]

It is all complete; or, rather, since there's no limit to such objects, all that is known in our continent and in the lands newly discovered by Captain Cook is represented here, arranged in order and maintained immaculately, with a care I have seen nowhere else. There is no doubt: this is the richest and most valuable collection of its kind in the world. The entrance-charge, for English and foreigner alike, is one écu[55] per head. The place is always crowded,[56] but the costs of maintenance are so enormous that the proprietor[57] is obliged to withdraw. I forgot to say that one can't enter the Museum – as a foreigner at least – without sending your name to the Lord Chamberlain, and you find written permission there next day: it is never refused.

Trade and Politics

I can't introduce the subject of London's trade better than by telling you that it absorbs almost an entire half of the nation's trade: and that doesn't include the trade of the Indies, which is exclusive to London. If to this external trade you add sales of goods not only for the consumption of a population as large as London's, but also for the counties in the provinces, the currency, stock-jobbing, sale of bank-notes, and all the business of handling the accumulated national debt – the immense debt almost all of which is negotiable – then you can have some idea of the liveliness of business in London.

In the city, the number, order, cleanliness and richness of the shops of all kinds always strikes foreign visitors and creates a high opinion of the luxury and wealth of the nation. But what, above all, is admirable is the good faith that prevails in every transaction. You may safely buy without advance knowledge of the prices: there's only one for each commodity. In consequence, there's never any haggling, and you can send a child to make a purchase with the same confidence you'd have in sending an adult.

The port of London is immense, and stretches from the port of London itself out to Deptford. Don't imagine, when I say 'port', I mean an artificial dock: it is the river itself. The buildings don't go above the Bridge, and downriver they go only as far as Deptford, which is a Royal Shipyard: its length is about seven miles. Often, from the Bridge for about a mile and a half, the number of ships is such that they

---

54 Pugin and Rowlandson's view of the staircase-well shows it cleared of all but two show-cases by 1808. A few individual antiquities are engraved in J. and A. van Rymsdyk's handsome work *Museum Britannicum*, in 1778, but there seems to be no general contemporary picture of e.g. a group of Pompeian objects from the Hamilton collection. I'm grateful to Miss Marjorie Caygill, of the Director's office, for her help in this enquiry (Pl. 50).

55 a crown, five shillings, 25 pence.

56 François, after their first visit in January 1784, said it was open only three hours a day for the limited number of ten people (*A Frenchman's Year in Suffolk, 1784*, p. 12). Was he describing January conditions of opening, or had there been a change of rules by May 1785?

57 ? Keeper, under the Trustees? (*Le propriétaire est obligé de s'en défaire.*)

51.   *Westminster. St James's Park, in front of the Queen's House (Buckingham Palace). Drawn Edward Dayes, draughtsman to HRH The Duke of York, 1790.*

52.   *Westminster. Pitt addressing the House of Commons on the outbreak of war with France, 1793. Karl Anton Hickel.*

are so packed together that there's hardly any channel down the middle of the river for boats to go up and down. The merchantmen go upriver with ease, but the Ships-of-the-Line don't pass above Deptford. Nor do those of the East India Company, which have to be partly unloaded before going any further. At certain times of the year, you can count more than ten thousand ships in the river.

On the left bank[58] are the quays, properly speaking, and on the right the mastyards, the shipyards and various kinds of warehouses are situated.

For the rest, the harbour is like that at Bordeaux, it isn't clad in masonry: the water isn't high enough for the ships to tie up at the quayside to be unloaded: so they are obliged to unload into lighters after the ship has been boarded by customs officers and they have discharged their duties. They managed, as at Bordeaux, to make a good big causeway for the convenience of carriages, but it is built up the whole length, and – as the river-basin is deep – the slope of the bank, especially on the left, is very steep. The warehouses are supported on piles at the water's edge: the piles come up to the same level as the road. Usually the last of these warehouses is occupied by sheds or stores into which goes the merchandise lifted over from the boats by means of pulleys mounted on a boom like the machines on the quay at Paris.

I shan't write of the three bridges, of London, Blackfriars and Westminster. You know that this was where *caissons*, to build dry under water, were first used; but we have greatly perfected the method.

London is two separate places: the ancient city of London, centre of trade, with Bank, Exchange, &c.; and Westminster, taking the name of the famous abbey, where are the palace and the Houses of Parliament.

WESTMINSTER

The King's palace [of St James] looks as much like a prison as a palace. It is large, in redbrick, so sad and unattractive that the King never lives there: he lives in a house built by the Queen at one end of St James's Park.[59] He lives there alone, as he does at Windsor: he comes to the palace only to give his audiences. His apartments are said to be extremely beautiful.[60] Soldiers in uniform and with arms are seen only on duty at the palace: they are lodged in the town and are rarely heard of.

PARLIAMENT

Parliament never meets away from Westminster, the ancient palace of William Rufus. The entrance hall, unfurnished, serves really only as promenade: it is the ancient hall

---

58 north bank.
59 Pl. 51. George III bought Buckingham House for his wife soon after their marriage in 1762: it was known as the Queen's House: later, of course, Buckingham Palace. New rooms were built in 1762, including a fine octagon for the library, which may explain Lazowski's belief that the Queen 'built' it.
60 George III was a man of remarkable taste, in books, in furniture, in pictures (Alan Ramsay and Gainsborough for royal portraits), and furnishing their new house must have given the King and Queen much pleasure: see J.H. Plumb, *Royal Heritage*, 1977, ch. 4.

in which William met his barons. A few steps from there and you enter various passages leading to record-offices and committee-rooms, offices of secretaries and ushers, &c. The room where Parliament sits is preceded by an ante-chamber which they call *Lobby*. It is a right belonging to members of Parliament to bring in one stranger. The Lobby is increasingly used for counting the votes of members as they leave the chamber.

The chamber is nothing remarkable, a fairly large room containing precisely – and closely packed – the members. It is square. The Speaker, charged with getting the business through the house and maintaining order, sits in a large and ancient chair, placed on the floor, not raised above it: about two-thirds of the way along the chamber. The space in front of the Speaker is filled with a great table on which all the papers lie. The Speaker always wears a large gown like those of Masters of Arts in our universities; also a long wig and a cap which he keeps on. He remains seated, and removes his cap only when speaking.

The two front benches round the table are occupied – those on the right by the Minister and members who have the talents and eloquence of their Party; and those on the left by the members of the Opposition who speak regularly. This is why you see in the debates that they refer to 'the gentleman opposite'. Don't imagine that there are places reserved for each member: no, each sits where he likes; but members who aren't orators don't take the best places so that those who are can speak conveniently. All the members wear hats and what clothes they please: on this point there is no etiquette; but when they speak they rise bare-headed.

You can find out all about the procedures and powers of the House of Commons in the *Commentaries* of Blackstone, an excellent work of the kind we and all the other continental nations lack. In this work you can find not only the entire working of the constitution, its progress, its present composition, one may say, its perfection; but also the system of civil and criminal law.

PITT VERSUS FOX UPON THE STATE OF THE REVENUE

I was present at the session when Mr Fox put the motion that he had tabled well in advance. He wanted to show that the Chancellor of the Exchequer's account of the finances was incorrect.[61] To soothe the multitude, the Chancellor hadn't uncovered

---

61 Fox's motion 'upon the State of the Revenue' was 'that a committee be appointed to inquire into, and state to this House, the annual net produce of each of the taxes'. He declared he had no confidence in Pitt's figures, and believed that the credit of the country rested on 'the publicity and clearness of our accounts'. Pitt was nothing if not a master in the country's financial business. And he had learnt the arts of debate from his father, perhaps the greatest orator in our parliamentary history. His maiden speech in 1781 earned delighted praise from Fox as well as Burke and North. In Cobbett's *Parliamentary History of England* (Vol. 25), this debate occupies 22 columns (492–514), and one can only wonder why Fox allowed his demagogic urges – opposing for opposing's sake – to lure him on to such dangerous ground. Pitt couldn't resist teasing him: 'heartily agreeing with him when he said that to impress the public with flattering hopes of the prosperity of the nation in point of revenue, when those hopes could only be supported by concealment or deceit, was a gross violation of duty in a minister'. The reporter

the symptoms that lay beneath the healthy appearance; nor had he once referred to them, in his entire speech; he was only prolonging the slumber and, the deeper that was, the more terrible the moment of awakening would be; all he needed was courage, for if the illness was a major one, the resources for its cure were even greater, and must be exploited: the nations must be shown that our fidelity to our under-takings would be, as always in the past, the basis of Parliament's conduct.

I am giving only the spirit of the motion, but as you see, you needed no deep financial understanding to follow it, nor was such understanding demonstrated by the party leaders, MM. Fox and Pitt, for all the brilliance of their eloquence.[62]

I didn't miss a moment of their speeches. They were long, so you see how much they affected me.

Mr Fox owes all that he is to nature; nothing to art, which he has studied above all in classical literature,[63] and which has corrected none of his defects as orator, yet which has reinforced to an eminent degree his valuable qualities – his natural talents. He has no sort of appearance: his bearing is without dignity or grace. His declama-tion, without being monotonous, is unstudied and artless: one may even say, incontrovertibly, that he is uncouth. His appearance expresses the depth of his genius, shows his peculiar strength, and, seeing this, one regrets that he hasn't drawn more closely on the ancient models whom he imitates so well in his rapid, impromptu, speech; in his skill in pleasing his audience, in anticipating and persuading before subjecting their minds to the empire of his reason.

But as a statesman, as eloquent orator, all these faults, however great, are more than atoned for. Never have I witnessed so prodigious a flowing together of ideas: they tumble over one another in such a flood that I can't begin to describe it. His genius is so vast: he has observed everything with such justice that this astonishing rapidity is a feature neither of orderliness nor of neatness: everything is classed in

noted that Mr Pitt 'paid some ironical compliments to Mr Fox for his zeal on the subject, which however, like that of all new converts, was more ardent than judicious'. The motion was 'negated without a division'. Lazowski failed to note that Burke spoke briefly on Fox's side and that Sheridan scored a good point against Pitt before going off at a tangent.

Pitt had begun the reconstruction of the tax system the previous year, and was well on the way to eliminating the national debt (half the annual expenditure) by the time the long wars started with Revolutionary France in 1793. Lazowski's English, good as it was, seems to have missed much of the subtlety of this classic, yet routine, debate.

62 He's right. In a sense they were putting on a sort of routine display, an oratorical duel, Fox for the exercise, Pitt content not to show his real power.

63 Lazowski seems unaware of the way some formidable orators of the French Revolution were themselves modelling their eloquence on Greece and Rome. He could hardly know in advance of the earliest reported demagogic experiment, in August 1785, of the young lawyer Hérault de Séchelles, who later caught the Queen's eye. Nor is he likely to have come across Simon Languet's book on *The Century of Alexander* as a standard for lawyer-orators. In his chapter on 'Projecting the Voice: the Echo of Antiquity', Simon Schama noted how ponderous Languet had found Westminster on a visit in the 1770s. In this brilliant chapter, Schama suggests how it is that, with the painter David, with Beaumarchais, and even with Rousseau, 'it was quite possible for the court, as well as for the grandest of *les Grands* to endorse what in hindsight appear to be the most subversive messages': *Citizens*, 1989, pp. 164, 166, 172.

the most natural way, at the same time the way most suited to carry conviction. Everything is spoken with warmth, energy, clarity. His ability to strike like a sudden, unexpected flash of lightning does not always leave him much time to round off his periods, but his conciseness, so invaluable in a statesman, is unfailing: never a wasted word, always the right one; never those studied phrases where the orator, to coax you, develops the full power of words, swarming with ideas. With him one doesn't make the commonplace comparison of a majestic river, overflowing and sweeping everything along with it: one compares him with an elephant, shaking with his mighty trunk a great and deeply rooted tree, and never ceasing his efforts until that tree is removed: that's the effect he had on me.[64] I've already said that the subject of his motion lent little to the deployment of his talents: one cannot be eloquent on the ponderous theme of financial estimates.

The character of Mr Pitt is altogether different. He presents an attractive appearance: and if his bearing, his gestures and his overall behaviour are not as poised and perfect as they could be, he has a sort of grace, the ease of a young man, and a voice of such beauty that one has to study it to discover that there are many things still lacking.

Unlike his opponent, in the matter of his eloquence as in his outward appearance, he doesn't try even to carry off by force of personality what he wants to bring about: he has none of the audacity and the energy of the other: as experienced and as well supplied with information as the other is deficient, he concentrates on speaking well and is much more a rhetorician than a statesman, balancing the great interests he is trying to satisfy; and it seemed to me that he perhaps went too far, pleased with his own pleasantries, his epigrams and even sarcasm. Sometimes he tries shamelessly to ridicule his opponents, and he doesn't get down to business until he has exhausted all his arts of seduction. Fine and subtle in discussion, he doesn't put a similar trust in the strength of his arguments. Everything irony can supply to the subject, he supplies. He says nothing that isn't precisely true, and this pursuit of precision leads him into diffuse qualifications: he won't sacrifice the grace of his oratory to a sudden bold idea. He listens to everything he says, and one must affirm that he speaks well: but I cannot dismiss the idea that his is the eloquence of a young orator, full of spirit and wit and grace, adroit and skilful in choosing what will please his party: a young orator fuller of words and oratorical tricks than of ideas. His eloquence tired me out: I had to analyse it too much in order to follow it. In a word, I saw in him only infinite spirit, and the attendant qualities. Yet nothing warmed me, moved me, astonished me; his personality isn't forceful: he looks for the place to insert his very sharp dagger. His discourse doesn't sparkle with the exuberance of ideas which astounds and pleases you in the other, because it instructs. The one has more the art of eloquence and words, the other that of things. One is a man of infinite spirit, the other has only genius.[65] One has all the qualities of an extraordinary young man: he triumphs too

---

64 Lazowski supplies an excellent illustration of the spell-binding exercised by Fox, clearly overwhelming on a first hearing through French ears.
65 Lazowski's own rhetoric tends to obscure his meaning.

much in his popularity, enjoying openly and with emphasis his successes. One walks proudly towards his goal, disdaining everything unconnected with it. The character of their respective spirits is much more marked than that of their political principles.

I hope you won't conclude from what I've said that I see in Mr Pitt some ordinary man: he is an astonishing phenomenon, carrying, at his age, the weight of a great empire in difficult times: the head and chief of a dominant party. These are miracles, and fill one with awe, but what adds too much to his awful difficulties has made his fortune. There is no lack of men of ability, but the number from whom the King could choose was limited: what was needed was a popular idol, but this idol was found in the mere name of Pitt. So much talent, and honest assurance, in a young man was bound to seduce the multitude. The good sense of the King in linking to his fortunes all the shareholders of the East India Company in making it appear like a subversion, a direct attack on the Constitution, a regulation, a new law, indispensably necessary, which had already been put to use at least for the party of which the King complained the most, a regulation which all the wise political people regard as the only remedy against the ills which unite slowly and surely the nation's empire in the Indies: – the King's good sense, I repeat, has brought Mr Pitt the majority of the nation's wealthy merchants. In the end, although Mr Pitt is obliged rather often to double back in his tracks; although he naturally lacks experience of men; although perhaps his day-to-day performance may upset people – it has to be recognized that he is one of those prodigies who appear only in free countries and at long intervals.

You have to see the nature of the operations of these two party-leaders in the light of their personal characters, which is why I write at such length about them: it does seem to me that, as one travels, people are just as interesting to observe as things are, and there is no doubt that, as public men, these two occupy the front rank.

I haven't heard Lord North speak, but opinion generally accords him the greatest talents, and he still has a great following in the nation. The American War is unjustly attributed to him, yet the War was demanded, begged for and undertaken with general approval, and the principle behind it dates from the time of lords Chatham and Rockingham.

It is time I stopped writing about the Commons. I've said enough for you to see that there is in this House a collection of brilliant men whose activity is generated as much by public debate as by the matters of the greatest interest that they are considering. There everything finds its level; talents emerge naturally. Admittedly, the credit, wealth and personal circumstances have a part in promoting an individual, but once he shows himself and his talents he is soon judged: with no talent his prestige ends. I think it even impossible that real talent fails to establish its rightful superiority not only because this superiority makes itself felt, and is sought by the parties, but because it is judged by the nation. This is through the Press, which prints reports of important committees, and moulds the reputation of those taking part and those who have conceived and directed them. But you know that one party in the House is without influence if it lacks popularity, if it lacks an elected majority. One effect is that it is the public opinion of the nation which decides the real state of operation of government.[66] It has to be consulted, clearly, on its true interests. It has the right to complain, and make itself heard through petitions. It has in its own bosom able men who sound the alarm through their writings: it is free. In a word, the right to active opposition is part of its constitution; and passive opposition exists in fact through the form of judgments by juries. The different parties, and the House in general, may thus dare everything and undertake everything with the nation, but without it nothing would work . . . [Lazowski rehearses Montesquieu and the division of powers, etc.]

Of all that I've told you about London, you rightly conclude that having – even more than Paris – an immense trade and a maritime trade, it is larger and more peopled. You'll have seen, in the course of my journal, that the nation is, generally speaking, richer and that the trade and its facilities are more extensive, that the agriculture is better, but, above all, more universally cultivated and respected, that their different establishments, whether in factories or manufactures generally, are grown larger and more perfect; so you conclude that the capital, which serves generally as model to the provinces is, in regard to capitals on the continent, as provinces are to its provinces. I will give you an example of such establishments, which will give you a means of comparison for judging the rest.

A GREAT LONDON BREWERY

You know the breweries of Flanders; and may have seen that of the Gobelins in Paris, and what a great undertaking it is. We have seen one of the London breweries,[67] in which Porter is brewed – a kind of strong beer, of which the recipe is a secret, but

---

66   In Paris in 1781, when François was 15 and Lazowski 32 and both of them 'politically aware', Jacques Necker, Louis XVI's best hope as a Finance Minister, made a famous experiment in 'open government'; and published 20,000 copies of the *Compte Rendu*, his statement of the ordinary expenditures and revenues of the Crown in balance – precisely the routine subject Fox had been raising here with Pitt. Simon Schama describes Necker's action as 'an exercise in public education, an attempt to form an engaged citizenry': Schama, *Citizens*, 1989, p. 95. He goes on to quote Necker's own observation, so close to Lazowski's: 'The strong bond between citizens and state, the influence of the nation on government, the guarantees of civil liberty to the individual, the patriotic support which the people always give the government in crisis, all contribute to make English citizens unique in the world'. However imperfect, Britain's representative institutions worked. When Necker was forced by the *Old Régimers*, Maurepas and Vergennes, to resign, there was a sudden sense of public calamity: 'people sadly pressed each other's hand as they passed'.

67   Pl. 53. Dr Peter Mathias, the leading authority on the history of brewing in Georgian England, has kindly read these paragraphs, and thinks that, on balance, this was Whitbread's Brewery, then as now in Chiswell Street, visited by George III in 1787. He says that the excise payment of £54,000 suggests either Whitbread or John Calvert (Peacock Brewhouse in White Cross Street). What really clinches the matter is Lazowski's description of the underground cisterns, which tallies exactly with those installed at Whitbread's, even to the timing (Mathias, *Brewing Industry in England, 1700–1830*, 1959, pp. 59–61): in May 1785, he says one of the cisterns 'was just being finished'.

53.   *London. Chiswell Street, Whitbread's Brewhouse. Painted by George Garrard, 1783. It celebrates Mansell, a favourite dray-horse: see note 71 opposite.*

54.   *Chelsea. The Physick Garden. D. Lysons,* Environs. *See p. 226 below.*

which contains laudanum and oil of vitriol.[68] I had heard of this brewery as something curious to see, but found it very much above what I'd heard or imagined.

There are always three coppers in action, each of which takes 25 *quarters* of malt, or about 50 *setiers*,[69] judging by their volume. They are clad in stonework reinforced with iron hoops. The water is fed in by pumps worked by horse-power. A hundred horses are needed for the working of this brewery.[70] In the same building you find the stables for all the horses and their provisioning, and the enormous shed for the housing of the coppers, with all the arrangements for emptying and cleaning them, and room for the carts to come and collect the rubbish (Pl. 53). Beside this immense shed,[71] which is the name they give to it, are weatherboarded granaries for storing the malt and hops which are kept at the top and facing the coppers. The stores are supplied from the corn-lofts above them. Beside them, the pumps have been installed for the supply of water[72] to the coppers. On the other side, there are immense reservoirs for cooling the beer. The beer enters the coolers through taps and barrels made of wood or leather; and from these coolers it descends into an enormous room with leather barrels, to be put into casks.

The cooperage is separate, and you can imagine what a sight it presents. As this kind of beer is not good till after eighteen months or two years, it ferments a lot and improves and blends in two great vats. They have conceived a method that would have frightened anybody who hadn't worked on this grand scale. They have built underground a great cistern of a hard freestone, jointed by cement of a new composition.[73] We went down into one of these cisterns that was just being finished. Its height and width are enormous, and its thickness must be considerable to withstand the pressure of the beer when it is full. The top of the vault is opened in the middle when the fermentation's over, with a sort of wooden trap-door, an opening protected above by a kind of iron lantern 3½ feet high and 2 feet in diameter, made

---

68 In his first-rate history of the Bury St Edmunds brewers, *Greene King*, 1983, pp. 24–25, Richard Wilson describes how commonly 'vitriol and copperas were used to bring beer into condition more quickly . . . and opium supposedly increased the strength of the beer. This was especially prevalent in porter, with its darker colour'.

69 An obsolete measure, varying according to place.

70 In 1785, James Watt (with young John Rennie as his assistant) was installing a steam-engine to do the work of these pumps. It is surprising that Lazowski did not comment on this engine, but, as it wasn't yet in action, they may not have been shown it. Whitbread's assistant Joseph Delafield reckoned in 1786 it was doing the work of 24 mill horses and almost covered in the first year its cost: £1,000. (Information kindly supplied by the company's archivist, N.B. Redman.)

71 *hangar*: one might have expected *magasin*. George Garrard's painting celebrates a favourite dray-horse, Mansell, as well as the trade through their wholesale porter merchant in Dublin, Thomas Haswell, whose initials appear on a barrel on the left. Dr Mathias, and Prof. Louis Cullen of Trinity College, Dublin, kindly explained these initals.

72 Brewers always refer to water as 'liquor'.

73 Robert Mylne, John Smeaton, Josiah Wedgwood and some anonymous ships' caulkers were all consulted or involved in this construction: the acid in new porter was corrosive to an alarming degree (Mathias, *loc. cit.*).

of good iron bars which can be locked. Each of the vats holds 5,000 tuns of beer, each tun representing about 250 bottles.

The cellars testify to the grandeur of this establishment, and the immense casks full of beer keep multiplying. The best way I can help you to imagine what prodigious casks a comparable enterprise might involve is by telling you that it pays the state in excise duty 54 thousand pounds sterling, or 54 thousand louis. The turnover must absorb more than 80 millions of our livres. Notice moreover that it isn't just a London enterprise; but in all the provincial towns there are breweries, and many – but many – individual breweries catering for local consumption.

CHELSEA PHYSIC GARDEN

I've told you too much and too little about London, but all I have left to tell you is about Chelsea. You know that it has the first, that is to say the most ancient, botanic garden in England.[74] I don't say it is the most beautiful and the best, but it is certainly the most useful. It gave the idea to the nation, and consequently to us. Today it belongs to the Society of the Apothecaries of London, so you would imagine it is complete in everything to do with pharmacy. But what it is famous for is the first cedars of Lebanon to be planted in Europe.[75] They are large, but not wonderful for their size or height; they are grafted generally, like apple-trees,[76] and produce cones, from which the seed raised in seed-beds is as good as that brought from Syria.

[74] Unfortunately, they missed the first, and most beautiful, when they were in Oxford, with gateways of 1632 by Nicholas Stone; but, as he wrote of their cursory look at Kew, 'there is nothing I am less well informed in than botany'. The Society of Apothecaries founded the Chelsea Physic Garden in 1673. Pisa University had opened a Physic Garden in 1543, then Oxford in 1621, then Edinburgh. In Paris, the Jardin des Plantes was opened as a Physic Garden in 1640. It is strange that Lazowski didn't know that. Admittedly Philip Miller, head gardener at Chelsea 1722–70, did make the Physic Garden one of the best-known general botanic gardens in Europe.

[75] Miss Ruth Stungo, of the research staff at the Physic garden, most kindly showed me the garden, and has a particular interest in cedars. The truth is that John Watts, head gardener here, brought back four cedars from Leiden and planted them in 1683. Ruth Stungo says it is now thought that the earliest in Britain were those at Wilton, ?c.1620, but many books *claimed* Chelsea's were the earliest. In 1771, two of the four were cut down because they caused excessive shading. (In the light of this, it seems unfortunate that, precisely a week after the storm damage of 16 October 1987, a new cedar was formally planted by a Secretary of State at the very centre of the garden, where its shade will one day create maximum harm.) By 1785, the remaining two had been pruned several times (Pl. 54).

[76] It might be that the pruning and/or damage by gales gave the trees the appearance of having been grafted. Philip Miller recorded that they were producing cones by about 1732 and were regenerating naturally by 1757. References to cedar-grafting in recent books F. J. Chittendon, *Dictionary of Gardening* and V. Chaudun, *Ornamental Conifers*, both 1956, seem to refer only to variegated forms of cedar. I'm most grateful to Ruth Stungo and Thomas Hutton for much help in these matters.

CHELSEA ROYAL HOSPITAL

Here at Chelsea, William III built his *Hôtel des Invalides* in imitation of Louis XIV.[77] Chelsea Hospital has nothing of the grandeur of ours, but it is on the maintenance and condition of the building that it must be judged, for its merit lies in its value to its individual inhabitants, the Pensioners. It is large: its front and two wings forming a long square of which one of the short sides is open to give entrance to the courtyard. Behind lies a great enclosure planted with trees for the Pensioners to walk under. They reckon 1,920 of them are housed and fed in the building. Each has his cubicle off a great corridor, each little room separated off by a partition. They have meat on five days a week and vegetables on the other two; one and a half pounds of bread, one of meat, a quarter of cheese and a jug of beer daily. Once a year they are issued with a uniform: a tunic, a pair of breeches, a hat, stockings and a pair of boots, a shirt and collar. They also have a shilling a week for laundry and maintenance.

Those soldiers on half-pay are spread throughout the counties, and not counted as pensioners. Every six months they send to the London office a certificate that they are alive, and during the following week they receive an order for their pay from the nearest Receiver of the Local Land Tax.

I will write of Greenwich on my way back to France.[78]

---

[77] In fact, Wren's remarkable building was begun in 1681 under Charles II and extended under James II, but opened in 1692, four years into William and Mary's reign: it was surely prompted by Louis XIV's *Invalides*, of 1670.

[78] My guess is that they saw Greenwich as part of a short excursion on horseback during their week in London.

12

The Dover Road

Looking back from Canterbury to London, Lazowski praised the flower-gardens and kitchen-gardens beyond the edge of the town, and the hay and mixed farming of Blackheath: vegetables in for the London market, horse-manure out for the vegetables. He found it hard to imagine that old sailors anywhere could be better off than the 3,550 housed at Greenwich Hospital: the Painted Hall 'rather rich than beautiful'.

At Chatham as at Mount Edgcumbe opposite Plymouth, they found a vantage-point from which they could see all parts of the dock, and count all the ships. The character of Kentish people, their independence and excellent farming, elicited Lazowski's most lavish praise, and led him into minute description of a seed-drill, horse-hoeing and hop-growing: Lazowski's in his element, revelling in social economy. The great Romanesque crypt beneath Canterbury cathedral was dismissed: 'of no use'. At Dover, within a few hours of sailing, he carefully records the local land-use before turning to the new harbour being built in front of the chalk cliffs.

Canterbury 9 May 1785[1]   We left London the day before yesterday, and I can't say it was without regret, even though we're now heading for home.

Some miles out of London you see only flower-gardens, kitchen-gardens and fields, many of which have been reclaimed from marshland by good drainage, as much underground field-drainage as in the form of ditches. Part of the fields is reserved for hay, the other is pasture for cows that supply cream and milk for London – the consumption of which must be immense. The view over this countryside is charming. These great fields intersected by ditches and green hedges, and with scattered houses and farms, sheds for the cattle, and gardens, are so very varied and agreeable. The soil is excellent, neither light nor heavy, mainly clay, well manured.

Here, Lazowski indulged himself (and the duke) in six pages of details on the excellence of the hay, how it was sheltered from rain, comparisons with Picardy, and so on, concluding: It is the best hay in all England: so important: so little considered in

---

[1]   In London on 6 May: 'We have been here for some days' – presumably from the evening of 28 April till 7 May. On the 9th they had left London 'the day before yesterday'. The amazing quantity of information Lazowski gathered about Kentish agriculture and society, not to mention the detailed layout of the defences of Chatham, by the time he came to write his letter in Canterbury on the 9th, provide a good reason for supposing that Greenwich had been seen on a separate excursion from London.

228

France. It would be a good thing to send some intelligent farmers over here during the hay-harvest.

More on the superb harvests of the Blackheath neighbourhood, where agriculture was mixed with market-gardening. All their vegetables are for the London market, sent by boat or on their carts, and returning with horse-manure. The work on these farms is immense: it isn't exceptional to take two harvests from the same field – for instance, after their summer cabbages they sow turnips or winter cabbage.

GREENWICH HOSPITAL

Greenwich is five miles from London, beside the Thames, and in the middle of the rich countryside I've been describing. We dismounted, left our horses beside the road, and entered the Park, with its fine, fully-grown trees, deer, cattle, and the riverside. To the left, the view is closed by London, a huge mass, forming its own enormous picture: to the right, the view is prolonged by the river, a most interesting contrast. Across the river lie the flatlands of Lower Essex.

Greenwich Hospital is superb, the architecture at once noble and elegant, an immense freestone building. All the sailors are maintained and fed like the Chelsea Pensioners, each with little rooms furnished according to their whim. Their furniture goes to their relatives when they die. Their rooms are kept extremely clean: the whole house is washed once a week. Some of their beds are made of iron to protect them from bugs: in time, all the beds will be of iron. There are 3,550 sailors, including the marine officers such as master-mariners, boatswain's mates, etc. All grades are distinguished by their uniforms and their weekly pay-packets.

Like me, you'll have heard of the great costs incurred here through abuses profiting the first officers. They seem to be inherent in all establishments run on this enormous scale. One condones such abuses when the objects of the institution are fulfilled: it's hard to imagine that old sailors could be better off. They qualify for admission by old age, the wounded having priority.

A terrace running the whole length of the building has been extended by the present King and Queen. All the ships going back and forth to London pass in front of this terrace; and all the warships of the port of Deptford, between London and Greenwich, pass before this hospital: so not only is it healthy, and comfortable, it is very pleasant.

I don't generally give you details of houses, but I must tell you of two of the main features of the hospital: the Chapel and the Hall.

The Chapel has been badly damaged by fire,[2] and they were at work on it, but I can give you its measurements: 100 feet long, 50 feet wide and 50 in height. It is difficult to imagine a room more grandly and beautifully proportioned.[3] The Hall

---

2   In 1779. It was reopened in 1789.
3   Cherry and Pevsner, 'Buildings of England', *London: South*, 1983, p. 264, say 'Athenian Stuart was surveyor, but most of the detailed work was done by his Clerk of Works, William Newton: it is of the highest order amongst any done in the new neo-Grecian spirit.'

is 80 feet long by 40 wide and 40 high. It is superb, and entirely painted. The ceiling makes an immense picture, perhaps rich rather than beautiful. The end and side walls are also painted in fresco: marine subjects, as you will easily believe, but I didn't think the painting matched the nobility of the architecture.[4]

Rochester is the first town along the road from London to Dover: however agreeable its situation on the Thames[5] – with the consequences for its trade – and although it has a fine bridge, it is an ugly town, badly laid out and meanly built. Its one main street, very long and narrow is so badly paved that one had to dismount and walk over it. It is expanding daily, like all English towns.

CHATHAM

Chatham stands next to Rochester. It is the third Royal Port of the kingdom. The town itself isn't very big, but when you join it to the dockyard, the barracks, storehouses, dwellings for the officers, etc., it occupies a considerable area. The dockyard, as in all the ports, is kept inexorably shut, so we didn't get in. But we found a vantage-point from which we could see all parts of the dock and count all the ships.[6] They were lined up, moored and made safe as at Plymouth.

The shipyard and whole range of buildings belonging to the King are aligned with the water's edge. The land slopes up steadily and appreciably. As the sea and the hinterland come close to the town, and the place is very easily arrived at, they have had to make a semicircular entrenchment round the whole of Chatham. The entrenchment runs east to a stone fort not yet quite finished: to take the fort would involve breaching the entrenchment. The fort, overlooking the countryside and flanking the entrenchment, would safeguard the dock and shipyard unless a body of troops arrived in force: it would be adequate to guard against sudden attack. The entrenchment might need more men to defend it than to attack it; it is weak and could be forced without artillery. It is in an almost shifting sand that would cave in at the least effort. But the fort overlooks the whole surrounding landscape and flanks the high ground in such a way as not to allow any thought of bringing up ships-of-the-line without taking it.

On the other side, approaching from inland, an attack must not be thought of unless an enemy disembarked in great strength: but before reaching here the Militia would have assembled on the riverside. It is not to be contemplated (a) because things are disposed otherwise than they were when Admiral Ruyter's Dutch fleet came to

---

4   Cherry and Pevsner, *loc. cit.*, rate Sir James Thornhill's famous work here, 1708–12, 'perhaps the most effective piece of baroque painting by any English artist, grand, abundant, and of a perfectly easy flow'. Sir John Summerson, *Architecture in Britain: 1530–1830*, 1953, p. 153, reckoned 'when Thornhill had finished painting the whole interior, he left it the most splendid thing of its kind in England'. Lazowski may well have been offended by one of Thornhill's subjects: Peace offering an olive branch to William III while Louis XIV, representing arbitrary power, crouches at his feet!
5   It is on the Medway, a tributary of the Thames.
6   Chatham is 30 miles from London. I imagine they spent the night of Sunday 8 May here.

burn the English ships in the Thames: the obstacles are much increased;[7] (b) because one would need to be absolute master of the seas; (c) because with ships-of-the-line it takes time to sail up the river, with the risk of being burnt in the night; and, finally, because the fort and batteries leave no ship-of-the-line with a chance of getting near – it would have no chance to use all its guns.

As to the different methods of agriculture between Rochester and Canterbury, I had little chance to enquire. *He then attempts a description of the distinctive historic character of Kentish society, and relates it to their excellent farming: tries to describe in precise detail a seed-drill, and dibbling, and horse-hoeing before going with enthusiasm into the economy of hop-growing, down to itemized costs per acre. The costs I shall be content to summarize, and the remaining descriptions I shall occasionally abridge. Most of it I include, for it displays the magnificent spirit of Lazowski's enquiries into the political economy of the English regions, and most particularly – as he declared – where it had a useful bearing on France. It was obviously in his nature to travel thus with his notebooks; it was entirely in line with the thinking and practice of Arthur Young, whose friendship he enjoyed from the previous year; and it was clearly in accord with the duc de Liancourt's intentions for the education of his two sons. It is remarkable that he kept up the pressure in the very last days and hours of their twelve-week tour, and fortunate for us. The boys had fallen silent at Salisbury and Windsor, but only, it may be assumed, so far as their notebooks were concerned.*

Kent is one of the best and richest districts in England. I don't know about its industry, but its wealth is soundly based: it is peopled by a branch of an ancient race of freeman.[8] When every husbandman was attached to the land [*glebe* was Lazowski's word], they were called yeomen: they are still farming their land today, comfortably-off, rich, independent and proud to be farmers. I don't know if there's a comparable race, such a distinctive people, in any other country in Europe, and this is not one of the least causes of progress in agriculture here. Their ambition is not limited to their farms, it is the pivot of their industry, the basis of the inheritance of their children, which must be augmented to create the dowries without too much dividing up of the land – which would make a good system of farming unthinkable. Their ideas centred on this one point; and, helped by a good education and sense of values, they dare to distance themselves from the general trends, are rich enough to try experiments, to wait for long-term profits – and they have succeeded.

They have character and public spirit perhaps more marked than in the rest of the nation. In Kent, they often find most resistance to the government's new ideas. In

7   The reference is to June 1667, when the government decided to economise by relying on coastal fortifications and failing to send a battle fleet to sea: the Dutch smashed through the boom defending Chatham, burnt four warships and calmly towed away the biggest ship, the Royal Charles, 80 guns.

8   Alan Everitt, *Landscape and Community in England*, 1985, expressed caution about the origins of Kent's wealth; says (p. 64): 'it is not in fact until the 1660s that we can be quite positive that Kent was among the five or six richest counties in England'. He confirms, though, of the Kentish Downland, that 'there are few areas of England where landscape and society have till recently remained so firmly moulded by their distant past' (p. 85). One wonders how Lazowski became aware of the peculiarity of Kent.

the last Election, for instance, they were not swept along on the general hatred of the American War, and the Fox-North Coalition: they voted for the War, and believed it constitutional. So they supported their old Member; and it seems it may be the only county to nominate a comparable Member.[9] They have a distinctive place in the nation, though this is a matter of opinion, and it is easier to give examples than to define. They do not belong to the Gentry – *gentilshommes* – but nor are they ordinary farmers; nor are they involved merely in trade.

Agriculture is not only not demeaning, it adds weight to the land-owners who practise it – from sentiment if not utility . . . It doesn't ennoble like the Church, the law, etc. The yeomen form a perfectly distinct race. They are proprietors and carry weight in a free government. William the Conqueror gave this part of the kingdom privileges, which were confirmed. One is an exception to the general rule of primogeniture (in which the eldest son inherits the estate): here, by right, it is equally divided among the children.[10] In practice, landed inheritances are rarely divided: the father generally settles the share of his children and – rather than divide his land or his farm – he assigns if possible a sum of money, which the eldest son has to make good. *Lazowski philosophizes for three pages.* Finally, although the law in Kent makes an equal division, the kind of yeomen I've told you of would not have perpetuated themselves unless they had practised a different system. I refer you to what you see in certain of our provinces, like Burgundy, where the régime produces a much greater industrial effort among the younger sons, who provide the artists, the merchants and often the real talents – effects which seem incontestable in England. These are subjects that could provide material for a long dissertation[!].

It is still one of my regrets to have been unable to follow the coastline and see Foulness, a place of great fertility and held on the best principles: in a word, not to have had an opportunity to study Kent in any depth. *Four pages on crop-rotations follows, and their method of growing peas.* Our backwardness results in a lack of terms. I use the verb *driller* [to drill] because it seems to me convenient to have one word for the process. A simple method is to adapt an ordinary plough. I will describe one: it is a funnel with four sides, like those used in milling. *Detailed measurements follow, and five pages of instructions on the use and maintenance of this seed-drill. In the fifth*

9   He had forgotten that each county elected – on a wider franchise than most Boroughs – two 'Knights of the Shire'. What he says applies broadly to both the Members returned, unopposed, for the county of Kent: the Hon. Charles Marsham 1774–90, and Filmer Honywood 1780–96, younger son of a Kentish baronet, who inherited estates in Essex. Both voted regularly in opposition to the government. Marsham worked at one time for a coalition between Pitt and Fox. George III wrote of him to Pitt: 'He will soon find the means of distressing government as an half friend.' Both men were devoted to the Whig principle of reducing the power of the Crown. (Their political biographies are outlined in Namier and Brooke, *History of Parliament: The Commons 1754–1790*.)

10   Gavelkind, a peculiar form of land tenure based on the partibility of inheritance, was recognised as the custom of Kent after the Norman Conquest, but goes back into greater antiquity. Professor Alan Everitt, the distinguished historian of Kent, affirms its importance to downland freedom, but admits that its origin remains mysterious: Alan Everitt, *Continuity and Colonization: the Evolution of Kentish Settlement*, Leicester U.P., 1986, p. 179.

page he uses the word dibblant, *his French version of* dibbling. *Three pages follow on the destruction of weeds by horse-hoeing, with a precise description of the hoe itself.* Horse-hoeing is another term we lack.

It remains for me to tell you of the cultivation of hops, greatly increased in this county. The best soil is a sort of deep black mould. At the beginning of spring, you transplant from the nursery to the hopfield three plants together. The first year you give them 5-foot poles; second year 12 or 14-foot; third, 18-foot. This is how the hop-ground is formed. Now for the cultivation. *Four pages of details.*[11] Immediately after August, it is time to pick the hops, which is done, very carefully, by the women or the young men, into baskets. Then the hops are dried on purpose-made drying-stoves. *Three pages of accounts, details of all the costs, and the summary.* So, farming a hop-ground and keeping it in good shape costs the farmer £32 11s 0d an acre before he gets any return: and farmers commonly have 20 acres of hops. The sale produces £39, so the profit is £6 an acre. But there is a lot of expense before the hopfield is in full production. Also this is the profit on the yield of excellent land. Other land yields scarcely £1 or £2 an acre. Hardly enough to encourage hop-growing, if hop-growing were not a kind of lottery: for sometimes the harvests are enormous, when an acre has been known to yield two tons (three times the yield discussed in the accounts above). So it is less by the growing of hops than by the wheat and the beans that serve as preparation that Kent is distinguished.

CANTERBURY

Canterbury is a town of modest size, which has lost its lustre since the Reformation. It has nothing remarkable but its cathedral, famous for the murder of Thomas Becket. It is a beautiful church, full of very ancient monuments that the antiquaries would find handsome. Here the Black Prince was buried: one still sees, above his tomb, his helmet, his gloves, his sword and his coat of mail. One is also shown a subterranean church, which is of no use [*n'est d'aucun usage*]. *So much for one of the most magic Romanesque buildings in Europe, but antiquities were uninteresting to the political economist: no use!*

Je . . . &c.

DOVER

uesday 10 May 1785   Here is the last letter I shall write you from England. We embark in a few hours. I'll employ them by writing about Dover, which I've had a good chance to see for the second time.

He can't resist three paragraphs on land use: light land, with a bed of hard chalk, hard to break up, even near the surface – sheep pasture – chalk mixed with manure

---

11   I have deposited my translation of Lazowski's full description of hop-growing, together with his detailed accounting, with the Museum of Kent Life, Cobtree Manor Park, Lock Lane, Sandling, Maidstone, ME14 3AU.

is left five or six months, the change in the mixture watched. The nearness of the town assures the land a considerable rent.

Anciently, the town and harbour lay at the foot of the tall hill which still carries the remains of a great, very strong castle . . . Nothing of the ancient port survives. At low tide, the river is silted up with mud, and there the masts are stored. The harbour proper – behind which a rear port has been made, separated from the basin by a bridge and a lock flushing the channel through – is now being built and covered with a fine terrace to form quays, supported by timbers and piles. The port is liable to silt up, particularly at its entrance, but as the waters pent up behind the lock will have plenty of slope and a straight run, I don't doubt they will produce the same result I've seen in France in the cleaning through of the harbour.

As the port has moved, you won't be surprised to hear that it has been pursued, with building along the river on all the land surrounding the harbour near the shore, and on land obviously reclaimed from the sea. Behind the town, the cliff is prodigiously tall, and cut down vertically, like that in the middle of Calais: it plunges down, exactly as in Normandy. It's the same hard chalk mixed with flint. In short, it is evidently the corresponding land-formation against which the sea comes hammering and undermining the base, just as it does, in our own time, on our coasts. Here it has withdrawn, depositing sands, and it's on this deposit that the new town has been built. You'd find the site most picturesque – town properly built along a line of great length, backing up against very tall cliffs, the view terminated by the enormous mass of the castle; it is interrupted by the masts of the ships, and has the sea for frame: a most agreeable picture. (Frontispiece).

I'll say nothing of the castle. In other times it would be, and was in fact, a place of great importance. It commanded the town and the harbour; its position, virtually inaccessible so long as it was defended, made it one of the keys of the kingdom. But now it serves no more than as somewhere to hoist signals or to maintain, still, a little garrison and a few pieces of cannon, more the remains of an old habit than objects of use.

Since the sea continues to carry away the sand, you can see that disembarking here is liable to be rough. To avoid this, on the moles that project into the sea, they have established good . . .

Here Lazowski's letter-book ends, mid-sentence, and presumably with a page or more missing as a result of the book's not being bound.

Epilogue: Back in France:
1785–92 and Beyond

'No epilogue, I pray you; for your play needs no excuse.' The Duke, in *A Midsummer Night's Dream*, was politely telling Bottom the Weaver and his fellow-entertainers that it was bed-time, and that they had gone on quite long enough. So, perhaps, have the La Rochefoucauld brothers and their companion; yet it might be thought infuriating to cut off their lives as abruptly as they broke off their journals. We can follow close behind them back to France, as their kindly Suffolk host, Professor Symonds, did in the summer of 1785. His lively description of Paris in that summer and autumn further explains their preoccupation – on their tour – with English manufactures and trade, gardens and farming.

In August, Symonds brought over his naval nephew, Jermyn, and settled him in 'a most agreeable house' at Pont-à-Mousson in Lorraine: to learn French and to be near his friend François, whose regiment was quartered in the town. A concrete bridge now spans the Moselle, and there is no hint of any former military presence; but there are still very agreeable houses, notably in rue St Laurent. Paris seemed 'wonderfully improved since 1770 when I was here'. He was received with more than reciprocal hospitality by François' and Alexandre's grand family. A letter to Arthur Young, in Suffolk, gives a vivid impression of his stay, which he extended till November, neglecting no opportunity: he dined twice with the great financier, Necker, out of office but not out of touch.

In July, just before Symonds arrived in France, Vergennes, the leading minister under the Controller-General Calonne, issued an *arrêt*, a prohibition of the import of all foreign cottons, muslins, gauzes and linens into France. Their aim seems to have been to push Pitt into a more general lowering of tariffs, which was finally agreed in the Treaty of September 1786. This was how Symonds described the scene he found in 1785 (BL. Add. MSS 35126, fols 296 ff.):

When the late *arrêt* was published, our commerce was to that of France as 53 to 10: Paris was overwhelmed with English goods, and MARCHANDISES ANGLOISES was written over all the shops. There was one milliner who did not sell less yearly than to the amount of £100,000 of them. Since the *arrêt*, no time has been lost to encourage the manufacture of common glass; the cotton manufactures upon Arkwright's plan; and the exploring of coal-mines. However, nine-tenths of the people are mad after our goods. The grand seigneurs must not only have English horses, with all their accoutrements, but English grooms also; and those who cannot get them are often so foolish as to oblige their own boys to wear slouched hats and cut their hair short in order to appear as English: Martin tells me he has often been deceived.

But the attention of the rich and great is still more given to English gardens. A walk ten times more winding than a snake, a ditch near it, and a bad piece of grass,

55. *Professor John Symonds, of St Edmund's Hill, Bury, in 1788. G.K. Ralph. Engraved J. Singleton.*

is dignified with the name of an English garden. Monsieur, the King's brother, not content with the Luxembourg Garden, has made a small one, in the taste described, that joins it, where there is an English cottage that has the appearance of a wretched necessary house.

Here Symonds described at length the walks round the lakes at the late J.-J. Rousseau's Ermenonville, and J.-J.'s favourite haunts there: 'they are for the most part such lovely sequestered spots as he describes in his *Héloise*' (cf. Nuneham, p. 139 above and cf. C. Quest-Ritson, *The English Garden Abroad*, 1992, p. 195). One easily sees how it occurred to François, during the dull summer of 1784 to gain some experience in designing and creating a new garden-walk for Professor Symonds at Bury; also how ready they were to appreciate the gardens at Blenheim, Nuneham, Clifton and Wilton.

Dining with Necker, Symonds found that he regarded Craufurd, the British commissioner at Versailles for drafting the Commercial Treaty, as discredited: he was duly replaced by Eden, who negotiated the final satisfactory treaty. Symonds then reported to Young something directly concerning the Duke and Lazowski: at the desire of Calonne an 'Assembly' was held. An 'Assembly' of the 'Administration of Agriculture' was the new official name of the old Royal Society of Agriculture, which was now expected to sift ideas and feed them to *l'Administration d'Agriculture*, a body like the Board of Agriculture, of which Young became Secretary at the outbreak of the war with Revolutionary France. The 'Administration' was created by the Physiocrat Du Pont de Nemours and the chemist Lavoisier in response to the drought in June 1785. Symonds described a meeting of the very academic 'Assembly', of which the Duke was a member:

The Duke of Liancourt carried thither a Memoire of Lazowski containing the best English farming practice. The Academicians pretended to know better, and an Abbé took the lead, who averred that he had learned in England himself the best agriculture. To him all the memoires were given. He instructed all the Intendants from this olio [hotch-potch], and the Intendants thought they had a right to alter the cookery.

This fiasco had an important consequence for Lazowski and Alexandre. In November, Symonds bore them off back to Bury St Edmunds for three months. They stayed at the Angel. On 19 January they were among the 43 guests of James Oakes at a private ball in Bury Guildhall: Mr Symonds brought two other guests (I owe Jane Fiske this unpublished item from the Oakes diaries). Then, on 14 March, they set out from the Angel with their two servants (Alexandre's was called Nelson) on a carefully planned tour of Scotland and Ireland. Alexandre was even more reluctant to leave Bury than he had been a year earlier: 'for the first time I felt as much at home in some English houses as I did in my father's', and he added a note on his self-education.

At the end of my stay in Bury, I read some novels, which made me astonished at my own use of language and dismayed at my own shortcomings. I hope this confession may reassure my father; and prepare him for reading this little work which needs his indulgence and patience. Mr Young had equipped us with tour-notes.

Again, they were setting out in 'snow and ice so thick that the road was hardly passable'. Lazowski and Alexandre were on horseback, the servants in the gig, and Dr Wollaston's son, one of Alexandre's friends, rode some way with them to show them one of his uncle's estates: in that weather! The Rev. Dr Frederick Wollaston, a prebendary of Peterborough, lived in Northgate Street, Bury, with two sons of about Alexandre's age. It was quite a testing itinerary, especially for the time of year: the Dukeries, Newcastle-on-Tyne, Edinburgh (where Adam Smith gave them an introduction to a Glasgow professor), right on up to Banff and Fort George on the Moray Firth and along to Fort William and a brief sailing adventure in the Western Highlands, over to Belfast and Dublin, and back through North Wales to London and home. At one stage, Lazowski expressed to Young his disappointment in Alexandre: 'He counts every day how many miles we have done, and his satisfaction is all wais in proportion to the number.' Young was probably amused at the complaint: all through France, he seldom failed to register his mileage at the end of each day's journal-entry, and Alexandre may easily have learnt the habit from him. Lazowski must often have been an exasperating companion to a lively, not very academic, 18-year-old aristocrat: from Glasgow he told Young he was writing for 'four hours at least every day'. Young's *Autobiography* gives his explanation of all that writing:

> Lazowski's employment was chiefly drawing up memorials upon political subjects for the duke's information, who was a vain man, and, without doubt, figured in conversation by this subsidiary assistance.

Young very well knew there was more to it than vain 'figuring in conversation'. For at this time, in April 1786, the Duke wrote to him from Paris to tell him he'd heard a few days earlier from 'our friend Lazowski in Edinburgh' that they were delighted with their tour, and that Lazowski, a few days before setting out from Bury, had sent him 'the most superb memorial on the agriculture of the two Kingdoms' (*loc. cit.*, fol. 335). This was clearly Lazowski's carefully prepared response to the fiasco last summer at the meeting of the 'Assembly', and what he had been labouring at while Alexandre took to reading novels in Bury.

This new memorial was presented by the Duke to the 'Assembly', together with his own *Extrait*; and an amalgamation of the two documents went forward on 9 June to Calonne over the signature of seven powerful and influential members of *l'Administration d'Agriculture* itself, including Vergennes, the dominant (though now terminally ill) foreign affairs minister, and Lavoisier the great scientist. It spoke of 'the infinitely estimable M. Lazowski who seemed to have neglected nothing in informing himself', and of the Duke's 'infinitely interesting Extract: we can only invite the Minister to read one or the other'.

Liancourt and Lazowski were clearly determined to circumvent that tiresome know-all of an Abbé and get through to the Minister, Calonne. Calonne was fairly desperately trying to operate what Simon Schama calls 'the nearest thing to a concerted economic policy since Turgot's in 1774–76' (*Citizens*, 1989, p. 231). But it was about to fail, and his own conspicuous nest-feathering lost him support all round: he was disgraced, and took refuge in England with a great trunk-load of apparently unsorted papers, including this large, close-written, highly statistical 18-page memorial produced by the Duke and Lazowski. There it is now, among the Privy Council papers in Chancery Lane, filed obscurely under PC 1/123 2946. Professor J.R. Harris kindly drew my attention to the original, and I find there is another copy in the La Rochefoucauld family archives. So it wasn't a mere matter of the Duke wanting to 'figure in conversation'. But how 'infinitely valuable' Lazowski's researches really were, or might have been, to France, has not, I think, been seriously examined; nor even whether Calonne did more than glance at them, though the American historian C.C. Gillispie included a general description of the 'Assembly' and the 'Administration of Agriculture' in his wide-ranging book, *Science and Polity at the End of the Old Régime* (Princeton, 1980).

At least Lazowski accomplished, as the powerful signatories pointed out, a 'singular rapport' between his own independent calculation of the French wheat harvest (dire in 1785, and a well-known basic element in the Revolution) and the Ministry's official calculations. This predisposed those serious politicians and scientists to look favourably on his mathematical presentation of the English agricultural economy – especially his estimates of the English farmer's outgoings, which he thought 'gave a more useful idea than endless detailed descriptions'.

It is those indefatigably detailed descriptions that, on the whole, endear him to us. Yet that Calonne memorial does reveal a political slant on the observant travelling of Lazowski, if not on that of his young companions. They were committed to travelling as education: it was their version of the Grand Tour; and that side of it, if not the companionship, appealed to both young men, especially the elder. Sons of an actively philanthropic duke embedded in the King's household can scarcely have doubted the 'political' relevance of so much English technology to their own country's needs: yet their descriptions were enthusiastically written for their father's eyes, and for their own in old age, as they occasionally reflected. If their father profited from their reports, that does not put them into the category of industrial spies. That he did, in a philanthropic way, profit may be gathered from Arthur Young's stay at Liancourt in September, 1787: 'At a village near Liancourt, the Duke has established a manufacture of linen and stuffs mixed with thread and cotton, which promises to be of considerable utility; there are 25 looms employed, and preparations for more. As the spinning for these looms is also established, it gives employment to great numbers of hands who were idle . . . Such efforts merit great praise.' By 1783, indeed, the Duke had established these small manufactures in Liancourt itself and seven neighbouring villages. (Pls. 56–57. Their value is discussed critically by J.-D. de La Rochefoucauld in *Le Duc de la Rochefoucauld-Liancourt*, 1980, pp. 106–39.) The nature of the La Rochefoucauld travels in England in 1785 differs little from that of Young's travels through France. It is not surprising, for they were all – including Lazowski – his pupils since their little tour together in Suffolk and Essex in July, 1784. In 1795, Alexandre did set up his own ambitious spinning-mill and cotton factory, with the aid of an expert 'Englishman' called Macklood (see p. 225 below). Even that (ultimately unsuccessful) enterprise cannot alter the essential 'innocence' of Alexandre's responses, ten years earlier, to what he saw in Derby.

56/57.   *Liancourt. View of cotton-mill and view of calico-factory established by the duke c.1783. Engraved by Wexelberg. See p. 239.*

Anyway, it is now clear that, for Lazowski, the 1786 tour of Scotland and Ireland with Alexandre was a serious extension of the work he had put in on the Calonne memorial: writing that memorial, he had been conscious that he was covering only England; that there was a large gap in his understanding of the economy of the United Kingdom. Poor Alexandre had to make the best of it. Among their surviving papers there may be just enough material for a slender book about the adventure into 'North Britain' and Ireland.

Back in France with all his new information, Lazowski evidently represented the duke at meetings of the agricultural 'Assembly'. C.C. Gillispie writes of him with notable absence of sympathy: 'His discourse tended to dominate the later sessions, marked more by Anglophilia than by agronomy' (*op. cit.*, p. 386). Lavoisier, prime mover in *l'Administration d'Agriculture*, and whose prodigious accomplishments included farming experiments on his own property (but did not, alas, save him from the guillotine), certainly seems to have been very much in line, in his assessment of what was wrong with French agriculture, with Arthur Young – who was admittedly English, and an agronome. He paid the Lavoisiers (Pl. 58) a visit in their Paris laboratory in October 1787. When a French translation of Young's *Travels in France* appeared in 1793, complete with its 'General Observations' on the French economy and the progress of the Revolution to the beginning of 1792, the far-from-Anglophile *Convention* ordered 20,000 copies to be printed and distributed free all over France.

While Lazowski attended meetings, Young was greatly enjoying the first of his incomparable French tours. (Constantia Maxwell's Cambridge edition, 1929, is the more fully annotated.) Lazowski had already, a year earlier (August 1786), chided him for not coming to join him and François at Pont-à-Mousson: his English was still idiosyncratic, but confident:

> Now you would live with a Regiment, and your insatiable curiosity would be furnished with a manner of living and some military details unknown in England. You would travel with us in the next month through Switzerland that you should be very amiable . . . the French will give you some of their transient fire which, mixed with the English reflexion, will be productive of good. Jermyn speaks now very well, yet [a year ago, when he came to Pont-à-Mousson] he could neither understand or write a single word.

In that same letter (BL. Add. MSS. 35126 fol. 351) he expressed some Adam Smith scepticism about the value of the imminent Anglo-French Treaty: 'they understand not, the richness of one nation must in the end enrich also the other . . . the interest of consumers is the interest of the nation'. He ended by expressing the warmth of his feelings for Young: '*Je vous embrasse de tout mon cœur*'.

Next year, April 1787, he pressed again, and Young came. The lure was an excursion as far as the Pyrenees, where François was obliged to go to take the waters at Bagnères-de-Luchon. It was a resort for people suffering from 'cutaneous eruptions', which sounds like eczema: it may be that the unspecified ailment detaining them in Bury between October 1784 and February 1785 was eczema, and its familiar companion asthma (see p. 11 above). On 25 May 1787, Young reached Paris.

58.   *Paris. The Lavoisiers, by Jacques-Louis David. See p. 241.*

The agreeable reception and friendly attentions I met with from this liberal family were well calculated to give me the most favourable impression – 42 miles. After a rapid excursion in Paris, with my friend Lazowski, spend the evening at his brother's.

(His brother Claude, born 1752, was an Inspector of Manufactures: there, Young met the energetic and agreeable secretary of the 'Assembly' – the Society of Agriculture – M. Broussonnet).

On the break-up of the party, went with Count Alexander post to Versailles to be present at the fête the day following – Whitsunday . . . Watched the King at dinner. If Kings do not live like other people, they lose much of the pleasure of life . . . The whole palace, except the chapel, seems open to all the world. But the officers at the door of the apartment where the King dined made a distinction, and would not permit all to enter promiscuously. Travellers speak much of the remarkable interest the French take in all that personally concerns their king, showing by the eagerness of their attention not curiosity only, but love.

Something changed all that, in five brief years. By a strange coincidence, two of the central figures in the La Rochefoucauld visit to England in 1784 and 1785 became principal recording witnesses in the fall of the French monarchy – Young in the crucial first stages in June and July 1789, and François on 10 August 1792. In his *Souvenirs du 10 Août 1792* (ed. Jean Marchand, Paris, 1929), François described, hour by hour, that terrible day when he, almost alone of the royal servants, stayed perilously close to the royal family in their walk through the Tuileries gardens and up the steps into the *Salle du Manège* – the young Louis XV's riding-school which was now the seat of the Legislative Assembly. All through that August day, as speakers declared the end of the monarchy, François waited, miserable and shocked, on a bench as near as he dared to the stifling reporters'-box in which the royal family were caged. In the evening, failing even to be able to smuggle a clean neckerchief to the Queen past the guard, and wearing a disguise given him by a waiter in the Assembly's refreshment-room, he withdrew into streets strewn with the bodies of the slain, the dying, and the drunk. Only a handful of Frenchmen showed any love for the King that day.

The opening stages in the Revolution Young saw and understood clearly on his third visit, in 1789, but that first tour in 1787 was relatively cheerful. His dismay at the wretchedness of French country inns – 'filth, vermin, impudence and imposition' – explains the delight of François and Alexandre in most English country inns. It also led Young, in Languedoc, to serious political comment:

In England, the friendly clubs [or Box Clubs, from which – see p. xix – the Savings Banks developed], the visits of friends and relations, the parties of pleasure, the resort of farmers, the intercourse with the capital and with other towns, form the support of good inns. In this journey through Languedoc, I have passed an incredible number of splendid bridges, and many superb causeways. But this only proves the absurdity and oppression of government. Bridges that cost £70,000 or £80,000, and immense causeways, to connect towns that have no better inns that such as I have described, appear to be gross absurdities. What traveller, surrounded by the beggarly filth of an inn, will not condemn such inconsistencies and wish for more comfort and less appearance of splendour?

Young went on to evoke the charm of his life with the La Rochefoucauld party in the Pyrenees. One wonders if poor François really subjected himself to the 'cure' that ostensibly brought them to Luchon. Young wrote: 'The present baths are horrible holes; the patients lie up to their chins in hot sulphureous water . . .' He complained, characteristically, of their hosts' dining at midday:

> Dividing the day exactly into halves destroys it for any expedition, inquiry or business that demands seven or eight hours' attention . . . What is a man good for after his silk breeches and stockings are on?

So Lazowski and he were 'early in the mountains' to seek out 'the more intelligent peasants'. They had many and long conversations with those who understood French.

As soon as he was back in Suffolk, in November, he saw that he had to return to extend his survey to cover the whole of France. From August to October 1788 he managed to tour the whole north-west and western side of the country. Meanwhile earlier, in June, Alexandre, not quite 21, married, more fortunately than he could have known, Adélaïde de Chastullé, a cousin of Joséphine de Beauharnais. His father, the Duke, spent 63,000 livres on the wedding-feast, clothes, etc., which may be compared with the 51,000 livres paid out on the long residence in England, 1783–86, of his two sons and Lazowski (La Rochefoucauld, Wolikow and Ikni, *Le duc de La Rochefoucauld-Liancourt*, Paris, 1980, p. 79).

On the second tour, in 1788, Young was prevented from seeing the dockyard at Brest – much as the brothers had been at Plymouth and Chatham in 1785 – despite 'Respectable letters to respectable people'. He recorded the recent making at Cherbourg of a great mole of insulated cones of timber and masonry, an enormous breakwater, a curious fore-runner of the 1944 Mulberry Harbour at Arromanches on that same shore: Mulberry, though, was a remarkable success; the cones a very expensive failure. He rounded off his 1788 tour with a visit to the duc de La Rochefoucauld whose murder in 1794 brought the La Rochefoucauld title to Liancourt. The friendly duke and duchess entertained Young for three days at their astonishing château at La Roche-Guyon, where the chalk cliff fronting the Seine near Vernon had been cut back steeply to make room for it. Young had enjoyed the ducal company in the Pyrenees, and their welcome here beside the Seine extended to letting him quiz their agent 'relative to the agriculture of the country'. (The fine 18th-century reception-rooms on the first floor have lately been restored, though not furnished, and are open to the public. A junior branch of the family, ducs de La Roche-Guyon, lived here from the early 19th century, and were much embarrassed, in March 1944, when the late Field-Marshal Rommel moved in with his Army Group B headquarters staff.) In July 1829, two years after his father's death, François bought this house from a cousin: it was his father's birth-place.

It is faintly surprising that Young managed to cover eastern France so thoroughly on his third tour (June 1789 – January 1790): during those first three weeks in Paris in June he saw the forces of revolution boiling up, shaping themselves round the question whether the commons should be isolated, one estate, one voice, among three; or whether its voice would prevail through the merging of the three estates. On *27 June* Young wrote:

The whole business now seems over, and the revolution complete. The King has been frightened by the mobs into overturning his own act of the Royal Session (on the 23rd), by writing to the presidents of the orders of the nobility and clergy, requiring them to join the Commons.

28 June. Having provided myself with a light French cabriolet for one horse, or gig *Anglois*, and a horse, I left Paris, taking leave of my excellent friend Mons. Lazowski, whose anxiety for the fate of his country made me respect his character as much as I had reason to love it for the thousand attentions I was in the daily habit of receiving from him . . . I had passed some time at Paris amongst the fire, energy and animation of a great revolution. And for those moments not filled by political events, I had enjoyed the resources of liberal and instructing conversations; the amusements of the first theatre in the world. The change to inns, and those inns *French*; the ignorance of everybody of those events that were now passing and which so intimately concerned them; the detestable circumstances of having no newspapers, with a press much freer than the English, altogether formed such a contrast that my heart sank with depression.

Young not only saw straight to the political heart of the matter, he described the human framework so vividly. (Schama's *Citizens* makes admirable use of him.)

The business in the pamphlet shops is incredible . . . one can scarcely squeeze from the door to the counter . . . The coffee-houses in the Palais-Royal present yet more singular, astonishing spectacles: they are not only crowded within, but expectant crowds are at the doors and windows . . . the want of bread is terrible.

Then he switches to dinner in the Duke's apartments in the palace of Versailles:

large party of nobility and deputies, among them the Duc d'Orleans, Abbé Sieyès, and M. Rabaut Saint-Etienne. They ate and drank, and sat and walked, loitered and smirked and smiled with that easy indifference that made me stare at their insipidity . . . It was not without disgust that I observed the Duc d'Orleans' small sort of wit and flippant readiness to titter.

But outside:

the language that was talked, by all ranks of the people, was nothing less than a revolution in the government, and the establishment of a republic . . . The supineness and even stupidity of the court is without example.

While the Bastille was being captured, Young was arriving in Metz, where he actually found a good and cheap inn, the *Faison*, and someone who agreed with him that it was 'now only by torrents of blood that we have any hope of establishing a freer constitution'. At Nancy, next day, he admired the architecture, heard that Mons. Necker had been 'asked to quit the kingdom' and went to look at the botanical garden by the Porte Sainte-Catherine: it was underfunded, as it is today. Then at Lunéville, Lazowski's old father made him very welcome, and expected him to stay some days. At Schlestadt, now Sélestat, in Alsace, on 22 July, he was warmly greeted by François, whose regiment, happily entitled the Champagne Light Horse (*chasseurs à cheval*) was quartered there. 'No attentions could be kinder than what I received

59. *Barthélemy Faujas de Saint-Fond, French Inspector of the furnace industry in 1784. Portrait anon., undated.*

60. *Birmingham. Priestley's house at Fair-hill after the mob sacked it, 14 July 1791. R.H. Witton, engraved W. Ellis. See pp. 248–9.*

from him; and he introduced me to a good farmer from whom I had the intelligence I wanted'.

On he went to Besançon and from there wrote to Lazowski, who replied on 2 August:

> I never was so uneasy in my life. The outcry against the English has been very high for a time. The people was convinced that you were paying *banditti* for creating disturbance . . . Every traveller is stopped and in the provinces they do not know what is to travel for the sake of travelling . . . You are a giddy head.

By then, Young had been in Dijon discussing Priestley's views on gas with the celebrated chemist and industrialist Guyton de Morveau, who vehemently disagreed with Priestley's theories. At Montélimar, Young was delighted with his reception by the eminent naturalist and expert on volcanic geology, Faujas de Saint-Fond. Saint-Fond, he says, received him 'with the frank politeness inherent in his character', and bore him off to visit his country-seat and farm, where he spent 'one of the richest days I have enjoyed in France'. It was 24 August (1789), and they had a proper harvest supper, 'drinking *à l'angloise* to the success of the PLOUGH . . . If M. Faujas de Saint-Fond comes to England, as he gives me hope, I shall introduce him to [my Suffolk farming friends]'. It is curious, and I think sinister, that Saint-Fond seems to have concealed from Young any reference to his highly business-like tour of Britain five years earlier, in 1784.

In Manchester, only five months before the La Rochefoucauld brothers' visit, the manufacturers allowed Saint-Fond to see their finished velvets in the warehouse, but despite his letters of introduction to Dr Percival, flatly declined to let him see the detailed processes the brothers were shown (B. Faujas de Saint-Fond, *A Journey through England and Scotland, 1784*, ed. A. Geikie, Glasgow, 1907, vol. II, p. 267, and cf. p. 62, footnote 13 above). In Edinburgh, Saint-Fond managed to get on to excellent terms with three leading scientists, and 'the venerable philosopher Adam Smith loaded me with polite attentions'. But at Prestonpans, the great sulphuric-acid works remained closed to him behind its high walls, and at the Carron Ironworks he was admitted, but firmly debarred from the large workshops where the cannons were bored (*Ibid.*, I, pp. 173–78). What Saint-Fond naturally kept very quiet about (so that even his editor in 1907 remained in ignorance) was that in 1784 he was a government-inspector of *Bouches à Feu*, 'cannon', the whole furnace industry (J.R. Harris, 'Industrial Espionage in the 18th Century', *Industrial Archaeology Review*, Spring 1985, p. 133). We may reasonably think that his delight in the geology of Fingal's Cave was more than offset by his failure to penetrate those workshops at Carron, for his business was not innocent espionage.

Young toured Italy from September to Christmas, returning to Paris on 3 January 1790, and staying with the Liancourts in the rue de Varenne. While Young was on his travels, the King had been brought from Versailles to live in the Tuileries. On 4 January Young wrote:

> After breakfast, walk in the gardens of the Tuileries, where there is the most extraordinary sight . . . The King, walking with six grenadiers of the bourgeois

247

militia, with an officer or two of his household, and a page. The doors of the gardens are kept shut in respect of him, in order to exclude everybody but deputies or those who have admission tickets. When he entered the palace, the doors of the garden were thrown open to all without distinction, though the Queen was still walking with a lady of her court. A mob followed her, taking off their hats whenever she passed. There is a little garden railed off for the dauphin . . . a very pretty, good-natured-looking boy of 5 or 6 years old: wherever he goes, all hats are taken off to him, which I was glad to observe. All the family being kept thus close prisoners (for such they are in effect) affords, at first view, a shocking spectacle.

During his sixteen January days in revolutionary Paris, Young was at the heart of things, dining mostly in the Tuileries apartments assigned to Liancourt as grand master of the wardrobe. Twice a week Liancourt gave a dinner to between twenty and forty of the deputies – nominally at 3.30 in the afternoon, though it was sometimes 7.00 before they dragged themselves from the business of the Assembly, just across the garden. Young was critical of the proceedings of the Assembly, most speeches being read, and therefore without precise relevance to one another. A year later, many of them were brilliantly relevant.

Who would be in the gallery of the English House of Commons if Mr Pitt were to bring a written speech to be delivered on a subject on which Mr Fox was to speak before him? The want of order, and every kind of confusion, prevails . . . utterly destructive of freedom of debate.

Two days before he left for England, two of the deputies carried Young off to the Revolution Club at the *Jacobins*, where he was introduced as the author of the *Arithmétique Politique*, and elected a member! 'Whatever passes in this club is almost sure to pass in the Assembly'.

He concluded his stay by reflecting on French cooking, feeding habits, fashions (which changed ten times more *slowly* than in England), very much the obverse, indeed, of the observations François recorded while he was in Bury St Edmunds (see *A Frenchman's Year in Suffolk, 1784*). On 19 January he waited on his friends to take leave. First the Duke de Liancourt:

His conduct in the revolution has been direct and manly from the very beginning . . . The decisive steps which he took at Versailles in advising the King, etc., are known to all the world. He is, undoubtedly, to be esteemed one of those who have had a principal share in the revolution, but he has been invariably guided by constitutional motives. He has been as much averse from unnecessary violence and sanguinary measures as those who were most attached to the ancient government.

His last evening in Paris Young spent with his friend Lazowski – 'he endeavouring to persuade me to reside upon a farm in France, and I enticing him to quit French bustle for English tranquillity'. But they didn't meet again. French bustle became a whirlwind, in which Lazowski appeared fleetingly, then vanished. English tranquillity was not immune. The painter John Eckstein, who was an eye-witness, showed how infernally the anti-Jacobin riot in Birmingham celebrated 14 July in 1791, destroying

Dr Priestley's house and laboratory (Birmingham Museums & Art Gallery): so did R.H. Witton and William Ellis (Pl. 60).

That quiet day Young had spent back in July of 1789 in Alsace with François and the officers of his regiment was one of the last François passed with that regiment. The Revolution was at once affecting the discipline in the regiment and the peace of the countryside. Alsace was overrun by *banditti*, out to burn down the châteaux: François was slightly wounded in leading an attack on them. Embarrassed by what he saw as his father's involvement in the revolution,

> I believed it my duty not to conduct myself publicly in such a way as to condemn members of my family. I made no move towards either the Princes or the *emigrés*. The only party left for me to adopt was that of the King. His misfortunes, the obligation so many of his servants felt to leave him, touched me greatly. I could join only those who resisted the Republicans.

His father's liberalism was not François' only worry. His only sister, Aglaé, not quite fifteen, died in 1789. His mother, ill with grief, sought solace first at the waters of Aix-la-Chapelle with Alexandre, then at Soleure in Switzerland, just south of Basle, where François, resigned from a regiment to which he'd been appointed by a King no longer free, joined her. She was bed-ridden for fifteen months, and she and her husband the Duke lived amicably separated from then on. In 1792 she bought the manor of Montfleury, near Gex and the Swiss frontier.

François described his own life during the Revolution in the book published in 1929, *Souvenirs du 10 Août 1792 et de l'Armée de Bourbon*, edited by Jean Marchand. It is a melancholy tale, conscientiously told, by the main author of this tour through England, which in retrospect must have seemed so politically calm and untroubled. Readers of French will want to read *Souvenirs* for themselves: I must limit myself to the bare outline.

Young's description of the King, Queen and Dauphin, 'caged', like creatures in a zoo, in the Tuileries garden in January 1790, makes it easy to see why they risked their 'flight' to Varennes in June 1791: their ineptitude in bungling their sole chance of gaining safety makes their final dreadful fate seem inevitable. François called it not the *flight*, but the *journey*, to Varennes, and thereupon decided that it was his duty to stay close to the King's person. Which is exactly where he was on 20 June 1792 when waves of people surged into the King's apartment, but withdrew without harming him. The events that began on 9 August took them by surprise. François captures the nightmare-quality that lasted throughout the next day. At about 6.00 on the morning of the 10th, the King left his apartments, where people were sitting on his chairs, tables and all over the floor; and went down into the courtyards. The Garde Nationale cried 'Vive le Roi!' – sounding even in good heart. 'And there I was glad to see my close friend, M. de Lazowski, with his brother'. (He had six brothers, ranging from 24 to 40 in 1792: this was probably the Inspector of Manufactures Young had met.) However, some people were shouting 'Down with the Veto' – one of the mob's rude names for the King. There was a lot more of that as the King walked out into the gardens to visit a guard-post on the south terrace, overlooking the quay and the Seine.

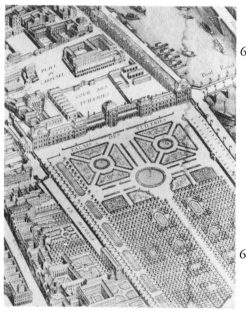

61. *Paris. Plan of Tuileries gardens, across the corner of which François walked with the royal family from the Palace to* Le Manège, *where the Assembly was in session, early on 10 August, 1792.*

62. *Paris. 10 August 1792, in the Legislative Assembly. Baron Gérard's dramatic picture, the royal family cooped up in the reporters' box behind the President of the Assembly. François was able to keep the royal family in view from a bench in a corner of the Assembly.*

It was about 8.30 that morning when François followed the King and Queen across the garden to the Assembly, the Princesse de Lamballe saying to him 'We shall never return', the little Princesse Royale sobbing. He went with them right into the hall of the Assembly, and heard the King pronounce, in a firm voice, that he had come to the Assembly with his family *'pour éviter aux Français un crime de plus'* – to spare the French people any further incrimination. Among the vivid events François described that day was one in which he saw through the door of the Assembly an old man lying spreadeagled on the steps, and bravely rescued him, binding his bloody head with the handkerchief he later wished he had to offer the Queen: it turned out to be the Marshal Viscount de Maillé, and François persuaded one of the deputies to help him safely home just across the Pont Royal. Meanwhile the National Guard was rapidly vanishing; in despair, François found a bench in the corner of the Assembly, and went over in his mind everything he'd seen. He'd been worried about Lazowski, and was overjoyed when suddenly he appeared – 'for one loves one's friends a hundred times more in the midst of great danger than in ordinary times'. Here he heard the end of the monarchy proclaimed, and knew that the King and the Dauphin were as good as dead. At 7.00 that evening he made his last attempt to help the King, who told him it was too dangerous to think of. That was when the Queen asked him, in vain, for a clean handkerchief. He left to find a bed in his brother Alexandre's house, in case his own house was watched. There he found Alexandre and his wife, eight months pregnant, and Lazowski. It was the last time all three – the brothers and Lazowski – were together. Next day someone came to warn them that mobs with pikes were coming along the boulevards to search his brother's house, normally occupied by one of the hated Swiss guards-officers.

Across the river, François headed for home in the rue de Varenne, but was intercepted by servants who had seen sinister individuals skulking outside. So he went to the home of the duchesse de Lévis, at the end of the rue St Dominique (running more or less parallel with the rue de Varenne). There, he instructed his servants to bring his saddle-horses to a place near the Ecole Militaire, beyond the Invalides, covering up the saddles to give the appearance of exercising them. He left Mme de Lévis's house with his English servant, talking to him loudly, in the hope that he'd be mistaken for English. Near the Ecole Militaire he saw his horses, asked his man to make his adieus to his family and friends, and leave him. He jumped on to the horse, drew a pistol in one hand, and left at a trot across the plain towards Versailles, avoiding towns and villages.

He called on his uncle at La Roche-Guyon, and at Rouen managed to persuade his father he was in urgent danger and must leave at once: *'Quelle drôle de chose –* how strange to find myself re-united with those who'd declared allegiance to the Constitution': in François' eyes, 'constitution' amounted to 'Revolution': in England in 1784 he wrote: 'the King of England is no king in a Frenchman's eyes' (*A Frenchman's Year in Suffolk, 1784*, p. 77). His father put his own point of view in a letter written from the safety of Bury St Edmunds on 30 October 1792, to Lazowski, presumably lying low in Paris. He clearly couldn't believe that he would have shared the fate of his cousin in Gisors if he had stayed in France, and he held François responsible for his escape!

My eldest son, against my judgment, despite my entreaties, joined the Army of the Emigrés: we nearly fell out over it, and I don't blame myself. I wasn't able to make him renounce the project, which was prompted by, *soufflé par, les petites dames et les petits messieurs de Paris.* I need only one malevolent witness to ensure that I incur the blame for his being in the emigré army, that I'm questioned in the matter, and put in the cruel dilemma of lying to no purpose (for his action is fairly common knowledge) or acknowledging and expressing my disapproval – which as you well know I would never do, whatever I might feel in my heart about his ineptitude.

This very long letter, a photocopy of which belonged to Jean Marchand, is touching for what it reveals of the Duke's *complete* confidence in Lazowski. In the last line he refers to Alexandre, and adds: 'At present not far from you', which showed that Alexandre was in no hurry to emigrate to San Domingo (see below). The Duke hoped to become a naturalized Englishman, but shortage of funds forced him to cross the Atlantic: see Duc de Liancourt, *Journal de Voyage en Amérique et d'un Séjour à Philadelphie*, publié par Jean Marchand, Paris, 1940.

At Le Havre, François reflected justly (it was 13 August, *before* the Massacres of September): 'One part of our nation is drunk with blood and capable of any excess . . .' His old friend from eight years earlier, M. Mistral, directed him to an Englishman, M. Lake, running a bar in the rue St Julien, who got him away. On 15 August, early in the morning, he reached Portsmouth, mooring alongside the *Hector*, man-of-war. By an extraordinary coincidence, Jermyn Symonds was serving on the *Hector*, and they were able to have lunch together before François left for London. One wonders if he ever heard that, on 16 December, old Mistral's body was found on the beach at Le Havre: no evidence was found as to whether it was accident, suicide or murder.

He stayed at Bates' Hotel in the Strand, and saw a good deal of the banker, Thomas Coutts and his family, whom he'd known 'for 5 or 6 years'. 'I was very happy every time I found myself in this excellent family.' (The banker had sent his three attractive daughters over to Paris to learn French in 1787.) Edna Healey's History of *Coutts & Co.* shows their profits at £27,000 in 1792, of which Thomas's personal share was £22,000. 'Everywhere the air of opulence offers a humiliating contrast with my country. The number of travellers on every road, and the number of elegant beautifully-equipped carriages, are what especially strike the new arrival from France.' The Couttses did all they could to prevent François going over to join the Duc de Bourbon's army in Belgium: offered to take him to spend a fortnight with the Montagus at Cowdray Park, and so on. Coutts gave him a letter of credit for £200 sterling: a sum he could well afford.

Over in the Bourbon army, he learnt that the English servant, Charles, who had seen him off as he mounted his horse at the Ecole Militaire and left Paris with pistol at the ready, had happily arrived in England with money and some of his belongings. He also learnt that Lazowski, 'mon meilleur ami', was well.

If I dared to write Memoirs of these times, I would spread myself with pleasure over all the circumstances of the retreat of the armies: I've spent so long with all the men who make up those armies. But I find that when one isn't a great writer [*une première plume*], so to say, one should limit oneself to the precise details of the actions one has witnessed, and so preserve the accuracy that can make a journal useful.

Well, he had had plenty of practice in his youth, in France, and in England, and with the example of his friend Arthur Young. We need not follow him through the distress and despair of the incompetent conduct of the armies facing Dumouriez, with his stiffening of the old French professionals. He does justice to the melancholy marching round in circles, in the plain of Fleurus, in early November. One episode we must note:

> On this march, I recognized one of the foot-sloggers, the brother of M. de Lazowski, and formerly an officer of the Regiment of Darmstadt. He had emigrated with his friends. They were fusiliers. Their company had always served in the vanguard of our army, so that I had never seen him, though I knew he was there. I found him sturdier, and even taller: he's a fine lad. All he wanted was to get to the firing-line – to see what we could do. He bravely shouldered his rifle, and was impervious to fatigue.

A fine lad – *beau garçon* – would have been a possible description of all three of Lazowski's younger brothers – but especially André, the youngest, at 24. Next day, 7 November, the generals had received no orders and had no idea what to do. The government was about to leave Brussels, and 'we were ordered to spend the night on the town ramparts'.

> Next day, 8 November, we headed eastwards for Louvain, Tirlemont, Maastricht. As we pulled out, our habitual discipline was all that kept us going – we were more a herd than a troop. Our line of four abreast was divided in two by the road, with vehicles passing down the middle of our columns. The men were worn out and wet through, sad and pensive. No one could imagine a scene more overwhelmingly desolate.

At Tirlemont, François was given a certificate of unlimited leave by the Duke of Bourbon, 'having taken part in the campaign of 1792 in my army'. It was dated 9 November, and as he left the Prince he saw the young Lazowski, a member of the guard; referring to him as 'M. de Lazowski' but clearly not meaning 'mon meilleur ami'. On the 14th, at Maastricht, he heard that Brussels had fallen: nothing now seemed impossible to the French army. He made for England as fast as possible, via Rotterdam.

In his *Souvenirs*, he couldn't resist a physical description of that remarkable town in the manner he had learnt and practised with his friends, Lazowski and Arthur Young. Again he was helped to a ship by an old acquaintance: this time James 'Fish' Craufurd, a banker friend of Thomas Coutts, and whom he'd often met at the Paris embassy. (He is not to be confused with George Craufurd, the commissioner at Versailles on the 1786 Trade Treaty.) Craufurd had a fine house in one of the most beautiful quarters of Rotterdam; and after the discomforts of his life adrift in a hopeless army, François rejoiced in his small inn 'with a fire in my bedroom'. The weather for the crossing was good, but it took five days. His *Souvenirs* ended on 1 December 1792 with these words:

> One of the greatest pleasures of my life has been to find myself on *terra firma* and in England, where, after escaping many dangers . . . I was sure to be able to wait calmly for better times – without being dislodged, time after time, and for ever hounded by the incredible progress of the French patriots, as those have been who stayed on the continent.

He wasn't one to sit about waiting calmly for better times, but soon joined the staff of the Duke of York, and took part in the successful siege of Valenciennes. We can only guess at the improvement in François' morale, for the journals he most probably kept have not emerged. Valenciennes fell on 28 July, and on 24 September, to the accompanying news of the massacres in Paris, he married at Altona, near Hamburg, Marie-Françoise de Tott, a young widow whose father, the baron de Tott, was a well-known writer and French ambassador in Istanbul. She was responsible for drawing him; apparently the only surviving portrait (Pl. 2). His journals, covering his life fairly fully up to the previous December, give no clue as to where and when they met. So far as they were settled in Altona, it was with the leading merchant-family Sieveking: at least that was their address – from which, five years later, he wrote to Young: 'My wiffe will give you some very good musique, for she is remarquable good musician' (BL Add MSS, 35128, fol. 489).

From the Duke of York's staff he transferred, still under York's command, to the Choiseul Hussars, whose colonel had been 2nd-colonel of the La Rochefoucauld Dragoons. He served as captain; then, in 1795, squadron-commander, at the Ile d'Yeu, at Quiberon, in Flanders, Holland, Westphalia and Hanover. Without his (presumable) journals, that is all we know. In 1796, a long letter from his father in Philadelphia to his mother in Switzerland expresses delight in the news of their eldest son, and determination that they should do everything they could to provide for his *aisance*. The same letter refers to '*la pauvre Lazowski*': presumably his widow, for he disappeared from the records in 1794–95: his intelligence, and the part he played with Lavoisier in the attempts to improve French agriculture were probably enough for the blood-drunk 'bureaucrat of death' Fouquier-Tinville to have him guillotined.

Liancourt's Philadelphia letter, in 1796, refers also, but less amiably, to Alexandre: 'he has played some rotten tricks on me, and made mischief (*a eu avec moi des vilenies*): perhaps if only he reflected, he could forgive himself as much as I feel disposed to do'. There is no hint, in the letter, of the nature of these *vilenies*. Alexandre had married in 1788. He joined Lafayette briefly as lieutenant-colonel, but resigned in 1792: as François wrote, in *Souvenirs*, 'it was clear, even to him, that one could *no longer* hold the King's commission without dishonour'. (That tartness seems to go back to the day in Bath, when François was shocked to find that his brother had bought a copy of the Bath Guide and had no intention of sharing it with him.) Meanwhile, late in December 1790, he had bought the recently 'nationalised' *ci-devant* priory of the Madeleine in Mello, a walled and picturesque mill-village beside the river Thérain, about 7 miles from the paternal estate at Liancourt.

Presumably the priory became their country seat. The great bell in the parish church, re-cast in the metal of its predecessors, bears the record that it was blessed by the *curé* of the parish in 1792, 'the 4th year of liberty', and named *Anastasie* by M. Alexandre de La Rochefoucauld, lieutenant-colonel, citizen of this town, and by dame Adélaïde his wife. The obscure Christian martyr Anastasie may have been chosen merely because the bell was re-dedicated on her feast-day, or because she wasn't one of the great – and thus in 1792 controversial – Christian figures.

Alexandre and Adélaïde's first three children were born in Paris. The second, their daughter Alexandrine, who was being carried at the time of that meeting of the two brothers and Lazowski late on 10 August, arrived during the September massacres, perhaps sensed what was going on, and died after fifteen days. They were again in Paris in September 1793, when the third child was born. Sometime in 1794 they withdrew to Adélaïde's family estates in Domingo: as émigrés, their possessions in Mello, including an armorial chest and the priory itself, were confiscated by the *Département* of Oise: 16 Vendémiaire (7 October). I owe these details of Alexandre's family history, and its connexion with Mello, to much kind help: from M. Georges Martin of Lyons, and his remarkable work of genealogy, *De la Maison de La Rochefoucauld*, privately printed; from Mme Geneviève Etienne, Director of the Archives of the *Département* of Oise; and from M. Robert Foubert, Deputy-Mayor of Mello.

Mme Etienne sent me a facsimile of a detailed departmental report of the state of factories and manufactures in the canton of Mello. The report was written in 'the year VI of the French republic, one and indivisible', i.e. 1797–98. It records that Alexandre's factory and spinning-mill had been set up 'some two and a half years ago by the citizen Delarochefoucauld', and described it as 'a very great resource for the canton, in which it employs several hundred hands'. Here was François' brother, probably as early as 1795, bringing his English experience to the benefit of the Republic.

The report continues: 'The spinning is done by machinery, which is a tremendous saving. There they make, *à la manière anglaise*, quilting and muslins, etc., more beautiful than those of all the other factories. Citizen Delarochefoucauld has procured at great expense an English workman named Macklood, already known to the government, to direct this organisation.' Presumably, he was a Scot, and this is a French effort at spelling Macleod. 'For the rest, the said Delarochefoucauld has sent the Minister of the Interior his trade-catalogue, *une carte de ses échantillons*, and has no doubt of his competitiveness with the English manufactures. Admittedly, the production is small, but there is reason to hope it will be more considerable with the peace.' This may be a reference to the Peace of Campo Formio of October 1797, at which Napoleon humiliated Austria and seemed for a while to have established French power across Europe.

Mme Etienne has also sent me the report by Louis Graves, published in the *Annuaire du Département de l'Oise* in 1828, with the disappointing information that Alexandre's factory, 'though extremely useful to the neighbourhood, could not sustain itself'. Craftsmen and workers were disbanded. In 1811, the surviving thirty, ten of them women, were housed in the stables, duly modified, of the château at

Mello, and were working without machinery. The stagnation of trade was blamed. The site is now occupied by Bowater's packaging plant. By 1811, Alexandre himself had long been otherwise employed. The priory has been demolished.

From 1801, as Napoleon established his power, he developed the most grandiose, glittering court in Europe, accumulating forty-four palaces for display and performance: it was more rigidly formal, and more astonishing, than the routine surrounding Louis XVI, whose natural instinct had been to simplify. Alexandre's wife was pressed by her cousin Joséphine into the prominent office of *dame d'honneur*, which she accepted with reluctance but performed with spirit and judgment: she had a place at Napoleon's coronation at Notre Dame. Himself hardly a model of lofty elegance, Napoleon was odiously rude about Madame de La Rochefoucauld's low stature and her lameness. But she became the leading authority on court etiquette, and Joséphine needed her. Napoleon made good use of Alexandre: in 1802, he was *chargé d'affaires* in Saxony; in 1805, ambassador in Vienna; and then helped in the negotiation of the Treaty of Tilsit with Russia.

The Hundred Days of Napoleon's return from Elba called for the best diplomatic talent of both the La Rochefoucauld brothers. They were experienced 'survivors' and re-established themselves comfortably in the quieter forms of French public life under the inept Bourbons. François' dogged Royalism must have been severely strained by Louis XVIII's and – even more –Charles X's treatment of his father, the philanthropic Duke, who died in 1827. François succeeded as duc de La Rochefoucauld-Liancourt and himself died at 83, just after the 1848 Revolution. Alexandre died in Paris in 1841, his travel-diaries from 1785 staying in his family's possession. One imagines his descendants glancing through them curiously from time to time; not at all easy to decipher, but now improved by collation with the journals of his two companions. François' journals, removed during the Revolution from his father's library and placed in the Republic's archive, were probably unread until the late Jean Marchand, distinguished Librarian of the National Assembly, transcribed them as part of his study of the two brothers, and left them for an English historian to translate and edit. The lives of the leading members of this ancient and resilient family may be followed through the 19th and 20th centuries in the four last brilliant chapters of *Les La Rochefoucauld* (Paris, 1992) by Solange Fasquelle, herself the daughter of the duchess Edmée de La Rochefoucauld, to whose inextinguishable spirit *Innocent Espionage* is dedicated.

Index

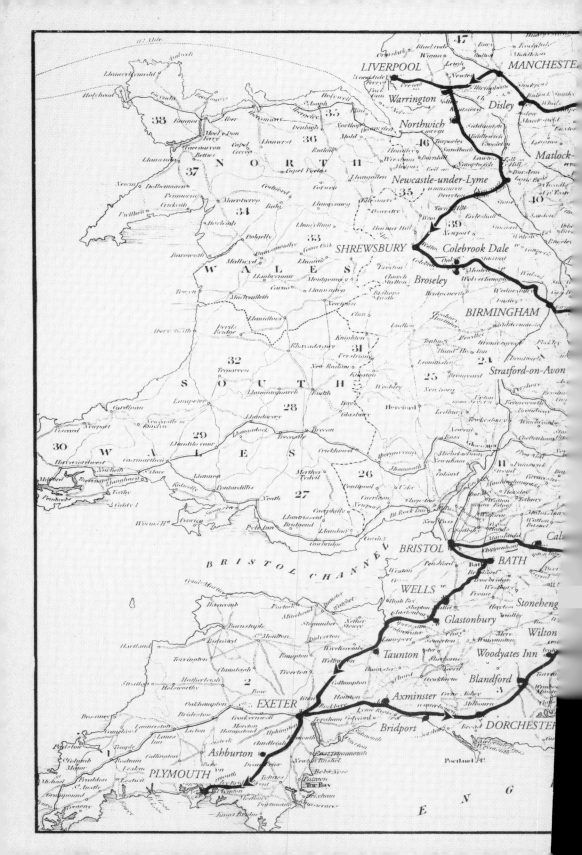